REMEMBERING
THE
COVENANT

A COMMENTARY ON
THE BOOK OF MORMON

VOLUME 1

Denver C. Snuffer, Jr.

Published in the United States by Mill Creek Press.
Mill Creek Press is a registered trademark of Mill Creek Press, LLC.
www.millcreekpress.com

ISBN-10: 0-9891503-0-5
ISBN-13: 978-0-9891503-0-9

Printed in the United States of America on acid-free paper.

First Edition

Cover design by Mill Creek Press.

CONTENTS

PECULIAR INDEED 1

GROW IN LIGHT 19

ANGELS AND MYSTERIES 43

WHAT GUARANTEE DO WE HAVE? 63

TRUTH IS INDEPENDENT 105

MY GLASSES AREN'T ROSE COLORED 147

D&C 132 155

GROW WHERE YOU ARE PLANTED 173

HUMOR REQUIRES UNDERLYING TRUTH ...187

THE TRADITIONS OF MEN 229

AWAKE AND ARISE 253

PHILOSOPHIES OF MEN......................................301

ISAIAH 53...335

THE SCRIPTURES HAVE ANSWERS..................353

SPEAKING PLAINLY.....................................363

A MESSAGE OF WARNING................................393

PREFACE

For several years I have maintained a blog on the Internet called "From the Desk of Denver Snuffer." That blog includes a discussion of a wide range of topics related to the Book of Mormon, the Restoration of the Gospel, church history and doctrine. Much of it is an important elaboration or extension of material in earlier books. To preserve this material in a form that is not vulnerable to Internet failure or website loss, I decided to put the blog contents into these volumes titled *Remembering the Covenant*.

The blog will remain up and available for anyone who wants to access the contents of this *Remembering the Covenant* series. It may be easier to search for a specific topic using the blog rather than the index that will be at the end of the fifth volume.

The content has been modified only in these particulars: First, the hot-links to scripture cites have been replaced by footnotes containing the scriptures. Second, some of the material has been reordered to bring together similar content. Third, some few spelling errors have been corrected, though it is likely some have been missed and will remain. Fourth, a small number (I think two) ambiguous statements have been changed to clear up confusion. Fifth, the material has been divided into chapters with chapter titles.

An earlier book was made available from the blog and published as *Removing the Condemnation*. That book remains in print. However, the entire content of *Removing the Condemnation* is included within these volumes, and therefore, if you have this series you do not need to have *Removing the Condemnation* as a separate book.

I want to thank Mill Creek Press for allowing all the content I write to be my own thoughts, without editorial censoring. I alone am responsible for what I write. I also appreciate the efforts of others who have contributed to the publication.

These volumes are to help us remember what the Restoration of the Gospel through Joseph Smith proclaims, despite the dwindling memory of our current Latter-day Saints. So long as the original, smoldering light remains, all that is required to ignite a new fire is the breath of the Spirit blowing on the spark. That breath of life comes from the word of the Lord. To the extent that these volumes reflect the Lord's word, the credit for stirring the reader to remember Him and His Gospel belongs to Him. Any errors or mistakes are mine.

Denver C. Snuffer, Jr., Sandy, Utah

VOLUME 1

PECULIAR INDEED

The Kingdom of Heaven Contrasted with Hell

It is a misnomer to speak of the "kingdom of the Devil" because the description presumes something more organized than is the case. It is difficult to organize when fear, hatred and anger are the primary motivations. Love is a far more cohesive, creative and loyalty producing motivation. All that Satan does is designed to destroy itself, as well as all those who follow him.

The Church of Jesus Christ of Latter-day Saints and Apologetics

I am a member of The Church of Jesus Christ of Latter-day Saints and am loyal to it as an institution and as the proponent of a faith. Although I am keenly aware of the flaws any body of men and women will display, those weaknesses inherent in the human condition do not diminish the greatness of an institution. I believe in constructive explanations about shortcomings, ways to understand or process what appear to be flaws. In that sense only do I believe in apologetics. To deny the existence of shortcomings is, I believe, to depart from the warnings given to us by Christ, Nephi, Mormon, Moroni, the Apostle Paul, Joseph Smith, Brigham Young, and others. I like the comment made by President Hugh B. Brown about us Mormons: "We are a lay church; and this gives rise to much mediocrity."

It helps to have a sense of humor if you're going to try to be a faithful Mormon. It also requires thick skin.

Words Matter

I worry about things being attributed to me from private conversations or speaking events where the public was invited. I choose words with great care. The difference between truth and error can be quite a fine line in some important matters. Therefore, when I say, teach, write or answer a question with exact language in mind, and the listener or reader does not retain the distinctions when they attempt to repeat what I've said, I wind up being confronted with things I never said, don't believe and would never teach. One of the reasons for this blog is so I can control what is attributed to me. I'm very willing to be held to account for what I teach or write. But I'm not willing to be held accountable for someone else's understanding or partial recollection of statements I have made.

I get asked a lot of questions. The other day someone asked how *"to write only what the Spirit directs?"*

That requires something quite subtle and hard to keep. The presence of the Spirit, its constant companionship, guidance and influence is so refined and difficult a matter to put into words that even the scriptures do not give an adequate account of the process.

Obedience is required, but there are obedient people who are utterly without the Spirit. Obedience can make a person rigid and unyielding, when they ought instead to be meek and pliable.

Discipline is required, but not if it makes a person dogmatic. The word "disciple" is derived from discipline, but a disciple *follows* the Master. A disciplined man can be on his own errand, rather than the Lord's.

These words, like so many others fail to capture just how great and fine a balance is required for the Spirit to provide direction.

Meekness is required, but not in the way the world thinks of meekness. I've tried to explain the true quality of meekness shown by the Lord and His followers in *Beloved Enos*. It involves power, strength, and certitude.

The process almost defies words. It is very real, in fact tangible. But the way in which you know it to be right involves an ability to feel the balance, taste the good, harmonize with the greater intelligence which pervades everything that is. It comes from Him. It is Him, in a very real sense. All things were made by Him, bear record of Him, and are a testimony of His way.

Writing the words of eternal life require someone to have eternal life. They can still be mortal, but they need the promise of eternal life. So I suppose the Lord's admonition: "Seek first the kingdom of God, and all things shall be added thereto" (see 3 Nephi 13:33 and Matthew 6:33) really answers the question. Or as told to Hyrum: "Seek not to declare my word, but first seek to obtain my word" (D&C 11:21). The one must precede the other. At least the statement of the Lord to His disciples, and the revelation to Hyrum Smith seem to indicate as much.

Principles and Rules

Q: What is the difference between "principles" and "rules"?

Assuming you define "Principles" as the underlying reason for the commandment, then you're also speaking about what the Apostle Paul called the "Spirit of the law" as opposed to the "letter of the law." He said the "letter killeth" but the "Spirit giveth life." I think he was right.

Any rule can be abused. Any rule can become broken even when it is being kept. Rules can become harsh taskmasters, inflicting punishment when they were designed to bless. The underlying principle, however, always seeks to bless. The underlying principle was designed as a blessing. When the rule begins to oppress, then is should be abandoned in favor of the principle.

Rules have and do change. But principles remain constant. The brutality of the rules was exposed by Christ when He healed on the Sabbath. He did that specifically to demonstrate the futility of ignoring the principle, while only adhering to the law/rule.

In the English common law tradition there were cases "at law" and cases "in equity." They divided the Courts into separate forums, where courts of law could not do equity. But courts of equity could ignore the provisions of law, modify them, or establish a higher principle which resolved fairly a dispute despite some legal impediment to the relief sought. That tradition follows the Lord's example.

Principles ennoble. Rules preoccupy.

Truth

When we receive truth we are expected to live our lives in conformity with the truth we've received. We shouldn't expect to receive more if we do not live what we've already been given. Living in conformity with such truth as you already have is also always required to avoid deception. It is simply not possible to harvest additional light while refusing to live the light already given. False spirits visit with those who invite them by their misconduct, rebellion or wickedness. Hence the need to constantly re-evaluate how you live and the choices you make.

Explanation

I was asked a question which provoked this explanation of the book, *The Second Comforter: Conversing With the Lord Through the Veil:*

The book was written to cause the reader internal reflection. There really isn't a "punch line" in the book. My testimony is essentially incidental; merely affirming that the principles taught in the book are true.

I worry that reading only the testimony, divorced from the explanation of how someone moves along in personal progress to the point they receive that personal witness, will make it just another "feel good" read. The book is a manual. It isn't designed to make people feel good. It is designed to get them to do something.

I worry that whenever people read of others' spiritual experiences they assume that because they have read about such things they are somehow "included" or "worthy" and that they are linked to God as a result. The book is designed to awaken people to their own lack of an existing link: then to cause them to resolve to establish that link for themselves.

So I think taking only the testimony alone contradicts the whole purpose for which it was written. The testimony was merely a brief, nine word ratification of the book's teachings. The focus was, and is, on receiving an audience with Christ. The book is a manual for the reader to do that for themselves. The reader, **not** the author, is the focus of the book. Indeed, with only brief exceptions, my personal presence intrudes into the book to highlight how to do something wrong. Then the book explains how to get it right.

What's in a Name

In response to a question asked today:

The Church of Jesus Christ of Latter-day Saints is a temporary institution which will cease to exist after this life. There is no vision, revelation, scripture or statement promising us that the church as an institution will continue to exist after mortality. What the scriptures, visions, and revelations do tell us about the eternal description of the saved is that it is "the Church of the Firstborn" or "the Church of the Lamb." Membership in that group is separate from membership in The Church of Jesus Christ of Latter-day Saints.

Nephi uses "Church of the Lamb"[1] to describe the latter-days group over whom the Lord will watch. Interestingly, although Joseph had this revelation before him when he organized the church, he did not choose the "Church of the Lamb" as the organization's name.

When modern revelation refers to those who inherit the Celestial Glory, it calls them members of the "Church of the Firstborn"[2]. Those who are chosen in our day to belong to the Church of the Firstborn are shown only one way in which that takes place. In a revelation given to Joseph Smith while translating the New Testament, Section 77, Joseph gave this explanation of the latter-day 144,000 saved persons in verse 11:

> "they are they who are ordained out of every nation, kindred, tongue, and people, by the angels to whom is given power over the nations of the earth, to bring as many as will come to the church of the Firstborn."

At the time Joseph received the explanation recorded in Section 77 (March 1832) the church had existed for over two years. When the

---

[1] 1 Nephi 14:12 "And it came to pass that I beheld the church of the Lamb of God, and its numbers were few, because of the wickedness and abominations of the whore who sat upon many waters; nevertheless, I beheld that the church of the Lamb, who were the saints of God, were also upon all the face of the earth; and their dominions upon the face of the earth were small, because of the wickedness of the great whore whom I saw."

[2] D&C 76:67 "These are they who have come to an innumerable company of angels, to the general assembly and church of Enoch, and of the Firstborn."
D&C 93:22 "And all those who are begotten through me are partakers of the glory of the same, and are the church of the Firstborn."

official name was given in 1838[3] the name chosen for the earthly, temporary organization was The Church of Jesus Christ of Latter-day Saints—not the Church of the Firstborn.

The Church of the Firstborn exists on the "other side" so to speak. You qualify to get there by how you live here. But you have to be invited into that church by the "angels to whom is given power" to extend that invitation.

Not for Entertainment

I was reading in the first volume of the *Joseph Smith Papers* and came across a letter written by Heber C. Kimball and Orson Hyde upon their return to Kirtland after their mission to England. During the interim things had broken down in Kirtland with lawsuits, cross accusations and apostasy. Although the missions had been a great success, with more than fifteen-hundred converts joining the Church, when they returned they found the existing Saints in disarray.

They were immediately confronted with criticism of Joseph and other Church leaders by the residents of Kirtland. In the letter to Joseph Smith, received on July 6, 1838, they responded to the criticism they were hearing with a comment which stood out to me. It would make a good motto:

"The faults of our brethren is poor entertainment for us." (*Joseph Smith Papers*, 1:280)

I like that. I think it is still good enough advice to remain true over a century and a half later: The faults of the Brethren are poor entertainment for any of us.

---

[3] D&C 115:4 "For thus shall my church be called in the last days, even The Church of Jesus Christ of Latter-day Saints."

Daniel

When Daniel saw the Lord he "alone saw the vision"[4] and not those who were with him. The others felt the great presence[5] but saw nothing. The physical effect upon Daniel was exhausting. He collapsed and had to be strengthened.[6] Three times he collapsed and three times he was touched by the Lord to strengthen him.[7] It was real and VERY physical. Yet he alone saw the Lord. It is always so. Hence Paul's comment "whether in the body I cannot tell; or whether out of the body I cannot tell".[8] It *is* physical. But those who are excluded merely feel the terrible presence, and see nothing. Those included are like Daniel and Joseph Smith, left exhausted from such encounters.[9]

---

[4] Daniel 10:7 "And I Daniel alone saw the vision: for the men that were with me saw not the vision; but a great quaking fell upon them, so that they fled to hide themselves."

[5] Ibid.

[6] Daniel 10:10 "And, behold, an hand touched me, which set me upon my knees and *upon* the palms of my hands."

[7] Daniel 10:10, 16, 18 "And, behold, an hand touched me, which set me upon my knees and *upon* the palms of my hands. And, behold, *one* like the similitude of the sons of men touched my lips: then I opened my mouth, and spake, and said unto him that stood before me, O my lord, by the vision my sorrows are turned upon me, and I have retained no strength. Then there came again and touched me *one* like the appearance of a man, and he strengthened me."

[8] 2 Corinthians 12:2 "I knew a man in Christ above fourteen years ago, (whether in the body, I cannot tell; or whether out of the body, I cannot tell: God knoweth;) such an one caught up to the third heaven."

[9] JS–H 1:48 "I shortly after arose from my bed, and, as usual, went to the necessary labors of the day; but, in attempting to work as at other times, I found my strength so exhausted as to render me entirely unable. My father, who was laboring along with me, discovered something to be wrong with me, and told me to go home. I started with the intention of going to the house; but, in attempting to cross the fence out of the field where we were, my strength entirely failed me, and I fell helpless on the ground, and for a time was quite unconscious of anything."

Valentine's Day

Today is Valentine's Day. Although I'm hundreds of miles away, my thoughts are with my wife. David and Solomon clearly never found a wife to be their equal, helpmeet, love and joy. I pity them. I have she who completes me; my queen and high priestess, love and companion, wise counselor and faithful friend. She is the standard against which all other women are measured, and all others found to be wanting. She is home.

I have yet to see a marriage I think the equal of my own.

The final parable in *Ten Parables* begins deliberately. I hope readers realize how important that discussion is to the way things really are.

Apostasy

I was asked whether those who are in the middle of an apostasy can detect that it is underway.

Yes and no: Yes, as to isolated individuals. No, as to the institutional mindset or they would have done something about it. The Great Apostasy began sometime during the second century. But you have to get down to the Protestant fathers in the 1500's and thereafter before there is any widespread shouting about what has been lost. For the intervening thirteen centuries people respected authority, and trusted that the leaders had the keys to save them.

I can't imagine the courage it took for Martin Luther to refuse to back down when he was confronted with thirteen centuries of history telling him he was wrong. We really do owe a debt of gratitude to him, and those who followed after, for ultimately establishing religious freedom. Americans more than any other people are the direct beneficiaries of that courage.

Two Women

A Parable by Denver C. Snuffer, Jr.

Once there were two women.

One was born to privilege, whose family had great wealth.

The other, named Martha, was born poor.

They both grew up and at length Martha married, but the woman of privilege never did marry.

As adults both women felt the need for motherhood.

Martha bore seven children.

The woman of privilege spent seven years in college studying child development and education, eventually receiving her Ph.D., but never married, nor had a child.

Now as coincidence would have it, the woman of privilege inherited her parents' home and moved back into the wealthy neighborhood in which she was raised.

Martha's family needed more room and searched for a house. They found a modest home located in wealthy neighborhood which had once been a servant's. Now the servant's home needed repairs, and few were interested in a home which, in comparison with the others around it, seemed merely a servant's residence.

Martha however, believed there was an advantage for her children to grow up among the children of greater privilege and therefore purchased the unwanted house.

And so it was that the woman of privilege and Martha came to live in the same neighborhood.

Martha, ever eager to learn more, had read books to better understand parenting. She was surprised to learn one of her favorite teachers lived in her neighborhood.

As coincidence would further have it, both the woman of privilege and Martha were called upon to serve together in teaching neighborhood children. They spent many hours together, but oftentimes did not agree.

For Martha, the experience of raising her own children led her to view things differently than the woman of privilege whose experience was based upon study, borrowed understanding and the science of others.

After six years, Martha concluded the conflicts between them were insurmountable.

In the seventh year, Martha concluded that if the woman of privilege could gaze into the eyes of her own children for but five minutes, she would know more than she did now, notwithstanding the many years of study which she had devoted to child development and education.

In the eighth year, Martha concluded it was her responsibility to teach the woman of privilege, and so the occupant of the servant's house undertook the burden of teaching the needy but unwilling.

It was a role that would require many years, with only limited success.

Pride is unbecoming in a pupil; and meekness ever required of a teacher.

In Response to a Critic

In response to a critic of the Church of Jesus Christ of Latter-day Saints:

I believe Joseph Smith was a prophet, and you do not. I'm content to let you disbelieve. Why are you not content to let me believe? One of us is clearly mistaken, but I am content with both my belief and your disbelief.

Of the two of us, I think your hostility toward my position reveals an underlying insecurity about your confidence in your position.

I am prepared to be everlastingly judged on the basis of my beliefs. I insist the Lord has every right to hold me accountable for what I believe, do, think, say and how I behave.

Infidelity

If a man is unfaithful to his wife, he will be dishonest in his business dealings and in his other relationships. Hence the saying: "an adulterer is a liar." The two go together.

Salesmanship

Recognizing a problem is not solving it in the same way that a diagnosing an illness is not treating it.

It is always the first step, however, to recognize a defect. We don't solve a lot of problems because we fail to acknowledge their existence.

Then there are those who will argue that a defect is not really a problem, but a feature. Don't be fooled by salesmanship. Defects are *never* features.

Personal Responsibility

I have tried to lessen the burden imposed upon Church leadership in the books I have written. The Saints need to be more accountable for their own progress and understanding. The books impose responsibility upon the reader to establish their own communication with God, and then to assume responsibility for their own progress.

Whatever intelligence we attain unto in this life will rise with us in the next. Seeking to gain in intelligence, or light and truth, is always individual, never collective.

BYU Visit

I need to preface my remarks below with this: My son attended a Catholic High School for a year and had the wonderful experience of being in the minority there. I have lifelong friends who are Catholic. My family was Baptist and my sister remains a devoted Baptist. I have friends of many faiths, or no faith at all. Some friends have been LDS, and lost their faith altogether. Some have converted from LDS to Catholic. All these wonderful people are valued friends. I attend annually a Presbyterian service blessing the Scottish clans with a dear friend. My friendships have nothing to do with the friend's faith.

Now, that having been said, I was down at BYU about a week ago. [While there, I was surprised to find that several of my books were for sale in the BYU Bookstore. Somehow I thought Benchmark Books in Salt Lake was THE local distributor.]

While walking about the campus I was reminded just how much I like being a Latter-day Saint. We're quirky, even peculiar people. There's a lot about us to laugh about. But underneath it all Latter-day Saints really try hard, in our strange way, to be good, decent people. The struggle to be that is met with frequent failure. But the exercise is good.

Devotion to any faith is good for the souls of mankind. In many ways we are not at all superior to other groups. I remember the talk given by Pres. Faust about the killings of the young girls in the Amish school a few years ago, which was followed by the compassion of the Amish victims' families to the widow and children of the murderer. If we were to hold up a contemporary group in the United States who most succeed in living a Christ-like life, it would likely be the Amish. Nevertheless, I really like being a Latter-day Saint and in fellowshipping and struggling with my fellow Saint. I find it joyful. I love the Saints. Even as I sense very keenly our many shortcomings. For me, it is still joyful to live as a Latter-day Saint.

Second Anointing

I've gotten numerous questions this last week on the subject of the "second anointing" or "second sealing." This is not a subject which I think invites a lot of open discussion. I've intentionally avoided it in my books.

Here's what I think is appropriate to explain: *The Second Comforter: Conversing with the Lord Through the Veil* is an explanation of what is required to get to the point you are prepared to meet the Lord. It is essentially a manual. It stops short of explaining what the Lord, in His on-going ministry to mankind, will do to prepare the individual for what comes next. That is His ministry. The Holy Ghost brings you to the Lord. The Lord brings you to the Father. That book was written to help you come to Him.

Beloved Enos is an explanation of what the results are, once some-one has received the Lord's ministry. It takes Enos' record and uses it as a basis for the explanation.

Between the text of *The Second Comforter* and *Beloved Enos*, what is omitted is a description of the sacred ordinances involved in what is termed "the second anointing." I do not feel inclined to go into that.

Who Can Be a Seer?

Q: "Who can become a seer?"

You could probably substitute "seer" for "prophet" in Moses' lament: "Would to God all men were [seers]". The purpose of seer-ship is the same as any other gift of the Spirit: to acquire knowledge of truth. And, assuming "God giveth liberally to all men," as James promised us,[10] it would follow this was among the things He in-tended all men to experience.

---

[10] James 1:5 "If any of you lack wisdom, let him ask of God, that giveth to all *men* liberally, and upbraideth not; and it shall be given him."

Read the description of the conditions of post-mortal residence in the presence of God given in Section 130. The "seership" experience there is commonplace. The "sea of glass," or earth on which they dwell is a great Urim and Thummim, as well as the "white stone" given to them. The result is that ALL occupants of that sphere are seers. Accordingly, we should assume that we obtain our first instructions here to prepare us for living there. Seership, being necessary for life there, is something we ought to expect to be included in the Lord's tutelage while we are all here.

ALL of us are to "covet the best gifts" on the one hand; and on the other "there is no gift greater" than seership. (That's Paul[11] and Ammon being quoted.)[12] It follows necessarily, therefore, that we should be seeking to have some experience with this gift here in mortality.

Peculiar

The gentiles seem determined to end their reign. According to an announcement from the Church this week, missionary work is being shifted from European and North American populations into Latin and South America, Africa and Asia.

I've thought for some time that the failing conversion rates are the inevitable result of the "marketing" system being used by the Church. What distinguishes the Restoration from other faiths is our doctrine. We have been de-emphasizing doctrine for years. We try to

---

[11] 1 Corinthians 12:31 "But covet earnestly the best gifts: and yet shew I unto you a more excellent way."

[12] Mosiah 8:15–17 "And the king said that a seer is greater than a prophet. And Ammon said that a seer is a revelator and a prophet also; and a gift which is greater can no man have, except he should possess the power of God, which no man can; yet a man may have great power given him from God. But a seer can know of things which are past, and also of things which are to come, and by them shall all things be made manifest, and hidden things shall come to light, and things which are not known shall be made known by them, and also things shall be made known by them which otherwise could not be known."

seem more and more like another Christian faith. We aren't. We are quite different. The reason to convert lies in our doctrinal differences.

No one is going to live the Latter-day Saint lifestyle who thinks that we are just another mainstream Christian church. To pay tithing, refrain from coffee, tea, alcohol, smoking and serve in Church leadership roles at considerable personal inconvenience and sacrifice requires our Church to be more than just another mainstream church. If that is all we are, most people (especially devoted people) are going to want an easier form of belief, like Methodism, Presbyterianism or Catholicism. If they offer the same doctrine as we do, then they will win.

I am a Latter-day Saint because I believe the doctrine. I am not a traditional Christian because I believe their creeds are false and they teach for doctrine the commandments of men. Unless someone comes to believe that, there is no reason to leave a traditional Christian denomination and become a Latter-day Saint.

Social and Cultural "Rights"

In the *Church News* there is an article about religious freedom being eroded by encroaching social and cultural "rights" which conflict with religious freedom. The case of *Perry v. Schwartzenegger* in California, which challenges the Proposition 8 vote was cited by Elder Lance Wickman, the Church's General Counsel (lawyer). In that case the public's decision to prohibit same-sex marriage is being challenged on the basis that voters cannot negate a fundamental right.

The Church is alarmed about the growing potential for conflict between social and cultural "rights" on the one hand, and the free exercise of religion on the other.

The deeper problem the Church has with their position on this legal conflict in California is the position taken on the Salt Lake City ordinance the Church endorsed a several weeks ago. In that decision, the Church announced that employment and housing were "funda-mental rights" which same-sex attraction could not forfeit. The Church endorsed the use of coercive governmental power to compel employers and property owners to permit homosexual employees and renters, upon pain of punishment by the Courts. This was an extraordinary departure from past positions of the Church, and rep-resented the first time the Church approved governmental compul-sion against employers and property owners to protect homosexual conduct.

The effect of the Church's change in view on the Salt Lake City ordinance was almost immediate. A follow-on state-wide survey after the Church's changed position showed that there was a dramatic shift in Utah's view of tolerance toward homosexual behavior. Essentially, Mormons all over Utah fell in line behind the Church's new attitude.

Now the Church is attempting to sound the alarm about legal encroachment of cultural/social views (read homosexuality) into other areas which will inevitably conflict with religious liberty. But the Church has already conceded the argument. By extension of the Church's position with respect to housing and employment, the only question to answer is what to define as a "fundamental right." If housing and employment, then why not marriage? How does that distinction get made? And if any judge, anywhere, or ultimately five of the nine Supreme Court Justices, decide that marriage is a "fun-damental right," then the result will follow that religion cannot pre-vent the practice. And if religion cannot prevent the practice of this "fundamental right" to marry despite a couple's homosexual orienta-tion, then the LDS Church cannot prohibit or limit homosexual mar-riage practices anywhere. Not even in their own marriage ceremo-nies. For to do so would invade a "fundamental right" of the persons involved.

It will take time for the arguments to wend their way through the courts. But ultimately the Church's position on the "fundamental right" of homosexuals to be employed and housed without discrimination, using the coercive force of the government to protect that "right" against employers and property owners, will be the same reason the government will force the LDS Church to be coerced into acceptance of homosexual marriage. The LDS Church's own words/press release and public relations spokesman's words will be the reason cited by the Court against the Church, at the time the decision is reached. The Court will announce that the LDS Church has already recognized the need for governmental power to be used to protect fundamental rights of housing and employment. The Court will rule the Church must, therefore, accept as a fundamental right marriage, as well.

What Have You Seen Lately?

Saturday my wife and I ate downtown in Salt Lake City. Instead of taking the Interstate back home, we meandered back to State Street and then down State Street. It was between 6:00 and 7:00 pm on a Saturday evening. I was surprised to see that there were eight tattoo parlors open at that time, all of which had customers and some of which were quite crowded.

I also saw that Salt Lake City hosted a three-day tattoo convention in February.

GROW IN LIGHT

Adam-ondi-Ahman

At the first great priesthood meeting held at Adam-ondi-Ahman, there was Adam, who conducted, and seven High Priests who were in attendance. The "residue" of those who were present looked on, but the meeting involved these seven High Priests and Adam.

The appearance of the Lord at that meeting was an appearance to the eight, who were involved in the ceremony in which Adam's calling and election was made sure. The on-lookers who were present did not see the Lord, although they could sense something important was underway when the Lord "administered comfort" to Adam. Only those who had been initiated into the High Priesthood were permitted to participate and to view the Lord as He appeared and ministered. You can read about this event in D&C 107.[13]

---

[13] D&C 107:53–56 "Three years previous to the death of Adam, he called Seth, Enos, Cainan, Mahalaleel, Jared, Enoch, and Methuselah, who were all high priests, with the residue of his posterity who were righteous, into the valley of Adam-ondi-Ahman, and there bestowed upon them his last blessing. And the Lord appeared unto them, and they rose up and blessed Adam, and called him Michael, the prince, the archangel. And the Lord administered comfort unto Adam, and said unto him: I have set thee to be at the head; a multitude of nations shall come of thee, and thou art a prince over them forever. And Adam stood up in the midst of the congregation; and, notwithstanding he was bowed down with age, being full of the Holy Ghost, predicted whatsoever should befall his posterity unto the latest generation."

We assume the great meeting to be held at Adam-ondi-Ahman in the future will involve a great crowd, and it may. However, if it is a repetition of the pattern from the first, there will be a small number, perhaps only seven or eight, who will see the Lord, with the residue merely sensing something of importance is taking place. (See my earlier post on Daniel's visitation with the Lord.)

Slippery

I pay close attention to the Church and its leadership. I take careful note of what is said, and by whom. The closer you listen, the clearer the Church's methods and means become. They really don't take a great deal of effort to conceal things.

The Church is quite important to me. It deserves my careful study. Therefore I do not mind giving it the attention which it requires to understand what the Church is doing to cope with the various pressures, trends, and difficulties it encounters daily.

The Church's study of public opinion is so careful, so well done, and so frequently updated, that in his October, 2006 General Conference talk, Elder Jeffrey Holland made the following observation:

> "Not often but over the years some sources have suggested that the Brethren are out of touch in their declarations, that they don't know the issues, that some of their policies and practices are out-of-date, not relevant to our times. As the least of those who have been sustained by you to witness the guidance of this Church firsthand, I say with all the fervor of my soul that never in my personal or professional life have I ever associated with any group who are so *in* touch, who know so profoundly the issues facing us, who look so deeply into the old, stay so open to the new, and weigh so carefully, thoughtfully, and prayerfully everything in between. I testify that the grasp this body of men and women have of moral and societal issues exceeds that of any think tank or brain

trust of comparable endeavor of which I know anywhere on the earth." [14]

This statement was based upon the Church's on-going public relations survey taking, opinion polling, and focus group studies. When I attended a valley wide leadership meeting, at which Elder Russell Ballard spoke, he mentioned that from the Church Office Building he had watched focus group discussions the day before which came in by video feeds from Chicago, Seattle, and several other cities (whose locations I do not recall).

When the Church changed its position and supported the same-sex attraction ordinance in Salt Lake City a few weeks ago, the Church's spokesman made the following public announcement of the Church's reasons for the change:

> "There are going to be gay advocates who don't think we've gone nearly far enough, and people very conservative who think we've gone too far; the vast majority of people are between those polar extremes and we think that's going to resonate with people on the basis of fair-mindedness."

This is the language of opinion polling. The words "going to resonate with people on the basis of fair-mindedness" are the words of social sciences. The decision was not a "revelation" but a change in position based upon the polling which showed the position change could be safely made. The *Salt Lake Tribune* made the following report on January 30, 2010:

> "When Salt Lake City embraced anti-discrimination ordinances for gay and transgender residents last fall—snagging a landmark endorsement by the LDS Church and widespread support from city officials—more shifted than public policy. Public opinion—throughout Utah—jumped, too. Support for

---

[14] Holland, "Prophets in the Land Again," General Conference, October 2006.

some gay rights, short of marriage, climbed 11 percentage points across the state from a year ago, according to a new *Salt Lake Tribune* poll, and shot up by 10 percent among Mormons. Two-thirds of Utahns (67 percent) favor employment protections and safeguards for same-sex couples such as hospital visitation and inheritance rights, up from 56 percent in January 2009, when pollsters asked the same question. (This year's survey of 625 frequent Utah voters has an error margin of plus or minus 4 percentage points; last year's was 4.5 percent.) Opposition dropped, overall, from 40 percent to 23 percent. Among LDS respondents, it plummeted from 48 percent to 28 percent. 'This isn't a gradual change of attitudes. This is a fairly dramatic jump,' says Matthew Burbank, chairman of the University of Utah's political science department. 'Clearly, the fact that the LDS Church was officially endorsing this position had an impact on people.' A similar number of respondents, 66 percent, also say they support expanding Salt Lake City's anti-discrimination policy—the first of its kind in Utah and already mimicked in Salt Lake County—throughout the state."

Venus

I was with John Pratt on Saturday and he mentioned his new article on *Meridian Magazine* called "Venus Testifies of Christ." I went home and read it and thought it was just delightful. He makes the case that Venus was the star which foretold all the great events in the Lord's life. You can find the article on *Meridian Magazine* online.

Consider This

When I joined the LDS Church there were approximately 3 million members. That was in 1973. We have now over 13 million. That means that there are approximately 10 million Latter-day Saints with less experience with the Church than I have. What an odd thing to consider.

President Monson, President Packer, and Elder Perry are the only remaining members of the Presidency and Twelve who were already in place when I joined the Church. All the others were added to the Twelve after I joined. Again, that is an odd thing for me to consider. I can't imagine a Church where all the Presidency and Twelve were called after I joined.

I was thinking about all those who were in the First Presidency and Twelve when I first joined:

It was (to me) terrible to lose President Kimball. I'd grown quite fond of him from a distance in New Hampshire and Texas. Then when I went to law school, his son Ed Kimball taught at the J. Reuben Clark Law School, and President Kimball would come to visit his son. We'd run into him in the elevator or hallway and I grew even more respectful and attached to him.

Who didn't absolutely love Elder LeGrand Richards? What a delight it was to listen to him.

Elder McConkie and Elder Peterson were doctrinal giants. I went to both of their funerals because I had such a personal sense of loss at their passing.

Visit to the Nephites

I was asked about the difference between **my** explanation regarding the timing of the visitation of the risen Lord to the Nephites in *The Second Comforter: Conversing with the Lord Through the Veil,* and the timing proposed by Bruce R. McConkie and Joseph Fielding Smith. I put the visit at the end of the thirty-fourth year, they put it immediately following Christ's resurrection. I responded as follows:

I won't respond or rebut the argument. I don't think it is important to resolve the matter. It is only important to understand the issue. From the things these men wrote, it is clear that Elders McConkie/Smith reason how it could have been immediate, despite the fact that the text says it was the difference between the beginning and end of the thirty-fourth year. The anchor of their argument is that the people were showing each other the great changes which took place during the destruction. They reason that this would have been immediately after the destruction, otherwise there would be no reason to be pointing it out.

I account for this by recognizing that the festival season caused a migration later in the year. At that time their presence at the Temple site would have introduced them to the destruction for the first time, despite the fact the great quaking and tempests had ended eleven months earlier. I also account for the various appearances of the Lord to "other sheep," as well as the forty-day ministry at Jerusalem in my reckoning.

However, I do not think it important for someone to disbelieve McConkie/Smith. It is only important how one decides to read the scriptures. Borrowed opinions are just that. People need to read the scriptures and decide what they mean for themselves.

In the book I refer to the "ceremony of recognition." This ceremony has a specific order. It begins with an embrace. The headnote (written by Elder McConkie) says "hands, feet, and side" as the order. The text, however, refers to the side, then the hands and feet. That ceremony, so far as it is appropriate to do so, is explained in the text of *The Second Comforter*.

It's All about You

I received an email over the weekend which finally helped me understand a reaction to *The Second Comforter: Conversing With the Lord Through the Veil*. Apparently there are readers who think that the book is about me. It isn't. It is entirely about the reader. If someone reads it trying to get to a 'punch line' or great ending, they are reading with the wrong intent. The book isn't about that at all. It is a manual. It's purpose is to provide the reader instruction while they are on their own path back to the presence of the Lord.

To the extent that there are any personal matters in the book, they are designed to illustrate common mistakes. My mistakes and errors are set out in the beginning of the chapters. Then the chapter explains how to get the principle right. Other than showing how poor a student I have been, my presence in the book is entirely secondary. I do bear testimony about the truth of the teachings, which I think is required for a book of that nature. But the book is entirely about you, the reader.

I reiterate several times in the text that it is not a book for every reader. It is not publicized, advertised, or promoted in any way. It is entirely a word-of-mouth book which will find appropriate readers without any effort on my part to promote it.

Truth—Anything More or Less

I'm in the unique position of being powerless. I preside over my family, nothing else. I write for all others only to persuade. I will not be penalized if someone who reads my writing rejects it. The question then is really not: "what is my motivation," but instead: does the Spirit ratify the things I have written to *you?*

There is an alarming statement in D&C 93. It follows the definition of *truth* found in D&C 93:24[15]: "Whatsoever is more or less than this is the spirit of that wicked one who was a liar from the beginning" (D&C 93:25); meaning that we are all required to find the truth. Anything *more* or anything *less* is evil and means we have been deceived. In addition, the follow up to the parable of the Ten Virgins found in D&C 45 warns everyone that the five foolish virgins who

---

[15] D&C 93:24 "And truth is knowledge of things as they are, and as they were, and as they are to come;"

will not take truth as their guide are going to be hewn down and cast into the fire.[16]

These decisions about what truth you must accept are important, but can only be made by trusting the Spirit. You should look to the Spirit for the answer to where and what is truth in this day of so much deception. Marketing, by its very nature, is deception.[17] All of modern commerce is based on deceiving you. Making you think you need something when you do not. Exciting your envy to get you to purchase something you really don't need. So when it comes to the truth, you will need to demonstrate some "sales resistance" to Satan, and not be fooled into rejecting truth although it comes from a lone voice, crying from the wilderness (as has been so often the Lord's pattern in the past).

Self Government and Self Discipline

Self-government implies self-discipline. Freedom requires self-restraint in conduct and speech. People are free to say whatever they want, but when they want to say things that endanger others, then you have to consider limiting speech. That is always unfortunate. Ultimately, unless people share common values, common beliefs, and a common sense of proper conduct you cannot have "freedom" and "self-government" because it will end in violence.

When everyone agrees on first principles, there is little need for speech-limiting laws. When, however, something is deeply offensive and insulting to one group, and valued highly by another, cycles of debate end in cycles of violence.

---

[16] D&C 45:56–57 "Verily, I say unto my servant Joseph Smith, Jun., or in other words, I will call you friends, for you are my friends, and ye shall have an inheritance with me—"

[17] See *The Marketing of Evil: How Radicals, Elitists, and Pseudo-Experts Sell Us Corruption Disguised As Freedom*, by David Kupelian.

The United States' Constitutional form of government presupposes an agreement on fundamental first principles. As that common consensus diminishes on fundamental principles, our form of government is increasingly less likely to work. If the "Elders of Israel" are going to save the Constitution, it will not be through legislation or litigation, but by conversion of people back to a common set of beliefs. Only then Constitutional government has a chance to survive.

Jumping Out a Window

When I first joined the LDS Church I thought every Latter-day Saint had revelations, visitations by angels, and miracles in their lives. I thought, the Joseph Smith story was the common experience for those who were members of this Restored Church.

It took a few years before I realized that it was the exception, not the rule, that such miraculous experiences took place. I learned that most saints were more akin to Hugh Nibley's description of his grandfather, a member of the First Presidency, who said that if he ever saw an angel he would "jump out the window."

I think there is a tendency to avoid discussing any contemporary occurrence of the miraculous in our individuals lives within the Church because of the frequent association of such things with deceivers and the deceived. In contrast to that fear, Moroni affirms that angels appear only to those with "a firm mind."[18] How odd it is that we have this juxtaposition: On the one hand, in our day it is viewed as being evidence of a weak mind, or dubious character, and on the other Moroni asserts it is evidence of a "firm mind." One or the other has to be incorrect.

---

[18] Moroni 7:30 "For behold, they are subject unto him, to minister according to the word of his command, showing themselves unto them of strong faith and a firm mind in every form of godliness."

I think such things are experienced less because we talk of them less. As we talk of them less, we increase our doubts about such things. Doubt and faith cannot coincide.

So was Christ weak-minded or of "a firm mind?" Was Saul of Tarsus deceived or a deceiver, or instead a godly man who received notice from heaven? What of Joseph, Alma, Moses, Peter, Mary, Elizabeth, Agabus, and John?

Today we prefer our miracles at a distance. When we do accept the occasional miracle, we want it to be separated by culture, time and reduced to written accounts from the deceased. We think it's safer that way. Society trusts that when the miraculous has been reduced to history alone it can then safely be the stuff from which PhD's and theologians extract the **real** meanings. After all, our scientific society only trusts education, certification and licensing; not revelation, visitation and ministering of angels. Well, even if that is not as it should be, it is at least as Nephi said it would be: "They deny the power of God, the Holy One of Israel; and they say unto the people: Hearken unto us, and hear ye our precept; for behold there is no God today, for the Lord and the Redeemer hath done his work, and he hath given his power unto men. Behold, hearken ye unto my precept; if they shall say there is a miracle wrought by the hand of the Lord, believe it not; for this day he is not a God of miracles; he hath done his work." (2 Nephi 28:5–6.)

A comment on Adam-ondi-Ahman

The description in D&C 107:53 refers to Adam giving a blessing to "them."[19] You have to determine to whom the word "them" refers.

---

[19] D&C 107:53 "Three years previous to the death of Adam, he called Seth, Enos, Cainan, Mahalaleel, Jared, Enoch, and Methuselah, who were all high priests, with the residue of his posterity who were righteous, into the valley of Adam-ondi-Ahman, and there bestowed upon them his last blessing."

I wrote elsewhere about Daniel and the way in which the Lord's appearance was veiled from others who were present, Daniel alone seeing the vision. The same is true of the Lord's contact with Saul of Tarsus on the road to Damascus. Those with him did not have the same open vision.

When Joseph and Oliver saw the vision in the Kirtland Temple, they were behind a drawn canvas veil, and others were in the building. They didn't see what Joseph and Oliver saw.

In the dedication of the Kirtland Temple, the visions which were opened to some were not to others.

There was an inner group of high priests for whom the Lord's appearance would be appropriate and they are named. Naming means something. The rest are referred to as "the residue" and are not named.

These patterns are very real. They are set out in scripture because they are real. There is a great difference between being one of "the residue" of good people and being a clearly named high priest, particularly when you encounter the number of seven for the meeting. The number is also important, as I've explained in books I've written.

The picture people get into their heads is difficult to remove. But this process is dependent upon the preparation of the individual, not membership in a group. I've associated importance with elements of the revelation which others may not think important. I believe naming the seven, the number of them (seven), identifying them as high priests, calling those others "the residue" and leaving their names out of the narrative, and the overall setting takes this incident and puts it into the Daniel/Kirtland Temple/Apostle Paul category of visions of the Lord. Where some present are excluded and only a specific group or individual whose presence was specifically invited by the Lord, are permitted to stand in His presence.

It is a terrible thing to enter into the presence of the Living God. Not all who are righteous are prepared for that. Hence my reading of the verses.

Increasing Light

Teaching is marred by the ineptitude of teachers. It does not matter how complex a subject being taught is, a good teacher will make is both simple and enjoyable to learn. When a subject becomes difficult to understand, more often than not it is because the teacher does not understand the subject well enough to make it simple.

For the Gospel, teaching is a matter of increasing light in the one learning. To do that the student must learn how to improve their obedience to true principles. Only someone's obedience to truth will lead them to greater truth. The teacher's obedience cannot and does not benefit the student of the gospel if the student is unwilling to receive greater light and truth by obedience.

The necessary obedience is not obedience to a man, or men, or a set of rules devised by men. It is not even obedience to a rigid set of commandments. Obedience and fidelity must be directed to the Lord. No matter how well someone may teach for doctrine the commandments of men, those who hear will never gain more than a form of godliness, without any power.

We all must progress in the same way Christ did. He grew from grace to grace, until as last He was called the Son of God. He had the fullness of grace and truth. Read John's testimony again found in the beginning of D&C 93. Pay attention to the first verse of Section 93, because it is the summary of what John's testimony will include.[20]

---

[20] D&C 93:1 "VERILY, thus saith the Lord: It shall come to pass that every soul who forsaketh his sins and cometh unto me, and calleth on my name, and obeyeth my voice, and keepeth my commandments, shall see my face and know that I am;"

The teachings are real. Increasing light is real. But each must gain it in the very same way as Christ and all those who have followed Him gained it.

A good teacher will always work himself out of a job by teaching how to find light without him. A bad teacher will call attention to himself, and try to make others dependent upon him. The worst teachers are those who want to control those who will listen to them and to dictate what they do, what they think, and how they must follow. Christ, and the light He brings, liberates, making each person an agent for themselves. Satan's plan is to put us into bondage, controlling us and making us fear.

What's in a Name?

The site we use for this blog has the unfortunate label of "Followers" for those who read the blog, or receive regular updates on new posts. The website comment goddess who works to manage this has attempted to change the name to "Readers" but can only do that within the fields open to be changed.

Now I realize those who follow this are "Readers" and only "followers" in the sense that they receive update notices. I acknowledge the insult given you by the Google label.

As an aside, if you really are a "Follower" then let me make one thing clear: You don't want to follow me. You should be a follower of Christ. He can really do something for you. I cannot.

That having been said, now let's go on being bemused at Google's unfortunate choice of monikers for those who read a blog.

I'm really appreciative of the ability this forum has to reduce the need for repetition with many people. I hope it is convenient for readers, too.

Baptism of Fire

The question has come up about how the Lamanites could receive the baptism of fire and "know it not" when it happened.[21] Whole books have been written on this subject and I can't do it justice in a blog. So I won't try. I'll make a brief comment:

The alternatives are:

1. They knew something happened, but didn't know what it was or what it should be called.

2. They didn't realize something had happened at all.

If the reason is 1, then the result is un-troubling because without a vocabulary to label the event it is easy to to understand whey they "know it not."

Much more troubling is reason 2. What if the baptism of fire is an event so subtle it could escape detection? And if that is the case, then how is one to know when or if they have experienced it?

Some writers have made the baptism of fire such a remarkable event that it connotes salvation, even exaltation itself. For those who accept that definition of the event, then to reduce it to an undetectable occurrence seems to somehow diminish it.

Joseph described the effects of the Holy Ghost on a Gentile (purges the blood and remakes them into an Israelite), and on a descendant of Israel (pure intelligence). [I'm not going to give the cite from the *Teachings of the Prophet Joseph Smith*, because I don't have a

---

[21] 3 Nephi 9:20 "And ye shall offer for a sacrifice unto me a broken heart and a contrite spirit. And whoso cometh unto me with a broken heart and a contrite spirit, him will I baptize with fire and with the Holy Ghost, even as the Lamanites, because of their faith in me at the time of their conversion, were baptized with fire and with the Holy Ghost, and they knew it not."

copy with me while I'm writing this. So you look it up.][22] Both effects
Joseph describes could be felt in a minimal way. Neither would require it to be dramatic.

"Fire" is a description of quickening, purging sin, and receiving
the love of God. [*Beloved Bridegroom* gives a great explanation of fire as
a symbol of the love of God.] If you are living in conformity with
such light as you have been given, receiving this kind of "fire" would
not necessarily be physically detectable. The real place where it would
begin to show would be as a person prays, and then begins to receive
answers, or "pure intelligence" as Joseph put it. "A sudden flow of
ideas," which the recipient knows is beyond their capacity to think of
or accomplish, would be another way in which the recipient would
recognize its presence.

I think it is altogether possible for either explanation to be true.
No matter which explanation, I don't believe it diminishes in any way

---

[22] "There are two Comforters spoken of . . . One of these is the Holy Ghost, the same
as given on the day of Pentecost, and that all saints receive after faith, repentance, and
baptism. The first Comforter or Holy Ghost has no other effect than pure intelligence.
It is more powerful in expanding the mind, enlightening the understanding, and storing
the intellect with present knowledge, of a man who is of the literal seed of Abraham,
than one that is a Gentile, though it may not have half as much visible effect upon the
body; for as the Holy Ghost falls upon one of the literal seed of Abraham, it is calm
and serene; and his whole soul and body are only exercised by the pure spirit of intelligence; while the effect of the Holy Ghost upon a Gentile, is to purge out the old
blood, and make him actually of the seed of Abraham. That man that has none of the
blood of Abraham (naturally) must have a new creation by the Holy Ghost. In such a
case, there may be more of a powerful effect upon the body, and visible to the eye,
than upon an Israelite, while the Israelite at first might be fare before the Gentile in
pure intelligence. The other Comforter spoken of is a subject of great interest, and
perhaps understood by few of this generation. After a person has faith in Christ, re-
pents of his sins, and is baptized for the remission of his sins and receives the Holy
Ghost, (by the laying on of hands), which is the first Comforter, then let him continue
to humble himself before God, hungering and thirsting after righteousness, and living
by every word of God, and the Lord will soon say unto him, Son, thou shalt be exalted.
When the Lord has thoroughly proved him, and finds that the man is determined to
serve him at all hazards, then the man will find his calling and election made sure, then
it will be his privilege to receive the other Comforter, which the Lord hath promised
the saints, as if recorded in the testimony of St. John, in the 14th chapter, from the
12th to the 27th verses." (*TPJS*, 149–150.) The Prophet then quotes verses 16, 17, 18,
21, and 23, and asks that they be noted in particular.

the importance of this baptism of fire and the Holy Ghost. It is, in my view, the event marking the beginning of the process by which someone becomes ultimately a new creature. It is not the end of the journey. I would use other words to describe that.

Popularity or Persecution?

A recent trend with Latter-day Saint scholars has been the publishing of several books that try to make Mormonism seem like Protestant Evangelicalism. I do not believe the Restored Gospel of Jesus Christ is much akin to anything in Historic Christianity, and thankfully very different from Protestant Evangelicals. It is instead a return of Primitive Christianity as found in the New Testament. That is quite a different thing than what Historic Christianity has become, and almost altogether alien to Evangelicalism.

I believe the Church will advance only by acknowledging the differences, explaining them and showing what great things Historic Christianity has lost. Unless we have something different and important to offer, there is no reason for anyone to become a Latter-day Saint.

The opening statement of Christ to Joseph Smith in the First Vision ought to be the point we most emphasize.[23] It was the many defects with Historic Christianity and its creeds which provoked the Lord to open the heavens again and start this great, final work. When we neglect that message, and try to seem like another brand of Protestantism we are neglecting the only reason for our Church's existence.

---

[23] JS–H 1:19 "I was answered that I must join none of them, for they were all wrong; and the Personage who addressed me said that all their creeds were an abomination in his sight; that those professors were all corrupt; that: "they draw near to me with their lips, but their hearts are far from me, they teach for doctrines the commandments of men, having a form of godliness, but they deny the power thereof.""

I know it is not up to me. And I do not challenge the right of the leaders, whom I sustain, to make decisions. But, if I could make a scourge of ropes and drive the social scientists out of the Church Office Building, I would. I think opinion polling and focus group results are worse than meaningless, they are misleading. It is an exercise in followship, not in leadership. If you see a trend through polling, and jump in front of it, that does not make you a leader. It makes you a clever follower.

I suppose this post is nothing more than proof of my tendency to err in judgment. But it is an honest and well meaning error which isn't being tried by the Church at present. When it was tried, in the early years, the newspapers railed against us, editorial cartoons mocked us, mobs persecuted us, and in turn the Church grew in numbers so dramatic that a single set of missionaries sent to England baptized nearly 7,000 converts. The distinction caused by the persecution was valuable. Certainly not in a public relations sense, but very much in a "harvesting of souls" sense.

Sharp distinctions give the disinterested a reason to consider our message. Persecution attracts the honest who want to know why the persecution is happening. Joseph believed, and history has proven that persecution is the heritage of the righteous. Its absence may not really be a good thing. The cost of trying to avoid it is at the expense of forward progress. This is evidenced by the decrease in convert baptisms we see at present.

I have never seen any statement in scripture affirming that becoming popular in the eyes of the world was good or desirable. On the contrary, I see the Book of Mormon listing that as one of the great evils.[24]

---

[24] 1 Nephi 22:23 "For behold, in that day that they shall rebel against me, I will curse them even with a sore curse, and they shall have no power over thy seed except they shall rebel against me also."

The Telestial

Here's a troubling thought to ponder: The Telestial are those who have received and bear testimony of their faith in prophets, such as Paul, John, Moses, Elias, Isaiah, Enoch, and Joseph Smith, but who "received not the gospel, neither the testimony of Jesus."[25]

Security therefore lies not in following men, even men identified in the verses who are true prophets, but only in following Christ and receiving His Gospel and testimony. What an absolutely uniform, individual obligation the Gospel imposes upon everyone.

Argument

I've never won an argument with the Lord.

A Tennessee Ward and the Lord

I have a friend in Tennessee who emailed me this week about a Latter-day Saint congregation he visited a few Sundays ago. The congregation was of mixed races, and the meetings were louder, more animated, and lively than the "typical" ward. He quite enjoyed it. His description of the visit made me long for the mission field again. In the mission field there are widely divergent congregations. But the Wasatch Front is far different in texture and tone than anywhere else. I think there are people here who believe a stoic face is required to be reverent.

---

[25] D&C 76:98–102 "And the glory of the telestial is one, even as the glory of the stars is one; for as one star differs from another star in glory, even so differs one from another in glory in the telestial world; For these are they who are of Paul, and of Apollos, and of Cephas. These are they who say they are some of one and some of another—some of Christ and some of John, and some of Moses, and some of Elias, and some of Esaias, and some of Isaiah, and some of Enoch; But received not the gospel, neither the testimony of Jesus, neither the prophets, neither the everlasting covenant. Last of all, these all are they who will not be gathered with the saints, to be caught up unto the church of the Firstborn, and received into the cloud."

My impression of the mortal Lord is that He was gregarious, lively, filled with life, and given to smiling often. He surely was challenged by serious men involved in conspiracies to have Him killed, and for them His responses were serious. But He was filled with life, and love, and humor. His many analogies drew from the common man's experience to teach with simplicity the deepest of ideas. I think He would have fit into the Tennessee ward my friend told me about.

I think when the scriptures note "He wept" it was because His normal demeanor was so upbeat, so positive, and hope-filled that weeping stood out by contrast.

I've only sensed that I genuinely offended Him once. All other errors and mistakes have merely "bemused" Him, even though I have felt terrible from my end. He is a patient Teacher. Who knows exactly when you are ready and then how best to teach.

Elder Oaks at Harvard

Elder Oaks spoke to law and divinity students at Harvard this week.[26] The talk was recorded and may be broadcast between General Conference sessions. He spoke for about 45 minutes then took questions. Among the comments he made was that neither the Church nor Evangelicals would identify Mormons as Evangelicals. He also noted the hostility of higher education to religious values and beliefs, despite the widespread religious convictions of Americans.

---

[26]Oaks, "Fundamental Premises of Our Faith", February 26, 2010.
http://www.mormonnewsroom.org/article/fundamental-premises-of-our-faith-talk-given-by-elder-dallin-h-oaks-at-harvard-law-school

Becoming One

The idea of being "one" (as Christ put it in His great Intercessory Prayer in John 17:20–23)[27] has been oftentimes misunderstood and the source of abuse. There should be nothing compulsory about this process. "Oneness" is a byproduct, and not an end. When we seek it as an end, then we have missed the opportunity to achieve it.

Believing "oneness" is achieved by making people think alike, look alike, be alike, or behave alike is so wrongheaded as to be Satanic. The ideal expressed by Christ as He prayed to the Father was that we should *each* attempt, in *our limited capacities*, to be more like Christ. The closer we approach that ideal, the more we become "one" as a byproduct. Merely giving a list of behavior as the way to "oneness" is not only foolish, but it is impossible. It must come from within, and cannot come from without.

Paul's 14th Chapter of Romans is actually the only way in which "oneness" can be attained. Let everyone decide what they believe will make them closer to Christ, and allow them the freedom to follow that path. Let all others refrain from judging the behavior of others. Whether they "eateth herbs" or "eateth meat" let each be free to do what they believe to be right before God.[28] "Judge not him that eateth: for God hath received him."[29] Let everyone do what in their own heart they believe is right before God, because God will respect

---

[27] John 17:20–23 "Neither pray I for these alone, but for them also which shall believe on me through their word; That they all may be one; as thou, Father, *art* in me, and I in thee, that they also may be one in us: that the world may believe that thou hast sent me. And the glory which thou gavest me I have given them; that they may be one, even as we are one: I in them, and thou in me, that they may be made perfect in one; and that the world may know that thou hast sent me, and hast loved them, as thou hast loved me."

[28] Romans 14:2–3 "For one believeth that he may eat all things: another, who is weak, eateth herbs. Let not him that eateth despise him that eateth not; and let not him which eateth not judge him that eateth: for God hath received him."

[29] Ibid.

anything done on His behalf. And let everyone else refrain from judging these honest efforts, but bear with one another.

This will give rise to widely diverse behavior. but will result in an absolute uniformity of intent. Everyone should be free to do what they believe God is asking them to do. And everyone should also respect the honest efforts of others.

Over time, perhaps over generations, behavior will grow closer as a result of the purity of the underlying intent. Not because someone is compelling uniformity, but because light and truth will eventually bring harmony.

Being "one"—just as building Zion—cannot be a goal in itself. It is always a byproduct of the kind of people which changed hearts produce.

In a private conversation with someone a few years ago he commented that he wished the definition of "Mormonism" would be changed. He thought that anyone who was willing to accept the ordinances of the Church ought to be regarded as being Mormon, no matter what else they may differ on. I've thought about his comment for years now. I'm inclined to see a great deal of wisdom in that idea. I've grown to see that those comments echo the earlier writings of the Apostle Paul.

Trials

On Friday Marie Osmond's son died in L.A. of an apparent suicide. My heart goes out to her. Some trials in life are not meant to be understood, but only to be endured. The suffering from unexplainable ordeals can bring us closer to the Lord, who alone can comfort us in such extremities.

In Chile there are over 200 dead and many missing. There is a race to rescue about 100 people trapped in a building. Aftershocks and injuries threaten those who are trapped.

There are no magic words to console those who endure tests in mortality. But we do have the promise from Him whose word is law and cannot return to Him unfulfilled: "God shall wipe away all tears from their eyes" (Revelation 7:17). If God intends to do this in the final day, the only God-like conduct we can imitate is to lessen the burdens felt by those with a sense of loss today.

Elder Oaks

My wife also suggested I add something about Elder Oaks' talk at Harvard, since some readers may not have access to the information:

When discussing our beliefs he explained that personal revelation is fundamental to Mormon beliefs. "some wonder how members of The Church of Jesus Christ of Latter-day Saints accept a modern prophet's teachings to guide their personal lives, something that is unusual in most religious traditions. Our answer to the charge that Latter-day Saints follow their leaders out of 'blind obedience' is this same personal revelation. We respect our leaders and presume inspiration in their leadership of the church and in their teachings. but we are all privileged and encouraged to confirm their teachings by prayerfully seeking and receiving revelatory conformation directly from God."

When asked by a Divinity School student why Joseph Smith was any more reliable than Mary Baker Eddy, he responded: "If you want to know go to the ultimate source. The answer to that question can only come from God himself. That's what I encourage anyone who asks me about it. I can't promise when it will happen with anyone, but I can promise it will happen."

Keep the Commandments

I was asked about a list of "commandments" to keep. The person was sincerely trying to keep the commandments, but lacked a comprehensive list of them.

It is not possible to list all commandments. In one sense there are only two: Love God. Love your fellow man. All others are extensions of those.

If you love God you will do what He asks of you. Whenever something comes to your attention He would have you do, you do it. For example, Christ was baptized and said to "Follow Him." So because of your love of God, you follow Him.

But Christ also showed repeatedly, that the second commandment was greater than the rules. Keeping the Sabbath day holy, for example, was subordinate to loving and freeing His fellow man. He freed men from sin on the Sabbath by forgiving sins. He freed them from physical injury or disease by healing on the Sabbath. Both were considered work, and therefore an offense to the commandment to keep the Sabbath day holy.

Your individual path back to God will begin with following the teachings of The Church of Jesus Christ of Latter-day Saints. At some point, however, you will find that individual service and obedience to God's will *for you* will create disharmony between you and others. Can't be avoided. If you're following Christ, you will find the same things He found. Helping someone in need will take you away from Church meetings on occasion. You can't make a list and keep it, because as soon as you do the list will interfere with loving God and loving your fellow man.

So the whole matter can be reduced to this: Follow Christ, receive the ordinances, accept the Holy Ghost, who will teach you all things you must do. Any list beyond that will inevitably result in conflicts and contradictions.

Cool Change

I think *Cool Change* was Little River Band's greatest song. I found this video on YouTube which couples the song with video of swimming dolphins and whales.

These are mammals in the video. They are warm blooded and breathe air. Because they must breathe they are required to return to the surface. But in the video they seem to be playing, jumping, enjoying the jump into the heavens and out of the waters where they live. One of the dolphins leaps and twists like one of the Olympic events we just finished watching.

The upward leap seemed a symbol to me of what all life here was intended to do: reach up joyfully to that God who gave us life. Hope you enjoy the video and song as much as I did as I watched it with a daughter last night.

ANGELS AND MYSTERIES

The Sacrifice

Abraham's great test in sacrificing his son Isaac was all the more difficult when you consider he was nearly sacrificed when he was younger, by his father, on an altar, in a false religious practice. When the true God whom he worshiped asked him to sacrifice his beloved son, Isaac, Abraham was put in the exact position he knew from his own past experience to be evil.

Despite this, Abraham complied.

Then God Himself provided a sacrifice.[30]

Not the ram found in the thicket on that day, but a living Son, later—in a direct corollary to what had first been asked of Abraham.

Many have stood back in amazement and considered the task given to Abraham to be outrageous, inexplicable, and offensive. It was. But it was designed to make us realize how outrageous, inexplicable and offensive the sacrifice of God's Only Begotten was on our behalf. Abraham was one of the few men whose experience allowed him to identify with God the Father.

---

[30] Genesis 22:8 "And Abraham said, My son, God will provide himself a lamb for a burnt offering: so they went both of them together."

His Words are Commandments

A great resource for understanding how to gain eternal life is found in D&C 1:38.[31] The Lord's word is law. What He says will not return void. It will all be fulfilled.

Immediately following his father's death, Moroni writes concerning the plates his father had made, which he was then completing. He recorded that the plates are "of no worth" in an economic sense, because of the Lord's "commandment."[32] He says the Lord had spoken the words: "no one shall have them to get gain."[33] This means that since the Lord had spoken that the gold plates could not be obtained for economic gain, this meant the Lord had "commanded" that the plates could not give a person any economic gain. The only gain to be had was "of great worth" to the soul.

Moroni equates the Lord's remark on the plates' lack of economic value to a "commandment." This is exactly how it works. This is what D&C 1:38 is affirming, as well: "What I the Lord have spoken, I have spoken, and I excuse not myself; and though the heavens and the earth pass away, my word shall not pass away, but shall all be fulfilled, whether by mine own voice or by the voice of my servants, it is the same."

Salvation consists in getting the word of the Lord spoken to you as a promise of eternal life. When you obtain that word, it cannot be broken. It becomes a "commandment" of the Lord's which cannot fail. This is the kind of commandment we should seek.

---

[31] D&C 1:38 "What I the Lord have spoken, I have spoken, and I excuse not myself; and though the heavens and the earth pass away, my word shall not pass away, but shall all be fulfilled, whether by mine own voice or by the voice of my servants, it is the same."

[32] Mormon 8:14 "And I am the same who hideth up this record unto the Lord; the plates thereof are of no worth, because of the commandment of the Lord. For he truly saith that no one shall have them to get gain; but the record thereof is of great worth; and whoso shall bring it to light, him will the Lord bless."

[33] Ibid.

I've tried to answer questions about "commandments" and I've tried to discuss the subject more fully in *The Second Comforter: Conversing with the Lord Through the Veil*. Instead of focusing on a list of things to do or not do, I would commend to you the idea of getting from the Lord those words which will assure you eternal life. Not His words spoken to others found in scripture, but words spoken by Him to you. If you obtain this from Him, then you have a sure promise, though the heavens and earth pass away. This more sure word guarantees you, by covenant from Him whose words cannot fail, that you will be granted life with Him.

Temple Work

In relation to the world's population there are statistically fewer LDS each year. Our birth rate is declining and our baptism rate does not even begin to keep up with world population growth. In other words, each year there is far more temple work to be done than there was the year before.

Judging

When Christ made His Twelve Disciples in the Americas "judges" over those people in the great Day of Judgment, He did not empower them to use their own discretion to reward or punish others. He said they would judge others "according to the judgment which I shall give unto you, which shall be just."[34] That same standard would apply to His Twelve Apostles in the New Testament.[35]

---

[34] 3 Nephi 27:27 "And know ye that ye shall be judges of this people, according to the judgment which I shall give unto you, which shall be just. Therefore, what manner of men ought ye to be? Verily I say unto you, even as I am."

[35] Matthew 19:28 "And Jesus said unto them, Verily I say unto you, That ye which have followed me, in the regeneration when the Son of man shall sit in the throne of his glory, ye also shall sit upon twelve thrones, judging the twelve tribes of Israel."

Christ Himself will provide the decision for us all; those Twelve will have the honor of announcing it.

I've often thought that with the standard set by the Lord in the Sermon on the Mount,[36] that any time a person is given the opportunity, they should forgive others, just as Christ admonished us.[37]

Those who think presiding over a ward or stake gives them an opportunity to dominate others are taking an extraordinary risk against their own eternal interests. My counsel would be to err on the side of forgiving, and never on the side of condemning. Even the woman taken in the act of adultery was told by the Lord: "neither do I condemn thee."[38]

Christ's teachings were meant to be applied internally to check our own behavior. Not externally as a means to judge or condemn others. If you see something amiss in other's conduct, then persuade them by your example to be better. Lectures are almost always useless. An example is compelling.

---

[36] Matthew 2:1–2 "Now when Jesus was born in Bethlehem of Judaea in the days of Herod the king, behold, there came wise men from the east to Jerusalem, Saying, Where is he that is born King of the Jews? for we have seen his star in the east, and are come to worship him."

[37] Matthew 6:14–15 "For if ye forgive men their trespasses, your heavenly Father will also forgive you: But if ye forgive not men their trespasses, neither will your Father forgive your trespasses."

[38] John 8:1–11 "Jesus went unto the mount of Olives. And early in the morning he came again into the temple, and all the people came unto him; and he sat down, and taught them. And the scribes and Pharisees brought unto him a woman taken in adultery; and when they had set her in the midst, They say unto him, Master, this woman was taken in adultery, in the very act. Now Moses in the law commanded us, that such should be stoned: but what sayest thou? This they said, tempting him, that they might have to accuse him. But Jesus stooped down, and with *his* finger wrote on the ground, *as though he heard them not.* So when they continued asking him, he lifted up himself, and said unto them, He that is without sin among you, let him first cast a stone at her. And again he stooped down, and wrote on the ground. And they which heard *it,* being convicted by *their own* conscience, went out one by one, beginning at the eldest, *even* unto the last: and Jesus was left alone, and the woman standing in the midst. When Jesus had lifted up himself, and saw none but the woman, he said unto her, Woman, where are those thine accusers? hath no man condemned thee? She said, No man, Lord. And Jesus said unto her, Neither do I condemn thee: go, and sin no more."

Declining Numbers

There was an article on *Mormon Times* about the declining baptism rate the Church is experiencing.[39] I thought it was odd to approach this subject in an article which maintains there is nothing unusual about a declining rate of baptisms.

The prophecy of Daniel was that the stone cut out of the mountains without hands would roll forth, grind to dust the prior world orders, become a great mountain, and fill the whole earth.[40] Daniel's interpretation included that God will establish a kingdom in the latter days which shall never be destroyed, nor left to other people. It will break into pieces and consume all other kingdoms and stand forever.[41]

To the extent the Church claims to be this kingdom, or rock rolling forth, it should be expected to increase in size, and momentum, as it rolls forth to fill the earth.

The Church ceased to distinguish between baptisms for "children of record" and "converts" some years ago. Numbers are given in April General Conference. Last April's conference statistical report included this statement: "Converts Baptized: 265,593." There was a separate category for "Children of Record" but there was no separate category for "Baptisms of Children of Record." That used to be

---

[39] http://www.mormontimes.com/mormon_voices/mckay_coppins/?id=12892

[40] Daniel 2:34–35 "Thou sawest till that a stone was cut out without hands, which smote the image upon his feet *that were* of iron and clay, and brake them to pieces. Then was the iron, the clay, the brass, the silver, and the gold, broken to pieces together, and became like the chaff of the summer threshingfloors; and the wind carried them away, that no place was found for them: and the stone that smote the image became a great mountain, and filled the whole earth."

[41] Daniel 2:44–45 "And in the days of these kings shall the God of heaven set up a kingdom, which shall never be destroyed: and the kingdom shall not be left to other people, *but* it shall break in pieces and consume all these kingdoms, and it shall stand for ever. Forasmuch as thou sawest that the stone was cut out of the mountain without hands, and that it brake in pieces the iron, the brass, the clay, the silver, and the gold; the great God hath made known to the king what shall come to pass hereafter: and the dream *is* certain, and the interpretation thereof sure."

a separate category. Since its elimination, I have had the impression that "Converts Baptized" included all numbers, including baptisms of "Children of Record." If that is so, then for the last recorded numbers of baptisms you would need to go back to eight years earlier, take the number of Children of Record, and subtract that number from the "Converts Baptized number to get the actual number of Converts. Eight years earlier from the number given in last General Conference, the statistical report announced that there was an increase of 81,450 Children of Record. So the actual number of baptisms of Converts alone would be 184,143. That appears to me to be the real number of Converts, exclusive of baptisms of Children of Record.

Now the Church hasn't provided this separate number for Children of Record for about a decade now. And I can't be certain that the "Converts Baptized" category is actually an amalgamation of the two. But I think it is. If so, the decline from the time of President Kimball to today is more than significant, it is catastrophic.

I believe the only reason to convert to our faith is our doctrine. Since the Church has de-emphasized doctrine, the trend of lowering missionary success has confirmed my belief in the necessity of teaching doctrine. Not just in the *Teach My Gospel* program, but in every aspect of the Church, from Sunday School and Primary to Stake and General Conferences. Doctrine is what distinguishes us.

Deseret Book has actually told me that "doctrine books do not sell." They are interested in fiction, which can be read in one or two settings.

Repent and Come Unto Me

There is this interesting statement by the Lord found in D&C 10:

"Behold, this is my doctrine—whosoever repenteth and cometh unto me, the same is my church. Whosoever declareth more or less than this, the same is not of me, but is against me; therefore he is not of my church." (D&C 10:67–68)

The statement requires us to

1. Repent, and then

2. Come unto Christ.

Repentance is a lifelong process. As we get further light and knowledge, we have to incorporate it into our lives and change behavior. Over a lifetime, this should be dynamic, not static.

The more difficult explanation is to "Come unto Him." It is my view that this includes fully receiving Him into your life as did the brother of Jared, Nephi, Enos, Enoch, Abraham, Moses, Joseph Smith, Daniel, Isaiah, Jacob, Mormon, Moroni, Alma the Younger, Paul, and so many others who have testified of Him. That is a subject so great that the entire body of scriptures exist to help us accomplish it.

Significant, too, is that whatever is "more or less" than this is not "of my church" according to the Lord. So we have to take great care to not overstate or understate this doctrine of His. Adding endless requirements by the commandments of men is "against Him." Similarly, any failure to declare the essential nature of coming to Him is also "against Him." I think the first verse of D&C 93 is a formula for coming to Him.[42] That formula declares that, when it is followed, you will see His face and know that He is.

---

[42] D&C 93:1 "VERILY, thus saith the Lord: It shall come to pass that every soul who forsaketh his sins and cometh unto me, and calleth on my name, and obeyeth my voice, and keepeth my commandments, shall see my face and know that I am;"

How Beautiful upon the Mountains

The feet of those who walk upon the mountains crying peace are beautiful[43] because they are clean from the blood and sins of their generation.

In the ancient ceremonies involving animal sacrifice, blood was shed upon the ground and the feet of those involved in the rites became bloody. The blood of the sacrifice upon the feet became a symbol of the sins for which the sacrifice was offered.

The feet of those who walk upon the mountains crying peace are cleansed from that blood. Christ's washing of His Apostles' feet was to symbolize this cleansing which He alone could provide. He employs no servant to provide such a cleansing.[44] These feet, washed by Him are, therefore, beautiful because they connote the sanctity of the one crying peace.

"Crying peace" because the only thing which stills the mind of man, and brings rest from the trouble of this world, is the atonement of Christ. That is why it is called "the rest of the Lord." When cleansed, it becomes the consuming desire of those who are clean to bring others to partake. Just like Lehi's dream, when those who had eaten of the fruit of the tree of life ate, they immediately invited others to come and join them.

"Upon the mountains" because the mountain is nature's symbol of the ascent to God. The climb represents repentance and purification of the soul. When a person stands upon the top of the mountain, she appears to be part of heaven itself and no longer earth-

---

[43] Isaiah 52:7 "How beautiful upon the mountains are the feet of him that bringeth good tidings, that publisheth peace; that bringeth good tidings of good, that publisheth salvation; that saith unto Zion, Thy God reigneth!"

[44] 2 Nephi 9:41 "O then, my beloved brethren, come unto the Lord, the Holy One. Remember that his paths are righteous. Behold, the way for man is narrow, but it lieth in a straight course before him, and the keeper of the gate is the Holy One of Israel; and he employeth no servant there; and there is none other way save it be by the gate; for he cannot be deceived, for the Lord God is his name."

bound. Her profile is with the sky, symbolizing the completion of the ascent back to God.

It is beautiful. All of it is beautiful. All of it is a reflection of the purity and intelligence of God, whose ways are higher than man's ways as the heavens are higher than the earth.[45]

True Blue, Through and Through

I've been thinking about an incident in the young life of Joseph F. Smith. He was outside a camp gathering firewood when a group of Mormon-haters rode into camp and scattered all the men. Joseph F. considered running for a moment, but then decided to go confront them. He walked with his armful of firewood back into the camp, right up to an armed man who was cursing the Mormons.

The man bellowed at Joseph F.: "Are you a Mormon?"

Joseph responded: "Yes siree; dyed in the wool, true blue, through and through."

The man was so disarmed that he grabbed Joseph F.'s hand and told him he was the "pleasantest man I ever met!" (with a few ob-scenities mixed in.)

I like that story. I consider myself a "true blue, through and through Mormon." Despite that, I know we have problems and many flaws. The scriptures foretell our many deficiencies. But human weaknesses and shortcomings are no impediment to the Divine origin of Mormonism; nor its ultimate destiny.

I think it is an error to have an unreasonably high opinion of ourselves. Conversely, it is an error to conclude that all is lost because of our shortcomings. We are full of sins and errors, slogging along making institutional and individual errors daily. But we are also, insti-

---

[45] Isaiah 55:8–9 "For my thoughts *are* not your thoughts, neither *are* your ways my ways, saith the Lord. For *as* the heavens are higher than the earth, so are my ways higher than your ways, and my thoughts than your thoughts."

tutionally and individually, called to be involved in God's work to redeem His children. He loves us all, with a love which can overcome our many failures.

An Emphasis on Doctrine

In addition to what I posted earlier about baptism rates, there is another number which is somewhat misleading. The total member numbers reported in General Conference never deducts for those who are excommunicated or who voluntarily ask to have their membership terminated. There is likely a doctrinal reason for that. When a person is excommunicated they are re-baptized to return to membership, but they are not re-ordained to the priesthood. They are given a blessing to reinstate their covenants and blessings, including authorization to begin using priesthood again. But they are not re-ordained. Although they are excommunicated, they retain some affiliation despite the severance. Nevertheless, most people do not assume someone who has been excommunicated would be counted in the number of total members, but it is my understanding that they are.

Also, I've heard estimates from as little as 25% to much more than that as the percentage of members for whom the Church has completely lost contact. That is, there is some significant number of members whose membership is so tenuous that the Church has nothing but a record. There is no address, no way to contact them, and no information about whether they are living or deceased. These people continue to be counted in the total membership number despite their complete absence of contact with or from the Church.

With the significantly lower fertility rate, and an aging population, the Church's future will not be anything like the projections of Professor Stark. That is, unless something changes.

I agree that there may be many reasons for the decline. However, the most prominent of reasons in my view is the de-emphasis on doctrine. As a convert to the Church I know what attracted me to become a Mormon. It had nothing to do with the formulaic discussions of the missionaries, slick marketing or good arguments. It had to do with doctrine. I *didn't want* to be a Mormon. Quite the contrary. But I knew I should become a Mormon because their doctrines came from God and answered questions other faiths could not begin to answer.

I'd like to see the trend return to a dramatic increase of numbers. In fact, I think there are many millions in the United States alone who are only kept from the truth because they do not know where to find it.[46] We won't attract them to the Church until we begin again to emphasize doctrine.

A Lifetime of Service

I do not know President Monson personally. But his history is well known to all of us. He was a Bishop while in his 20s, a Stake President shortly thereafter, and then called in his late 30s to be a member of the Quorum of the Twelve. He worked for Deseret News before becoming a full time General Authority. Essentially his entire life has been church service, both in his profession and in his calling.

If you want to see what The Church of Jesus Christ of Latter-day Saints would produce if a life were entirely the product of the institution and experiences derived from serving in and under that institution, you have that in President Monson.

It is clear to me that he absolutely trusts the system which produced all his significant life experiences. The last two vacancies in the Twelve were filled by the senior president of the Seventy. This would

---

[46] D&C 123:12 "For there are many yet on the earth among all sects, parties, and denominations, who are blinded by the subtle craftiness of men, whereby they lie in wait to deceive, and who are only kept from the truth because they know not where to find it—"

make Elder Ron Rasband the next one in line to fill a vacancy in the Twelve. He (Elder Rasband) is a member of my stake.

Heeding the Warning

There is an interesting article in *Meridian Magazine* about the Chilean earthquake.[47] The Mission President and his wife went about preparing the missionaries for the earthquake before it happened. This was because they had received a prior warning.

What is most interesting to me is that the warning came to the wife, not the husband. He respected her revelation, and they went together to proclaim the warning. *Meridian Magazine* published this article. It delights me when there is recognition of the entirely democratic way in which revelation comes to us. And when we find a married couple without jealousy about such things.

Institutional Charisma

There was an article in the Church News about a symposium at BYU dealing with the "Organization and Administration of the LDS Church."[48] The article mentions a paper delivered by Professor Bushman titled "Joseph Smith and the Routinization of Charisma." Among other things, Professor Bushman asserts the church's "genius can be largely explained in the fact that the expectation of divine revelation has been built into the very administrative structure and offices of the Church, an expectation attributable to the Prophet himself." This is what he asserted also in *Rough Stone Rolling*.

From the two thousand year example of the Roman Catholic Church, I fear presumptions like these. There is a profound difference between actual revelation and an "expectation of divine revela-

---

[47] http://www.ldsmag.com/churchupdate/100303chile.html

[48] http://www.ldschurchnews.com/articles/58903/Symposium-deals-with-the-institution-of-the-Church.html

tion ... built into the very administrative structure and offices of the Church." He uses comments from Joseph Smith to support the assertion, while ignoring the revelation in Section 121 cautioning that while many may be called, few are chosen.[49] He ignores the revelation that it is the nature and disposition of almost all men, as soon as they get a little authority as they suppose they begin to immediately exercise unrighteous dominion. Without confirming revelation given to every member of the Church, as a constant check on abuse, the destiny of Mormonism will be a repeat of the history of Catholicism. A Holy American Empire will replace the Holy Roman Empire, both of which have or will resort to blood and horror as the means to reign over mankind. The bedrock of the Gospel is the testimony of Jesus. The testimony of Jesus is the spirit of prophecy.[50] That is the charisma the scriptures tell us to trust.

There is absolutely no historical precedent we can point to which confirms that charisma can be safely institutionalized. There are an abundance of examples, however, of men abusing religion to gain control over others to satisfy their pride, to exercise control and dominion over others, and to gratify their vain ambition. The only check against this are the individual testimonies of the few, humble followers of Christ. Nevertheless, we are told that in our day even they are going to be led into error oftentimes by those who teach them the precepts of men.[51]

---

[49] D&C 121:34, 40 "Behold, there are many called, but few are chosen. And why are they not chosen? Hence many are called, but few are chosen."
D&C 95:5 "But behold, verily I say unto you, that there are many who have been ordained among you, whom I have called but few of them are chosen."

[50] Revelation 19:10 "And I fell at his feet to worship him. And he said unto me, See *thou do it* not: I am thy fellowservant, and of thy brethren that have the testimony of Jesus: worship God: for the testimony of Jesus is the spirit of prophecy."

[51] 2 Nephi 28:14 "They wear stiff necks and high heads; yea, and because of pride, and wickedness, and abominations, and whoredoms, they have all gone astray save it be a few, who are the humble followers of Christ; nevertheless, they are led, that in many instances they do err because they are taught by the precepts of men."

Angels

There is a system by which men learn the mysteries of heaven and are saved. That system is set out in Alma 12:29–30:[52]

- First, angels are sent to prepare men/women.
- Second, they are allowed to behold the Lord's glory.
- Then they converse with the Lord, at which point they are taught the things which have been prepared from the foundation of the earth for their salvation.
- All of which is driven by the man/woman's faith, repentance and holy works.

This is in keeping with Joseph Smith's revelation about those chosen to become a member of the Church of the Firstborn. They are chosen by the holy angels to whom the keys of this power belong.[53]

If this isn't happening, then faith does not exist on the earth any longer.[54]

Ministering angels are an indispensable part of the Gospel of Jesus Christ. That is why those keys were restored so early on in this

---

[52] Alma 12:29–30 "Therefore he sent angels to converse with them, who caused men to behold of his glory. And they began from that time forth to call on his name; therefore God conversed with men, and made known unto them the plan of redemption, which had been prepared from the foundation of the world; and this he made known unto them according to their faith and repentance and their holy works."

[53] D&C 77:11 "Q. What are we to understand by sealing the one hundred and forty-four thousand, out of all the tribes of Israel—twelve thousand out of every tribe?
A. We are to understand that those who are sealed are high priests, ordained unto the holy order of God, to administer the everlasting gospel; for they are they who are ordained out of every nation, kindred, tongue, and people, by the angels to whom is given power over the nations of the earth, to bring as many as will come to the church of the Firstborn."

[54] Moroni 7:37 "Behold I say unto you, Nay; for it is by faith that miracles are wrought; and it is by faith that angels appear and minister unto men; wherefore, if these things have ceased wo be unto the children of men, for it is because of unbelief, and all is vain."

dispensation, and are so widely disseminated into the Church membership.[55]

Wo, Wo, Wo

Enoch's powerful testimony to his condemned contemporaries included this question: "why counsel ye yourselves, and deny the God of heaven."[56] Men in that day preferred to have the counsel of men instead of the word of God, from God.

Nephi spoke of the "Zion" of our time and said:

"Wo be unto him that hearkeneth unto the precepts of men, and denieth the power of God, and the gift of the Holy Ghost." (2 Nephi 28:26)

Now having one "wo" pronounced upon a people is a warning of condemnation in this life. Their ways do not prosper and they suffer setbacks because they listen to the precepts of men. They fall back. More concerning is when three "wo's" are pronounced upon a people. The connotation being a condemnation which will last beyond this life and into eternity. So I take the following statement with some considerable seriousness:

"[T]hey have all gone astray save it be a few, who are the humble followers of Christ; nevertheless, they are led, that in many instances they do err because they are taught by the precepts of men. O the wise, and the learned, and the rich, that are puffed up in the pride of their hearts, and all those who preach false doctrines, and all those who commit whoredoms, and pervert the right way of the Lord, wo, wo, wo be unto them, saith the Lord God Almighty, for they shall be thrust down to hell." (2 Nephi 28:14–15)

Three "wo's" pronounced and three names of God used to make that warning. False doctrines and whoredoms are an equivalent in this passage. That is, you are "whoring" after other false gods, and betraying the true Lord God Almighty, when you preach false doctrines which assure you, in your pride, that you are safe, elect, chosen and better than others. Such teachers are condemned three-fold.

What an interesting problem we have in front of us. No-one can trust in any man or men. All of us are required to hear God's voice, and follow Him.

In My Opinion

I think Alma 41:8 should be cross referenced with D&C 130:7.[57]

The footnote at Alma 41:10b should include Deuteronomy 32:8–9.[58]

Alma 41:15

Alma 41:15 includes this thought: "For that which you do send out shall return unto you again."[59] Profound thought. I do not be-

---

[57] Alma 41:8 "Now, the decrees of God are unalterable; therefore, the way is prepared that whosoever will may walk therein and be saved."
D&C 130:7 "But they reside in the presence of God, on a globe like a sea of glass and fire, where all things for their glory are manifest, past, present, and future, and are continually before the Lord."

[58] Alma 41:10 "Do not suppose, because it has been spoken concerning restoration, that ye shall be restored from sin to happiness. Behold, I say unto you, wickedness never was happiness."
Deuteronomy 32:8–9 "When the most High divided to the nations their inheritance, when he separated the sons of Adam, he set the bounds of the people according to the number of the children of Israel. For the Lord's portion is his people; Jacob is the lot of his inheritance."

[59] Alma 41:15 "For that which ye do send out shall return unto you again, and be restored; therefore, the word restoration more fully condemneth the sinner, and justifieth him not at all."

lieve you have to await the afterlife or Judgment Day to realize the truth of this statement.

Therefore, I try to take care what I "send out" for fear of how it may return unto me again.

My Scriptures

I have several sets of scriptures. The one I prize the most used to be my every-day set. Into this copy I have added only additional cross-references and footnotes. There are no other marks. I suspect that I have added between 11,000 and 15,000 additional cross references and footnotes in red pencil to this set. It has become so valuable a study set that I do not take it out of my home.

I have a "retired" set which is literally falling apart. I used that set to teach from 1980 to 2000. It is tattered, and has very little, if anything, marked or added to it. I keep that set in my desk drawer at work.

Then I have a new set which has become my every-day set. I take it to Church with me.

None of these sets have thumb-indexing on the pages. I HATE that stuff. It distracts me when I use the scriptures. Both of the first two sets were "Type A" sets which Deseret Book used to publish without thumb-indexing. You can't get a "Type A" set like that anymore. I tried. Even talked with the management at Deseret Book. Can't be done.

So I bought a "Type B" set, which is the same paper as a "Type A" but just not genuine leather bound. Much cheaper set. Then I took that set to Schafer Bindery in Salt Lake and had them bind it with a real leather cover. So I have a "Type A" set, without thumb indexing, and it only cost in total about $20 more than if Deseret Book made a proper set and sold them.

With Respect to the Leaders of The Church of Jesus Christ of Latter-day Saints

I balance my deep respect for these men, and profound aware-ness that no-one is really equal to the burden which WE impose upon them, with the knowledge that I alone am responsible for con-firming through revelation all truth. Now, I say "the burden which WE impose upon them" to distinguish between what the Lord and scriptures says are their duties on the one hand, and the mythological duties which we have put upon them. The scriptures and the Lord do NOT make them omniscient. As a group the Saints do. That is the first great error, and it is not the leader's error but the saints'.

I've seen many, many mistakes made by the Brethren. But I loved them and sustained them and have refrained from being overtly criti-cal of them.

It is not an institution which will be saved. Indeed, the institution is doomed to be confined to this world, and not pass into the next. But, it is the individual who will be saved. Individuals, however, must receive what the institution offers to obtain salvation. Therefore re-spect for the church is necessary. It's role is essential. It's authority from the Lord.

Genius

Joseph Smith was the first, great restorer of lost light in this Dis-pensation. He restored doctrine, authority, ordinances, scriptures and the organization for the Church. His ministry was one of the greatest among men in any age.

The second great restorer was, in my view, Hugh Nibley. He shed light on antiquity using the scholar's tools while calibrating the recov-ery of ancient truth using the restored doctrine, authority, ordinances and scriptures which Joseph had bequeathed him. Hugh Nibley's legacy as a restorer of lost truth from the past is second only to Joseph Smith's.

Joseph's genius was unique and inspired. So was Hugh Nibley's. In the case of Hugh Nibley, he inspired a whole generation of students and produced a small army of those who intended to follow his example. It is not as easy as it seems, however. From scholarly disciples, to FARMS to now the Maxwell Institute, the effort has produced some good fruit. but you cannot institutionalize genius. The great contribution of Brother Nibley is simply something that cannot be replicated or continued.

Genius will always be (as Will Durrant put it while intending to be derisive): "isolated and unruly." It could not be tamed in the schools of Greece, nor can it be captured in the halls of BYU. Credentials will never become a substitute for inspiration.

WHAT GUARANTEE DO WE HAVE?

Nadab and Abihu

I was asked about the relationship between Nadab and Abihu's death and the Day of Atonement ceremony. I responded as follows:

Remember that these two saw the Lord in sacred space (on top of Sinai with Moses) earlier in their lives.[60]

Despite their earlier audience with the Lord, they were not authorized to enter the Holy of Holies. Only the chosen High Priest, and then once an year, only on the Day of Atonement.[61]

---

[60] Exodus 24:9–11 "Then went up Moses, and Aaron, Nadab, and Abihu, and seventy of the elders of Israel: And they saw the God of Israel: and *there was* under his feet as it were a paved work of a sapphire stone, and as it were the body of heaven in *his* clearness. And upon the nobles of the children of Israel he laid not his hand: also they saw God, and did eat and drink."

[61] See Leviticus 16. Also Leviticus 23:26–32 "And the Lord spake unto Moses, saying, Also on the tenth *day* of this seventh month *there shall be* a day of atonement: it shall be an holy convocation unto you; and ye shall afflict your souls, and offer an offering made by fire unto the Lord. And ye shall do no work in that same day: for it *is* a day of atonement, to make an atonement for you before the Lord your God. For whatsoever soul *it be* that shall not be afflicted in that same day, he shall be cut off from among his people. And whatsoever soul *it be* that doeth any work in that same day, the same soul will I destroy from among his people. Ye shall do no manner of work: *it shall be* a statute for ever throughout your generations in all your dwellings. It *shall be* unto you a sabbath of rest, and ye shall afflict your souls: in the ninth *day* of the month at even, from even unto even, shall ye celebrate your sabbath."

They entered into the Holy of Holies when they were not authorized, and burned incense contrary to the Day of Atonement ceremony. They were not authorized to be there nor to do what they did.
Therefore they were struck down.[62] The Lord reminded Moses after
their death that those who are going to enter into that place must be
"sanctified" before entering, hence the Day of Atonement ceremony
being a prerequisite for entry.

Later Jewish tradition required the High Priest to have a rope tied
to his ankle when he entered the Holy of Holies, so that his body
could be recovered if he were struck down without the necessity of
others entering the room.

Raising the Bar

The name of the policy which eliminates a large population of
desirous young men from serving a mission was really unfortunate.
"Raising The Bar" implies that these young men do not measure up.

Repentant young men who have been involved with serious sexual transgressions during their teens are by and large denied the opportunity to serve. So, also, are young men with medical conditions
which require significant treatment or medications.

As a result of this program, there have been tens of thousands of
young men who have not served. The missionary force dropped
from the high 60,000's to the low 50,000's and has remained there.
Those who have been excluded who wanted to serve have quite often felt judged and alienated as a result. Many have either left activity
or left the church altogether. They form a body numbering now in
excess of 100,000, and as they marry, have children, and raise their

---

[62] Leviticus 10:1–3 "And Nadab and Abihu, the sons of Aaron, took either of them his
censer, and put fire therein, and put incense thereon, and offered strange fire before
the Lord, which he commanded them not. And there went out fire from the Lord, and
devoured them, and they died before the Lord. Then Moses said unto Aaron, This *is it*
that the Lord spake, saying, I will be sanctified in them that come nigh me, and before
all the people I will be glorified. And Aaron held his peace."

posterity outside the church they will eventually number in the millions.

Calling this program "Raising The Bar" has essentially precluded a change. You can't "Lower The Bar" without seeming foolish, or to invite 'ner do well's.

I've seen what this program has done to young men who wanted to serve, and who would have been allowed to serve before the program was announced. I've tried to overcome their sense of rejection by the church, and have succeeded in only one case. The others have essentially all told me that the church had rejected them and therefore they intended to stay away.

Equinox

The Vernal Equinox is Saturday, March 20th. It is that moment that arrives every year where everything is in balance, light and dark are balanced and nature everywhere from pole to pole is showered equally with the light and life of heaven. It occurs twice a year, and not again until the Autumnal Equinox in the Fall.

The First Vision aligned with the Spring, the date of which is not recorded. However, as Michael Quinn noted in his work (using borrowed research), the Smith family in general and Joseph in particular, would have associated power with the event. It is not unlikely that the First Vision occurred on the Vernal Equinox, just as Moroni's visits always coincided with the Autumnal Equinox.

For our day, the Autumnal Equinox is the more significant. The Vernal is associated with life, birth, beginnings, restoration and newness. The Autumnal is associated with death, closing, judgment and endings. We live on the cusp of the end times. Though there remain a great many things to be done, our era is the time when history is about to close out.

Observing the Vernal, Autumnal and Solstices was something done from ancient times, in ceremony and in ritual. Whole cities were built aligned to the cardinal directions of the compass and the lights of heaven. The lights of heaven were given to us first as "signs" and secondly as "seasons."

Don't let them pass by unnoticed. Otherwise you note less than even the plants and the animals whose life cycles and behavior acknowledge the passing of such events.

Reincarnation

Yesterday at lunch I heard a great line from the Maharaja: "Reincarnation is only for the ignorant." Made me laugh.

All Things Bear Testimony

In reflecting back on John Pratt's recent article on Venus and its tie to the Lord's life, I have concluded that the phrase "under the earth" as used in Moses 6:63 is referring to the cycles of the "wandering stars" or planets.[63] It does not refer to the subterranean composition of the earth's mantle.

Venus disappears on the horizon, taking it "under the earth." Then it reappears again, symbolizing the resurrection of the Lord. Venus being the great symbol of Christ, as John Pratt has shown.

As Val Brinkerhoff has also shown in his *The Day Star—Reading Sacred Architecture* volumes, the orbit of Venus tracks a pentagram in the sky over its eight year cycle.

Toyotas and light beer are of more interest to us than the procession of the equinoxes through the zodiac. All things do bear testi-

---

[63] Moses 6:63 "And behold, all things have their likeness, and all things are created and made to bear record of me, both things which are temporal, and things which are spiritual; things which are in the heavens above, and things which are on the earth, and things which are in the earth, and things which are under the earth, both above and beneath: all things bear record of me."

mony of God. But we prefer the billboards on the side of the highway.

Ordinances

Oddly, ordinances were intended to communicate an inner message of redemption and holiness. Instead, they get looked upon as credentials. They aren't. Possession of ordinances without inner holiness is meaningless. On the other hand, D&C 137 shows that possession of inner holiness, while lacking the ordinances, will not be an impediment. (We can send anyone with a card to the temple to take care of the ordinances. But how infrequent it is that we produce a redeemed and acceptable soul to our God and Father.)

Christ's Victory

Christ's great victory was won by this simple formula: "He suffered temptations but gave no heed unto them." (D&C 20:22)

A Little Leaven

Sometimes it is the thinnest of threads which keeps a people from judgment. A "little leaven" or a "little salt" can save a whole lump. The want of "five righteous" has and can destroy a whole city. When you consider so thin a thread as that, you must surely realize there are no private sins. Each life has cosmic meaning.

Patriarch Smith

The Patriarch of the Church is Eldred G. Smith, now aged 103 years. His office used to ordain the President of the Church of Jesus Christ of Latter-day Saints using the hereditary priesthood line running back to Father Smith, Joseph and Hyrum.

Eldred G. Smith was made Emeritus in 1979, but continues to have an office in the Church Office Building.

Powerful Doctrines

I've been reading Alma's teachings on priesthood in Alma 13. There are some startling things in there. We underestimate the depth of doctrine preserved in the Book of Mormon. Pre-earth life is unmistakably taught there.

Ordination to the high priesthood reckons from before the foundation of the earth. Power in that priesthood is derived from heaven (as D&C 121 teaches).

These powerful doctrines are not even imagined by other faiths or traditions. Among us it is hardly understood, and we possess the scriptures that teach it.

Seriously

There's an article which estimates that 16% of the population (teens to 49 yrs.) of the United States has genital herpes.[64]

Now there's an advertisement for the law of chastity . . .

or anti-itch Gold Bond...

or a wire hair brush to scratch with . . .

The woman/man has not been born who is worth forfeiting what is lost by breaking covenants with the Lord.

Patriarch

When I first joined the church we sustained the Patriarch of the Church, along with the First Presidency and the Quorum of the Twelve as a "Prophet, Seer and Revelator." I would expect that at some point Patriarch Smith will be succeeded by his oldest, direct, descendant, unless there is still a living sibling of his upon whom the office would devolve (which I doubt).

---

[64] http://www.reuters.com/article/idUSN0923528620100309

When the office was established, it formed an independent line of priesthood authority. This line was not be dependent upon selection by temporary office holders drawn from many family lines. Instead the Smith family, through whom the church was restored, would hold this hereditary office forever. It will be interesting to see how this office is handled in the future.

Do We Have a Guarantee?

I've been thinking about the "guarantee" we have as Latter-day Saints that God takes peculiar delight in us. We're His "chosen" and He looks down from heaven and grins broadly when He considers our enlightened advantage over our fellowman. I'm not sure I can reconcile that happy view of our circumstances with His frank assessment of us in D&C 112:23–26.[65]

I'm thinking that the first order of the day for me is repentance.

Judgment

Since the Lord reserves to Himself alone the final judgment,[66] I think we overstep our privileges when we presume our judgment of others is our right. In fact, the irony of judging while holding priesthood office is that the one judging may be the one really on trial. They hold office, are given "keys", and are upheld by other saints to

---

[65] D&C 112:23–26 "Verily, verily, I say unto you, darkness covereth the earth, and gross darkness the minds of the people, and all flesh has become corrupt before my face. Behold, vengeance cometh speedily upon the inhabitants of the earth, a day of wrath, a day of burning, a day of desolation, of weeping, of mourning, and of lamentation; and as a whirlwind it shall come upon all the face of the earth, saith the Lord. And upon my house shall it begin, and from my house shall it go forth, saith the Lord; First among those among you, saith the Lord, who have professed to know my name and have not known me, and have blasphemed against me in the midst of my house, saith the Lord."

[66] 3 Nephi 27:27 "And know ye that ye shall be judges of this people, according to the judgment which I shall give unto you, which shall be just. Therefore, what manner of men ought ye to be? Verily I say unto you, even as I am."

see whether they will execute the assignment in conformity with D&C 121, using gentleness, meekness, persuasion, kindness and love unfeigned. If they don't, they fail the test, and in the process establish the criteria and means by which they will be judged.

Ironically, the one judging is the one really on trial, and the one being judged will be a witness against (or for) them.

Things are different than we think. And that is as it should be. Otherwise the hearts of men could not be put on display here in this life, and the proving that this estate was designed to accomplish would fail.

We should be afraid to hold office over others. We should have pity or compassion for those who are called to these positions. Instead, we envy those who hold offices in the church. Nephi counseled against this.[67]

Now is the great day of deception when darkness covers so much of the social order that madness reigns. If you just turned the light on and saw our day as clearly as Nephi did you'd marvel at the abundant foolishness, vanity and errors we entertain. To do that you only need to read what Nephi wrote and realize he's talking to and about US; not those who will never read the book.

We're being tested. More importantly, I'm being tested. So I need to "work out my salvation with fear and trembling before the Lord" just as Paul suggested.[68]

It's *Your* Eternal Salvation

When it comes to the subject of one's eternal salvation, I can't understand why someone would simply trust others and leave it to

[67] 2 Nephi 26:21 "And there are many churches built up which cause envyings, and strifes, and malice."

[68] Philippians 2:12 "Wherefore, my beloved, as ye have always obeyed, not as in my presence only, but now much more in my absence, work out your own salvation with fear and trembling."

them to tell them what is necessary. I should think everyone would study this matter night and day, and reach their own conclusion about what is important, what is not, what will save, and what is simply foolishness.

Joseph said he advised all to go on and search deeper and deeper into the mysteries of God. Alma said about the same thing.[69]

When it comes to sacred knowledge, the absence of curiosity and relentless inquiry is evidence of apathy and indifference. Joseph posed the question in the *Lectures on Faith* of how we can hope to inherit the same reward as the ancients without following the same path as they did. Great question, that. Brings to mind Abraham's description of his own relentless search to find God.[70] I think that is the formula. As is also D&C 93:1.[71]

Important

I think this is interesting history. I should like to know more of this kind of thing:

---

[69] Alma 12:9–11 "And now Alma began to expound these things unto him, saying: It is given unto many to know the mysteries of God; nevertheless they are laid under a strict command that they shall not impart only according to the portion of his word which he doth grant unto the children of men, according to the heed and diligence which they give unto him. And therefore, he that will harden his heart, the same receiveth the lesser portion of the word; and he that will not harden his heart, to him is given the greater portion of the word, until it is given unto him to know the mysteries of God until he know them in full. And they that will harden their hearts, to them is given the lesser portion of the word until they know nothing concerning his mysteries; and then they are taken captive by the devil, and led by his will down to destruction. Now this is what is meant by the chains of hell."

[70] Abraham 1:2 "And, finding there was greater happiness and peace and rest for me, I sought for the blessings of the fathers, and the right whereunto I should be ordained to administer the same; having been myself a follower of righteousness, desiring also to be one who possessed great knowledge, and to be a greater follower of righteousness, and to possess a greater knowledge, and to be a father of many nations, a prince of peace, and desiring to receive instructions, and to keep the commandments of God, I became a rightful heir, a High Priest, holding the right belonging to the fathers."

[71] D&C 93:1 "VERILY, thus saith the Lord: It shall come to pass that every soul who forsaketh his sins and cometh unto me, and calleth on my name, and obeyeth my voice, and keepeth my commandments, shall see my face and know that I am;"

Joseph Smith, by revelation, established two presiding offices: The President of the High Priesthood and the Patriarch of the Church. The President (Joseph Smith) presided. But the Patriarch stood by with keys to ordain the next President and provide for orderly transition from one President to the next.

The Patriarchal office is by lineage or descent. That way it cannot be stolen by an interloper; thereby creating a separation of power inside the one Church (or kingdom).

Joseph became President through divine ordination by the Lord and messengers sent by the Lord.

Brigham Young was sustained as President, relying upon his ordination as an Apostle.

John Taylor was also sustained, relying also upon his ordination as an Apostle.

These precedents were relied upon through Joseph F. Smith, who had an ordinance/ordination accompany his assumption of the office of President of the Church. That ordination was performed by his half-brother, John Smith, the Patriarch of the Church.

Heber J. Grant was conflicted about the Patriarch because he considered himself a descendant of Joseph Smith by sealing and the Patriarch was competition to that; and therefore he did not want the Patriarch to ordain him president. He had the Twelve ordain him. He also initiated the name change from "Presiding Patriarch" to "Patriarch to the Church."

Heber J. Grant's practice continued thereafter.

Interestingly the term "Prophet" was not applied to a living man holding the office of "President of the Church" until 1955, during the administration of David O. McKay. The term "Prophet" until that time always meant exclusively Joseph Smith, and not the office holder of President. Before then it was "President Young" and "President Taylor" and "President Woodruff" and so on. However, in 1955 the Church News began a new practice of referring to the living President McKay as a "Prophet." It was felt that changing the reference to the living President would result in quicker acceptance of direction from him, and less criticism of the President. (President Grant was the most unpopular Church President in the Church's history, and that was something they hoped to avoid happening again.) It worked. No-one wants to reject counsel from a living prophet of God.

So since that time the practice has been for living Presidents to continue to be referred to by the title "Prophet" by all General Authorities and other leaders. However, I have noticed that the President never refers to himself as "Prophet" in any declaration I have been able to find. He accepts that term as used by others, but does not apply it to himself.

The recorded times when a Church President was asked if he was "a Prophet" include testimony by Joseph F. Smith when asked by the Senate Committee in the hearings to seat Senator Smoot. His response was "my people sustain me as such." President McKay was asked by a reporter and his response was "look me in the eye and tell me I'm not a prophet." President Lee essentially repeated the same response to a reporter as President McKay. And when he was interviewed by the Press President Hinckley essentially repeated Joseph F. Smith's response, saying in effect: "I'm sustained by the Church as such." There may be others, but those are the ones I recall at the moment.

All of which is, I suppose, interesting history. I of course, sustain as "prophets, seers and revelators" the First Presidency and Quorum of the Twelve every Ward Conference, Stake Conference, General Conference and temple recommend interview.

Accuser of Our Brethren

There is really no reason to complain about the church. That is a role I would never want to assume. Satan's title is "the accuser of our brethren".[72] Of what does he accuse them? The answer is of all their natural failings, mistakes, shortcomings and errors. We are all ample examples of such shortcomings. No matter how good a life we may lead, we all fall short. The answer to this problem is not to accuse others but to forgive them. We cloak others in a robe of charity, and we in turn merit charity.

This is why Christ requires us to forgive all others. We get forgiveness as we give forgiveness to others. There is an extensive discussion of this in *Come, Let Us Adore Him*. It is true doctrine.

I think avoiding the role of "accuser" and filling the role of patient forbearance with others' shortcomings is the only wise course in life.

The Lord Is in Charge

I was asked if there was a day coming when men/women will be required to condemn those in the church whose conduct does not measure up. I responded:

There is certainly a day of separation coming. Angels are already begging to begin that process. The Lord has told them "not yet" but promised them it will happen "by and by" as His preparations continue.

The Lord is in charge. We needn't worry about how His purposes will all be fulfilled. Patience with the larger picture is easier when we realize that for each of us the smaller, individual picture is what is important. We have plenty to do individually to receive our invitation

---

[72] Revelation 12:10 "And I heard a loud voice saying in heaven, Now is come salvation, and strength, and the kingdom of our God, and the power of his Christ: for the accuser of our brethren is cast down, which accused them before our God day and night."

into the Church of the Firstborn. As we do what is necessary to receive that invitation, then we will become more effective ministers of
salvation for others. Worrying about the salvation of all others before being saved ourselves is a needless thought.

The evil of this day is sufficient[73] because it really is enough to
live well one day at a time. Eternity will be composed of living well
one day. For God all is as one day.[74] When we have done that, we are
ready to receive eternity. Until then, worrying about the larger and
more chaotic picture of what is going on keeps us from changing the
only environment over which we have any influence or control. That
is the environment of our hearts.

Sampson

I teach the Young Men tomorrow and will be discussing Sampson's life and example. He conforms to one of the great patterns of
men sent by the Lord to deliver His people. That often repeated pattern includes:

- A couple or woman who cannot bear a child because of
  some infirmity, age, infertility, barrenness, or lack of marriage.
- A promise made that a son will be sent.
- The woman/couple receive a son despite the infertility
  problem before.
- The son then comes and plays a role which alters the course
  of the Lord's people.

This was the case with Abraham and Sarah, to whom Isaac came.
Manoah, to whom Sampson came. Elkanah and Hannah, to whom

---

[73] Matthew 6:34 "Take therefore no thought for the morrow: for the morrow shall take
thought for the things of itself. Sufficient unto the day *is* the evil thereof."

[74] Alma 40:8 "Now whether there is more than one time appointed for men to rise it
mattereth not; for all do not die at once, and this mattereth not; all is as one day with
God, and time only is measured unto men."

Samuel came. Zechariah and Elizabeth, to whom John was sent.
Mary and Joseph, to whom Jesus came.

There have been many others, but their stories are not always
recorded or known.

Sampson was a Nazarite, the covenant terms of his dedication to
the Lord is set out in Numbers 6. Among other things, a Nazarite
was not to cut his hair during the time of the covenant. This was the
reason Sampson's hair cutting was so significant. It represented the
final break of the covenant.

Sampson was a Messianic figure. He foreshadowed the Lord.

There is a statement in Matthew that Christ was to be called a
"Nazarene."[75] That conflicts, however, with the later inquiry of Na-
thanael recorded in John 1:46: "Can any good thing come out of
Nazareth?" The more likely statement Matthew was referring to was
that the Lord was to be "called a Nazarite" meaning he was under
the covenant in Numbers 6.

I've written a parable about the way in which Sampson's life mir-
rored the Lord's in *Ten Parables*.

I believe that if we had a full account of the Lord's life we would
realize just how much Sampson's life foreshadowed the Lord's. A
hint of that is contained in that parable in *Ten Parables*.

Different Traditions, Different Interpretations

In Stephen's testimony just prior to his martyrdom in Acts, he
gives an account of Moses which does not appear in our version of
the Old Testament. In Stephen's explanation, he attributes to Moses
the knowledge that he was going to be a deliverer of Israel even be-

---

[75] Matthew 2:23 "And he came and dwelt in a city called Nazareth: that it might be
fulfilled which was spoken by the prophets, He shall be called a Nazarene."

fore he killed the Egyptian.[76] According to Stephen, Moses was frustrated that the Israelites failed to recognize him as their deliverer.

Our account instead tells us that Moses was called by God, to his surprise. When called, Moses responded:

> "Who am I, that I should go unto Pharaoh, and that I should bring forth the children of Israel out of Egypt?" (Exodus 3:11)

This goes to show that there were different traditions reflected in the biblical accounts. Just as there are references to scriptural books which we no longer possess.

The relevance of personal revelation, and the need for continuing revelation, remain apparent even if you want to understand the very scriptures we believe in. Hence the almost immediate reaction of Joseph and Oliver to receiving the Holy Ghost and how scriptures took on new, even previously hidden meanings.[77]

I was taught from the New Testament all my childhood by a mother who was a Baptist. When hands were laid upon my head after baptism, I re-read the New Testament and thought it was a new book.

---

[76] Acts 7:24–25 "And seeing one *of them* suffer wrong, he defended *him,* and avenged him that was oppressed, and smote the Egyptian: For he supposed his brethren would have understood how that God by his hand would deliver them: but they understood not."

[77] JS–H 1:74 "Our minds being now enlightened, we began to have the scriptures laid open to our understandings, and the true meaning and intention of their more mysterious passages revealed unto us in a manner which we never could attain to previously, nor ever before had thought of. In the meantime we were forced to keep secret the circumstances of having received the Priesthood and our having been baptized, owing to a spirit of persecution which had already manifested itself in the neighborhood."

True and Living

The Lord's reference to the Church in a revelation received on November 1, 1831 as "the only true and living church upon the face of the whole earth"[78] was true for the following reasons:

First, the Church was established by revelation, visitations from angels, and delegation of authority.

Second, it was "living" because the authority and gifts were present and unfolding; and new scripture and revelations were being received.

Third, it would continue to grow in knowledge, light and truth as further ordinances and rites were restored.

Finally, it was "true" because it taught the doctrines which gave converts the tools with which they could grow in light and knowledge until the perfect day.[79]

The Lord's description in 1831 is what we should aspire to have said about us still, today. But, of course, that would require us to also be "true" and "living" in the same way as the Church in 1831.

Concourses of Angels

The object of this mortal existence is to develop faith. We need adversity and a sense of isolation from God in order to develop the character necessary to be like God. There is a test underway. But it is conducted by a benign and friendly heavenly host, whose primary purpose is to develop in us a godly character and charity toward one another.

---

[78] D&C 1:30 "And also those to whom these commandments were given, might have power to lay the foundation of this church, and to bring it forth out of obscurity and out of darkness, the only true and living church upon the face of the whole earth, with which I, the Lord, am well pleased, speaking unto the church collectively and not individually—"

[79] D&C 50:24 "That which is of God is light; and he that receiveth light, and continueth in God, receiveth more light; and that light groweth brighter and brighter until the perfect day."

Men and women may see Christ in vision or in an appearance as a solitary personage. But no person has ever seen God the Father without also seeing a host of others. They are referred to in scriptures as a "heavenly host," or "numerous angels," or "concourses of angels." There is a reason that a company is always shown at the appearance of the Father. You should look into the matter. Within the answer lies a great truth about God the Father.

Shepherds of Israel

In Ezekiel 34 it is written:

> "Son of man, prophesy against the shepherds of Israel, prophesy, and say unto them, Thus saith the Lord God unto the shepherds: woe be unto the shepherds of Israel that do feed themselves! should not the shepherds feed the flocks? Ye eat the fat, and ye clothe you with the wool, ye kill them that are fed: but ye feed not the flock." (Ezekiel 34:11–12)

This description could be applied with several layers of meaning. However, the one I like best is the interpretation which relates "feeding" to teaching truths. Shepherds were given the calling of teaching the "flocks" of Israel higher truths which would exalt them. However, they instead focused their ministry upon things which were trivial, did not raise the inner lives of the "flocks," and stirred up those who followed them into envy and strife. These shepherds were unworthy, condemned with the pronouncement of "woe" upon them and warned by the prophet.

Fortunately, Ezekiel's message goes on to promise that in the latter-days the Lord will "both search [His] sheep, and seek them out. As a shepherd seeketh out his flock in the day that he is among his sheep that are scattered; so will I seek out my sheep, and will deliver them out of all places where they have been scattered in the cloudy and dark day."[80] We are in that latter-day time now. He is seeking. But notice that throughout the description of His latter-day work, He alone takes credit for finding and feeding.[81]

When He has gathered enough to establish again His kingdom, He will then make a new day in which "my servant David" will be the "one shepherd" over them, in that Millennial Day.[82]

We're supposed to be getting gathered now in anticipation of becoming numerous enough for there to be a Millennial King provided for us. We're supposed to be in contact with the Lord as He alone gathers us in this latter-day. It is a glorious vision for which we should rejoice.

---

[80] Ezekiel 34:11–12 "For thus saith the Lord God; Behold, I, *even* I, will both search my sheep, and seek them out. As a shepherd seeketh out his flock in the day that he is among his sheep *that are* scattered; so will I seek out my sheep, and will deliver them out of all places where they have been scattered in the cloudy and dark day."

[81] Ezekiel 34:13–17 "And I will bring them out from the people, and gather them from the countries, and will bring them to their own land, and feed them upon the mountains of Israel by the rivers, and in all the inhabited places of the country. I will feed them in a good pasture, and upon the high mountains of Israel shall their fold be: there shall they lie in a good fold, and *in* a fat pasture shall they feed upon the mountains of Israel. I will feed my flock, and I will cause them to lie down, saith the Lord God. I will seek that which was lost, and bring again that which was driven away, and will bind up *that which was* broken, and will strengthen that which was sick: but I will destroy the fat and the strong; I will feed them with judgment. And *as for* you, O my flock, thus saith the Lord God; Behold, I judge between cattle and cattle, between the rams and the he goats."

[82] Ezekiel 34:22–24 "Therefore will I save my flock, and they shall no more be a prey; and I will judge between cattle and cattle. And I will set up one shepherd over them, and he shall feed them, *even* my servant David; he shall feed them, and he shall be their shepherd. And I the Lord will be their God, and my servant David a prince among them; I the Lord have spoken *it.*"

Amos Was No Prophet's Son

In a vision given to Amos, the Lord showed him a plumb line. This was the method used to establish a straight wall.[83] When Amos delivered the message he received, the king threatened him. Amos' answer was succinct:

> "I was no prophet, neither was I a prophet's son; but I was an herdman, and a gatherer of sycomore fruit; And the Lord took me as I followed the flock, and the Lord said unto me, go, prophesy unto my people Israel. Now therefore hear thou the word of the Lord: Thou sayest, Prophesy not against Israel, and drop not they word against the house of Isaac. Therefore thus saith the Lord; They wife shall be an harlot in the city, and thy sons and they daughters shall fall by the sword, and they land shall be divided by line; and thou shalt die in a polluted land: and Israel shall surely go into captivity forth of his land." (Amos 7:14–17)

Prophets in the past have come from obscure places. They quite often resisted delivering a message which the audience wanted to hear. Instead they corrected the behavior of a fallen people. There were no opinion polls, no focus groups to shape the message they delivered. Their words corrected, jarred, condemned and served as a warning which could allow the faithful to change the path they were on whenever needed. The Apostle Paul coined a term for teachers who taught doctrines that reassured those who ought to be con-

---

[83] Amos 7:7–9 "Thus he shewed me: and, behold, the Lord stood upon a wall *made* by a plumbline, with a plumbline in his hand. And the Lord said unto me, Amos, what seest thou? And I said, A plumbline. Then said the Lord, Behold, I will set a plumbline in the midst of my people Israel: I will not again pass by them any more: And the high places of Isaac shall be desolate, and the sanctuaries of Israel shall be laid waste; and I will rise against the house of Jeroboam with the sword."

demned. He said such people "heap to themselves teachers, having itching ears".[84] I presume "heap" means they get quite a few of them.

I'm pleased we live in a day of living prophets again, and that we receive stern warnings from time to time from those who know the Lord. Such occasions provide us all the opportunity to be warned, repent, change our ways and approach nearer the mark of the high calling of God, in Christ Jesus.[85]

Daylight Savings

We celebrated Daylight Savings by neglecting to reset the clocks and missing Sacrament Meeting. Apparently this was a widespread celebration in our ward, with less than half making it to the meeting on time. I sense a family tradition in the making here.

Disgraced

Both the Republican leaders of the Utah Legislative Senate and House were forced to resign this year. The Senate leader because of a DUI. The Representative leader because of a sexual relationship with a minor many years ago, which he paid $150,000 campaign money to buy her silence. In connection with the latter scandal, the church-owned Deseret News was aware of the sexual misconduct eight years ago, but kept silent until other news of the matter became public.

The problem with any political machine owning a state is the same everywhere. It really does not matter if that machine controls the city of Chicago or the State of Utah, the result is the same. People do "favors" for the insiders, and the public suffers as a result.

---

[84] 2 Timothy 4:3 "For the time will come when they will not endure sound doctrine; but after their own lusts shall they heap to themselves teachers, having itching ears;"

[85] Philippians 3:14 "I press toward the mark for the prize of the high calling of God in Christ Jesus."

Utah's reputation as "the reddest of red states" is well deserved. The competition to fill these seats for the two involved in the scandals is internal to the Republican Party. The result of doing so will not be unlike what has long been the case here in Utah, where only one side controls everything.

Both of these men were Latter-day Saints. They are victims of the corrupt political domination every bit as much as the public has been. Without a healthy opposition party, there is no real check upon misbehavior and excesses.

I've always thought that opposing views and people speaking their mind is healthy. Without some criticism of a person's plans and ideas you simply get a chorus of "yes men" chanting how inspired or worthy or good all ideas are, no matter how flawed or foolish. Utah's two fallen leaders are "family men," one of whom was known as a champion of "family values." It's almost as if he had shopped with focus groups to know what words to use to get elected, without any regard to what was within his heart.

Now is the great day of opinion polling and focus group directed marketing, in which the substance of any group of political leaders is always hidden behind the carefully crafted message intended to market image. Indeed, image is everything in this day of deceit.

So, choose your leaders carefully. They will all sound the same. It will not be the vocabulary which will distinguish the evil and corrupt from the true and good. It will only be what lies within them that will differ.

Christ's Touch

Ceremonial uncleanness under the law of Moses could be spread from the unclean to the person who came in contact with them. Uncleanliness could be spread.

A tradition grew among the Jews that the altar of the Temple could not be profaned, and that if an unclean person came into contact with it, the altar did not become unclean but instead the person coming into contact with the altar became clean. We have two examples of persons relying upon this tradition in the case of Joab in the Old Testament and Zacharias in the New.

Joab was to be killed by Solomon, and he knew he was to die. To die in contact with the altar was to die clean, and so Joab fled to the tabernacle, took hold of the altar and was killed there. The ones sent to kill him hesitated because they also knew they were killing a clean man, and had to be told a second time to kill him by Solomon.[86] Solomon did not care that Joab would die clean.

In the case of Zacharias, his death is not recorded other than in a passing reference by Christ as He confronted the scribes and Pharisees.[87] Joseph Smith said this reference was to John's father.

In the case of Christ, the tradition had fulfillment. He touched the unclean, but communicated cleanliness to them. Whether it was

---

[86] 1 Kings 2:28–34 "Then tidings came to Joab: for Joab had turned after Adonijah, though he turned not after Absalom. And Joab fled unto the tabernacle of the Lord, and caught hold on the horns of the altar. And it was told king Solomon that Joab was fled unto the tabernacle of the Lord; and, behold, *he is* by the altar. Then Solomon sent Benaiah the son of Jehoiada, saying, Go, fall upon him. And Benaiah came to the tabernacle of the Lord, and said unto him, Thus saith the king, Come forth. And he said, Nay; but I will die here. And Benaiah brought the king word again, saying, Thus said Joab, and thus he answered me. And the king said unto him, Do as he hath said, and fall upon him, and bury him; that thou mayest take away the innocent blood, which Joab shed, from me, and from the house of my father. And the Lord shall return his blood upon his own head, who fell upon two men more righteous and better than he, and slew them with the sword, my father David not knowing *thereof, to wit,* Abner the son of Ner, captain of the host of Israel, and Amasa the son of Jether, captain of the host of Judah. Their blood shall therefore return upon the head of Joab, and upon the head of his seed for ever: but upon David, and upon his seed, and upon his house, and upon his throne, shall there be peace for ever from the Lord. So Benaiah the son of Jehoiada went up, and fell upon him, and slew him: and he was buried in his own house in the wilderness."

[87] Matthew 23:35 "That upon you may come all the righteous blood shed upon the earth, from the blood of righteous Abel unto the blood of Zacharias son of Barachias, whom ye slew between the temple and the altar."

the woman with an issue of blood, a leper, or the dead, touching them did not make Him unclean, rather it made those whom He touched clean.

Common Consent

My car insisted it was 5:36 this morning as I drove my daughter to Seminary. The Honda was not yet in on the collective conspiracy to sustain the loss of an hour by our common consent.

My daughter got out the owner's manual while we were driving and helped me convince the car to sustain the new hour. Now the Honda is also in on the conspiracy by common consent to change our bearings in the universe.

It still gets light and dark as before, but we call it something different. Happily, the Honda does not contradict that illusion anymore.

We cannot control the reality in which we live, but we can use our collective agreements to pretend it is otherwise. Now we awake and arise at a different time, but call it an hour later. Common consent is a powerful thing. It can be used to change how we look at time itself.

Why a Teleprompter?

My wife and I were watching a KBYU broadcast of a speaker using a teleprompter to deliver a talk to students there. What a remarkable difference there is between an extemporaneous talk, given from the heart, and someone reading a teleprompter.

I think it is high tribute to President Obama that his use of a teleprompter is so casual and conversational that you cannot detect he is reading the comments. He actually seems to be speaking spontaneously when he uses one. That is a great gift, unfortunately not shared by many other public speakers.

When a talk is read off a teleprompter and sounds like reading, the speaker sounds insincere, even robotic. I wonder why we see them used so often anymore, even at BYU Education Week, among small audiences. When you rob a speaker of spontaneity, you deprive the audience of a connection which might have been made.

I can't read a talk. I can try, but I always drift off into a conversation and leave the script behind.

Valiant

Those who receive a Terrestrial estate include "they who are not valiant in the testimony of Jesus; wherefore, they obtain not the crown over the kingdom of our God" (D&C 76:79). This means that they actually did have a testimony of Jesus, were on the right path, received the Gospel and accepted it, but failed to be "valiant" in their testimony.

I do not believe this means rigid, dogmatic, insistent or bellicose. In fact, the religious people having these qualities have historically been the greatest persecutors of the few, humble followers of Christ in all generations.

I believe this means they were willing to suffer much for the Lord. To follow Him in meekness, gentleness, kindness, persuasion, and love unfeigned. To bear the crosses of this world, and to return good for evil. Valiance is measured by the patience you show to your fellowman when they say all manner of evil against you falsely, for His sake. It is measured by the things you suffer willingly and without complaint.

It is not to get a reward in this life. Nor is it to be given acclaim, recognition, applause or chief seats.

It is to minister to others, rather than to be ministered unto.

When I think of the greatest examples of such conduct as would be truly described as "valiant," I think of mothers and what they have done and do to bring, bear, love and raise children in this world.

Creation itself is renewed every time a new, innocent life is brought into this world.

Ask, Seek, and Knock

James promised the Lord would answer those who lack knowledge and ask with a sincere heart.[88] The Prophet Jeremiah made a similar promise. In Jeremiah's promise the words are a quote from the Lord. He said:

> "And ye shall seek me, and find me, when ye shall search for me with all your heart." (Jeremiah 29:13)

He is approachable. He wants us to approach Him.

Faith, Belief, Knowledge

The psalmist's words, "by the word of thy lips I have kept me from the paths of the destroyer" (Psalms 17:4), refers to all the words of God. Not just those in scripture alone, but also those that came from "thy lips" O Lord. The Lord visited with the psalmist as he recorded: "thou hast visited me in the night."[89]

This idea of God's visitation with those who follow Him is as ancient as creation itself. Belief was always intended to grow into faith. Faith was always intended to grow into knowledge.

---

[88] James 1:5–6 "If any of you lack wisdom, let him ask of God, that giveth to all *men* liberally, and upbraideth not; and it shall be given him. But let him ask in faith, nothing wavering. For he that wavereth is like a wave of the sea driven with the wind and tossed."

[89] Psalms 17:3 "Thou hast proved mine heart; thou hast visited *me* in the night; thou hast tried me, *and* shalt find nothing; I am purposed *that* my mouth shall not transgress."

Adam and Eve

Adam and Eve could not have children while they were in the Garden of Eden. They lacked the capacity to bear children in the innocent state in which they then existed.[90]

They had been given the gift of childbearing as an endowment from God. The endowment of the capacity did not mean they had the means or understanding at the time to act upon it. Without the fall, they would not have been able to act on the endowment. They were like little children who are born male and female with the capacity to one day become parents, but who are immature and innocent, and therefore unable to bear children.

The great offense was in Satan's control of the timing. Had they remained in the Garden throughout the Sabbath day of rest then they would have received the commandment to partake of the fruit in the Lord's timing. At this point they would have moved from their innocent state into a condition not unlike the Millennial day. The "fall" would have transitioned to a Terrestrial state, rather than a Telestial state.

It Is Enough for One to Seek Him

The Gospel of Jesus Christ, in a fullness, with power to save and exalt, remains intact on the earth. Whenever there are those who come to Him, He will quickly come to them.

Since salvation is always an individual event, the failure of others to search for and obtain the great blessings which He makes available to His followers is not and never has been predicated upon the success of a group.

---

[90] 2 Nephi 2:23 "And they would have had no children; wherefore they would have remained in a state of innocence, having no joy, for they knew no misery; doing no good, for they knew no sin."

It is enough for one to seek Him. But when two or three are gathered in His name, He will not leave them comfortless, but will respect their faith, heed and diligence.

Lamenting about the decay all around you will not help you draw closer to Him. If you detect that decay, then your eyes have been opened, and you should do something about it in your *own* life. Condemning the failure of others has not advanced a single soul in history. It is true enough that the Lord may require by the constraint of the Spirit that people be "reproved betimes with sharpness" but only "when moved upon by the Holy Ghost."[91] But the Gospel of Jesus Christ consists in gathering light and truth, which is not accomplished by focusing upon the failings of others.[92]

Strangers and Angels

Here was my thought to the kids last night as they were getting ready to for bed:

> "Be not forgetful to entertain strangers: for thereby some have entertained angels unawares." (Hebrews 13:2)

I believe that. I think it happens more often than people generally believe or even think possible.

Nicodemus

When Christ taught publicly and could be heard daily, there was no need to approach Him at night in private. However, Nicodemus, a Pharisee member of the Sanhedrin, came to Jesus to examine Him

---

[91] D&C 121:43 "Reproving betimes with sharpness, when moved upon by the Holy Ghost; and then showing forth afterwards an increase of love toward him whom thou hast reproved, lest he esteem thee to be his enemy;"

[92] D&C 93:28 "He that keepeth his commandments receiveth truth and light, until he is glorified in truth and knoweth all things."

"by night" without his peers knowing that he was making this contact. Christ knew the heart of Nicodemus, and put the matter squarely to him:

> "Verily, verily, I say unto thee, Except a man be born again, he cannot see the kingdom of God." (John 3:3)

The assertion made here is:

"*Verily, verily*"—meaning Christ was capable of announcing truth.

"*I say unto thee*"—meaning that Christ was capable of making commandments, establishing conditions, announcing the requirements for salvation. Indeed, Christ was putting Himself into the position of Moses, becoming a lawgiver.

"*Except a man be born again, he cannot see the kingdom of heaven*"— meaning that if Nicodemus intended to see heaven, Christ was declaring the condition for entry. Becoming a new creature was essential. Without newness, new birth, a new approach to life, all things which Nicodemus followed would lead away from the kingdom of heaven.

Nicodemus responded:

> "How can a man be born again when he is old? Can he enter the second time into the mother's womb, and be born? " (John 3:4)

This isn't a rhetorical or meaningless question, nor does it announce ignorance. Nicodemus is testing Christ. If this is a new lawgiver, and possessed the capacity to announce conditions for entry into heaven, then He needs to explain His meaning. This is a Pharisee Rabbi, asking a young, new Rabbi to set the matter plainly.

Christ responded:

> "Except a man be born of water and of the Spirit, he cannot enter into the kingdom of God. That which is born of flesh

is flesh: and that which is born of the Spirit is spirit. Marvel not that I said unto thee, Ye must be born again. The wind bloweth where it listeth, and thou hearest the sound thereof, but cannot tell whence it cometh, and whither it goeth: so is every one that is born of the Spirit." (John 3:5–8)

Now it is put plainly:

Born as a new man, by water (baptism) and Spirit (receive Holy Ghost) is required to "enter into the kingdom of God." Without receiving these new ordinances from the new officiators (John the Baptist and Christ), the old ordinances will no longer be accepted. This is a call to Nicodemus to receive the new prophets then preaching. Without accepting these new prophets, he could not enter into God's kingdom.

Flesh is just flesh. What is required to be able to go where God is will require every person to receive a new Spirit, new life, and become connected with heaven.

Heaven is unruly, unpredictable and blows without predictability. The Spirit is unruly, requiring things which men do not anticipate. It takes you places you have not been before. You cannot just sit within the councils of the Sanhedrin and reason with men's understanding. You must become inspired by a higher source. You must accept that new direction from above, or you will never enter into God's kingdom.

Brilliant. Christ taught the teacher. Now the matter is put to him: Will he receive a new life, and leave the old one? Will he become born again.

How hard it must have been for a man in Nicodemus' position to approach Christ. The fact he came at night testifies to the discomfort of his circumstances. Yet Christ, in patience, told him how to receive eternal life.

What a revealing encounter. We are the richer in our understanding for it having occurred.

Twelve Oxen

The Temple of Solomon had a "sea" for washings of the priests. The description of that "sea" is found in 1 Kings 7.[93] Significantly the "sea" sat upon the backs of twelve oxen.[94] Three were facing north, three facing west, three facing south, and three facing east.

In the time of the First Temple, these twelve oxen foreshadowed the scattering of Israel to the four corners of the earth. The destruction of the First Temple completed the scattering, which began at the death of Solomon, who was responsible the construction of the First Temple. When he died, the kingdom was divided north and south. The northern kingdom contained ten tribes, which would be taken into Assyrian captivity at about 725 B.C., and then be lost to history as they scattered northward. The remaining two tribes of the south were taken captive by Babylon at 600 B.C., and then a "remnant" returned. They were finally dispossessed of their land at 70 A.D. by the Roman destruction of Jerusalem, and scattered throughout the Roman Empire.

We also build fonts in Temples with twelve oxen bearing the font of water used for baptisms for the dead. These twelve oxen are also divided into groups of three facing north, west, south and east. Now, however, the oxen signify the gathering of scattered Israel. They also signify by their number, three, the concept of presidency or organization under restored priestly authority. The circle of twelve also are

---

[93] 1 Kings 7:23–26 "And he made a molten sea, ten cubits from the one brim to the other: *it was* round all about, and his height *was* five cubits: and a line of thirty cubits did compass it round about. And under the brim of it round about *there were* knops compassing it, ten in a cubit, compassing the sea round about: the knops *were* cast in two rows, when it was cast. It stood upon twelve oxen, three looking toward the north, and three looking toward the west, and three looking toward the south, and three looking toward the east: and the sea *was set* above upon them, and all their hinder parts *were* inward. And it *was* an hand breadth thick, and the brim thereof was wrought like the brim of a cup, with flowers of lilies: it contained two thousand baths."

[94] Ibid, verse 25.

a symbol of restored, reorganized Israel in the latter-days to once again exist as a united people upon the earth.

How I Study the Scriptures

I was asked about how I study. It was a good enough question I thought I ought to address it here.

First, I spent over 20 years teaching Gospel Doctrine weekly. To prepare for a class I would read the assigned scriptures on Sunday evening. Beginning Monday I would research in commentaries what others had said about the passages in the assigned lesson. Then before going to bed I would re-read the scriptures for the next lesson.

I would continue this process daily until Thursday. Beginning Thursday I would start to outline what I intended to cover in the lesson on Sunday.

Throughout the week I would listen to the relevant scriptures for the next lesson on tape/CD whenever I was in my car. So on the way to and from work I would listen and re-listen to the scriptures.

On Saturday I would pray then put a final lesson plan together. It took about 10 hours a week for me to prepare a 50 minute lesson.

In all the time I taught I never repeated a lesson. I tried to go deeper and deeper into the meaning of the material every time I taught it.

Today with that background I read books and scriptures daily. However, I take what I learn back into my scriptures and add cross-references or margin notes to make scriptural passages more meaningful for me. My scriptures have very little underlining and no coloring, but there are many notes and cross-references in them.

I try to tie any new concept I learn, no matter the source, back into the scriptures. Lately I have also taken to using an electronic version of the scriptures to help locate material or passages which relate to a topic.

Weekend Movie

I watched a new DVD we bought from Deseret Book titled *One Good Man.*

If it was satire or intended as irony then it was quite good. If it was just a straight up drama then I hated it. Since it was an LDS product, and sold at Deseret Book, I assume it wasn't meant as irony or satire.

It offended me because the lead character was called to be a Bishop. This makes the hero a church leader. The hero treats one of his ward members as disposable, but goes out of his way for non-members and widows. It resulted in the inactivity of an entire family whose sole outreach by the bishop was to go Christmas caroling with his family on their porch. While there, he tells the wife that he "hadn't seen them in church lately."

It was depressing. As irony it shows how a "good" man can't always do good. Life is riddled with conflicts and unintended harm. So I like it as irony.

Dumbing Down?

I had a friend suggest to me that the Lord was requiring the church to "dumb down" the curriculum. I absolutely reject that idea. It's just preposterous. The Lord always offers light and truth to any who come to Him. It is men who turn away from what is offered.

Satan Fell from Heaven

Satan was not thrown out of heaven until after this earth was created. Jesus remarked, "I beheld Satan as lightning fall from heaven" (Luke 10:18). Similarly, John's revelation records that Satan "which deceiveth the whole world: he was cast out into the earth, and his angels were cast out with him" (Revelation 12:9). From this we know that Satan was not cast out until after the creation of this earth had prepared a place into which Satan could be cast.

Several of the astronauts who walked on the moon during the Apollo project reported having deeply spiritual experiences when they left the earth. One of them became a full-time minister.

C.S. Lewis wrote a science fiction trilogy in which the first volume titled *Out of the Silent Planet* made this earth isolated from the heavenly chorus because of its wickedness.

> "Therefore rejoice, ye heavens, and ye that dwell in them. Woe to the inhabitants of the earth and of the sea: for the devil is come down unto you, having great wrath, because he knoweth that he hath but a short time." (Revelation 12:12)

Continual Worship

After Christ's resurrection, when He had ministered to His disciples, and proven that it was He who had been crucified, Luke makes this interesting observation:

> "And they worshipped him, and returned to Jerusalem with great joy; and were continually in the temple, praising and blessing God." (Luke 24:52–53)

First, it is interesting because Christ had fulfilled the Law of Moses. Therefore, the rites of the temple of Herod were no longer necessary. Yet Christ's disciples returned to the temple "continually" to worship Him. Second, the temple was under the control of those who conspired to kill the Lord. Despite this, Christ's disciples were "continually" in the temple.

True worship by a true disciple is never impaired by the circumstances. We should not allow anything to distract us from our own "praising and blessing God." If it can be done in the temple of Herod after the crucifixion of Christ, it can be done today.

Prophets and Entropy

I have been struck by how much of the message which Samuel the Lamanite and Abinadi both deliver have previously been the subject of Nephi's prophecies. Almost every bit of Samuel the Lamanite and Abinadi's messages are first included within Nephi's message. It is possible that both of these later Book of Mormon prophets were "restoring" to new generations the message originally taught by Nephi which had fallen into neglect.

The entire message of Joseph Smith was to restore what had been here before and become lost. The work of scholar Margaret Barker suggests that Jesus Christ was restoring First Temple theology and earlier lost traditions.

If the gospel was originally preached to Adam (and I think it was) then every prophet from that day until now has simply been restoring what was once here. Prophets fight the law of entropy. Mankind keep losing truths and prophets keep bringing them back.

One of the great "signs" that there is a true prophet on the earth is the restoration by them of truths which have fallen into disuse or neglect. True prophets are at war with entropy and decay.

Witch of Endor

King Saul lost his counselor-prophet when he died of old age.[95] Saul's unstable conduct and unfaithful behavior precluded him from getting an answer from the Lord. "And when Saul enquired of the Lord, the Lord answered him not, neither by dreams, nor by Urim, nor by prophets" (1 Samuel 28:6). So Saul went to visit a woman who could conjure the dead. Saul had the woman conjure the deceased Samuel.

---

[95] 1 Samuel 25:1 "And Samuel died; and all the Israelites were gathered together, and lamented him, and buried him in his house at Ramah. And David arose, and went down to the wilderness of Paran."

Saul had prohibited conjuring as a matter of law within the kingdom.[96] So think about what he's doing:

- it's illegal to go see a conjurer, so he's breaking his own law.
- he goes to see the witch of Endor in order to get access to the dead prophet.
- so are we to trust the witch? or are we to trust the spirit that the witch conjures to be reliably Samuel?

Life really gets complicated for the superstitious and foolish.

Stake Conference

Stake Conference weekend! That means that I'll be helping to minimize the crowds in the parking lot at the Stake Center by leaving my car at home. I'll also help out with the crowded seating problems at the Stake Center by leaving some seats open. I know it is a sacrifice to do this, but it's one I'm willing to make.

It's the equinox. I'm going to do something memorable.

On a Scale of 1 to 10

I've figured out part of the problem I have in discussing Mormon issues with others. Oftentimes there is a disconnect between how important the two parties view the subject being discussed. To illustrate the point, I'm proposing a completely arbitrary method of ranking an issue on a 10 point scale of ascending importance as follows:

1. Completely meaningless
2. Trivial
3. Relevant
4. Somewhat significant
5. Significant

---

[96] 1 Samuel 28:3 "Now Samuel was dead, and all Israel had lamented him, and buried him in Ramah, even in his own city. And Saul had put away those that had familiar spirits, and the wizards, out of the land."

6. Very significant

7. Important

8. Very important

9. Critical

10. Essential to salvation

When I think a subject is "1" and someone else thinks it is "10" then naturally I don't care about the point. They think I must be convinced of the point or I am going to forfeit salvation itself. When that is the case, we don't connect very well. If we do reach an agreement, I don't think the agreement amounts to much. They on the other hand, think they've won a major point, or provided a valuable service. I would likely be bored with the discussion, and since I didn't value the subject's importance would probably offend the other party by my disinterest.

On the other hand, views change. At one point I am convinced that some behavior or conduct is either 9 or 10, only to later realize that it is more likely a 3 or 4. That change in attitude may be due to nothing more than living longer, getting more experience and developing a little humility about life and its challenges.

I think that a lot of discussions, disagreements and strong arguments are rooted in an assignment of different levels of importance to the subject.

For example, when I was an Elder's Quorum President, Home Teaching by Quorum members was something between an 8 and 10. I'm not an Elder's Quorum President any longer, and I go home teach my families because I really care about them. I like them. I want to be with them. I find them interesting. I've been 100% for many months and, if I miss at all, it is due to either their absence during the month or mine. But I try to keep in close touch, not because of some "assignment" but because I like them. If I were to assign a level of importance to home teaching now, based on the scale above, I would candidly give it a 5 or 6.

There are people who believe the center piece of the relief society room during a lesson is a 10. I don't relate well to that. And there are those who think President Monson's General Conference Addresses are a 1. I don't relate well to that, either.

Before a discussion begins about gospel subjects, I think it is always helpful to first find out how important the subject is to the person with whom you are speaking.

Priesthood

The Priesthood is separate from the church. For example, when someone is excommunicated they are told to stop using their priestly authority. When they are re-baptized they are never re-ordained. They are simply given authorization to now begin using their authority again.

We do not re-ordain someone when they are re-baptized because re-ordination is unnecessary. They held priestly authority even while they were not a member of the church.

Priesthood preceded the church and is the basis upon which it was organized. It will last beyond the church, at least in the final, Patriarchal form. That priesthood will endure into eternity, for it is the basis upon which the eternal family is predicated. The eternal family is the government of God, not the church. After this life, the church will come to an end. But the family, as a form of government, and priesthood of a Patriarch and Matriarch, presiding as a king and queen, priest and priestess, will endure.

Heroes

I've been reflecting on the frailty of the human experience. We are buffeted and torn from the time of birth, tempted and beckoned to choose poorly, subject to hunger, fatigue and loneliness. The wonder is not that we see so much failure and frustration in mankind. Rather the wonder is that we see occasionally such heroic lives that shine like a brilliant star while lived among us.

The *Deseret News* had an article and pictures of the young Utah lives cut short by service in the military. For the families of these valiant men and women who died for our country's interests, the loss will be lifelong. They will hardly take a breath from the day of their son or daughter's death that the memory of their child does not stay with them.

I don't think we do enough to express our collective gratitude for those who have lost their lives for others. Whether they are in the military, police service, firemen or others who die trying to render noble service for the rest of us, we owe a debt of gratitude to these families.

The Importance of Personal Revelation

In Section 19 the Lord explains what the words "endless torment" and "eternal damnation" mean. They are words of art, and are essentially proper nouns referring to God's punishment.[97]

---

[97] D&C 19:4–12 "And surely every man must repent or suffer, for I, God, am endless. Wherefore, I revoke not the judgments which I shall pass, but woes shall go forth, weeping, wailing and gnashing of teeth, yea, to those who are found on my left hand. Nevertheless, it is not written that there shall be no end to this torment, but it is written *endless torment*. Again, it is written *eternal damnation;* wherefore it is more express than other scriptures, that it might work upon the hearts of the children of men, altogether for my name's glory. Wherefore, I will explain unto you this mystery, for it is meet unto you to know even as mine apostles. I speak unto you that are chosen in this thing, even as one, that you may enter into my rest. For, behold, the mystery of godliness, how great is it! For, behold, I am endless, and the punishment which is given from my hand is endless punishment, for Endless is my name. Wherefore— Eternal punishment is God's punishment. Endless punishment is God's punishment."

This is an enormous help in understanding the scriptures generally. Words are chosen carefully, and the Lord is deliberate in how He puts a message across. Things may not mean what we initially think they mean.

The scriptures are designed to reveal *and* conceal. They are able to reveal even very hidden and mysterious things to the understanding of mankind when we understand what is being discussed. Until the reader has been prepared for this understanding, reading the messages will not necessarily result in greater insight.

It is almost as if you have to know the answer first, or have it revealed to you. Then, while in possession of the truth, you can see that prophets and seers have been speaking about these matters since the beginning of time.

How often do we reflect on Christ's "opening the scriptures" to His followers? This is something that ought to make us all think about how little understanding we obtain without first receiving light and truth from Him. Once again it points to the absolute necessity of personal revelation.

The Problem with Too Much Praise

I think criticism is necessary to the human condition. When a great public official in Rome was given a victor's parade, there would be a companion in his chariot whose responsibility it was to tell the man being celebrated that all fame is fleeting. Rome had it right on that score.

Sometimes a sincere and devoted man can offer his help best by giving criticism to someone he loves. When the only response which is tolerated is that the person is "doing great" or is "wonderful" there is stagnation and failure.

I love baseball. All young men should play baseball. It is a game of failure. If you only fail 70% of the time as a batter, you can become a Hall of Fame player. No amount of praise will compensate for a .110 batting average. Criticism is unnecessary.

One of the *Simpson's* *"Treehouse of Horrors"* episodes had Bart being omni-powerful. Because of his great powers, whenever anything bad happened people would say, "it's good Bart did that." This was to appease the all-powerful Bart. It only made him worse. Funny episode involving a cartoon character, but with a powerfully true underlying message. Too much praise corrodes. Worship of demigods inevitably risks making demons of them.

Near Death Experiences

I was asked about Near Death Experiences and their interface with conversion. Here's my take:

The advantage is that they know there is a continuation of life after the death of the body. However, whether they use that knowledge to advance in light and truth or not is individually determined.

Some have used NDE's to become guru's and sell books or give talks. That may detract from getting more light and truth. The thing about growing in light and truth is that it is always directly connected with the humility of the person. Humility or openness to new ideas and greater understanding is required to move from wherever you may be at present to a position of greater truth. It is that openness to new ideas which is indispensable to gaining knowledge of God.

Closed minds, particularly those that may grow out of religious experiences or beliefs, are not benefited by what great things God has to offer in the continuing education of His children. Joseph Smith once commented that it will be "a great while after we have left this life before we will have learned" enough to be saved. It is not all to be understood in this life.

Openness to ideas and further instruction is necessary to continue in the path of truth and light. A NDE may open one's eyes to some truths, But the fullness of what is to be taught or gained from God is not given in a single experience or in a brief tutelage from missionaries. It is a lifelong quest.

TRUTH IS INDEPENDENT

Godliness

I was asked about godliness.

The ordinances are helps, symbols *and* requirements. "Helps" in that they establish milestones that memorialize passage from one stage of development to the next. "Symbols" in that they point to a deeper meaning or spiritual reality almost always grounded in the Atonement of Jesus Christ. "Requirements" in that they mark the defined route taken by Christ as a mortal to fulfill all righteousness.

The power of godliness is tied to opening the heavens and receiving assignments, confirming revelation, or blessings from God. Promises given to others are not promises to you. Men are rarely reliable sources from which to attain the Word of God. It is the unfortunate condition of mankind that, so soon as the are given a little authority they begin to use unrighteous dominion. Heaven, on the other hand, does not dictate, abuse, misuse authority or entice you to do evil.

All power is tied to heaven. When the powers of heaven are withdrawn from someone, then their authority comes to an end and they have no power.

The ordinances as symbols point to the real thing. The real thing is Jesus Christ and His Gospel.

If you want to have the power of godliness in your life, it must be gained through Jesus Christ; access to whom is available to all men on equal terms.

The Education of All of Us

I've been marveling at the irrelevance of higher education to the process of receiving light and truth.

PhDs are generally so schooled in their discipline that they view the Gospel in the light of their educational training. A scholar studies economics and then everything looks to him like it can be explained in economic terms. Or a scholar studies philosophy and then everything looks like it can be fit into a paradigm matching their school of thought.

I suspect the only book Nephi or Lehi had for their migration was the brass plates containing a version of the Old Testament. Slim library pickings for what great things those two prophets were able to receive through their lives. It isn't the volume of the books we possess which helps our search into deep truths. Indeed, our libraries may well interfere with knowing God. It is the depth of how we live the basic principles contained in the scriptures which let the light of heaven shine into our lives.

Joseph Smith's early education was so limited that our children have a comparable education at the conclusion of fourth grade. But what he learned from on-high, by revelation, made him a towering pillar of light and truth.

Joseph once commented that if you could gaze into heaven for five minutes you would know more that if you read everything that had ever been written on the subject. Now imagine the libraries that are filled with material written by the world's scholars and theologians about heaven. Those who have written include such luminaries as St. Thomas Aquinas, St. Augustine, Dante, Rabbi Bacharach, and Buddha. Yet five minutes of "gazing" would supplant all they had to offer.

The wonder of it all is that so few are willing to trust a prophet's advice. We read endlessly uninspired books written by the uninformed, and bypass the process commended to us by the scriptures.

A bad education (which is most educations) is worse than no education when it comes to the things of heaven. When men are learned they think they are wise, and therefore have little reason to trust in God or revelation from Him to correct their misunderstanding. I think the Book of Mormon had something to say about that.[98] I consider myself a fool. (That is the one advantage I have over those who also hold doctorates. I know it does not provide me with any advantages, but does impose considerable disadvantages because of its corrosion to my thinking.)

Heaven is an endless source of surprises. There's nothing mundane going on there.

---

[98] 2 Nephi 9:28–29, 42 "O that cunning plan of the evil one! O the vainness, and the frailties, and the foolishness of men! When they are learned they think they are wise, and they hearken not unto the counsel of God, for they set it aside, supposing they know of themselves, wherefore, their wisdom is foolishness and it profiteth them not. And they shall perish. But to be learned is good if they hearken unto the counsels of God. And whoso knocketh, to him will he open; and the wise, and the learned, and they that are rich, who are puffed up because of their learning, and their wisdom, and their riches—yea, they are they whom he despiseth; and save they shall cast these things away, and consider themselves fools before God, and come down in the depths of humility, he will not open unto them."

White Stone and a New Name

I was asked whether the white stone and new name in D&C 130 are the same as the Second Comforter.[99] It was an interesting question and I thought I'd put the answer up here:

There are some equivalents (i.e., if A=B and B=C, then A=C) in the Gospel when it comes to this subject. The ministry of the Second Comforter is to bring those to whom He ministers to the Father, and have them accepted by Him. This means that the Father accepts them as a member of the Heavenly Family, or in other words, promises them exaltation.

Since the end of that ministry is to have the person accepted by the Father as a son or daughter of God, then an equivalency can be drawn between the final outcome and the Second Comforter. This is what is done in D&C 88:3–5.[100] Joseph Smith did something similar in a statement he made in which he put the voice declaring a person's exaltation first, and the visit of Christ and the Father with that person second. You can read about it in the *Words of Joseph Smith*, pages 3–6, but the most relevant excerpt is found below:

> The other Comforter spoken of is a subject of great interest & perhaps understood by few of this generation, After a person hath faith in Christ, repents of his sins & is Baptized for the remission of his sins & received the Holy Ghost (by the laying on of hands) which is the first Comforter then let him

---

[99] D&C 130:10–11 "Then the white stone mentioned in Revelation 2:17, will become a Urim and Thummim to each individual who receives one, whereby things pertaining to a higher order of kingdoms will be made known; And a white stone is given to each of those who come into the celestial kingdom, whereon is a new name written, which no man knoweth save he that receiveth it. The new name is the key word."

[100] D&C 88:3–5 "Wherefore, I now send upon you another Comforter, even upon you my friends, that it may abide in your hearts, even the Holy Spirit of promise; which other Comforter is the same that I promised unto my disciples, as is recorded in the testimony of John. This Comforter is the promise which I give unto you of eternal life, even the glory of the celestial kingdom; Which glory is that of the church of the First-born, even of God, the holiest of all, through Jesus Christ his Son—"

continue to humble himself before God, hungering & thirsting after Righteousness. & living by every word of God & the Lord will soon say unto him Son thou shalt be exalted. &c When the Lord has thoroughly proved him & finds that the man is determined to serve him at all hazard. then the man will find his calling & Election made sure then it will be his privilege to receive the other Comforter which the Lord hath promised the saints as is recorded in the testimony of St John in the XIV ch from the 12th to the 27 verses Note the 16.17.18.21.23. verses. (16.vs) & I will pray the father & he shall give you another Comforter, that he may abide with you forever; (17) Even the Spirit of Truth; whom the world cannot receive because it seeth him not, neither knoweth him; but ye know him; for he dwelleth with you & shall be in you. (18) I will not leave you comfortless. I will come to you (21) He that hath my commandments & keepeth them, he it is that loveth me. & he that loveth me shall be loved of my father. & I will love him & will manifest myself to him (23) If a man Love me he will keep my words. & my Father will love him. & we will come unto him, & make our abode with him.

Now what is this other Comforter? It is no more or less than the Lord Jesus Christ himself & this is the sum & substance of the whole matter, that when any man obtains this last Comforter he will have the personage of Jesus Christ to attend him or appear unto him from time to time. & even he will manifest the Father unto him & they will take up their abode with him, & the visions of the heavens will be opened unto him & the Lord will teach him face to face & he may have a perfect knowledge of the mysteries of the kingdom of God, & this is the state & place the Ancient Saints arrived at when they had such glorious vision Isaiah, Ezekiel, John upon the Isle of Patmos, St Paul in the third heavens, & all the Saints who held communion with the general Assembly & Church of the First Born &c. (This is an excerpt from Willard Richards' Pocket Companion contained in *The Words of Joseph Smith*)

Since the white stone and new name mentioned in D&C 130:10–11 are referring to the state of exaltation and inheritance,[101] and since the promise which the Second Comforter (Christ) is working to obtain for those to whom He ministers is the promise of exaltation, that equivalency may also be made. The difference as I see it is that those described in the verses in D&C 130 are in a future state, in which they have actually inherited the condition of exaltation, have entered into the Celestial Kingdom to dwell there and possess the white stone on which their new name is written; whereas the promises Joseph speaks of in the quote above and the promises in D&C 88 are given to a mortal and are to be realized fully in the future.

Now the promise of the Lord is reality itself. What He **says** will happen. His Word becomes the law of the universe.[102] Therefore when viewed with the eyes of faith, the Word is the reality, and the inheritance is immediate for those with faith. This is the reason why Joseph said when a man receives "this last Comforter he will have the personage of Jesus Christ to attend him or appear unto him from time to time. & even he will manifest the Father unto him & they will take up their abode with him, & the visions of the heavens will be opened unto him & the Lord will teach him face to face & he may have a perfect knowledge of the mysteries of the kingdom of God[.]"

Finally, since the mortal who receives these things is already in company with the Lord and the Father, they are already occasional visitors in a Celestial Kingdom although they are still here in mortal-

---

[101] D&C 130:10–11 "Then the white stone mentioned in Revelation 2:17, will become a Urim and Thummim to each individual who receives one, whereby things pertaining to a higher order of kingdoms will be made known; And a white stone is given to each of those who come into the celestial kingdom, whereon is a new name written, which no man knoweth save he that receiveth it. The new name is the key word."

[102] D&C 1:38 "What I the Lord have spoken, I have spoken, and I excuse not myself; and though the heavens and the earth pass away, my word shall not pass away, but shall all be fulfilled, whether by mine own voice or by the voice of my servants, it is the same."

ity, required to endure to the end, suffer death and then await resurrection. Despite this, they are celestial and their lives are punctuated by contact with celestial beings from time to time, as the Lord determines is appropriate or necessary.

First Principles of the Gospel

Someone asked this question:

In one part of *Come, Let Us Adore Him* you talk about the Dispensation in the Meridian of Time. How "Men of good faith and sincere desire doing their best to follow after God, lost the light of the Spirit, then lost sound doctrine, and ultimately lost their covenant status and drifted into darkness." Did you mean this collectively? Over time as a group? As an individual of good faith, sincere desire, doing their best to follow after God, losing the light of the spirit, then sound doctrine and later drifting into darkness . . . How tragic. If after all that they still failed, what then is our hope for an individual now, in our dispensation? Are we doomed to the same outcome? I see many following the same course as anciently.

My answer:

It is troubling. It is the terrible problem of mortality. We are all prone to drift and fail. It is only by constant renewal of faith that we can hope to succeed. No matter how far we have come, what great things we have obtained, we are still subject to failure. This is why the FIRST principles and ordinances of the Gospel are: "faith, repentance, baptism and laying on of hands for the gift of the Holy Ghost." We never outgrow these FIRST principles.

I believe them to be "FIRST" in the sense of primacy, not a singular event which happens and then you can take them off the list of stuff to do. They are primary. They are foundational. They are required to be used constantly. Therefore, they are "FIRST."

So, we always go forward in *faith*. No matter how much we already know, we must use faith to go forward. We live within the limitation of linear time. We experience things in a flow that happens without our control. Life unfolds as an unknown to us, and we must cope with all it hands us from day to day. That requires faith to confront this uncontrolled, unfolding stream of time in which we are presently confined.

Repentance is required because even if we are doing what we should be doing we are always going to learn more. It is the nature of the Gospel that our light should increase. Whenever we learn more, we must change to reflect what we have just gained. Change is the heart of repentance.

Baptism is to have sins washed away. If you are already baptized, then the ordinance does not need to be done again, but the remission of sins and washing them away is required repeatedly. For those already baptized, this is done through the Sacrament. It is still required for us to have sins remitted.

The *Holy Ghost* is should be a regular participant in our lives. Its renewed companionship is also primary. Its witness to us that we are on the right path is the only way to wage the necessary war against entropy which seeks to take you into darkness. It is the source of renewed light that always enlightens when it comes.

These are the only means by which we can avoid the same dismal fate as all others of all prior dispensations. We must do this individually. It does not matter if it is done collectively. I've yet to see any reason in the scriptures to expect great collective success by the Gentiles who inherit the Gospel in our dispensation. There are individual promises to the few Gentiles who will repent, have faith, be baptized, enter into the covenant and remain faithful. But the collective outcome is not particularly rosy.

Truth

There is "truth" which exists independent of what we think or believe. (I use the word in the same sense as D&C 93:24–25.[103]) Our collective forgetfulness does not erase truth. Nor does our vain imagination alter truth.

Whenever a doctrine is changed because of man's planning or arguments, then we are teaching for commandments the doctrines of men; just as Christ complained to Joseph in the First Vision.[104]

During the 3rd and 4th Centuries the debates over "adoptionism" were causing doctrinal havoc for the Christian movement. As they solidified control over the movement, the leaders of the developing Historic Christian faith had a plan to cure the schism involving arguments that Christ was just a man who had been "adopted" at His baptism to become the Son of God. The original words spoken at His baptism came from Psalms 2:7.[105] These words supported the "adoptionist's" arguments. The answer was simple—change the text of the Gospels. So they edited the words and changed them from saying, "Thou art my son, this day have I begotten thee" to instead, "This is my beloved Son, in whom I am well pleased" (Matthew 3:17). That drove a stake in the heart of the "adoptionist" arguments.

Bart D. Ehrman has shown how this, and other controversies, affected the text of the New Testament in his book *The Orthodox*

---

[103] D&C 93:24–25 "And truth is knowledge of things as they are, and as they were, and as they are to come; And whatsoever is more or less than this is the spirit of that wicked one who was a liar from the beginning."

[104] JS–H 1:19 "I was answered that I must join none of them, for they were all wrong; and the Personage who addressed me said that all their creeds were an abomination in his sight; that those professors were all corrupt; that: "they draw near to me with their lips, but their hearts are far from me, they teach for doctrines the commandments of men, having a form of godliness, but they deny the power thereof.""

[105] Psalms 2:7 "I will declare the decree: the Lord hath said unto me, Thou *art* my Son; this day have I begotten thee."

Corruption of Scripture: The Effect of Early Christological Controversies on the Text of the New Testament.

Patterns in history have a way of repeating themselves. Men almost always find it easier to change doctrine than to conform to the truth; and to edit books to fit their failures than to follow direction. Our challenge is to learn the right lessons from history. We should not succumb to the easy advantages of changing the principles our religion is founded on, in order to accomplish "good" and repel criticism by adapting to meet the critics' arguments.

Truth is immutable and unchanging. We either conform to it or apostatize from it. We can't change it.

How grateful I am to still have prophets among us.

Abinadi's Message

The significance of a prophet's message can never be measured by the extent to which he is accepted or even acknowledged by his peers. In the case of Abinadi, he was an outcast whose origins and even ethnic affiliation are unknown. He is the only person in the Book of Mormon with this name. His lineage cannot be determined from the name, and whether he is Nephite, Lamanite, or some "other" is not disclosed.

His only credential was his message. He came to announce warnings, was rejected, and ultimately killed. He had no success with the people, and made only one convert.

Abinadi is a hinge character around whom the entire remainder of the Book of Mormon will center. His one convert, Alma, will become the spiritual leader of the Nephites, and that convert will become the leading writer of the Book of Mormon. Then his posterity will be the focus of the remaining history of the Book of Mormon.

Abinadi's prophecies were cited from the time he delivered them to the end of the Book of Mormon. But measured by the events of his life, he failed. His one convert fled persecution and hid in the wilderness.

However, measured by the full sweep of history, he is the pivotal character, the central figure from the time of his appearance until the end of the Book of Mormon.

I think there's a profound lesson in Abinadi's appearance and legacy. If the Book of Mormon was edited by those who "saw our day," and was edited to foreshadow our own history, then we ought to be cautious about discarding a message from someone like Abinadi.

The only meaningful credential is the content of the message. Trappings of office, genealogy, name, status, and standing were all irrelevant to Abinadi.

Central America or North America?

I used to view the subject of where the events in Book of Mormon took place as one of those trivial matters (2 on my earlier scale). However, I've found that FARMS has become quite animated about the subject. They are quite critical of the North American model. This has somewhat raised the subject's importance in my view.

There are two views. One is that the events took place in Central America. The other is that they occurred in North America. The best explanation of the Central American setting is John Sorenson's book: *An Ancient American Setting for the Book of Mormon*, published by FARMS. The best defense of the North American setting is Bruce Porter and Rod Meldrum's book *Prophecies and Promises—The Book of Mormon and the United States of America*. FARMS gave a very critical review of the Porter/Meldrum book.

I used to think this subject was unimportant enough to allow it to remain undecided. After reading both sides' arguments, I am inclined to believe it has more significance if you accept Bruce Porter and Rod Meldrum's view. If you accept their view, then Joseph Smith knew something more about the Book of Mormon's events than Sorenson advances. Also the fit of Book of Mormon prophecies into a highly focused unfolding of events also follows. In fact, the D&C comes into sharper focus when you accept the Porter/ Meldrum view.

I am inclined to now view this as an important or very important issue (7 or 8 on my earlier scale). I think everyone ought to read those two books and decide the subject for themselves. Since the Sorenson book was written first, and the Porter/Meldrum book is somewhat a response to it, I think they should be read in that order.

HBO and Politicians

My wife has become a Republican County Delegate again. I stayed home.

Given the sorry state of the current political class, I'm just glad when the political scandal of the day doesn't involve sodomy of a parrot.

Sobbing politicians blubbering how sorry they are for the DUI/ nude hot-tubbing with underage girls/oral sex or drug use require me to then explain to my kids things I would rather defer until they are older. What good is it to not buy HBO when the evening news features Republicans and Democrats confessing sins as sordid as anything we get in R-rated movies?

All Is Well in Zion

According to the Joseph Smith's First Vision, the Restoration occurred because of the apostasy of Historic Christianity. All churches "were wrong" and their "professors were all corrupt." "All their creeds were an abomination." The people who inhabited these churches "draw near [to God] with their lips, but their hearts are far from" Him.[106]

This is the historic moment which justifies the Restoration. It forces a choice upon the world. Mormonism is either correct, or it has no reason to exist.

This forces The Church of Jesus Christ of Latter-day Saints into a dilemma. It must either proclaim that it is the only repository of saving truth, or it must strike a compromise which betrays the reason for its existence.

Jesus Christ did not intend to let those who follow the work He was to commission through Joseph Smith to become popular, successful, or live in peace. He intended to put them at odds with all the rest of the world. The very reason for His strange act was to notify anyone who heard about it that they were to repent, change, accept new truths, or remain "corrupt" and with "hearts far from Him." It is an instant challenge to the world.

When we shape the message of the Restoration into a vocabulary which does not offend, we miss the point. We are REQUIRED to offend. We are REQUIRED to sound the alarm to "Awake! Arise!" When the message to those who accept the Historic Christian faiths is that "you're OK" we are contradicting Christ's opening statement to Joseph Smith.

All of this is only true if what we are doing is continuing the work begun by Joseph Smith. If we have abandoned what he restored, then never mind. We can fit in and get along. In fact, we can not only fit in and get along, but we can even mimic the other mainstream faiths of the day. We can adopt a positive mental attitude, and

---

[106] JS–H 1:19 "I was answered that I must join none of them, for they were all wrong; and the Personage who addressed me said that all their creeds were an abomination in his sight; that those professors were all corrupt; that: "they draw near to me with their lips, but their hearts are far from me, they teach for doctrines the commandments of men, having a form of godliness, but they deny the power thereof."

proclaim: "All is well in Zion, Babylon, Athens, Rome, and Nineveh. In fact, all is well everywhere. Don't get up. Stay asleep. We're just here to help make you feel better about yourself."

An Explanation

This came to me through an email and I thought I should address it here. This is the email I received:

> "I got information through the grapevine about a woman who is claiming that Denver ordained her to do something and that he put his hands on her head and set her apart for some type of work. I don't know all the details, but I was not happy when I heard that. I know that he wouldn't do that but thought that Denver should know that this woman is going around telling people this."

I thought I would put it on the blog and explain.

First, I don't have any idea what woman this is referring to; nor for that matter who wrote the information in the email. It was just forwarded to me, and I was given permission by the one who forwarded it to use it on the blog.

Second, I've not "ordained" a woman to do anything. Nor do I intend to "ordain" a woman to do anything.

Third, I have given blessings to my wife, daughters, home teaching assignments who are sisters, and other women who have asked from time to time, just as others do who hold priesthood and are asked to give a blessing. That has never involved "ordaining" a woman to some assignment or work.

Finally, the only women I have "set apart" for an assignment was done while I served in a Bishopric at BYU, or while serving on the High Council. Apart from that I haven't "set apart" any woman. I've done numerous "setting apart" assignments in Elder's Quorums, and other assignments, but those were men.

Have You Heard Christ Sing?

I had the following article brought to my attention.[107]

It is my view that Christ's Sermon on the Mount was actually a hymn. It was announced as a form of "new law" or higher path. Those to whom He addressed it would have readily recognized the propriety of it being sung, as the article above reflects.

I was then asked if I had heard Christ sing. I replied, "We all have, but only a few can now remember it."

The Word of God

We have a whole different mindset than did the ancients. We view things through the prism of Aristotle. We think that "reality" is what we can observe and touch and measure. However, there was once a mindset where what is "reality" was what God said. The Word of God alone was enough to make the reality.

When God said or promised something that was enough to make what God said true, real, and eternal.

God says: "You are my son, this day I have begotten you" (Psalms 2:7). When that occurred, it was enough to make a man a son of God. I don't know if we even believe that possible now.

Today we assume if it is to happen at all it will be in the afterlife. To the ancients, the person to whom this promise was made was instantly a son of God, even though he may have to live out a life in mortality before entering into the kingdom promised him.

The "king-making ceremonies" of the Egyptians, for example, made the Pharaoh a son of Horus and a God. He was a God on earth even though everyone knew that he needed to eat and breathe to survive. He would eventually die and be buried. He was a mortal— but he was a God. The promise was everything. The words of the

---

[107]http://www.templestudy.com/2010/03/22/universal-creation-song/

ceremony, the effect of the anointing, the commitment to the man was enough to make him a God.

This concept of man becoming God hails from a different culture and time. One untainted by the "head of gold, arms of silver, belly of brass, etc." It is from a time when the Eastern mind, (words are eternal, everything here is temporary and an illusion) was in place among those who are talking with God.

Christ took the Father's words so seriously that Christ became the literal embodiment of God the Father's words. He, Christ, was known as the "Word of God" because He remained true to every word spoken by the Father. If you want to know what the Father said, look to Christ.

So believing/accepting the words of God are critical to getting the true reality of what this life is all about.

Adoptionism

I wrote a post about altering or rewriting scriptures to resolve doctrinal disputes. The example used was taken from the time before the New Testament settled into its final form. That example, "adoptionism" was rejected by the majority view, and ultimately the text of the New Testament was changed to make the doctrine "false" from the text. That change was made during the Third and Fourth Centuries as a result of what is now called the Christological debates.

Someone asked if I thought Christ was adopted. That wasn't the point of the blog post. But as long as the question was asked, here's my view:

No, He was the Son of God. However, even as the Son of God He still was required to be acknowledged by Him in mortality to be saved. Once He entered into mortality, took upon Him blood, He was subject to the Fall. Despite being subject to the Fall, He lived His life in such a way that the Fall could not have a proper claim upon

Him. It was unjust He should die. When, therefore, death overtook Him, it was unjust. That injustice was the reason He could resurrect. The grave could have no just claim upon Him, and therefore death could be reversed in Him. The Father accepted Him as His Son while He was still in mortality. This was done because as a mortal, subject to the Fall, inhabiting a body with blood and the elements of corruption, Christ needed to receive the Father's acknowledgment as His Son, even though He was indeed His Son.

Now the adoptionist theory was contrary to this. They held the view that Christ was just another man and got adopted to become the Son of God. He was God's Son solely as a result of that adoption and not in any other way. I reject that idea. But I accept that He needed, just as everyone else needs, to be baptized, receive the Holy Ghost, proceed through the ordinances of the Gospel, and ultimately receive His calling and election made sure. He said He needed to "fulfill all righteousness" and He did all that was required of any of us. God acknowledged Him as His Son. This is required for anyone to be saved. Christ showed the way and walked the path. So in that sense He, just as all of us, needed to be "adopted." Him because He was mortal. Us because we are conceived in sin.

Joseph's First Vision

I was asked if Joseph Smith saw more than two personages in his First Vision. In the account written in 1835 Joseph stated: "I saw many angels in this vision."

The account in the Pearl of Great Price (written in 1838) omits any mention of this detail.

Process Not Event

Almost everything about the Gospel plan is a process and not an event. There are events to be sure, but for most of us and for most of the time we are only working through the process.

A great deal of the scriptures have been written by those who have been through the process, and who are trying to give us instruction to repeat it in our own lives. "Events" which occur are in the scriptures, as well. But we will never arrive at the "events" unless we first realize there is a process and we begin to participate actively in that process.

The first chapter of Abraham, second and third verses, describes a lengthy process. It took decades to unfold. It was not merely that Abraham determined to do something and then it happened. He's giving a recitation of the process whereby he became at last a "rightful heir" and a "prince of peace" who had "received instructions" and "held the right belonging to the fathers."

His quest began in "the land of the Chaldeans." His ordination would not occur until he was transplanted nearly a thousand miles to the place where Melchizedek would at last ordain and endow him.[108] Shem was the "great high priest" we know as "Melek" (king) and "Zadok" (priest), or in other words, Melchizedek.[109]

[Bruce R. McConkie and President Joseph Fielding Smith taught that Shem was NOT Melchizedek. They reasoned that the meaning of words "through the lineage of the fathers, even till Noah" meant that there were generations between Noah and Melchizedek. And that since Noah was Shem's father, there were no generations. I do not think the words refer to the "generations" after Noah, but to the

---

[108] D&C 84:14 "Which Abraham received the priesthood from Melchizedek, who received it through the lineage of his fathers, even till Noah;"

[109] D&C 138:41 "Noah, who gave warning of the flood; Shem, the great high priest; Abraham, the father of the faithful; Isaac, Jacob, and Moses, the great law-giver of Israel;"

generations before Noah. In other words, Noah received the priesthood through the generations going back to Adam, and then having that priesthood which began in the first generations, he conferred it upon Shem, whose new name was Melchizedek. It was this "great high priest" who conferred the priesthood on Abraham. You should be aware that I am differing from what McConkie and Smith have taught on this issue. I'm confident in my position and not persuaded by their reasoning, but you are free to believe who you choose.]

When we read the quick summary of Abraham,[110] we can wrongly presume that this was a quick event, not a long process. It was lengthy. It did not unfold without decades of desiring, seeking, receiving promises and then having them fulfilled.

A great deal of what we read in the scriptures is quickly describing the process. They can be misleading in that respect. Nephi's early account of his visionary experiences suggests instant clarity and understanding. However, Nephi took decades to unravel what he had been given. We are reading his third account. He first wrote it when it happened. Then he recorded it a second time on his large plates. It was not until he had received the commandment to prepare the small plates (on which he wrote the account we read in 1 & 2 Nephi) that he finally gave us the third, refined, and completed account. This was decades later. He had "pondered continually upon the things which [he] had seen and heard" (2 Nephi 4:16) during the intervening dec-

---

[110] Abraham 1:2–3 "And, finding there was greater happiness and peace and rest for me, I sought for the blessings of the fathers, and the right whereunto I should be ordained to administer the same; having been myself a follower of righteousness, desiring also to be one who possessed great knowledge, and to be a greater follower of righteousness, and to possess a greater knowledge, and to be a father of many nations, a prince of peace, and desiring to receive instructions, and to keep the commandments of God, I became a rightful heir, a High Priest, holding the right belonging to the fathers. It was conferred upon me from the fathers; it came down from the fathers, from the beginning of time, yea, even from the beginning, or before the foundation of the earth, down to the present time, even the right of the firstborn, or the first man, who is Adam, or first father, through the fathers unto me."

ades. The account we have reduces the decades of reflection into a single, cogent statement.

The Lord does no magic. He aids us in our growth. We have to grow and overcome. Nephi's vision was something which, without decades of pondering, he could not state with clarity to a reader of his testimony. It is always required for us to conform to the Lord's understanding and abandon our own.

The comment by Moses[111] shows how, despite the vision, he could not understand. He had to ask, "Tell me, I pray thee, why these things are so, and by what thou madest them?" It would take great effort to be able to catch up with the things he witnessed.

The Lord lives in a timeless state.[112] We live inside time. When the Lord shows things to prophets from His perspective, it takes a while for men to comprehend what they have been shown. It is a process. Our effort is also required.

Men are not perfected in an instant. We do not learn, even with a Perfect Teacher, without applying ourselves. It sometimes takes, as in the cases of Abraham and Nephi, decades of pondering in order for us to understand and finally receive what has been given to us. In the mean time, the Lord gives us experiences in life which will allow our minds to open to what He has done for us.

---

[111] Moses 1:27–30 "And it came to pass, as the voice was still speaking, Moses cast his eyes and beheld the earth, yea, even all of it; and there was not a particle of it which he did not behold, discerning it by the spirit of God. And he beheld also the inhabitants thereof, and there was not a soul which he beheld not; and he discerned them by the Spirit of God; and their numbers were great, even numberless as the sand upon the sea shore. And he beheld many lands; and each land was called earth, and there were inhabitants on the face thereof. And it came to pass that Moses called upon God, saying: Tell me, I pray thee, why these things are so, and by what thou madest them?"

[112] D&C 130:7 "But they reside in the presence of God, on a globe like a sea of glass and fire, where all things for their glory are manifest, past, present, and future, and are continually before the Lord."
Alma 40:8 "Now whether there is more than one time appointed for men to rise it mattereth not; for all do not die at once, and this mattereth not; all is as one day with God, and time only is measured unto men."

Joseph's First Vision was originally his own conversion story. By the time of the third account (the one we have in the scriptures) it had changed into the opening of a dispensation for all mankind. It changed from Joseph's conversion into the herald call from heaven to all mankind. The years from 1820 to 1838 were required for Joseph to understand the difference. Same vision. Much different understanding.

So it is with all sons of God.

It is a process which unfolds. It unfolds, as we will finally come to realize, in perfect order, perfectly. If you want to read about it I have tried to describe it beginning with *The Second Comforter: Conversing with the Lord Through the Veil.*

President Packer's Testimony

I have enormous respect for President Boyd K. Packer. To me he is one of the great lights in the church. I know he had a role in the excommunication of seven "intellectuals" years ago, and that controversy remains today. One of those affected was a fellow who attended law school at the same time as I did. I feel for both him and President Packer. I do not feel inclined to criticize him, nor have I. I do wish the breach between my friend and the church were healed.

President Packer has given many important talks in his career. Perhaps one of the most significant was given in the October 1977 General Conference. In it he made the following explanation of his testimony and of the testimonies of General Authorities. He is speaking of the time when he was first interviewed to be called as a General Authority by President :

President McKay explained that one of the responsibilities of an Assistant to the Twelve was to stand with the Quorum of the Twelve Apostles as a special witness and to bear testimony that Jesus is the Christ. What he said next overwhelmed me:

"Before we proceed to set you apart, I ask you to bear your testimony to us. We want to know if you have that witness."

I did the best I could. I bore my testimony the same as I might have in a fast and testimony meeting in my ward. To my surprise, the Brethren of the Presidency seemed pleased and proceeded to confer the office upon me.

That puzzled me greatly, for I had supposed that someone called to such an office would have an unusual, different, and greatly enlarged testimony and spiritual power.

It puzzled me for a long time until finally I could see that I already had what was required: an abiding testimony in my heart of the Restoration of the fulness of the gospel through the Prophet Joseph Smith, that we have a Heavenly Father, and that Jesus Christ is our Redeemer. I may not have known all about it, but I did have a testimony, and I was willing to learn.

I was perhaps no different from those spoken of in the Book of Mormon: "And whoso cometh unto me with a broken heart and a contrite spirit, him will I baptize with fire and with the Holy Ghost, even as the Lamanites, because of their faith in me at the time of their conversion, were baptized with fire and with the Holy Ghost, *and they knew it not*" (3 Nephi 9:20; emphasis added).

Over the years, I have come to see how powerfully important that simple testimony is. I have come to understand that our Heavenly Father is the Father of our spirits (see Numbers

16:22; Hebrews 12:9; D&C 93:29).[113] He is a father with all the tender love of a father. Jesus said, "For the Father himself loveth you, because ye have loved me, and have believed that I came out from God" (John 16:27).

Some years ago, I was with President Marion G. Romney, meeting with mission presidents and their wives in Geneva, Switzerland. He told them that 50 years before, as a missionary boy in Australia, late one afternoon he had gone to a library to study. When he walked out, it was night. He looked up into the starry sky, and it happened. The Spirit touched him, and a certain witness was born in his soul.

He told those mission presidents that he did not know any more surely then as a member of the First Presidency that God the Father lives; that Jesus is the Christ, the Son of God, the Only Begotten of the Father; and that the fulness of the gospel had been restored than he did as a missionary boy 50 years before in Australia. He said that his testimony had changed in that it was much easier to get an answer from the Lord. The Lord's presence was nearer, and he knew the Lord much better than he had 50 years before.

There is the natural tendency to look at those who are sustained to presiding positions, to consider them to be higher and of more value in the Church or to their families than an ordinary member. Somehow we feel they are worth more to the Lord than are we. It just does not work that way!

It would be very disappointing to my wife and to me if we supposed any one of our children would think that we think

---

[113] Numbers 16:22 "And they fell upon their faces, and said, O God, the God of the spirits of all flesh, shall one man sin, and wilt thou be wroth with all the congregation?"
Hebrews 12:9 "Furthermore we have had fathers of our flesh which corrected *us,* and we gave *them* reverence: shall we not much rather be in subjection unto the Father of spirits, and live?"
D&C 93:29 "Man was also in the beginning with God. Intelligence, or the light of truth, was not created or made, neither indeed can be."

we are of more worth to the family or to the Church than they are, or to think that one calling in the Church was esteemed over another or that any calling would be thought to be less important.

Recently, one of our sons was sustained as ward mission leader. His wife told us how thrilled he was with the call. It fits the very heavy demands of his work. He has the missionary spirit and will find good use for his Spanish, which he has kept polished from his missionary days. We also were very, very pleased at his call.

What my son and his wife are doing with their little children transcends anything they could do in the Church or out. No service could be more important to the Lord than the devotion they give to one another and to their little children. And so it is with all our other children. The ultimate end of all activity in the Church centers in the home and the family.

As General Authorities of the Church, we are just the same as you are, and you are just the same as we are. You have the same access to the powers of revelation for your families and for your work and for your callings as we do.

It is also true that there is an order to things in the Church. When you are called to an office, you then receive revelation that belongs to that office that would not be given to others.

No member of the Church is esteemed by the Lord as more or less than any other. It just does not work that way! Remember, He is a father—our Father. The Lord is "no respecter of persons."

We are not worth more to the on-rolling of the Lord's work than were Brother and Sister Toutai Paletu'a in Nuku'alofa, Tonga; or Brother and Sister Carlos Cifuentes in Santiago, Chile; or Brother and Sister Peter Dalebout in the Netherlands; or Brother and Sister Tatsui Sato of Japan; or hundreds of others I have met while traveling about the world. It just does not work that way.

And so the Church moves on. It is carried upon the shoulders of worthy members living ordinary lives among ordinary families, guided by the Holy Ghost and the Light of Christ, which is in them.

I bear witness that the gospel is true and that the worth of souls is great in the sight of God—every soul—and that we are blessed to be members of the Church. I have the witness that would qualify me for the calling I have. I've had it since I met the First Presidency those many years ago. I bear it to you in the name of Jesus Christ, amen."

I believe President Packer means it when he says his testimony was "the same as I might have in a fast and testimony meeting in my ward." When someone in a position of Church leadership has an audience with Christ, we hear about it. Joseph Smith told us. Oliver Cowdery told us. Sidney Rigdon told us. So did President John Taylor, President Joseph F. Smith and David B. Haight. Their calling is to bear a witness of Him. When they have an actual audience, I believe they tell us.

The calling of the Twelve is to "bear witness" of Christ.[114] Because of that calling, they must proclaim they have a "witness" even if it could be more correctly described as a testimony born of the Spirit. I accept their "witness" of Christ and believe it is authoritative. However, I do not read into their testimony what they do not put there themselves.

---

[114] D&C 107:23 "The twelve traveling councilors are called to be the Twelve Apostles, or special witnesses of the name of Christ in all the world—thus differing from other officers in the church in the duties of their calling."

I accept the "witness" of the living Apostles, although it is a rare exception when one has an audience with Christ. In recent talks Elder Scott has gone to some length to testify and describe his own spiritual experiences. I trust in them. I trust him. I believe him to be an Apostle. It is not necessary for an Apostle in The Church of Jesus Christ of Latter-day Saints to have a personal audience with Christ.

Years ago Elder Mark Peterson said he did not think it possible for a gentile to receive an audience with Christ. He thought that was confined to pure-blooded Israelites. Since he was a gentile apostle to a gentile church, he did not believe it possible for him to receive such an audience. As I understand it, that is the general view among the brethren. The charge given by Elder Oliver Cowdery to the Twelve (telling them they must receive an audience with Christ for their ordination to be complete) was discontinued in 1911 by President Smith. It was discontinued because so few had received that audience. But that does not make these men any less apostles.

I trust President Packer. I accept his testimony. I believe it is enough to qualify him for the work, just as President McKay told him. I am impressed with his humility in explaining his testimony in General Conference. It increases my trust in him as a servant of the Lord.

Boyd K. Packer's Testimony, Part2

Because of a question contained in the comments section under an earlier post, I am adding this explanation:

Elder Mark E. Peterson explained his view regarding the Second Comforter (a visitation by Jesus Christ with a believer) in conversations of his which have been repeated to me. He had been asked about the issue, and explained his view to those who asked. He believed that the Second Comforter experience was not available to Gentiles. He quoted 3 Nephi 15:20–24 as the basis for his view, which includes this statement by Christ to the Nephites at the time of His appearance at the Temple in Bountiful:

> "they understood not that the Gentiles should be converted through their preaching. And they understood not that I said they shall hear my voice; and they understood me not that the Gentiles should not at any time hear my voice—that I should not manifest myself unto them save it be by the Holy Ghost."

I interpret the above quote differently than Elder Peterson. It is my view that this statement made by Christ was explaining His immediate post-resurrection appearances. Those were limited to the scattered sheep of Israel. These scattered sheep were unknown to each other, and therefore "lost" from each other's knowledge. However, they remained (just as the Nephites) in organized and believing bodies of scattered Israelites. It was to these organized bodies alone that the risen Savior's ministry extended immediately following His resurrection.

In contrast, in the latter-days the prophecies are to the contrary. In the latter days, Christ's appearances as the Second Comforter have been without regard to any limitation of who may be visited. Now, those who believe who are identified with the Gentiles, are grafted into the branches of Israel and become part of the covenant people.[115]

With respect to the Gentiles in our day, it is promised directly to them by the Lord, through Nephi, that His appearances will include Gentiles, in very deed:

---

[115] 1 Nephi 10:14 "And after the house of Israel should be scattered they should be gathered together again; or, in fine, after the Gentiles had received the fulness of the Gospel, the natural branches of the olive-tree, or the remnants of the house of Israel, should be grafted in, or come to the knowledge of the true Messiah, their Lord and their Redeemer."

"And it shall come to pass, that if the Gentiles shall hearken unto the Lamb of God in that day that he shall manifest himself unto them in word, and also in power, in very deed, unto the taking away of their stumbling blocks—" (1 Nephi 14:1)

This is that day.

Believe It Is Possible

The first step in the path back to God's presence is to believe it is possible. Without this, the rest of the path does not exist.

Cycles

I've been impressed with Isaiah the last few weeks. His words are timeless. He describes patterns which recur whenever people seek to follow God. It is little wonder Nephi chose to adopt many of Isaiah's words to describe what he (Nephi) had seen in vision.

I'm struck by how often one prophet will adopt the words of another prophet as his own. One of the great moments in scripture is when Jacob has his people come up to the temple, promising to give them a prophecy. When they arrive, he reads them the words of Zenos, found in Jacob Chapter 5. Then, after this long recitation of Zenos' words by Jacob, he adds the following:

"As I said unto you that I would prophesy, behold, this is my prophecy—that the things which this prophet Zenos spake, concerning the house of Israel, in the which he likened them unto an unto a tame olive tree, must surely come to pass." (Jacob 6:1)

That's it. His great prophecy: What Zenos said will happen!

I like that. Succinct. No messing around. Just telling these folks that this prophecy he read from another prophet was from God.

It's a profound message. We endlessly lose light. Then assignments come to prophets to bring back a little (or a lot) of it, and they restore again. We've been in the process of restoring truth since Adam. This is because we have also been in the process of discarding truth since Adam. It's a race between the discarding and the restoring. Mostly discarding seems to win.

God of Truth

I was asked about the meaning of the statement in scripture that "God cannot lie." It is an important concept and it has a highly specific application. I have dealt with it at length in the book *Beloved Enos*. I would suggest reading the discussion there. If there are still questions, send me another inquiry.

"dried up with thirst"

Isaiah prophesied about the effect of losing knowledge about God. He wrote:

"Therefore my people are gone into captivity, because they have no knowledge: and their honourable men are famished, and their multitude dried up with thirst." (Isaiah 5:13)

This is an apt description of people when they are not "fed" with truth and light.

In contrast, Nephi wanted the Latter-day followers of Christ to have a "feast" to consume while toiling in this fallen, difficult time. But Nephi notes the "feast" will come to us from hearing the words of "angels" and not from the "arm of flesh." Nephi taught us:

"Angels speak by the power of the Holy Ghost; wherefore, they speak the words of Christ. Wherefore, I said unto you, feast upon the words of Christ; for behold, the words of

Christ will tell you all things what ye should do." (2 Nephi 32:3)

Whether we are to "feast" or be "famished" is up to us. Seek, ask, knock: it will be opened. Stay content, do not ask, seek, or knock: you will remain dried up with thirst.

The Fruit at the Bottom of the Bowl

When I was in 9th grade the teacher asked me to read a short story aloud to the class while she went to the office. She asked that I do it because the class would likely listen if I were the reader, but if I were not then they would be out of control. Mostly because I was not a good listener at that age.

In any event, I read the story aloud. Despite the intervening years I still recall the thing. It was by Ray Bradbury and was titled *The Fruit at the Bottom of the Bowl*. The character in the story killed someone, and was cleaning up fingerprints from the murder scene. The cleaning went on as the story was narrated, and at some point it became apparent that the character had gone insane.

The story ended with the police coming and finding the person still there cleaning up fingerprints. The cleaning included the fruit at the bottom of the bowl. Fruit that had never been touched. The character was simply mad.

I think of that phrase whenever I see something completely mad. Particularly when I see behavior which is inexplicable. I've had a few "fruit at the bottom of the bowl" moments while on the High Council. I try not to have them while at home.

It just isn't necessary (or possible) to micro-manage your children's lives. Nor is it wise to try to micro-manage millions of other people's lives. Whether as a parent, as a government leader, business leader, or as a church leader, Joseph Smith's advice is still timely. He said the way he managed the church was to "teach them correct principles and let them govern themselves." I'd like to see a return to that. In all parts of daily life.

The Lamb and the Lion

There is only one place in scripture where the Lord is identified as both the "Lamb" and the "Lion" in successive verses.[116] In verse 5 He is referred to as "the Lion of the tribe of Juda."[117] In verse 6 He is called "a Lamb as it had been slain."

The moment when the "Lamb" and the "Lion" lay down together is the time of His great return. He is both. A Lamb to those who are prepared at His coming. A Lion to those who are not prepared, for whom judgment will be poured out.

When you see that painting of the Lamb and Lion lying down together (we have one in our Stake Center), you are seeing the two great symbols of the Lord's Millennial reign.

General Conference

April General Conference is upon us. I'm hoping to be able to see or hear some of it while at an out-of-state baseball tournament set for this weekend.

We have a tradition of attending General Priesthood meeting at the BYU Marriott Center. I'm worried that I won't be back in time for that session. I always like to attend with a larger group, and since you don't need tickets to attend at BYU, I like going there. All my sons grew up with this tradition.

---

[116] Revelation 5:5–6 "And one of the elders saith unto me, Weep not: behold, the Lion of the tribe of Juda, the Root of David, hath prevailed to open the book, and to loose the seven seals thereof. And I beheld, and, lo, in the midst of the throne and of the four beasts, and in the midst of the elders, stood a Lamb as it had been slain, having seven horns and seven eyes, which are the seven Spirits of God sent forth into all the earth."

[117] Ibid.

If you're in Utah County or Salt Lake County, I recommend it. Outside of the Conference Center itself, I think it is the largest single body of priesthood attending that session of conference.

Pollutions

The great latter day "pollutions" referred to by Mormon[118] are the behaviors of men; not environmental waste. Mormon identifies what those "pollutions" are "murders, and robbing, and lying, and deceivings, and whoredoms, and all manner of abominations."[119]

Those are harsh indictments. But it becomes even more harsh when Mormon identifies *US* as the culprits. He calls us "pollutions." He tells us we have polluted the "holy Church of God." That can only mean the Restored Church. Sobering indeed.

> "O ye pollutions, ye hypocrites, ye teachers, who sell your-selves for that which will canker, why have ye polluted the holy church of God?" (Mormon 8:38)

Remember that Mormon saw us. Jesus Christ showed Mormon US. He was in a unique position to accurately tell us what ails us.[120]

So why do we think ourselves in good spiritual condition? Why are we confident we aren't condemned by the Lord? Why do we presume that as Latter-day Saints we are safe. Why do we think Mormon is talking to all those other churches; churches who will never read his book, and therefore cannot be warned by it? It defies common sense, really.

---

[118] Mormon 8:31 "Yea, it shall come in a day when there shall be great pollutions upon the face of the earth; there shall be murders, and robbing, and lying, and deceivings, and whoredoms, and all manner of abominations; when there shall be many who will say, Do this, or do that, and it mattereth not, for the Lord will uphold such at the last day. But wo unto such, for they are in the gall of bitterness and in the bonds of iniquity."

[119] Ibid.

[120] Mormon 8:35 "Behold, I speak unto you as if ye were present, and yet ye are not. But behold, Jesus Christ hath shown you unto me, and I know your doing."

We are in a lot of trouble. He's trying to help us. How foolish to think we can line up beside him and point the finger away from ourselves. He won't let us do that, you know. He's pointing the finger right at us.

Just the Commandments

According to the Moses account of the creation, at the time the commandment was given to "not eat of" the tree of knowledge of good and evil, the woman had not been created.[121] It was after giving Adam this commandment that the woman was created.[122]

Eve's knowledge of the commandment came from Adam, not from God.

God's commandment to Adam was: "Of every tree of the garden thou mayest freely eat. But of the tree of the knowledge of good and evil, thou shalt not eat of it, nevertheless, thou mayest choose for thyself, for it is given unto thee; but, remember that I forbid it, for in the day thou eatest thereof thou shalt surely die." The restriction placed on Adam was to "NOT EAT" of the fruit of that tree.

Adam's explanation to Eve was different. Eve explained her understanding to the serpent when the serpent tempted her: "God hath said—Ye shall not eat of it, neither shall ye touch it, lest ye die." (Moses 4:9.) Eve's understanding of the commandment varied from

---

[121] Moses 3:15–17 "And I, the Lord God, took the man, and put him into the Garden of Eden, to dress it, and to keep it. And I, the Lord God, commanded the man, saying: Of every tree of the garden thou mayest freely eat, But of the tree of the knowledge of good and evil, thou shalt not eat of it, nevertheless, thou mayest choose for thyself, for it is given unto thee; but, remember that I forbid it, for in the day thou eatest thereof thou shalt surely die."

[122] Moses 3:21–23 "And I, the Lord God, caused a deep sleep to fall upon Adam; and he slept, and I took one of his ribs and closed up the flesh in the stead thereof; And the rib which I, the Lord God, had taken from man, made I a woman, and brought her unto the man. And Adam said: This I know now is bone of my bones, and flesh of my flesh; she shall be called Woman, because she was taken out of man."

what had been given to Adam by the addition of the words: "NEI-THER SHALL YE TOUCH OF IT."

Adam added to the Lord's commandment. This additional precaution was the error which set the transgression in motion. For when Eve saw the serpent touching the fruit and not dying, it lent credibility to the assertion that "ye shall not surely die."[123] Being innocent, and therefore vulnerable to deception, Eve could not know she was confronting a lie. Instead she saw with her own eyes that the commandment "not to touch" clearly did not result in death.

One of the great lessons of the Moses account is that adding to the commandments of God, no matter how well intentioned, is going to lead to error if not tragedy. We do as He asks. Without adding to, nor subtracting from what He has bid us to do, we should follow what we are asked by Him.

We cannot improve on His commandments. We cannot build a fence around His commandments by adding other precautions, gestures, supplements, or restrictions. When we do that we produce excess, rigidity, unintended consequences and error. We teach for doctrines the commandments of men. Inevitably leading to a form of godliness without any power. It's an historic path to failure, diminishing power in the priesthood until it is gone altogether. Detracting from our spiritual as well as physical health. Removing our strength. Corrupting our posterity, as they are distracted from what they should receive as they seek for what they cannot attain by "some other way."

I rather like Moses' account.

---

[123] Moses 4:10 "And the serpent said unto the woman: Ye shall not surely die;"

Tithing

The Church of Jesus Christ of Latter-day Saints has a three-year system for collecting and spending tithes.

In the first year the funds are collected.

In the second year the funds remain invested while a budget is prepared for spending the tithing.

In the third year the funds are spent.

During the time when the funds are collected (first year), they are put to use in investments or deposits which yield a return. Similarly, while they remain invested during the second year, they also yield a return. When the third year arrives, and the funds are being spent on budgeted expenses, until the day they are spent they continue to collect interest or a return.

The amount of tithing collected in the first year is the amount designated "tithing" contributions. This is the amount that is budgeted and spent in the third year. All of the return on tithing yielded in the form of interest or return on investments is treated as "investment income" not tithing.

When the church spends "tithing" on temples, chapels, publications, etc. those monies are confined to the original amount collected as "tithing" only.

When the church spends "investment money" those include the interest, return, etc. collected on the tithing money during the three year cycle from when originally collected until the time it is spent. It also includes the returns on the returns as they accumulate over the years.

Therefore, when the church announces that a project (like the large reconstruction of downtown Salt Lake City) is not "tithing" but is "investment income" of the church, this is the distinction which is being made.

Repent and Be Humble

As the Apostle John closes his Gospel, he adds this comment:

"And there are also many other things which Jesus did, the which, if they should be written ever one, I suppose that even the world itself could not contain the books that should be written." (John 21:25)

In D&C 7's headnote we read that Section 7 is a "translated version of the record made on parchment by John and hidden up."

In D&C 93 we read, "John saw and bore record of the fulness of my glory, and the fulness of John's record is hereafter to be revealed. And he bore record, saying: . . . " (D&C 93:6–7). From verses 7 through 18 it is an excerpt from John's more complete, and as yet unrevealed account.

[Bruce R. McConkie concluded that this was the testimony of John the Baptist, and not John the Beloved. I have accepted Elder McConkie's position in books I have written; however, I believe the account in Section 93 is more likely John the Beloved's record. Since the issue is only a 3 to me on the earlier scale I proposed, I have simply accepted Elder McConkie's view in what I have written.]

John likely had a good deal more to add concerning the Savior, but deliberately withheld it. Similarly, we have the sealed portion of the Book of Mormon as a reminder that not everything has been revealed to us which prior generations had given to them.

We ought to have a bit more humility about our "Restoration" than we have. The fact is, we have never been given what the ancients were trusted to possess. We have never been equal to them. We certainly aren't now. Until we take seriously the Book of Mormon (which will require us to both repent and become more humble than we've ever been), we aren't qualified to receive more.[124]

Of what then do we have to boast?

Various Creation Accounts

There are different versions of the creation. The Moses, Abraham, and Genesis accounts are similar in putting Adam alone at the point when the commandment was given to not partake of the fruit of the tree of knowledge of good and evil. The Temple account does not preserve this.

All the accounts are intended as initiation ceremonies. In the Abraham account, for example, there are directions given to the players who perform the ceremony. They are all "endowment" documents.

Each ceremony can be viewed as a separate revelation. The fact that there are differences means nothing. All of them are intended to highlight or emphasize different teachings. It is foolish to ask "which one is right" because they are all right.

---

[124] 3 Nephi 26:7–12 "But behold the plates of Nephi do contain the more part of the things which he taught the people. And these things have I written, which are a lesser part of the things which he taught the people; and I have written them to the intent that they may be brought again unto this people, from the Gentiles, according to the words which Jesus hath spoken. And when they shall have received this, which is expedient that they should have first, to try their faith, and if it shall so be that they shall believe these things then shall the greater things be made manifest unto them. And if it so be that they will not believe these things, then shall the greater things be withheld from them, unto their condemnation. Behold, I was about to write them, all which were engraven upon the plates of Nephi, but the Lord forbade it, saying: I will try the faith of my people. Therefore I, Mormon, do write the things which have been commanded me of the Lord. And now I, Mormon, make an end of my sayings, and proceed to write the things which have been commanded me."
D&C 84:54–58 "And your minds in times past have been darkened because of unbelief, and because you have treated lightly the things you have received—Which vanity and unbelief have brought the whole church under condemnation. And this condemnation resteth upon the children of Zion, even all. And they shall remain under this condemnation until they repent and remember the new covenant, even the Book of Mormon and the former commandments which I have given them, not only to say, but to do according to that which I have written— That they may bring forth fruit meet for their Father's kingdom; otherwise there remaineth a scourge and judgment to be poured out upon the children of Zion."

The creation (or transplant of man onto this world) is not really the reason for the various ceremonial accounts of the event. They are intended to orient us to how we got here (by a deliberate, planned act of God), why were are here (to find our way back to God) and why conditions here are difficult (to gain knowledge of good and evil). The accounts are really about us. Each of us was born innocent in the beginning, gradually become accountable, feel ourselves outside the presence of God, and must work to return.

Where Do Your Fast Offerings Go?

The ward I live in has been an exporter of fast offering donations for decades. I don't think there has been a time since it's beginning when we haven't exported fast offering donations. Two weeks ago in a meeting with the Priest's Quorum, our bishop remarked that we are using nearly all the fast offering contributions inside our own ward to meet family needs of our own neighbors.

This economy has affected the church's "breadbasket" along the Wasatch Front. The church is able to project international efforts because of the tithing of the saints in Utah. When Utah's economy falters, the church is affected.

The last report the US Government released (that I saw) announced that tax collections were down 40%. If tax revenues are down by this much, tithing contributions must bear some proportion near to that.

The US has been blessed for the sake of the church. When we do not merit blessings, judgments follow. The economic prosperity of the US has not been because we are better than other people, but because it furthers the Lord's purposes. When you view our current circumstances in moral terms, then we should ask what we need to do to merit further blessings from the Lord.

There are no private sins. We have only the illusion of privacy. All eternity looks on at us, at times in complete wonder at our astonishing pride and vanity.

Ideas and Thoughts

Ideas are things. Real things. They come into existence as we create them. They will become subject to the judgment of God, because our thoughts are perhaps the most real part of us.[125]

We should guard our thoughts as we guard the lives of our children. Our thoughts hold the key to everything else.

This is so important a matter that the Lord tied knowledge of priesthood itself to the thoughts we entertain in the privacy of our minds. Only when our thoughts are worthy are we able to bear the presence of God.[126]

If you study the scriptures and then meditate upon them also. You will only develop power within as you do so.

Las Vegas

We returned from Las Vegas.

I have an assortment of observations:

They didn't have a law school there just a few years ago, and lawyers were scarce. They've been able to make up for the shortage I can tell from the billboards. Lawyers do traffic tickets for $50 and DUI's for $700. They get catchy phone numbers like 444–4444; and

---

[125] Alma 12:14 "For our words will condemn us, yea, all our works will condemn us; we shall not be found spotless; and our thoughts will also condemn us; and in this awful state we shall not dare to look up to our God; and we would fain be glad if we could command the rocks and the mountains to fall upon us to hide us from his presence."

[126] D&C 121:45 "Let thy bowels also be full of charity towards all men, and to the household of faith, and let virtue garnish thy thoughts unceasingly; then shall thy confidence wax strong in the presence of God; and the doctrine of the priesthood shall distil upon thy soul as the dews from heaven."

if you want a "half-priced" one he's 400–4000. Not sure what a half-priced lawyer amounts to.

Sex still sells, apparently. At least the advertisers think so. I wonder if Lot would live in Las Vegas were he alive today.

I walked through the casino to the hotel elevator carrying my scriptures, baggage and in company with my wife and four daughters. I assume we were as much a spectacle to the patrons as the patrons were to us.

While there must be a few folks for whom gambling offers some sort of glamor, I did not detect much of that. Mostly you could see boredom or desperation on the faces of the typical patron.

They don't pay the girls who deal on the blackjack tables enough to dress properly. Poor things only have a tiny remnant of a pair of Levis on, not enough to cover their underwear. Their exposed garters and fishnet stockings betray a style dating back to the 1960's. They were practically unclad on top, as well. I assume these hallmarks of poverty betray an employer who is exploiting their labor without appropriate remuneration.

The baseball was fun, but Alta went 2–2. Still searching for the right combination in the batting lineup and trying to fill a gap at 3rd base still, too. They'll get there. Now we're back in Salt Lake for some more 'snowball.

General Conference was broadcast live on the TV, but I couldn't find either an AM or FM station carrying it on the radio. I wondered why that was.

The LDS Temple is pointed out on the top of the Stratosphere Hotel as a point of interest. I thought that was interesting.

I noticed an older couple wearing newly-wed attire. They both had enough miles on them to make them either eternal optimists about the state of matrimony or habitual about their marital affairs. I like to think them optimists.

Creation Ceremonies

I was asked about the creation account being tied to ritual initiation ceremonies. All the ancient accounts of creation were given in connection with initiations or ceremonial rites. That is true of the Egyptians, Babylonians, Israelites, Babylonians, Hopis, etc. The ritualized explanation of the origin of human life is tied together with the meaning of life, and obligations about how life was to be lived, and what the afterlife will hold. The restored Temple rights are consistent with the most ancient of traditions.

Interestingly, the rites of the Masons do not have this basic orientation, and are therefore not part of the tradition from which the endowment ceremony springs.

MY GLASSES AREN'T ROSE COLORED

What It Means and What It Does Not Mean

I was asked about the meaning of receiving the Second Comforter. There is a chapter in *The Second Comforter: Conversing with the Lord Through the Veil* titled "What it Means and What it Does Not Mean" that summarizes the matter.

Life here is complex and sometimes difficult. You have both moral and legal obligations which every one of us owe to society, to employment, to friends and neighbors, the Church, the government, the civil and criminal law and taxing authorities. Some obligations are not "moral," but nevertheless binding and controlling. Being taxed, for example, is not a moral matter, but it is a legal matter. Governments obligate their citizens to pay them and all citizens are required to do so. No matter what your standing before God may be, you are going to have to pay taxes. Christ made that clear when He paid taxes and responded to the question about taxes by confirming the obligation.[127]

The promises of God are helpful in enduring to the end. But they have no value here apart from peace of mind. They are not "property" which this world will value highly. They are for the coming life.

Encouragement and Example

All the prophets can do is offer encouragement to others. They can affirm that the path back to God exists and can be walked even in a day of sin like today. They cannot do the walking for anyone other than themselves. Each person is obligated to walk on the path for him or herself.

Examples of others offer encouragement, but can never replace the obligation devolving upon each individual.

It would be easier for a person to live in harmony with God in obscurity than with public notice. Sometimes, however, the Lord requires a person to take a public stand as part of the trial or obligation imposed upon the them. Whether the person complies with that duty is a measure of the person's sincerity.

---

[127] Matthew 22:15–22 "Then went the Pharisees, and took counsel how they might entangle him in *his* talk. And they sent out unto him their disciples with the Herodians, saying, Master, we know that thou art true, and teachest the way of God in truth, neither carest thou for any *man:* for thou regardest not the person of men. Tell us therefore, What thinkest thou? Is it lawful to give tribute unto Caesar, or not? But Jesus perceived their wickedness, and said, Why tempt ye me, *ye* hypocrites? Shew me the tribute money. And they brought unto him a penny. And he saith unto them, Whose *is* this image and superscription? They say unto him, Caesar's. Then saith he unto them, Render therefore unto Caesar the things which are Caesar's; and unto God the things that are God's. When they had heard *these words,* they marvelled, and left him, and went their way."

Unique and Individual Experiences

Every life is a miracle. Every lifetime unique. How amazing is life and the wondrous experiences we are privileged to receive while here. We cannot really see what is inside another person because their experiences have been unique to them and cannot be shared.

We should resolve all doubts about someone's motivation or heart in favor of them. It is always best to be slow to judge and quick to forgive.

My father would say: "I never spoke a word in anger that I didn't later regret." He was a wise man. I think that is good advice for all of us.

April 6

It is April 6th. This is the day Latter-day Saints regard as the birth date of the Lord. His coming into the world in the springtime symbolized the new hope found in Him. Creation begins anew with the return of light, warming of the earth, flowering of trees and plant life. Springtime is when the sheep, cattle and other animals bring their young into the world. It is a time of hope in the cycles of nature. His coming at this time confirms His role as the Bringer of Hope.

He came to redeem the world that all may be saved by Him.

Why I Admire President Monson

Christ's denunciation of the Scribes and Pharisees included the caution that the outward observances of the law were less important than the "weightier matters of the law, judgment, mercy, and faith."[128]

---

[128] Matthew 23:23 "Woe unto you, scribes and Pharisees, hypocrites! for ye pay tithe of mint and anise and cummin, and have omitted the weightier *matters* of the law, judgment, mercy, and faith: these ought ye to have done, and not to leave the other undone."

James, the brother of Jesus and Presiding Bishop of the New Testament Church, whom I regard as the unidentified "Teacher of Righteousness", taught:

> "Pure religion and undefiled before God and the Father is this, To visit the fatherless and widows in their affliction, and to keep himself unspotted from the world." (James 1:27)

Thomas Monson's lifelong ministry to the widows, elderly and fatherless is sincere, real and lasting. One of the widows to whom he paid a visit a few short months ago was my wife's grandmother, the great-grandmother to my children. At the time, she was confined to an assisted-living home. Without any advance notice President Monson showed up on a stormy Sunday afternoon. Due to the weather conditions, the care center had decided to cancel their Sacrament Meeting. He came through the storm, put the meeting back into place, and conducted this Sabbath celebration for the confined, elderly widows and widowers.

He lives that "pure religion" which includes the "weightier matters" that, above all else, we ought not leave undone.

Virtues are worthy of recognition. I like to take a lead from the Egyptian judgment scale and to weigh a man's heart against a feather to decide another man's worthiness before God. For with what judgment we judge we shall be judged.[129]

Presiding Patriarchs

I was asked the names of the various Presiding Patriarchs of the church.

First, Joseph Smith, Sr., the father of Joseph Smith. Served from 1833 to 1840.

---

[129] Matthew 7:2 "For with what judgment ye judge, ye shall be judged: and with what measure ye mete, it shall be measured to you again."

Second, Hyrum Smith, older brother of Joseph Smith. Served from 1841 to 1844.

Third, William Smith, brother to Joseph Smith. Served from May 1845 to October 1845.

There was an interval between 1845 and 1847 while the Church moved west when the office was not filled. John Smith was called in 1847 and served until 1854.

Fifth, John Smith, who served from 1855 until 1911.

Sixth, Hyrum G. Smith, who served from 1912 until 1932.

Seventh, Joseph F. Smith II who served from 1942 to 1946.

Eighth, Eldred G. Smith who began in 1947 and still serves, although as emeritus since 1979.

D&C 46:13–14

I was asked whether D&C 46:13–14 meant that only some could see the Lord while others would have to rely on their testimony.[130]

It could mean:

1. Some (and only some) will know Him, and others will be able to believe on their words (but will not know Him).

or,

2. Some, initially less than all, will know Him, and others will, initially, believe on their words. But if the others who believe on their words follow the same path as those who know Him, they will also grow to know Him as well.

The correct choice between these two is described in Nephi's account where he could not believe his father, Lehi. Then he prayed and the Lord "visited" him by softening his heart so he could believe his father's words. Then he developed faith to receive stronger im-

---

[130] D&C 46:13–14 "To some it is given by the Holy Ghost to know that Jesus Christ is the Son of God, and that he was crucified for the sins of the world. To others it is given to believe on their words, that they also might have eternal life if they continue faithful."

pressions, and acted consistent with them. Then he was able to "hear" the Lord by continuing on that path. Finally he had angels minister to him and prepare him to receive an audience with the Lord. And, after remaining true and faithful to the path, he at last received an audience with the Lord.

Nephi's spiritual development is described in detail in the early chapters of *The Second Comforter: Conversing with the Lord Through the Veil*.

D&C 93:1 says "every soul", not just a few.[131] Not just a select group. But "every soul." I believe it means all. Not just a few; while others are relegated to believing on their words.

D&C 46:14 is talking about where people begin. Not where they finish.

"Schizophrenic?"

I was asked why there are sometimes "criticisms" of the church on my blog and in the books I have written. Someone would like to know whether or not the views I advance weren't "schizophrenic" by both criticizing and defending the church, and what my true belief about the church was. I responded:

I have had many people with whom I have "ministered" as a Gospel Doctrine Teacher, Ward Mission Leader and High Councilor who have become disaffected with the church. I've worked to help them come back. What I write reflects this history with these strug-gling Latter-day Saints. There are many people who have left the church (or have given up on the church) who have read what I write and come back to activity again.

There are those who are in the process of realizing that the church has flaws who now want to quit. There are people who have

---

[131] D&C 93:1 "VERILY, thus saith the Lord: It shall come to pass that every soul who forsaketh his sins and cometh unto me, and calleth on my name, and obeyeth my voice, and keepeth my commandments, shall see my face and know that I am;"

begun to encounter problems who just don't know how to process them. It doesn't do any good if I pretend there aren't problems. Many of these saints have a crisis underway because they have been pretending, and now they find they cannot cope with the tension any longer.

One of posts at the beginning of this blog describes what my attitude is. I recognize weaknesses, have no intention of avoiding them, and am not an apologist in the traditional sense. But I believe in the church, accept its authority, and think its role is necessary and even critical to the work of the Lord.

Acknowledging the flaws is admitting the obvious. But getting those who are discouraged, losing their faith, or have left the church to reconsider that decision is another thing. They cannot be reached spiritually without some acknowledgment of the problems in the church. They aren't going to be deceived by offering a clever polemical argument.

Once the varnish comes off the institution of the church, for many, faith dies. But that is not necessary. Nor is it inevitable. It is possible to see the frailties of men and still also see the hand of God.

I've had many conversations with what would be regarded as leading Mormon educators, writers, and authorities who have essentially lost their faith and continue to hold on to being a "Latter-day Saint" because of the culture or employment or family. I'm trying to help them and any others in a similar spot. I'm trying to say that the church may be flawed, but despite that, it is worthy, worthwhile, necessary and good. I have had some success.

I've had a number of men and women tell me that I've helped rescue them from their faithlessness. What I have written has helped them balance their attitudes. People who have had their names removed voluntarily, or who have been excommunicated, or who have drifted into inactivity have been persuaded by what I've written to see what they have lost by that disassociation from the Church.

It may be that someone who has "rose colored glasses" will find some of what I write difficult to take in, particularly if they haven't encountered any particular criticism about the church before. I regret when that happens. However, all of us are going to need to confront the growing array of arguments against the church and its leadership as time goes on. Some of the church's most effective critics are former members. Indeed, with the internet, the arguments against the church are multiplying, as are the number of critics. I try not to gloss over the flaws or ignore their existence or to pretend that there aren't legitimate questions being asked about what has or is happening within the institution of the church. I'm saying that we can and should have faith anyway. The church matters and its mission has always been possible to accomplish.

I also want those who sense we've retreated from the original scope of doctrine and practice to realize the fullness of the Gospel of Jesus Christ remains on the earth. It is as accessible to anyone living today as it was while Joseph was here. The failure of others does not impose any limitation upon the individual who sincerely seeks, asks and follows. We are not dependent upon others or even the institution itself to receive that fullness. Although the ordinances offered by the church remain the foundation upon which the fullness must be built.

D&C 132

I have written that it is my view that Section 132 is not a single revelation, but as many as five. I was asked about how I divide Section 132. Before I respond a few words of explanation:

First, the version we have was written in 1843 at the request of Hyrum. He (Hyrum) intended to take it to Emma and persuade her it was from God. Hyrum knew this revelation had been a continuing source of friction between Joseph and Emma and he offered to try and get Emma to accept its truthfulness. So Joseph agreed to dictate it. The scribe was summoned, and Hyrum asked if he should retrieve the Urim and Thummim. Joseph responded that he could recite it from memory, and then dictated it as it now appears in Section 132.

There were two copies made. The one Hyrum took to Emma was burned by Emma. The second came west and was ultimately made public in the 1850's and added to the scriptures.

The dating of the revelation is uncertain, but the headnote to Section 132 notes that "the principles involved in this revelation had been known by the Prophet since 1831" (Section 132, headnote). Given the uncertainty of dating, the typical approach by scholars has been to date it from when the first practice began. I think that is wrong. I would date it from the time Joseph translated Jacob 2, in 1829. Joseph prayed during the translation of the Book of Mormon to receive the visitation of John the Baptist and the ordinance of baptism. I see no reason why the translation of Jacob 's comments on plural wives would not have provoked a similar inquiry and revelation.

We know the information was suppressed from at least 1831 to 1843. What we do not have is an earlier version from which to reconstruct the entire process; we only have the finished product in 1843. With that, I think the revelation divides into sections as follows:

First, the original revelation begins in the first verse and continues until verse 40. This is concerned with one subject and provides the doctrinal and historical basis for the practice of plural wives. However, the subject changes in verse 41 and comes in response to another inquiry regarding the subject of adultery.

The answer to the question on adultery is a separate revelation beginning in response to Joseph's inquiry in verse 41 and continuing through verse 50. That revelation confirms upon Joseph the sealing authority by the voice of God (a separate issue altogether) and pronounces Joseph's calling and election sure. This is the voice of the Lord to Joseph confirming his exaltation and it is unlikely to have happened at the same time as the original revelation in 1829 or 1831. [It is important that this conferral of authority to seal, and his calling and election are contemporaneous events. This is not well understood by the church today, but nevertheless true.]

Verses 51 through 56 are a revelation to Emma which appears to be separate as well. It makes no sense to have this revelation given to instruct, warn and counsel Emma until after she learns of the first revelation and has reacted to it. Once that has happened, a separate revelation to her about her reaction makes sense.

Because of Emma's refusal after her warning, the final section from verses 61 through the end is a new explanation of the law. It talks about how to proceed in light of her (or any woman's) rejection of the principle.

These are four of the potential five sections which appear to me. It is possible that verses 64–66 are also separate from verses 61–63, which would then make five total revelations which are grouped into this single section of the D&C.

Now, what is important about this revelation being in separate parts (to me at least) is that first, the subject was not fully understood by Joseph when first received. He encountered practical and doctrinal questions even after the first revelation came on the subject. That is commonly experienced by all who receive revelation from God. Additionally, it is important that the sealing authority was given to Joseph by the word of the Lord, in revelation to him, apart from the events in the Kirtland Temple. This is consistent with how that authority came to Helaman in Helaman 10, as well. The voice of the Lord speaking about exaltation and conferring authority at the same moment is the Lord's way of doing things. It was no different for Joseph.

Now, least anyone be confused or begin asking questions about plural wives, I do not believe in the practice. It was discontinued and we do not practice it. I have addressed the polygamists' claims to the right to continue the practice in *Beloved Enos* and my position is as I stated there.

D&C 132, Part 2

There was a question about Section 132 received. The previous post on D&C 132 did not address the underlying subject of the section. I only discussed the text divisions and timing of the document's creation. The question I received asks about the substance of the revelation, and in particular, the status of women in plural marriage.

I have a few observations which color my views of this subject. This will take a few posts, but below is my first set of observations:

When plural marriage was first introduced publicly in the 1850s, the brethren were rather candid about the history of monogamy. They explained that the societal and governmental institution of monogamy was intended to exploit women. By depriving women of husbands, it resulted in an excess number of women who could be prostituted. Men could then have one wife, for whom they bore the burden of support and shared parenting responsibilities, while other women could be used without any burden of support or shared parenting duties. The brethren also explained that one of the reasons Rome was originally opposed to Christianity was because it was a cult that threatened to spread the practice of plural marriage throughout the Empire. Their comments are in the Journal of Discourses and you can read these explanations there if you are interested.

So as the practice of plural marriage was introduced publicly, it was accompanied by an attack on monogamy; claiming that women were exploited and disadvantaged by the practice of monogamy. This inverts the argument against plural marriage. The claims against it were based in large measure upon the notion that it exploited women and made them subservient. So the argument turns on its ear the "exploits women" card.

When introduced, the practice of plural marriage ran counter to nearly two thousand years of cultural practice. It was decidedly counter to the Elizabethan mores of the age. It was shocking to the Latter-day Saints who learned of the practice. Not only was it foreign in concept, but the Saints had absolutely no basis for implementing it successfully. They had no history, no example, no trial-and-error wisdom. There were no previous examples that they could select behaviors from that would help solve obvious issues arising from the practice. So they began the whole trial-and-error sorting out.

Unfortunately. the practice was introduced in 1853 (publicly) and died in 1890 (publicly). It began secretly in 1831 and died secretly in 1904. Whether you take the public bracket of time or the secret bracket, that isn't enough time for the process to have resulted in handed-down wisdom gained by living that kind of lifestyle.

Those who are outside the Latter-day Saint community (fundamentalists, etc.), and have continued to practice of plural marriage do not really provide a basis for inter-generational wisdom. They live a "bunker-like mentality"—always under siege and never allowed the social and cultural opportunity to practice this form of marriage freely and openly. The results of these efforts are tainted by the hostility, rejection and prosecution by the population at large towards those who try to live this kind of marital relationship.

How the view of women changes under this practice is something that we are not in a position to evaluate accurately. We have a cultural bias, an historic bias and religious bias that colors our view. We do not have a reasonable framework from which to make a neutral evaluation of the subject. The only contemporary societies that have plural marriage in any significant numbers are so socially ill, so backward and violent that a liberal, democratic and open society cannot take any wisdom from them to judge this matter. We are left to look backward into biblical times for clues about the practice. Unfortunately, even there we do not get much guidance or many examples of happy outcomes. Hagar, a princess from Egypt, was at odds with Sarah and ultimately so incompatible that one had to leave. Jacob's wives were competitive and jealous. The account we have seems to make Jacob responsible for exploiting these ill-feelings. David's relationships were unsteady. Solomon was ultimately led into idolatry by his foreign, political marriages. The biblical record does not seem to give any hope of a happy outcome (or at least not much hope). So when trying to evaluate it, there is little happy news or basis for celebrating it as a triumph of matrimony.

Then there is the underlying exploitation of young women. These women are married and pregnant so early in life that they are essentially obligated to remain in the marriage. I think that is a reflection of the unhappiness that is anticipated by such unions. The younger bride syndrome seems to be a tacit admission that unless you put the women into this kind of difficult bind (choosing between their children or fleeing), then women won't remain in the marriage. This is an interesting admission seen in both the Muslim communities and in the Fundamentalist communities. It betrays a similar state of unease about women's desire to remain in such relationships.

All in all the practice does not seem to offer (in this life) much advantage to either husband or wife. Nor does it seem to produce happiness here. You can read the book *In Sacred Loneliness* as an account of our own history with the difficulties of the practice.

Now that doesn't address the "doctrinal" question asked. I'll post again on that issue. However, when you consider the revelation, this is the first point that should be on the table. It is a terrible sacrifice. No society appears to have had much success in implementing it. The "practical" verses the "ideal" is something that tells us important information.

Humanity has not been able to create a widespread social experiment using this form of marriage, notwithstanding its basis in doctrine. At least not one that has been well documented, with wisdom to guide the way. There are of course societies where the economic order consists of a widespread slave class supporting a socially dominant, wealthy class. In these societies, escape from hunger and enslavement requires a plural marriage arrangement. In these circumstances, plural marriage is greeted as a form of liberation. I do not consider those worthy examples. We don't want or expect to build Zion on the backs of a slave class.

D&C 132, Part 3

Joseph taught that we can't expect to achieve the same glory as the ancients if we do not make a similar sacrifice as they did. It's all in Lecture 6 of the *Lectures on Faith*. I've quoted that stuff in several books and won't repeat it here. If you don't have a copy you should get one. *And read it.*

Anyway, it is quite important to note the necessity of sacrifice to produce the kind of faith which saves. Joseph's explanation required us to sacrifice all things to be able to lay hold on saving faith. Without the knowledge that we would give up everything, even our own lives if necessary, we cannot receive eternal life. We have to trade this life for the next. No trade, no exaltation.

So when a man or woman reaches the point where she/he can be tested, the Lord will supply a test to them to prove (to themselves) that they will sacrifice all things. [The Lord already knows, but we don't. And it is OUR faith which is required to be tested.]

For most women, they make this kind of sacrifice when they marry. They literally "give up their lives" and become a wife. Even to the point they surrender their prior name and become known by a new name and begin a new life. The sacrifice for them is completed in childbirth, where they risk their life and then shed their blood to bring a new person into the world. For women, therefore, this estate provides a ready-made opportunity for the development of this faith. For men that is much different. That is why we produce so few men worthy of preservation into the next life in an exalted state.

Joseph Smith succeeded in receiving his calling and election. His promise of eternal life appears within Section 132. That is no accident. If the revelation is a series of communications, beginning in either 1829 or 1831, and continue through nearly the time of the recording in 1843, all of which are on the same subject, then they are all interrelated.

Joseph's sealing authority is confirmed in verse 46 and his calling and election is confirmed in verse 49. This would have been after Joseph had received the beginning of Section 132 and had actually begun to live it. Meaning that Joseph was doing what he was commanded to do, and that in so doing he was sacrificing everything. Even his own life was being sacrificed. He was developing the faith necessary to know he would surrender everything to God by this principle. Later, when he would go to Carthage and die, it was not as difficult for him to do because he had earlier lived a principle which proved to him that he would obey God at all costs. Death under such circumstances was not a test, merely a confirmation of what Joseph already knew.

Plural marriage was so difficult for Joseph that it was THE means by which he advanced in faith to the point he knew he would surrender all things to God. It was the key to his exaltation. Not because plural wives are needed, but because of the difficult sacrifice this practice imposed upon him.

Now if that were true for Joseph, then we should not think the practice of plural marriage, with all its difficulty and sacrifice, something desirable to undertake. Nor should we be fooled into thinking that Joseph wanted or welcomed it. The revelation belies this notion.

Therefore I take it as a given that plural marriage was introduced as a test. Not as a reward or as a holiday for Joseph Smith and his close associates. It was a difficult, trying ordeal.

Now there's more to be said, so I'll add another post at some point on this as well.

D&C 132, Part 4

This brings us to some details that need to be understood. The clarifications in verses 41–44 were a result of the "mechanics" of how the practice was implemented.[132] The various efforts to "fulfill the law" while still keeping up Elizabethan appearances included performing a "sealing" for time and eternity to one man, while the woman was married for time to another man. This relieved the eternal husband/companion of any duty to have conjugal relations with, or provide financial support for the woman while here. It allowed her to live a "normal" married life with her husband, while still committed eternally to another. A sort of nod in the direction of the plural wife revelation, without any real commitment to actually practice it here. There were other forms of compromise attempted, as well.

The defining of what was and what was not "adultery" was necessary in light of the troubles on the ground, so to speak. Confusion began to multiply as these compromise efforts were attempted by people who really didn't want to get this thing going in the way David and Solomon had done.

Also, verse 51 grew out of a specific incident in which Joseph and Emma were arguing.[133] She protested his secret addition of

---

[132] D&C 132:41–44 "And as ye have asked concerning adultery, verily, verily, I say unto you, if a man receiveth a wife in the new and everlasting covenant, and if she be with another man, and I have not appointed unto her by the holy anointing, she hath committed adultery and shall be destroyed. If she be not in the new and everlasting covenant, and she be with another man, she has committed adultery. And if her husband be with another woman, and he was under a vow, he hath broken his vow and hath committed adultery. And if she hath not committed adultery, but is innocent and hath not broken her vow, and she knoweth it, and I reveal it unto you, my servant Joseph, then shall you have power, by the power of my Holy Priesthood, to take her and give her unto him that hath not committed adultery but hath been faithful; for he shall be made ruler over many."

[133] D&C 132:51 "Verily, I say unto you: A commandment I give unto mine handmaid, Emma Smith, your wife, whom I have given unto you, that she stay herself and partake not of that which I commanded you to offer unto her; for I did it, saith the Lord, to prove you all, as I did Abraham, and that I might require an offering at your hand, by covenant and sacrifice."

more wives (beyond those she had approved) and was complaining to him about it. In response to the arguments, Joseph offered to have her marry William Marks (the Nauvoo Stake President) as well. This is what is referred to by the oblique reference: "that she stay herself and partake not of that which I commanded you to offer unto her." This, again, was an event in the 1843 time frame. It could not possibly have been part of what was happening in either 1829 or 1831 when the first part of the revelation was received. Showing once again this was an amalgamation of several revelations, and not a single transcript.

Not everyone in Nauvoo knew what was going on. Nor was everyone who practiced this principle discrete enough to escape notice. Enter John C. Bennett, who had abandoned his wife and children and come to Nauvoo pretending to be something more than he was. He got added to the First Presidency and elected mayor of Nauvoo. He learned of the commandment, and then began to let his libido go in Nauvoo. He produced a system of seducing other men's wives under the practice of "spiritual wifery" which he would later blame upon Joseph Smith. Indeed, John Bennett's account of Joseph's exploits seem more autobiographical of Mr. Bennett, with Joseph given credit for Bennett's wrongdoings.

As I said before, this was not a culture into which this commandment fit neatly. It was awkward. They just didn't know how to do it, nor what would work or not work. Even so basic a matter as the definition of "adultery" became hard to sort out. The half-way measures Joseph tried to implement in order to avoid the outright practice were not working. They were producing such confusion that these verses were needed to sort the mess out.

Trying the souls of those who were involved, indeed! Proving whether you have faith to sacrifice everything for God, indeed! This was terrible, difficult stuff. Not the license for a libido that critics were trying and still try to make it seem. Even Bushman has mentioned how few offspring Joseph Smith produced as a result of the plural wife system. It seems that the only offspring Joseph ever fathered were through Emma. (Of course we have the tale of Eliza Snow's miscarriage, but that child did not live. So far as has been documented, all Joseph's living descendants came through Emma, despite DNA testing of other living descendants from putative children.)

Look, we should have compassion and empathy for these people. They didn't want it any more than a normal, mature and moral person living today would want this. They were draftees, not volunteers. It was quite hard for them and even harder on them.

Anyway, I still am not to the answer to the question, just laying the groundwork to understand the answer first. I'll write some more on this as I have time.

D&C 132, Part 5

Words have unique meanings when used in scripture. The Lord has given us great insight into word usages in D&C 19:4–12. He uses words as proper nouns which then change meanings.[134]

Part of the question raised concerns the word "destroy" as used in Section 132. I have described the meaning of destroy or destruction in footnote 225 on page 161 of *Nephi's Isaiah*. It does not mean

---

[134] D&C 19:4–12 "And surely every man must repent or suffer, for I, God, am endless. Wherefore, I revoke not the judgments which I shall pass, but woes shall go forth, weeping, wailing and gnashing of teeth, yea, to those who are found on my left hand. Nevertheless, it is not written that there shall be no end to this torment, but it is written *endless torment.* Again, it is written *eternal damnation;* wherefore it is more express than other scriptures, that it might work upon the hearts of the children of men, altogether for my name's glory. Wherefore, I will explain unto you this mystery, for it is meet unto you to know even as mine apostles. I speak unto you that are chosen in this thing, even as one, that you may enter into my rest. For, behold, the mystery of godliness, how great is it! For, behold, I am endless, and the punishment which is given from my hand is endless punishment, for Endless is my name. Wherefore— Eternal punishment is God's punishment. Endless punishment is God's punishment."

annihilate. It means to divest of government or control. In the context of Section 132, to be "destroyed" does not mean to be killed, or obliterated, but rather it means to lose your order, your government, or covenant. The form of government that will endure into eternity is the family. Without a family connection, you remain separate and single, without exaltation. Therefore to be "destroyed" is to be severed from the family unit, or marriage relationship which the section of the D&C is establishing.

It is also necessary to understand that the role of the woman in the establishment of an eternal family unit is critical. It is central. Some of what is involved in understanding the relationship between the man/woman and covenant making is just not appropriate to be set out in public. Therefore I won't do it. To the extent it is appropriate, I have given a basis for someone who wants to understand in several things I have written. The closing chapters on sealing authority/power in *Beloved Enos* is part of what should be understood. The tenth parable in *Ten Parables* is also critical to understanding what and why an eternal relationship would be preserved. The chapter on "Sacred Ordinances" in *Come, Let Us Adore Him* gives some further information. I'd commend you to that information.

I also found this in Hugh Nibley's latest book, which helps with understanding, also. Particularly in light of the information contained in the tenth parable referred to above:

> "Sarah, like Isis, is the ageless mother and perennial bride; with the birth of Isaac she becomes young again—'Is any thing too hard for the Lord?' (Genesis 18:14). The woman who stands behind Osiris on the throne is Isis, sustaining him in his office with uplifted hand; it is Isis, 'fused' with Hathor as the 'king-maker,' as Jan Assmann puts it." (*One Eternal Round—The Collected Works of Hugh Nibley*, 156)

"Neither is the man without the woman, nor the woman without the man, in the Lord," wrote Paul (1 Corinthians 11:11). You cannot have an eternal marriage without both. In the relationship, the woman's role in creating a king is central, for it is the woman who will establish him on his throne. In turn, it is the man who will then establish her on her throne. Her act precedes his, and his act confirms and blesses the new government or family unit as his first act as king. For king without consort is doomed to end. Together they are infinite, because in them the seed continues. They may still be mortal as the events take place, but because they continue and produce seed, they are as infinite as the gods.

The role or importance of the woman in the eternal family unit is not diminished in any respect by the confusion and sorting out being done in the later verses of Section 132. The information there is attempting to restore order to the chaos that had developed through the half-hearted attempts to comply with the new order without actually engaging in a fully public, acknowledged marital relationship involving a man and multiple wives.

As to the reference to serial marriage of "virgins" in the later verses, this was a return to the original intent. When you marry a virgin, you are getting someone who does not already have a spouse. Using innovations, like sealing a second "wife" to a man when she was already married to another, was never the intent. These verses about marrying virgins returns to the foundation of a first marriage for the woman. She was to be involved with a direct, actual marriage, not to be in some half-hearted compromise relationship where the relationship was not truly and fully a marriage for her. She was to acquire a husband and mate. She would have all the rights and the husband would owe all the obligations, as if he were married to her alone. She was "his" and therefore he was obligated to her for support, maintenance and duties as a husband. There could be no sharing. There could be no half-way measures. This was to be his wife in very deed.

Now I've taken perhaps too long to answer the question, and it may in turn raise other questions, but I've tried to bring some clarity to this rather confused and messy circumstance. It was the confusion of the early practice that brought about the need for multiple updates and clarifications which all got amalgamated into the single Section 132. Part of the revelation comes from the attempts to work around the earliest portions of the revelation, received between 1829 and 1831. The clarifications don't make as much sense when separated from the conduct that resulted in the clarifications.

There is a reason we don't have much from the church about this section. Right now the whole thing has become an embarrassment. We (the LDS Church) have become the chief antagonists of the polygamists in the west. We want to clearly draw a line between "us" and "them." The church learned its lesson by hard experience. Now the lesson learned is going to be constantly reapplied to show all the world that we have abandoned the practice. We do that by constantly denouncing the polygamists. As part of that campaign we can't really go back and give Section 132 a wholesome treatment. That would seem to contradict what we now preach and practice. Such are the results of history.

D&C 132, Conclusion

Which brings us to the question of why Section 132 would be given in the first place. I don't think it is enough to say "Joseph asked the question" as the full reason for it being revealed. Joseph could have received the revelation without the requirement to live it. We could have an understanding that this was a correct principle, but that we had no obligation to comply with it (just as we do now).

However, we were at one time given it and, commanded to live it. So the questions is "why?" Here's my take:

We are witnessing the end of the times of the Gentiles. There is a worldwide collapse of the Gentile populations. (Gentiles being the white, European populations.) Although we have scattered Israelite blood in us, the LDS Church was founded by those who are "identified with the Gentiles".[135] But their (our) time has run its course.

The God of this land (North America) is Jesus Christ. When people reject Him, they lose their claim on the land and are swept away.[136]

We have now, by the popular vote of the Gentiles who possess this land, chosen a leader who proclaimed on April 6, 2009 (the Lord's birth date) that "we are no longer a Christian nation."

Birth rates among Gentiles have collapsed. The European social democracies require a large working class to support the retiring

---

[135] D&C 109:60 "Now these words, O Lord, we have spoken before thee, concerning the revelations and commandments which thou hast given unto us, who are identified with the Gentiles."

[136] 2 Nephi 1:7–10 "Wherefore, this land is consecrated unto him whom he shall bring. And if it so be that they shall serve him according to the commandments which he hath given, it shall be a land of liberty unto them; wherefore, they shall never be brought down into captivity; if so, it shall be because of iniquity; for if iniquity shall abound cursed shall be the land for their sakes, but unto the righteous it shall be blessed forever. And behold, it is wisdom that this land should be kept as yet from the knowledge of other nations; for behold, many nations would overrun the land, that there would be no place for an inheritance. Wherefore, I, Lehi, have obtained a promise, that inasmuch as those whom the Lord God shall bring out of the land of Jerusalem shall keep his commandments, they shall prosper upon the face of this land; and they shall be kept from all other nations, that they may possess this land unto themselves. And if it so be that they shall keep his commandments they shall be blessed upon the face of this land, and there shall be none to molest them, nor to take away the land of their inheritance; and they shall dwell safely forever. But behold, when the time cometh that they shall dwindle in unbelief, after they have received so great blessings from the hand of the Lord—having a knowledge of the creation of the earth, and all men, knowing the great and marvelous works of the Lord from the creation of the world; having power given them to do all things by faith; having all the commandments from the beginning, and having been brought by his infinite goodness into this precious land of promise—behold, I say, if the day shall come that they will reject the Holy One of Israel, the true Messiah, their Redeemer and their God, behold, the judgments of him that is just shall rest upon them."

older class. The older retiring class did not have a birth rate that would supply the needed taxpayers, and therefore they are importing a younger working class throughout Europe. The younger working class is drawn from third-world people who have much higher birth rates. Those people are primarily Muslim. As a result there are many European nations whose demographic picture leads to the inevitable change from Gentile/Christian nations to Muslim nations within the next twenty to fifty years. The Danish peoples will be among the first. France has a majority of their school-age children now who are Muslim. All of them are threatened by a religion that rejects Jesus Christ as the Son of God and Redeemer of mankind. They are, in a word, anti-Christ.

In the US, the birth rate is is only a replacement rate. But social programs require growth. That population growth is the only way to amortize the governmental spending. Increased government spending requires in turn a surge in population to support by taxation the necessary payments. This is being accomplished by the deliberate failure to police the immigration of foreign populations. It is a fiscal plan, not a demographic, social, religious or political plan. The government will not be able to pay for itself if large working-class people aren't found and brought into the US. Fortunately, most of those who are coming to the US are already Christian, and only a small fraction are Muslim. However, the Gentiles who are identified with the white population are declining, and being displaced by those who are identified with Book of Mormon remnant populations (although perhaps not THE remnant destined to build Zion—that's a whole different subject).

The church's birth rate has also declined rapidly. At present it is only a small fraction above the larger US rate. There result is the same loss of Gentile momentum in the building of the church. The

Gentile population of the church is collapsing just as it is throughout the world.

What the revelation in Section 132 offered to the Gentiles was an opportunity, while the Gentile's day was still in full bloom, to create a much larger population from which to build Zion. I've seen some estimates that, had we lived the principle of plural wives from when it was restored until today the resulting population of Latter-day Saints would have been in excess of 150 million. The Latter-day Saint population would essentially have political control of the United States. That didn't happen, and now the time of the Gentiles has passed. We can't make up for lost time now. Nor are we exhibiting any desire to do so, as our declining birthrates demonstrate. Indeed, large families have vanished as a subject for General Conference. The Brethren seem to have forgotten the message once preached to "not artificially limit the size of your families." That message was spoken in General Conference as recently as President Kimball's time. Their examples are also important and telling. (Taking only the most recently called of the Twelve: Elder Bednar has three children, President Uchtdorf two. President Eyring has six. Elder Anderson has four, Elder Christopherson has five children. Now we don't always know the reasons why people have the number or children they do, so I do not read too much into this. However, there was a time when the reason all did not have six or more children would get attention, and an explanation would be offered. Now we don't even notice and it is simply not an issue. We presume that larger families are optional and completely unrelated to living the Gospel of Jesus Christ.)

Well, as with all things in the Gospel, we are handed opportunities. What we do with them is up to us. However, these opportunities are gifts from the Lord. We are now a tiny fragment of what we might have been at this point in history. We are vulnerable as a people in a way that we could have avoided with living the principles in

Section 132. The results are going to play out in conformity with the rather pessimistic view of the Gentile's failed stewardship foretold by Nephi, Mormon, Moroni and modern revelation.

There's always a back up plan. That plan will rely upon a "remnant" to take things over and return to what was once offered to the Gentiles. And to the extent that a few Gentiles will follow the covenant, they are invited along and included as covenant people. But by and large they will be left behind.

Now Section 132 was an opportunity, not a burden. We never got enthusiastically behind the opportunity and the earlier posts explain why. I think the reasons for the failure are perfectly understandable. I think it was reasonable. But it is a fact that we failed with the opportunity. Worldwide we have a little less than 4 million active Latter-day Saints and an estimated total population of approximately 14 million. Those results are not what might have been. The Gentile Saints are vulnerable in a way they would have avoided had they taken the opportunity and done more with it.

But of course, that is true in a much larger sense, as well. The promise of an "innumerable posterity" presumes that the one receiving the promise realizes that it is a great blessing, and not a curse or burden.

OK, those are my thoughts. It's taken a bit to lay out. And I probably should add that there are those who would disagree with much of what I have said. However, I've given enough thought and study to the matter to have reached these conclusions, and I offer them to you for whatever you want to make of them.

GROW WHERE YOU ARE PLANTED

Outgrowing the Church

I was told by someone that they "had outgrown the church, didn't get anything out of meetings, and therefore did not attend anymore."

I responded: "As to your 'growth,' that may or may not be true. However, even if it is true, then the church needs you all the more for what you have to offer. Continuing service inside the church will always take a person to still greater peace and light."

What I did not say is that whenever one assumes their own spiritual or intellectual superiority to others, they have lost light and become a fool. Spiritual development here distinguishes the best from the worst by so little that God regards us all as equal. What this world views as intellectual achievement is more often than not a hindrance to finding and following God.

Creation Accounts

All ancient accounts of the creation of life here came through a presentation intended either as an initiation or an ordinance. The various accounts we have are also from such settings. Genesis is the ritual account given through Moses. The words "God said" should better be rendered "the Gods shall say" (meaning that this is telling the players what to do). Similarly, the Abraham account saying that one "like unto the Son" or "like unto God" is describing the player's role. It is a dramatic presentation.

There is no need to read into any of the various texts something which isn't there. Hence the earlier post dealing with the creation accounts and how Eve was left out of the original statement of the commandment regarding the fruit of the tree of knowledge of good and evil. The account sets it out with the commandment coming before Eve's creation in all but the current Endowment presentation. Our version has been changed from time to time to accomplish various efficiencies as we have adopted filming, and other innovations to make the Endowment fit within new formats and time constraints.

Holy Ghost

The equivalents made in Moses 6:61 are very interesting. The definition of the Holy Ghost includes these various equivalent descriptions of the Holy Ghost:

1. The record of heaven.

2. The peaceable things of immortal glory.

3. The truth of all things.

4. That which quickeneth all things.

5. That which maketh alive all things.

6. That which knoweth all things.

7. That which hath all power according to wisdom, mercy, truth, justice and judgment.

These seven equivalents are the Holy Ghost. It is this which "dwelleth in you."[137] Seven being the number of perfection. The Holy Ghost being the Third Member of the Godhead. And, of course, we hope to join them in exaltation.

Finally, Christ promised the Holy Ghost would "teach you all things" and "bring all things to our remembrance."[138]

Christ truly said: "The Kingdom of Heaven is within you" (Luke 17:21). That is, of course, so long as you have taken the step of "receiving the Holy Ghost." You were admonished to do that by someone with authority at your baptism. The power of doing so (as President Packer pointed out in General Conference last Saturday) is entirely left to you.

That Was Funny

I was driving my daughter home from baseball practice and the car in front of us began driving erratically. It slowed down. Then wandered from side to side. The driver was clearly distracted and we could see him looking down at the seat next to him and fiddling around with something.

My daughter said, "What's he doing?"

I replied, "He spilled his Coke and is trying to put it out with a fire."

She thought about it for a minute then laughed long and hard. Funny what can strike your kid's sense of humor. I take it as a sign of intelligence when word play can amuse.

---

[137] D&C 130:22 "The Father has a body of flesh and bones as tangible as man's; the Son also; but the Holy Ghost has not a body of flesh and bones, but is a personage of Spirit. Were it not so, the Holy Ghost could not dwell in us."

[138] John 14:26 "But the Comforter, *which is* the Holy Ghost, whom the Father will send in my name, he shall teach you all things, and bring all things to your remembrance, whatsoever I have said unto you."

Why Not the Cross?

I was asked about the cross as a religious symbol and why I thought it inappropriate. Here's my response:

When Christ described what He accomplished for us in His Atonement, He referred exclusively to the suffering in Gethsemane.[139] Therefore, in the Lord's own explanation, He used the suffering of Gethsemane as the exclusively to let us know the price He paid.

I know that among others, James Talmage and Bruce R. McConkie, have said that the suffering in Gethsemane was renewed on the cross. I have a different view, and I explain that in *Come, Let Us Adore Him*. I will not repeat that here. I expect that since this is my personal view, there will be many who do not share it with me. However, it is my view that the cross was the means of death; and His death became possible by what He went through in Gethsemane. Had He not been weakened through the ordeal in Gethsemane, He could not have died on the cross. But when He arrived at the cross, all that was left to accomplish was His death, while fulfilling the inspired, prophetic foretelling of the event in conformity with the 22nd Psalm.

The original Saints who belonged to the Primitive Church (New Testament Church) regarded the great symbol of Christ as the fish. That symbol was used in the first centuries following Christ. It was supplanted by Constantine. Constantine adopted the cross as a symbol for the new, Roman state religion which changed the Primitive Church into the new, Historic Christianity. It would undergo a name

---

[139] D&C 19:15–19 "Therefore I command you to repent—repent, lest I smite you by the rod of my mouth, and by my wrath, and by my anger, and your sufferings be sore—how sore you know not, how exquisite you know not, yea, how hard to bear you know not. For behold, I, God, have suffered these things for all, that they might not suffer if they would repent; But if they would not repent they must suffer even as I; Which suffering caused myself, even God, the greatest of all, to tremble because of pain, and to bleed at every pore, and to suffer both body and spirit—and would that I might not drink the bitter cup, and shrink— Nevertheless, glory be to the Father, and I partook and finished my preparations unto the children of men."

change to the Catholic Church (meaning Universal Church), then the Roman Catholic Church as it was entrenched as the state religion of the Roman Empire. It has also been referred to as the Holy Roman Empire. All those names are suitably descriptive. The adoption of the cross as a religious symbol for this new Historic Christianity, supplanting the earlier fish symbol, is one of the reasons I think it not appropriate. It symbolizes the change of Primitive Christianity into a new religious form significantly different from what it was when it began.

The cross symbolizes the newer form of the faith, which adopted many of the earlier Roman state myths and simply gave Christian names and references to them. The celebration of Sol Invictus mid-winter became the celebration of Christmas. Spring fertility rites, including use of the egg and rabbit symbols of fertility were con-verted into a "Christian" holiday of Easter. Local deities no longer hailed from Olympus, but semi-deified "Saints" could be prayed to just as the earlier veneration of local deities. The full panoply of changes would require books to explain, but for me these changes are symbolized by the adoption of the cross as the great symbol of the new Historic Christian movement. Hence the reason I think it inappropriate as a symbol for a restoration of Primitive Christianity.

Fast and Testimony

In our ward yesterday we heard testimonies from ward members who rarely speak. It was delightful. One of the best testimony meet-ings I can recall. One fellow who spoke was so moved by what he was telling us that he had to choke back tears. His elderly mother has Alzheimer's disease and he could not be certain what was getting through to her. She responded to him touching her hand, rubbing her back, and whispering to her during his last visit. His comments focused on charity toward others, and the great example he pointed to was the group responsible for caring for the people at the facility where his mother was located. They were primarily Hispanic. They labored with smiles on their faces and showed such genuine care for the people that he had to thank someone as part of his last visit. He spoke with a woman working there, and thanked her and the whole staff through her for the kindness, charity and love they show while providing care for the people they serve. The woman was grateful for his comments. His whole testimony was about charity and caring for others. It was quite moving, and a reminder again of how many opportunities there are to provide service to others.

Another fellow spoke about his baptism, long ago in the South. He was baptized in a "muddy stream" when he was young, and he can remember how cold it was on that day. It was the first time my children had heard him speak, although we have been in the same ward for nearly two decades. They all were surprised he had a southern accent. And they all said they now "really loved the guy" because of what he said and how he said it. Before they hardly noticed him because he was so very quiet.

What a wonderful thing a ward family is. There hasn't been a ward I've attended that hasn't been quirky, diverse, interesting and at times trying. It's a good thing we are divided by area and cannot choose where to attend. We have no choice but to associate with a diverse lot of people. I think that is healthy.

Current State of Things

I was asked why I do not sound the alarm about the current state of society more often. My view is that fixing problems on a large scale is not helpful. The fix should occur at the individual level. We fix the whole of society with individual conversions, not by better legislation. I do have a view about the state of the world at present. It comes from Moroni, and other modern revelations. I might as well lay out that view, briefly:

Satan does not create. He cannot. He only destroys what others create.

Since life itself is sacred, and he cannot create life, he shows his "great power" by taking life. This is the reason he taught murder to Cain, because if life is among the greatest of gifts from God, Satan's secret work of murder attacks the power of creation.[140]

If you want to know where Satan's great work is prospering anytime in history, look for those groups who organize to kill others. Those who preach hate, lead to violence, lead to murder and ultimately mass killing. These are the ones who do not create, nor do they respect the great gift of creation given by God to mankind. These are they who are overcome by the devil, who love a lie, who

---

[140] Moses 5:29–32 "And Satan said unto Cain: Swear unto me by thy throat, and if thou tell it thou shalt die; and swear thy brethren by their heads, and by the living God, that they tell it not; for if they tell it, they shall surely die; and this that thy father may not know it; and this day I will deliver thy brother Abel into thine hands. And Satan sware unto Cain that he would do according to his commands. And all these things were done in secret. And Cain said: Truly I am Mahan, the master of this great secret, that I may murder and get gain. Wherefore Cain was called Master Mahan, and he gloried in his wickedness. And Cain went into the field, and Cain talked with Abel, his brother. And it came to pass that while they were in the field, Cain rose up against Abel, his brother, and slew him."

make war with God and will ultimately succeed in completely rejecting what He has offered to them.[141]

"Destroyer" is one of Satan's names.[142]

Murder of the innocent is one of the unpardonable sins.[143] It is
so offensive because it undoes the great gift of life given by God. It
is a direct challenge to God's authority. He alone holds the keys of
life and death. Killing directly invades God's authority.

We live at a time when there are organized efforts to form groups
for the sole purpose of killing others. This behavior is so directly
analogous to the Gadianton conspiracy within the Book of Mormon

---

[141] D&C 76:28–37 "And while we were yet in the Spirit, the Lord commanded us that
we should write the vision; for we beheld Satan, that old serpent, even the devil, who
rebelled against God, and sought to take the kingdom of our God and his Christ—
Wherefore, he maketh war with the saints of God, and encompasseth them round
about. And we saw a vision of the sufferings of those with whom he made war and
overcame, for thus came the voice of the Lord unto us: Thus saith the Lord concerning all those who know my power, and have been made partakers thereof, and suffered
themselves through the power of the devil to be overcome, and to deny the truth and
defy my power— They are they who are the sons of perdition, of whom I say that it had
been better for them never to have been born; For they are vessels of wrath, doomed
to suffer the wrath of God, with the devil and his angels in eternity; Concerning whom
I have said there is no forgiveness in this world nor in the world to come— Having
denied the Holy Spirit after having received it, and having denied the Only Begotten Son
of the Father, having crucified him unto themselves and put him to an open shame.
These are they who shall go away into the lake of fire and brimstone, with the devil
and his angels— And the only ones on whom the second death shall have any power;"

[142] D&C 61:19 "I, the Lord, have decreed, and the destroyer rideth upon the face
thereof, and I revoke not the decree."

[143] D&C 132:19 "And again, verily I say unto you, if a man marry a wife by my word,
which is my law, and by the new and everlasting covenant, and it is sealed unto them by
the Holy Spirit of promise, by him who is anointed, unto whom I have appointed this
power and the keys of this priesthood; and it shall be said unto them—Ye shall come
forth in the first resurrection; and if it be after the first resurrection, in the next resurrection; and shall inherit thrones, kingdoms, principalities, and powers, dominions, all
heights and depths—then shall it be written in the Lamb's Book of Life, that he shall
commit no murder whereby to shed innocent blood, and if ye abide in my covenant,
and commit no murder whereby to shed innocent blood, it shall be done unto them in
all things whatsoever my servant hath put upon them, in time, and through all eternity;
and shall be of full force when they are out of the world; and they shall pass by the
angels, and the gods, which are set there, to their exaltation and glory in all things, as
hath been sealed upon their heads, which glory shall be a fulness and a continuation of
the seeds forever and ever."

that the lessons there should serve as notice to us. Moroni interrupted his translation of the Book of Ether to give us this warning:

> And now I, Moroni, do not write the manner of their oaths
> and combinations, for it hath been made known unto me that
> they are had among all people, and they are had among the
> Lamanites. And they have caused the destruction of this peo-
> ple of whom I am now speaking, and also the destruction of
> the people of Nephi.
>
> And whatsoever nation shall uphold such secret combina-
> tions, to get power and gain, until they shall spread over the
> nation, behold, they shall be destroyed; for the Lord will not
> suffer that the blood of his saints, which shall be shed by
> them, shall always cry unto him from the ground for venge-
> ance upon them and yet he avenge them not.
>
> Wherefore, O ye Gentiles, it is wisdom in God that these
> things should be shown unto you, that thereby ye may repent
> of your sins, and suffer not that these murderous combina-
> tions shall get above you, which are built up to get power and
> gain—and the work, yea, even the work of destruction come
> upon you, yea, even the sword of the justice of the Eternal
> God shall fall upon you, to your overthrow and destruction if
> ye shall suffer these things to be. Wherefore, the Lord com-
> mandeth you, when ye shall see these things come among you
> that ye shall awake to a sense of your awful situation, because
> of this secret combination which shall be among you; or wo
> be unto it, because of the blood of them who have been slain;
> for they cry from the dust for vengeance upon it, and also
> upon those who built it up. For it cometh to pass that whoso
> buildeth it up seeketh to overthrow the freedom of all lands,
> nations, and countries; and it bringeth to pass the destruction
> of all people, for it is built up by the devil, who is the father of
> all lies; even that same liar who beguiled our first parents, yea,
> even that same liar who hath caused man to commit murder
> from the beginning; who hath hardened the hearts of men

that they have murdered the prophets, and stoned them, and cast them out from the beginning.

Wherefore, I, Moroni, am commanded to write these things that evil may be done away, and that the time may come that Satan may have no power upon the hearts of the children of men, but that they may be persuaded to do good continually, that they may come unto the fountain of all righteousness and be saved. (Ether 8:20–26)

Having said the foregoing, let me add that I do not think knowing our awful circumstance does a thing to fix it. What fixes it is to have more people come to the Lord, develop love for their fellow man, and live the commandments given by Him. That is something done one person at a time. I despair when I think in larger numbers than the individual. I rejoice when I think of the single person. For anything is possible with each person, no matter what their circumstances.

Follow Christ in All Things

I was asked:

Nephi invites us to follow Christ in all the ordinances starting with baptism. The endowment clearly requires us to follow Adam in seeking more light and truth, receiving ordinances and making covenants. Finally, when we arrive in the sealing room we seek to follow and obtain the blessings of Abraham Isaac and Jacob. Ultimately we follow Christ in all things, but I wondered if you could comment on this.

My response:

Nephi followed Christ. Adam followed Christ. Abraham, Isaac and Jacob followed Christ. We get examples from sacred writings (and ordinances) which incorporate reference to earlier disciples of Christ, but always in the context of showing the need to follow Christ.

There is no jealousy about using a man who followed Christ as an example to follow. One of the reasons the Melchizedek Priesthood is named after a man rather than retaining the original "Holy Priesthood after the Order of the Son of God" was to prevent the frequent repetition of the Son of God name.[144] This was respectful of the Son of God, while using the man Melchizedek as the example for using the authority which comes from the Son of God.

However, the one we follow is Christ and we follow His Gospel. When we decide to follow only a disciple of His, even if it is a true disciple, we miss the mark and fall to a Telestial state and are no better than the liars and thieves.[145] So even when it is a man whose example we list or refer to, it is only to the extent that the man illustrates the correct manner to follow the Son of God.

The God of the Telestial Kingdom (in which we are presently situated) is the Holy Ghost. The God of the Terrestrial Kingdom (which the Millennium will reflect) is Jesus Christ. The God of the Celestial Kingdom is God the Father.[146] The Holy Ghost brings us

---

[144] D&C 107:2–4 "Why the first is called the Melchizedek Priesthood is because Melchizedek was such a great high priest. Before his day it was called the Holy Priesthood, after the Order of the Son of God. But out of respect or reverence to the name of the Supreme Being, to avoid the too frequent repetition of his name, they, the church, in ancient days, called that priesthood after Melchizedek, or the Melchizedek Priesthood."

[145] D&C 76:98–104 "And the glory of the telestial is one, even as the glory of the stars is one; for as one star differs from another star in glory, even so differs one from another in glory in the telestial world; For these are they who are of Paul, and of Apollos, and of Cephas. These are they who say they are some of one and some of another—some of Christ and some of John, and some of Moses, and some of Elias, and some of Esaias, and some of Isaiah, and some of Enoch; But received not the gospel, neither the testimony of Jesus, neither the prophets, neither the everlasting covenant. Last of all, these all are they who will not be gathered with the saints, to be caught up unto the church of the Firstborn, and received into the cloud. These are they who are liars, and sorcerers, and adulterers, and whoremongers, and whosoever loves and makes a lie. These are they who suffer the wrath of God on earth."

[146] See D&C Section 76.

to Christ. Christ brings us to the Father. The Father extends the promise of exaltation by making you a son or daughter of God.

The plan of redemption brings us from our current, fallen state back to a state of awareness of our condition, and then by cleansing us, elevates us in light and truth. The primary God with whom we deal here is the Holy Ghost. However, the association with Christ is promised by Him in Chapter 14 of John. Joseph Smith explained that when the promise given by Christ in that chapter of John is realized, then the Father and Son will visit with the person from time to time. He also clarified that the visit referred to is actual, not just something "in the heart" of a believer.[147]

Abraham is the example used in the sealing ordinance because Abraham's covenant with the Lord is the prototype of what the Lord promises all those who follow Him. Those promises include eternal increase (posterity), land (inheritance) and eternal life.

Missionary in Kenya

There's a family I home teach whose son is on a mission in Kenya. They ride a motorcycle to teach outlying areas. Three at a time on the bike through the rain and on muddy roads. They are in a city of 75,000 and not a road is paved in the entire city. Sort of like Sandy, Utah right now. Comparable size and dirt roads everywhere while they do their "stimulus" spending on roadways.

They baptized four new converts last week. My young elder (he's mine because I still home teach him over the internet) did two of the baptisms. It was quite a milestone in his young life.

The pictures are quite interesting. Here's this 6 foot white, smiling kid standing with a crowd of shorter, very dark faces all with the

---

[147] D&C 130:3 "John 14:23—The appearing of the Father and the Son, in that verse, is a personal appearance; and the idea that the Father and the Son dwell in a man's heart is an old sectarian notion, and is false."

look of joy and kinship on their countenances. He's sort of a spectacle to the people there. Not only his height, but his light skin and blonde hair. Kids ask if they can touch him (and he lets them).

What an adventure this young man is on. What fun it is to share it by reading his emails sent back home. It reminds me of just how small the world is after all. I guess Disney got that right . . .

HUMOR REQUIRES UNDERLYING TRUTH

THE Remnant

The subject of THE "remnant" is too great to undertake in a post here. I've attended meetings lasting two days in which the subject was the sole matter being discussed. I've had discussions, read a manuscript, exchanged emails and spent years on this subject with people who know more about the details than do I. Therefore my conclusion is that it exceeds the parameters of this venue.

Identification of the "remnant" was critical to Joseph Smith. Although we've discarded the issue, it was of central concern to the early Brethren. So much so that the "remnant" was what drove the movement westward near the "borders of the Lamanites" The first missionaries were sent to the "Lamanites" as part of the Restoration's concern with the promised "remnant" of the Book of Mormon people.[148] The Saints were required to move west to be near these people as part of locating Zion.[149]

---

[148] D&C 32:2 "And that which I have appointed unto him is that he shall go with my servants, Oliver Cowdery and Peter Whitmer, Jun., into the wilderness among the Lamanites."

[149] D&C 54:8 "And thus you shall take your journey into the regions westward, unto the land of Missouri, unto the borders of the Lamanites."

The Book of Mormon is filled with promises addressed to the "remnant" of those people. Modern revelation promises they will blossom as a rose.[150]

The first Temple built in the west after the exodus was in St. George to be near the suspected "remnant" to be reclaimed. The first company in that Temple's first session included a Chief from the Hopi tribe. Brother Nibley was partial to the Hopi as the "remnant" or at least a part of the "remnant" and he wrote a good deal about them.

This is an important subject. Worthy of study. But it is too great a subject for treatment in a limited venue like this. To do it justice would require this forum to become devoted to that subject for many days. By the time it was finished, I doubt anyone would still be reading. So I'll just reaffirm the subject is important, and there are many passages in the Book of Mormon dealing with the "remnant" of the Book of Mormon people. Promises extended to them have not yet been fulfilled. But all those promises will be fulfilled. As they are, the role of those people will change from what we see it today into something much more central to the Church.

The Individual and Truth

There are two propositions I believe have the potential for defining our lives here in mortality.

First, the importance of the individual.

I really do believe in the importance, centrality and power of the individual. What happens everywhere in the world begins with interpersonal relationships and the individual. More can be done, and is done to change the course of history by the actions of individuals than anything else.

---

[150] D&C 49:24 "But before the great day of the Lord shall come, Jacob shall flourish in the wilderness, and the Lamanites shall blossom as the rose."

There's that old saying that when God wants to change the world, He sends a baby. Whether that baby is Buddha, or Gandhi, or Abraham Lincoln, or Henry Ford, or Thomas Beckett, or Jesus, the world changes when babies enter mortality. All lives matter. No one matters more than another in my view. The accumulation of lives well lived is the stuff of history. How many unnamed artisans were required to build the Parthenon?

Our day is the great day of the individual. Now your thoughts can be sent by electronic means anywhere in the world. Your audience can include every living person who has a connection to the internet. I think there is a purpose there.

You matter. All of us do. Good ideas can now spread on eagle's wings, so to speak. A spark kindled today can light the whole world.

Second, the primacy of good.

I believe truth will triumph. To be here on the earth required an initial "screening," which was conducted before the people who are born here were permitted to come. All those who live here came from a shared God and Father of us all. Therefore, we have something in common.

Truth is recognizable. It must be fought to be suppressed. Although some will wage that fight and succeed in blighting **their** sense of the truth and light, the overwhelming majority will not. The "light of Christ" given to all mankind as a commonly shared inheritance persists here.

The result is that truth will win. In free exchanges of ideas, it will be truth that will ultimately triumph. I believe the truth will win even if it is only spoken as a whisper in a hurricane of opposition. It will win.

It is unnecessary for truth to come from authorized sources. It is irrelevant for it to be opposed by authorized sources. It will always triumph. Crush it, burn it, send it into the wilderness and crucify those who believe it—it will triumph.

Record Keeping

Joseph touches on a principle in his letter on September 6, 1842 that is quite important. It relates to keeping record and the day of judgment.

After quoting Revelation 20:12, Joseph explains there are two kinds of records kept.[151] One is on earth, recording what men have done here. The other is kept in heaven. The one agreeing with the other.[152] He goes on to explain how these two records are related.

What is recorded on earth is recorded in heaven. What is not recorded in earth "shall not be recorded in heaven."[153]

This principle was extended by President Spencer W. Kimball in a talk he gave in October, 1975 while President of the Church. His comments included this:

---

[151] Revelation 20:12 "And I saw the dead, small and great, stand before God; and the books were opened: and another book was opened, which is *the book* of life: and the dead were judged out of those things which were written in the books, according to their works."

[152] D&C 128:7 "You will discover in this quotation that the books were opened; and another book was opened, which was the book of life; but the dead were judged out of those things which were written in the books, according to their works; consequently, the books spoken of must be the books which contained the record of their works, and refer to the records which are kept on the earth. And the book which was the book of life is the record which is kept in heaven; the principle agreeing precisely with the doctrine which is commanded you in the revelation contained in the letter which I wrote to you previous to my leaving my place—that in all your recordings it may be recorded in heaven."

[153] D&C 128:8 "Now, the nature of this ordinance consists in the power of the priesthood, by the revelation of Jesus Christ, wherein it is granted that whatsoever you bind on earth shall be bound in heaven, and whatsoever you loose on earth shall be loosed in heaven. Or, in other words, taking a different view of the translation, whatsoever you record on earth shall be recorded in heaven, and whatsoever you do not record on earth shall not be recorded in heaven; for out of the books shall your dead be judged, according to their own works, whether they themselves have attended to the ordinances in their own *propria persona,* or by the means of their own agents, according to the ordinance which God has prepared for their salvation from before the foundation of the world, according to the records which they have kept concerning their dead."

"Get a notebook, my young folks, a journal that will last through all time, and maybe the angels may quote from it for eternity. Begin today and write in it your goings and comings, your deepest thoughts, your achievements, and your failures, your associations and your triumphs, your impressions and your testimonies. Remember, the Savior chastised those who failed to record important events." (Originally printed in October, 1975 *New Era*; reprinted in *New Era*, Feb 2003, 32)

Why would angels quote from your personal journal? It would be based on the same principle given by Joseph Smith in Section 128. Recording here those sacred events which happen in your life is necessary for the same events to be recorded in heaven. The personal records of disciples of Christ have become scripture, but they began as a personal journal. Nephi's record was his journal. Alma's, Abraham's, Enoch's and many others were also. Section 128 is a letter. Most of the New Testament consists of letters. These were written to or for family members or friends.

Do not underestimate the significance of what you record on earth in your own records. If you record sacred events, written under the influence of the Holy Ghost, angels may not only quote from it (as Pres. Kimball suggested), but they may regard it as scripture itself.

My Calculations

I was asked about the numbers in activity used in an earlier post. That calculation was one I made based on the statistics we were given by the Mission President on our area.

By way of background, I did a two year stint as the Ward Mission Leader, followed by five years on the High Council over missionary work in my stake. During the last two years on the High Council we would meet quarterly with the mission presidency. During those meetings we would be updated on the numbers throughout the mission and the church. The numbers worked out to approximately 37%

activity rate church-wide. *However*, the definition of "active" included anyone who attended a single sacrament meeting during a quarter. This had the effect of inflating the number by all those who attended during Easter and Christmas (because they all became instantly "active" during two quarters of the year). They also were affected by the count of sacrament meeting attendees who came for missionary farewells and missionary homecomings.

I did a count of my own to try and come up with a "distortion" number to attempt to calculate who was really carrying the load as an average. I couldn't get a consistent result using my own ward to allow for Easter/Christmas and missionary farewell/homecoming additions. But it appeared to me the distortion was somewhere between as little as 5% and as much as 10%. I took a mid-point between the two and made my overall estimate of 4,000,000 out of the total church membership as those who are really serving regularly, attending regularly, and who are not merely "active" by virtue of quarterly appearances in a sacrament meeting. I hope that serves your purposes.

A Parable

A parable—for which I borrow Hindu and Buddhist notions to make it possible to tell.

There was a certain man who feared not God nor regarded his fellow man; who was filled with ungoverned lust and anger. He married, fathered a child, and abused his son daily, for he was without compassion. In the course of his abuse, he injured his son frequently. When the child was a young boy, in a fit of anger, the man killed his son. He was arrested, convicted of the murder, and executed.

Time is known only to man, but not to God, for all things past, present and future are before Him at all times in one eternal "now." God, who is merciful and whose purpose is to improve His children, to bring about their immortality and lead them into eternal life, needed this man to understand within his heart how his acts affect others. For the man regarded not his fellow man and could not feel compassion for his wicked deeds. With God all things are possible, and therefore the man was sent back again to mortality for further instruction.

When he returned, the man was born as the son of a certain man who feared not God nor regarded his fellow man. His father was filled with ungoverned lust and anger. His father abused him daily and in the course of abuse he was frequently injured. One day the father killed him.

When men die they return to God, who gave them life, and so the child, who had once been a wicked man, returned again to God. The Lord asked him upon his return: "Do you now understand?"

The man replied, "Yes. I have been both. I have been the victim and I have been the perpetrator. I have been the father and I have been the son. I have released my uncontrolled anger and I have been the victim of it. I remember abusing and I also remember being abused. I see now that when I was ungovernable and unkind it was only myself who I abused. What I have given has returned to me and I have caused my own suffering."

The Lord said, "It is well. Now let these experiences work in you, for without the opportunity to use them to live aright, you are not yet ready."

Having been the wicked father and the abused son, the man returned again to the same time and place to now be a neighbor of the wicked man and the abused son. How, then, ought the neighbor act so as to show he had truly learned?

What we do to another, we only do to ourselves. We will all find in the end that we are indeed our brother's keeper. We are our fathers, and we are our sons, and we ought to be One with each other.

Mark Twain

Mark Twain had a greater influence on my childhood development than any other writer. Here are a few of his quotes:

"It ain't what you don't know that gets you in trouble. It's what you know for sure that just ain't so."

"Loyalty to petrified opinion never broke a chain or freed a human soul."

"It's no wonder that truth is stranger than fiction. Fiction has to make sense."

Benjamin Franklin and Mark Twain gave Americans their sense of humor. Whether you've ever read anything written by them or not, they form the underlying basis for our American humor. Deep inside all their wit lies the truth.

The Battle Is the Lord's

I had an interesting conversation yesterday. It provoked this comment.

When Julius ended the Republic by crossing the Rubicon with the 13th Legion from Gaul, he established a dictatorship that would change into the Empire thereafter. The Republic was dead. The Empire lived on.

Julius' great nephew is regarded as the first fully recognized Emperor of the Roman Empire. He ruled until his death in 14 A.D. as dictator for life.

Rome dominated the world, subduing other peoples who were considered inferior to Romans. They believed it was Rome's right to rule the world. Roman control was benefiting others. This was the Pax Romana, or peace of Rome. It came at the point of a spear. Such is the peace offered by the leaders of this world.

Among the lands under Roman control was the Judean province in which Jesus Christ was born. The place of His birth was directly affected by Augustus' taxing.[154] He was a Jewish subject to the vassal king of the Herodian family. His life was lived between two Roman controlled provinces.

Jesus was asked if it was lawful to give tribute to Rome. He responded by asking for a coin, noting Caesar's image on it, and remarking "give unto Caesar the things that are Caesar's; and unto God the things that are God's."[155]

Jesus never challenged Roman authority. He submitted to it. When the time comes for the establishment of Zion, it will not be necessary for us to deviate from Christ's example. Those who are in the promised latter-day Zion will be protected by the "the terror of the Lord." The residents will be those who "will not take up arms against their neighbor."[156] There is no need to overthrow the world.

---

[154] Luke 2:1–6 "And it came to pass in those days, that there went out a decree from Caesar Augustus, that all the world should be taxed. (*And* this taxing was first made when Cyrenius was governor of Syria.) And all went to be taxed, every one into his own city. And Joseph also went up from Galilee, out of the city of Nazareth, into Judaea, unto the city of David, which is called Bethlehem; (because he was of the house and lineage of David:) To be taxed with Mary his espoused wife, being great with child. And so it was, that, while they were there, the days were accomplished that she should be delivered."

[155] Matthew 22:17–22 "Tell us therefore, What thinkest thou? Is it lawful to give tribute unto Caesar, or not? But Jesus perceived their wickedness, and said, Why tempt ye me, *ye* hypocrites? Shew me the tribute money. And they brought unto him a penny. And he saith unto them, Whose *is* this image and superscription? They say unto him, Caesar's. Then saith he unto them, Render therefore unto Caesar the things which are Caesar's; and unto God the things that are God's. When they had heard *these words,* they marvelled, and left him, and went their way."

[156] D&C 45:66–71 "And it shall be called the New Jerusalem, a land of peace, a city of refuge, a place of safety for the saints of the Most High God; And the glory of the Lord shall be there, and the terror of the Lord also shall be there, insomuch that the wicked will not come unto it, and it shall be called Zion. And it shall come to pass among the wicked, that every man that will not take his sword against his neighbor must needs flee unto Zion for safety. And there shall be gathered unto it out of every nation under heaven; and it shall be the only people that shall not be at war one with another. And it shall be said among the wicked: Let us not go up to battle against Zion, for the inhabitants of Zion are terrible; wherefore we cannot stand. And it shall come to pass that the righteous shall be gathered out from among all nations, and shall come to Zion, singing with songs of everlasting joy."

It will overthrow itself. The Lord will not permit the wicked to destroy the righteous.[157] It is the wicked who destroy the wicked.[158]

We live in a world today in which Pax Americana has established controlled violence the world over. The fear of destruction holds forces at bay which would gladly destroy one another if permitted. The key to replacing the current world order with another one, as many insurgencies the world over recognize, is the destruction of Pax Americana by destroying American hegemony. A lot of people are working on that, both inside and outside the United States.

Latter-day Zion will not need to take up the sword to defend themselves. The Lord will be their shield and protection. Since the wicked are responsible for killing the wicked, you join them when you decide to take up arms. You also exclude yourself from those who are to come to Zion—for that group will be composed only of those who refuse to take up arms against their neighbor.[159]

---

[157] 1 Nephi 22:16 "For the time soon cometh that the fulness of the wrath of God shall be poured out upon all the children of men; for he will not suffer that the wicked shall destroy the righteous."

[158] Mormon 4:5 "But, behold, the judgments of God will overtake the wicked; and it is by the wicked that the wicked are punished; for it is the wicked that stir up the hearts of the children of men unto bloodshed."

[159] D&C 45:68 "And it shall come to pass among the wicked, that every man that will not take his sword against his neighbor must needs flee unto Zion for safety."

Read again how Zion was protected in the days of Enoch.[160] It wasn't an army or arms which protected them. It was the Lord who dwelt among them.

Our challenge as a people is to live so the Lord can dwell among us. He will "take up His abode" with us as the Second Comforter, if we are prepared to receive Him. This is why I have written what I have written. Zion will be a byproduct of a prepared people. It never has been and never will be the result of a violent, armed, and politically motivated insurrection by people who want to isolate themselves from the world. Such people will only be a part of those who take up arms, and acting as part of the wicked, join in the destruction of the wicked, including themselves.

This does not mean that some righteous will not be required to die. The Lord's ability to protect us will require His hand move in "justice and mercy" to fulfill His promises. Those who die will die unto the Lord. Those who live will live unto the Lord. But the battle is the Lord's.

---

[160] Moses 7:13–17 "And so great was the faith of Enoch that he led the people of God, and their enemies came to battle against them; and he spake the word of the Lord, and the earth trembled, and the mountains fled, even according to his command; and the rivers of water were turned out of their course; and the roar of the lions was heard out of the wilderness; and all nations feared greatly, so powerful was the word of Enoch, and so great was the power of the language which God had given him. There also came up a land out of the depth of the sea, and so great was the fear of the enemies of the people of God, that they fled and stood afar off and went upon the land which came up out of the depth of the sea. And the giants of the land, also, stood afar off; and there went forth a curse upon all people that fought against God; And from that time forth there were wars and bloodshed among them; but the Lord came and dwelt with his people, and they dwelt in righteousness. The fear of the Lord was upon all nations, so great was the glory of the Lord, which was upon his people. And the Lord blessed the land, and they were blessed upon the mountains, and upon the high places, and did flourish."

Mosiah 18:8–10

I was asked why the language of Mosiah 18:8–10 related to membership in the church, and not to others outside the church. Here's my response.

These verses are talking about entering into a covenant and becoming "the fold of God."[161] This fold will be "called his people."[162] The fold, who have this covenant, and who are called His people, are to be "willing to bear one another's burdens, that they may be light."[163] The whole passage is relating to the interrelationship between those who are of the covenant, the fold, and who are God's people as a result of this covenant. These are the duties owed internally to the fold.

It continues to explain that these people should be "willing to mourn with those that mourn."[164] The word "those" should be read in the context of the covenant, the fold, the people and the obligation arising from within the group.

These verses are church/fold/covenant people related, and govern the obligations which those who come into that fold owe to each other. It arises out of the covenant of baptism.[165]

---

[161] Mosiah 18:8 "And it came to pass that he said unto them: Behold, here are the waters of Mormon (for thus were they called) and now, as ye are desirous to come into the fold of God, and to be called his people, and are willing to bear one another's burdens, that they may be light;"

[162] Ibid.

[163] Ibid.

[164] Mosiah 18:9 "Yea, and are willing to mourn with those that mourn; yea, and comfort those that stand in need of comfort, and to stand as witnesses of God at all times and in all things, and in all places that ye may be in, even until death, that ye may be redeemed of God, and be numbered with those of the first resurrection, that ye may have eternal life—"

[165] Mosiah 18:10 "Now I say unto you, if this be the desire of your hearts, what have you against being baptized in the name of the Lord, as a witness before him that ye have entered into a covenant with him, that ye will serve him and keep his commandments, that he may pour out his Spirit more abundantly upon you?"

The obligation owed within the church membership to one another on the one hand does not eliminate other obligations owed to your fellow man. Indeed, it is one of the chief obligations owed to all humanity to cry repentance and bring others into the fold. Christ also extended the obligation to care for others without regard to their status, including in His parable of the good Samaritan. So to say there is one duty owed within the church is not to say there are not other obligations owed to others outside the church.

Forward or Backward

I got asked about loss of teachings or practices within the LDS community. My response is as follows.

It makes no difference whether it is an individual or a community, we are all on a single path that goes two ways—forward or backward. We are either gaining, or we are losing. We cannot stand still.

Whether a group or a person, we are either gaining (restoring) light and truth, or we are losing (apostatizing) from light and truth. This world is a world of change. Nothing remains the same. Everywhere you see either growth, or decay. These forces are at work everywhere. They are also at work within you.

You either search out new truth, find it, live it, and thereby become restored to truth, or you back away from it. If you are backing away, losing it, neglecting it, and discarding it, you are in the process of apostasy.

In a restoration process, there are moments along the way which are marked and notable. Having the inspiration of the Spirit, or feeling the remission of your sins, or receiving revelation, or having a visit of an angel are notable. The culmination of the restoration would be to return to God's presence. Should that happen, through the Second Comforter's ministry, then you have been restored in full.

In an apostasy process, you also have a few momentous events. Having a loss of sympathy for others, feeling progressively more critical of others, becoming neglectful of prayers, failing to associate with fellow saints, neglecting the sacrament are early along the path. Ultimately asking to have your membership terminated, engaging is drug abuse, patronizing the sex industry, are strong signs someone has departed from moving in one direction and has begun to move quickly into the other. (I'm not saying that these are related, nor that someone who leaves the church voluntarily is doomed to addiction, immorality or worse. There are many people of good faith who struggle with the church. That is a different subject.) It is clear, however, than when a person has become a murderer, seeking to kill the saints, as we have seen in history, such a person has finished the course of apostasy and is beyond feeling.

These are examples which try to quickly illustrate the point on a personal level. Quickly, at the institutional level, we have at one end of full restoration, a return to Zion, and the Lord dwelling among them. At the other we have a society whose wickedness and abuse of children is so far spread that fire comes down from heaven to destroy them. Complete restorations and complete apostasies are rare. What history is made up is the description of struggling along the path. We ebb and flow back and forth, without becoming fully ripe either way.

Christ promised at the end of time there there would be a ripening. "Wheat" and "tares" will ripen. Then there will be a harvest.[166] However, the haphazard manner of the harvesting makes a full re-

---

[166] Matthew 13:37–42 "He answered and said unto them, He that soweth the good seed is the Son of man; The field is the world; the good seed are the children of the kingdom; but the tares are the children of the wicked *one;* The enemy that sowed them is the devil; the harvest is the end of the world; and the reapers are the angels. As therefore the tares are gathered and burned in the fire; so shall it be in the end of this world. The Son of man shall send forth his angels, and they shall gather out of his kingdom all things that offend, and them which do iniquity; And shall cast them into a furnace of fire: there shall be wailing and gnashing of teeth."

turn of Zion before His coming seem unanticipated by the Lord's teachings.[167] Modern revelation gave us that opportunity. We clearly have not done so, and at present seem clearly not interested in doing so. That is a subject for another time, however. As Christ put it, we need to seek for our individual, complete restoration because the group will not.

There are two ways—forward or backward. It is not required that you finish the course in a day; but times are coming in which the environment will require of you a greater commitment as "wheat" on the one hand, or leave you to descend into becoming a "tare" on the other. So the direction you are on now is quite important. Either you are restoring truth or you are discarding it.

A Confession

Confession of sins is supposed to be good for the soul. So I figure I'll make a confession of my attempted arson. I offer no defense for this crime, since I need none. The statute of limitations having run many years ago.

When my friend decided he no longer wanted to make payments on his new 1969 Chevy Nova, I offered to total the car for him so he could collect the insurance money. As we were speeding along getting ready for me to wreck it into a collection of roadside boulders, he chickened out. So we never destroyed it that evening. Within a few days, however, he returned to his despair over making payments. We discussed it for some time without any resolution to the problem.

Because of some movie (I think with Steve McQueen, but for the life of me I can't recall what it was about), we came up with a solution: We'd burn the car. Surely insurance would total it if burned.

---

[167] Matthew 24:39–40 "And knew not until the flood came, and took them all away; so shall also the coming of the Son of man be. Then shall two be in the field; the one shall be taken, and the other left."

So we parked it behind the Mountain Home Newspaper office, where we worked, and set the plan in motion. My friend soaked the front seat with kerosene, lit a cigarette, tucked the lit cigarette into a match-pack, set it on the soaked front seat, and we went inside. We were waiting for the cigarette to burn down to the matches, the matches to ignite, the ignition to set the kerosene afire, and the fire to destroy the car. We waited. And waited. And nothing seemed to be happening. We stayed in the front of the newspaper office, wanting to appear surprised when the news of a burning car was brought to us, but nothing happened.

I think it was an hour or more before we went to the rear of the building to check on how our felony was progressing, and noticed that in the upper glass block skylight there was flashing red lights, clearly showing flames licking upward from a burning Chevy Nova. We thought it worked! Now someone needed to notice it and call the police. But we couldn't be the ones who discovered it. So we retreated again to the front of the building and settled in to wait out the discovery.

When another hour or so had passed we again peeked into the back of the building and again saw that same flickering red light. We retreated again.

Another hour later and still no sirens, no commotion, nothing. We checked again and sure enough the red flickering was still underway. We wondered what it was about a Chevy Nova that would let it burn for hours once ignited. Then concluded that if no-one else was going to make the grim discovery, we could at least see the results of our handiwork directly instead of through glass block skylight reflections.

So we opened the back door and there sat the Chevy Nova completely undisturbed. Intact, fully operational and not even singed. Puzzled, we wondered at what we'd been seeing flickering these past hours. It turned out to be the outdoor sign of Jovial Jerry's bar, whose sign was on the sidewalk outside the bar with which the Mt. Home News shared a parking lot.

Well the Nova didn't burn. When we inspected our crime scene it turned out that kerosene will put out a lit cigarette without igniting. The cigarette was there, soaked with the seat, and the matches were unusable as well. The only damage was a cigarette burn to the front seat upholstery.

Well my friend had suffered so much from the hours of anticipation and was so relieved at the failure, that he determined to just keep the Nova. However, from that day till the day he sold it it always stank of kerosene.

There, confessing my sin does make me feel better. Maybe I'll cover some others in the future.

LDS Books

I was asked to recommend some books. I am going to first discuss some of what I've read over the years.

The first year after joining the church I was eager to learn what the religion was about. I began reading whatever I could find to inform me about the new faith. I started with the following, which I obtained from a bookstore inside the home of a woman in the ward:

- *A Marvelous Work and a Wonder*, by LeGrand Richards.
- *The Autobiography of Parley P. Pratt*
- *Life of Heber C. Kimball*
- *Teachings of the Prophet Joseph Smith*
- *Jesus the Christ*
- *Documentary History of the Church by Joseph Smith* (all volumes)

I was transferred by the Air Force to Texas, and continued to read there until my discharge from the military. While there I read the following:

- *The Life of John Taylor*
- *Comprehensive History of the Church of Jesus Christ of Latter-Day Saints* by BH Roberts (all volumes)
- *Evidences and Reconciliations*
- *The Gospel Kingdom*
- *Mormon Doctrine*
- *The Promised Messiah*
- *The Articles of Faith*
- *The House of the Lord*
- *The Mortal Messiah* (all volumes)
- *Ensign, Conference Report, Journal of Discourses* (not all volumes read)
- *Doctrinal New Testament Commentary*
- *The History of Joseph Smith by His Mother Lucy Mack Smith Discourses of Brigham Young*
- *Brigham Young: American Moses*
- *Doctrines of Salvation* (3 volumes)
- *Answers to Gospel Questions* (5 volumes)
- *Gospel Doctrine* by Joseph F. Smith
- *Messages of the First Presidency* (6 volumes)

By the time I arrived at BYU, I thought I was beginning to understand the faith, at least as it was taught and understood at the beginning. There was a debate between BH Roberts and the Chaplin of the United States Senate which I really liked. It was titled *"The Mormon Doctrine of Deity: The Roberts and Van Der Donckt Debate."* Nibley's book *The Timely and the Timeless* came out and I still have my original copy. During law school I also discovered Hugh Nibley, and found an actual Deseret Book store. Back then Deseret Book sold doctrine. In fact, almost everything they sold or printed was doctrine or history. I bought and read until I couldn't find an early or contemporary work about church history or doctrine I hadn't read. I have acquired a library since joining the church that includes every significant LDS doctrinal book as it became available in print. I still try and keep up with all the current reading that I believe is worthwhile. But the new stuff is getting thinner and thinner in material, importance, and doctrine. In fact, it is quite rare that a new book isn't disappointing to me, particularly when it comes from Deseret Book. *The Joseph Smith Papers* project is the exception; however, it is coming out under the Church's new publication arm (a division of Deseret Book.) A good example of the foolishness to which Deseret Book has descended is that *Odds Are You're Going to be Exalted* book that came out a couple of years ago.

That having been said, I was asked by someone what I thought was absolutely essential reading. Here's my list:

The scriptures (first, foremost, and without peer)

- *Teachings of the Prophet Joseph Smith*
- *Lectures on Faith*
- *Words of Joseph Smith*
- *Approaching Zion*, by Hugh Nibley
- *The Second Comforter: Conversing With the Lord Through the Veil*

I think if you study those six books, you will understand the Gospel.

Egypt and Egyptian

The brass plates of Laban were also in Egyptian. Mosiah 1 discuss the education of Mosiah's sons.[168] They were taught "in all the language of his fathers." That phrase gets explained. But before clarifying what "all the language" included, the brass plates are mentioned in verse 2.[169] These plates contained the commandments that the sons of Mosiah needed to understand and were not possible for father Lehi to remember. Therefore it was necessary for them to possess the brass plates to stimulate their memory of the commandments.

Continuing on with the explanation, and addressing specifically the brass plates, it is written:

> "it were not possible that our father, Lehi, could have remembered all these things, to have taught them to his children, except it were for the help of these plates; for he *having been taught in the language of the Egyptians therefore he could read these engravings,* and teach them to his children." (Mosiah 1:4, emphasis added)

---

[168] Mosiah 1:1–4 "AND now there was no more contention in all the land of Zarahemla, among all the people who belonged to king Benjamin, so that king Benjamin had continual peace all the remainder of his days. And it came to pass that he had three sons; and he called their names Mosiah, and Helorum, and Helaman. And he caused that they should be taught in all the language of his fathers, that thereby they might become men of understanding; and that they might know concerning the prophecies which had been spoken by the mouths of their fathers, which were delivered them by the hand of the Lord. And he also taught them concerning the records which were engraven on the plates of brass, saying: My sons, I would that ye should remember that were it not for these plates, which contain these records and these commandments, we must have suffered in ignorance, even at this present time, not knowing the mysteries of God. For it were not possible that our father, Lehi, could have remembered all these things, to have taught them to his children, except it were for the help of these plates; for he having been taught in the language of the Egyptians therefore he could read these engravings, and teach them to his children, that thereby they could teach them to their children, and so fulfilling the commandments of God, even down to this present time."

[169] Ibid.

This somewhat changes the picture of Jerusalem at the time of Lehi's departure. The record of the brass plates included what we would recognize as the Old Testament record, from Moses' five books down to the time of Lehi's exodus.[170] For the entire Old Testament account to have been written in Egyptian onto the brass plates means that Egyptian was a preferred language. It wasn't just an efficient language that Nephi selected for his own record, but instead a preference that was widespread among the Jews throughout Jerusalem at the time of Lehi's departure.

By the time Mormon took over abridging the record, the language had been further modified for efficiency and reduced effort in carving the record onto metal plates.[171] It was a more efficient, though less exact, form of language than Hebrew.

The Egyptian influence upon ancient Jerusalem and our own Bible should be studied. The presence of Egyptian hieroglyphs in

---

[170] 1 Nephi 5:10–16 "And after they had given thanks unto the God of Israel, my father, Lehi, took the records which were engraven upon the plates of brass, and he did search them from the beginning. And he beheld that they did contain the five books of Moses, which gave an account of the creation of the world, and also of Adam and Eve, who were our first parents; And also a record of the Jews from the beginning, even down to the commencement of the reign of Zedekiah, king of Judah; And also the prophecies of the holy prophets, from the beginning, even down to the commencement of the reign of Zedekiah; and also many prophecies which have been spoken by the mouth of Jeremiah. And it came to pass that my father, Lehi, also found upon the plates of brass a genealogy of his fathers; wherefore he knew that he was a descendant of Joseph; yea, even that Joseph who was the son of Jacob, who was sold into Egypt, and who was preserved by the hand of the Lord, that he might preserve his father, Jacob, and all his household from perishing with famine. And they were also led out of captivity and out of the land of Egypt, by that same God who had preserved them. And thus my father, Lehi, did discover the genealogy of his fathers. And Laban also was a descendant of Joseph, wherefore he and his fathers had kept the records."

[171] Mormon 9:32–34 "And now, behold, we have written this record according to our knowledge, in the characters which are called among us the reformed Egyptian, being handed down and altered by us, according to our manner of speech. And if our plates had been sufficiently large we should have written in Hebrew; but the Hebrew hath been altered by us also; and if we could have written in Hebrew, behold, ye would have had no imperfection in our record. But the Lord knoweth the things which we have written, and also that none other people knoweth our language; and because that none other people knoweth our language, therefore he hath prepared means for the interpretation thereof."

our scriptures (Book of Abraham, Facsimiles 1–3) also puts us on notice that we need to look into Egyptian matters. Hugh Nibley has written a number of books on the matter, the most recent of which was released as *One Eternal Round* on the occasion of Nibley's 100th year from birth. *Abraham in Egypt* was an earlier work also on this subject. And there has been a three volume set on the *Early Life of Abraham* published through BYU (quite an expensive set to own). It is interesting how much Egyptian influence there has been in our faith. Remember that the Egyptians sought to preserve the faith which existed before the flood and was practiced from Adam to the time of Noah.[172] It may have become eroded and drifted, but it nevertheless preserved truths from the beginning. Abraham was sent to them to help restore the original faith which they originally tried earnestly to preserve.

Whether we like it or not, we have an interest in knowing more about ancient Egypt than any other Christian faith.

Violence and the Violent

There has been an abundant outpouring of vitriol by those who disagree with my view about "the battle is the Lord's" (an earlier post). The comment moderator has asked me about them, because she's reluctant to put some of them up. They claim the view I hold is either Satanic or else I have been deceived by the Devil. They insist I have a duty to kill people rather than refrain from doing so when there is a threat of violence directed at me or my family. They claim Brigham Young and Joseph Smith both require me to begin killing

---

[172] Abraham 1:26 "Pharaoh, being a righteous man, established his kingdom and judged his people wisely and justly all his days, seeking earnestly to imitate that order established by the fathers in the first generations, in the days of the first patriarchal reign, even in the reign of Adam, and also of Noah, his father, who blessed him with the blessings of the earth, and with the blessings of wisdom, but cursed him as pertaining to the Priesthood."

enemies under appropriate circumstances, rather than submitting to being killed.

From time to time someone writes something which they later regret and they send another message asking for the comment to either not be put up or to be deleted if it had already been posted. I reminded her of that and suggested that she wait a few days and see if people decide to withdraw them before making any decision. Ultimately I leave it to her to decide.

I did want to add a comment about the use of violence. First, I trust the inspiration of a non-violent man, constrained against his will, when he determines the Lord requires him to act far more than I would trust the judgment of someone prone to violence when they suggest the need to kill, take violent action or attack. Throughout history all those who have made claims their violence was excused claimed they were "defending" themselves. There is a chapter on this subject in *Eighteen Verses*, which covers the topic a bit more than I am inclined to do again here.

I would comment about the Mountain Meadows Massacre and its sad legacy. The recent publication by the Assistant Church Historian as co-author of yet another new treatment of the unfortunate moment when Brigham Young's clamor for "defending" the Saints got out of hand. The book is called *Massacre at Mountain Meadows*. The book reiterated how mistaken and regrettable that moment was in LDS history. It is the great example pointed to by anti-Mormon sources as proof that Mormons are capable of all the depredations of Historic Christianity, Roman Catholicism and Puritanical excesses that killed those who offended them. The church has issued an official apology, and President Hinckley visited the site and dedicated a monument as an act of Latter-day Saint contrition and regret.

That single moment in church history is something which all our prayers cannot take back. We cannot restore those lives which were taken. We cannot explain we are really Christ's disciples to the descendants of that party of victims. They continue to hold resentments which have festered for generations and still call out condemnation for our act of violence and murder.

If we had suffered then, as we had in Missouri and Illinois we would have been better. If given the opportunity to suffer again for our faith, we would be better remembered by history if we learn the lesson of Mountain Meadows. We are ennobled by our sacrifices. We are detested for our revenge and violence.

In General Conference a few sessions back, President Faust gave a talk titled "The Healing Power of Forgiveness."[173] Unfortunately, his great example came from the Amish, whose young daughters were killed by a murderer, whom they forgave. It was not taken from our own conduct. I would commend that talk as a more recent and more reasoned statement on violence and the violent than the comments of Brigham Young who Latter-day Saint historians now admit had some role in the Mountain Meadows Massacre. Not because he approved it, he did not. Indeed, he sent a message to let the entrapped party go. But his message arrived too late. The violent attack had already taken place. The violence having been rationalized, at least in part, by Brigham Young's own militant comments in the preceding years.

I am not trying to persuade anyone. Go ahead and resolve this issue for yourself. I am only setting out my own view. Take it for what you think it is worth. If you think it is "of the Devil" or "Satanic" then of course you ought to reject my view. But I have considered the quotes of Brigham Young before reaching my view, and find them in a context which even I believe he grew to regret.

---

[173] Faust, "The Healing Power of Forgiveness", General Conference, April 2007.

A Student of the Lord

Our obligation is to conform our opinions to the Lord's instruction. That requires us to be careful about how we listen, how hard our hearts are, how much we want to let in, and how loyal we choose to be to traditions. It is rare for any man to be an eager student of the Lord's. The scriptures give us only isolated examples. Abraham was one of them. He *wanted* to receive and obey commandments.[174]

Resistance to truth prevents us from obtaining it. The Lord will not force us to understand Him or His ways. Instead He invites us to come and learn from Him. Joseph Smith made this remarkable statement:

> "We consider that God has created man with a mind capable of instruction, and a faculty which may be enlarged in proportion to the heed and diligence given to the light communicated from heaven to the intellect; and that the nearer man approaches perfection, the clearer are his views, and the greater his enjoyments, till he has overcome the evils of his life and lost every desire for sin; and like the ancients, arrives at that point of faith where he is wrapped in the power and glory of his Maker and is caught up to dwell with Him. But we consider that this is a station to which no man ever arrived in a moment: he must have been instructed in the government and laws of that kingdom by proper degrees, until his mind is capable in some measure of comprehending the propriety, justice, equality, and consistency of the same." (*TPJS*, 51)

Closing your mind to the Lord's agenda before He has had an opportunity to fully instruct you is damnation. Damnation merely

---

[174] Abraham 1:2 "And, finding there was greater happiness and peace and rest for me, I sought for the blessings of the fathers, and the right whereunto I should be ordained to administer the same; having been myself a follower of righteousness, desiring also to be one who possessed great knowledge, and to be a greater follower of righteousness, and to possess a greater knowledge, and to be a father of many nations, a prince of peace, and desiring to receive instructions, and to keep the commandments of God, I became a rightful heir, a High Priest, holding the right belonging to the fathers."

means the end of progress. So when we fail to progress in our understanding, we voluntarily damn ourselves.

The Lord's system, however, involves gentleness, meekness and love unfeigned. It requires patience and pure knowledge.[175] Before we can elevate anyone else's understanding we have to stand on higher ground. To lead a soul to salvation, as Joseph put it, required the following:

> "Thy mind, O man! if thou wilt lead a soul unto salvation, must stretch as high as the utmost heavens, and search into and contemplate the darkest abyss, and the broad expanse of eternity—thou must commune with God." (*TPJS*, 137)

Given this requirement for a man to be able to lead another soul to salvation, it would seem that few are really qualified.

Choose your teachers carefully. Accept any truth you are offered and you will be offered more. Reject a truth given to you and you close down the opportunities given to you for learning.

Someone asked the question a bit ago: "Humility = light?" and I haven't responded till now. The answer is humility allows someone to be taught. We are all ignorant, but not all are willing to let in new understanding. We must be taught about the things we do not yet know for us to be saved. Without humility we cannot be taught, and therefore we cannot gain light. Humility is so fundamental a requirement for gaining further light and truth that without it we cannot grow. The two are so intimately linked together they form a near equivalency.

---

[175] D&C 121:40–42 "Hence many are called, but few are chosen. No power or influence can or ought to be maintained by virtue of the priesthood, only by persuasion, by long-suffering, by gentleness and meekness, and by love unfeigned; By kindness, and pure knowledge, which shall greatly enlarge the soul without hypocrisy, and without guile—"

BYU Women's Rugby

The BYU women's rugby team forfeited the championship opportunity because of required competition play on Sunday. An article was written about the event.[176]

I applaud anyone who puts principle ahead of self. Sacrifice is still required.

Pax Americana

Prof left a comment on my post "The battle is the Lord's":

> I'm particularly interested in what you mean by this: "We live in a world today in which Pax Americana has established controlled violence the world over. The fear of destruction holds forces at bay which would gladly destroy one another if permitted. The key to replacing the current world order with another one, as many insurgencies the world over recognize, is the destruction of Pax Americana by destroying American hegemony. A lot of people are working on that, both inside and outside the United States."
>
> Do you support "American hegemony" in order to maintain "Pax Americana"? And from what source did you get these terms?

Those are really several questions. I will try and answer briefly. This is a very cursory explanation to the inquiry.

With the fall of the Soviet Union, there followed the universal recognition that there only one surviving super-power. I think the truth was that even prior to the Soviet breakup there was only one real superpower, but the international propaganda machine and the eastern European subjugation by the Soviets essentially formed such

---

[176] http://www.fanhouse.com/2010/04/18/to-pray-or-play-that-is-not-a-question/?ncid=webmaildl5

a land barrier and controlled such a population base that they were accepted as a second super-power. The reality was somewhat different, but in this world perception is everything and so long as everyone believed there were "two" the world acted consistent with their being two.

Now the world acts consistent with there only being one. As a result of there being one, political pacts, economic alliances, trade, military alliances, treaties, social mores, entertainment, language, corporate interests and sea lanes are all governed by what the United States tolerates or accepts. Even China has so limited a military sphere of influence that they can "control" Tibet and the upper Korean Peninsula, but have no ability to project power over active American resistance. That does not mean they aren't working on it. They are. But they can't compete at present.

Whatever other strengths other nations may possess, they cannot compete with the total inventory of American power. Economically the entirety of Europe is not able to compete with American economic power. There are other members of the nuclear power states, but none with the delivery systems, proven capabilities and demonstrated will to use nuclear weapons in combat.

A full elaboration of the unique American combination of power is far too great a subject to cover here. Just one other example: Al Jazzera was launched as a counterpart to CNN, Fox News and the BBC. These networks dominate international news. An earthquake in Istanbul happens and residents there turn their TV's to CNN, Fox News or the BBC to find out what is happening. Al Jazzera is an attempt to get another cultural perspective different from an Anglo-American vantage point. To possess the dominate vantage point in the news is to possess the advantage.

Why are Turkey and Greece not in combat with one another despite their long lasting territorial disputes? They are members of the

North Atlantic Treaty Organization (NATO) founded by the US at the end of WWII to attempt to avoid another land war in Europe. Why is the Korean Peninsula not back in combat? The fear is that it would draw the US and China into direct conflict and that would be a disaster for the whole world. So an uneasy peace endures. Why is Taiwan not overrun at present by China, when they claim sovereignty over it? It is because China has not yet reached a point of development where they feel safe to have a direct conflict with the US. Again, there could be many examples, but the world stage is set by American interests which dominate other considerations.

The resentments pile up and attempt to organize. Chavez has high hopes in Venezuela, just as Castro had high hopes in the 1950's in Cuba. But just like Castro, Chavez is having a difficult time keeping the lights on in his energy rich country.

The current American president candidly admitted "whether we like it or not, American is the world's sole superpower." He's taking flack for that right now. But it was a correct statement. America is the dominant power, and its interests influence the world over. Foreign aid props up many countries which would not exist without it.

There are many people who would like to see American power end. You would have to have never seen the news to not hear that rhetoric coming from critics the world over. And inside the American political landscape there are those who want to see an end of American foreign entanglements. The most outspoken may be the Libertarian Party, whose candor about the need to withdraw from the world stage is part of their every campaign.

I have not evaluated the wisdom of the reality. I've only commented on its existence. How America got here is a product of history and decisions made in past generations. President Washington's Farewell Address cautioned against "foreign entanglements" which would cost us lives and treasure. He was right about what he foresaw.

President Eisenhower warned against the "military industrial complex" (a term he coined), and how it would eventually control such economic interests that it would skew our national policies and priorities. I think he was right as well.

The terms are taken from Roman history and applied to American history. We are re-living the Roman model, without borrowing wisdom from those who saw its decline and fall. Gibbon is still good history, and a model for modern historians as well. The parallels between these two empires are so striking that even the element used by the Lord in Daniel's interpretation of Nebuchadnezzar's dream are similar. The Roman being iron, and the American being iron and clay. The parallels are unmistakable to any student of history.

We repeat history. We are living with the past and cannot see ourselves outside the forms we have inherited from our past. Tradition controls even the way we read scripture. Therefore we are blind to what they tell us until it has been fulfilled, at which point we see in hindsight only what things we have forfeited. Zion is alien here, and therefore we have a difficult time envisioning it without putting it into Babylonian/Roman form. Zion, however, is without ambition, competition and aggression. It has fled.

Seeking For and Obtaining Gifts—Part of the Expected Pattern

I received this comment and question:

As I have learned more about the scriptures, I have come to find many "anomalies" in the lives of the prophets are actually not anomalous but part of the expected pattern. Examples of things I once thought exceptions which I now believe are expected steps along "the way" include Moses' struggle with the devil, the 2nd Comforter, the sealing power, Christ's willingness to give Nephi anything he asks, John's vision of all,

Abraham's astral journey, and John's entering into the temple in heaven.

The appearance of the Liahona in the Book of Mormon seems anomalous, a physical object of divine origin given to aid his servant in completing his journey. But is the Liahona, in fact, an anomaly? Or can any righteous member expect physical tokens from heaven to aid them on their own journey before they arrive in the celestial kingdom?

I would agree that there is a pattern, it is universal, and the prophets are trying to give that pattern to us in the history they record, the examples they teach, the parables they offer and the commandments they reveal. There is one, universal system which everyone will receive as part of their journey back to God. In order to pass the angels who stand as sentinels along the path you must proceed in an orderly fashion through the veil. It will be one by one.

Yes, I agree there are physical tokens given as an aid to getting there. Take the gift of seership, as an example. We know there was an instrument given to Joseph to aid him at the first. He used it to gain an understanding even before the translation of the Book of Mormon plates commenced. He would tell his family stories about the ancient inhabitants, their customs, manner of dress, etc. His mother, Lucy Mack Smith records this in her history. This understanding came as a result of Joseph's possession and use of the Urim and

Thummim, making him a "seer" in the sense of the term used in Mosiah.[177]

Eventually Joseph developed the independent gift of seership, and no longer required the physical instrument to be used in order to exercise the gift. He became, like Enoch, able to "see" without use of the instrument.[178]

We tend to think this a great rarity and grand exception. Yet we also find that everyone who enters into the same state of exaltation as God will be required to possess this same gift.[179] If possession or

---

[177] Mosiah 8:13–17 "Now Ammon said unto him: I can assuredly tell thee, O king, of a man that can translate the records; for he has wherewith that he can look, and translate all records that are of ancient date; and it is a gift from God. And the things are called interpreters, and no man can look in them except he be commanded, lest he should look for that he ought not and he should perish. And whosoever is commanded to look in them, the same is called seer. And behold, the king of the people who are in the land of Zarahemla is the man that is commanded to do these things, and who has this high gift from God. And the king said that a seer is greater than a prophet. And Ammon said that a seer is a revelator and a prophet also; and a gift which is greater can no man have, except he should possess the power of God, which no man can; yet a man may have great power given him from God. But a seer can know of things which are past, and also of things which are to come, and by them shall all things be revealed, or, rather, shall secret things be made manifest, and hidden things shall come to light, and things which are not known shall be made known by them, and also things shall be made known by them which otherwise could not be known."

[178] Moses 6:35–36 "And the Lord spake unto Enoch, and said unto him: Anoint thine eyes with clay, and wash them, and thou shalt see. And he did so. And he beheld the spirits that God had created; and he beheld also things which were not visible to the natural eye; and from thenceforth came the saying abroad in the land: A seer hath the Lord raised up unto his people."

[179] D&C 130:5–11 "I answer, Yes. But there are no angels who minister to this earth but those who do belong or have belonged to it. The angels do not reside on a planet like this earth; But they reside in the presence of God, on a globe like a sea of glass and fire, where all things for their glory are manifest, past, present, and future, and are continually before the Lord. The place where God resides is a great Urim and Thummim. This earth, in its sanctified and immortal state, will be made like unto crystal and will be a Urim and Thummim to the inhabitants who dwell thereon, whereby all things pertaining to an inferior kingdom, or all kingdoms of a lower order, will be manifest to those who dwell on it; and this earth will be Christ's. Then the white stone mentioned in Revelation 2:17, will become a Urim and Thummim to each individual who receives one, whereby things pertaining to a higher order of kingdoms will be made known; And a white stone is given to each of those who come into the celestial kingdom, whereon is a new name written, which no man knoweth save he that receiveth it. The new name is the key word."

development of this capacity is expected for all those who reside with God, then the gift is intended to be universal among the exalted. Therefore, we should not delay seeking this as one of the best gifts to desire.[180]

Since whatever principle of intelligence we attain unto will rise with us, and you will have so much more the advantage if you have gained greater light and truth by your heed and diligence than others who have failed to show such diligence, there is no reason to delay. Just as Moses wished all men were prophets, I wish all men were seers.

Your proposition is right.

Truth = Truth

Truth is a knowledge of things as they were, as they are, and as they are to come (see D&C 93:24). As a result, truth is really not subject to debate. We either know the truth or we are deceived. If we know it, we have an obligation to declare it. If we are deceived, we have an obligation to be humble enough to at least consider the truth before we reject it.

When we dispute in anger, we move away from truth.

> "For verily, verily I say unto you, he that hath the spirit of contention is not of me, but is of the devil, who is the father of contention, and he stirreth up the hearts of men to contend with anger, one with another." (3 Nephi 11:29)

The truth is not being taught when men argue in anger with one another. When they do, the Spirit withdraws and learning ends.

Truth should appeal to the heart and mind. It should bring joy.

---

[180] D&C 46:8 "Wherefore, beware lest ye are deceived; and that ye may not be deceived seek ye earnestly the best gifts, always remembering for what they are given;"
1 Corinthians 12:31 "But covet earnestly the best gifts: and yet shew I unto you a more excellent way."

"Verily, verily, I say unto you, I will impart unto you of my Spirit, which shall enlighten your mind, which shall fill your soul with joy;" (D&C 11:13)

I do not believe there is any past scriptural precedent for angry people bearing a threatening message about vengeance and revenge who then proceeded to build Zion. I doubt we will see such an unprecedented and unscriptural event occur in the future.

Words that describe Zion include:

- Humble
- Meek
- Submissive
- Contrite
- One
- No poor among them
- Presence of God among them
- Peaceful
- Only people not at war
- Singing songs of everlasting joy
- Of one heart

It is an odd thing how those who learn about the possibility of Zion think that possessing that awareness entitles them to live there. Before anyone will be admitted to Zion they will necessarily have to bring it into their own lives. Gathering a crowd without considering first who has been chosen by the angels who possess the keys for this gathering, and those who have been sealed in their foreheads by those angels, is just another foolish and futile act.[181]

---

[181] D&C 77:11 "Q. What are we to understand by sealing the one hundred and forty-four thousand, out of all the tribes of Israel—twelve thousand out of every tribe?
A. We are to understand that those who are sealed are high priests, ordained unto the holy order of God, to administer the everlasting gospel; for they are they who are ordained out of every nation, kindred, tongue, and people, by the angels to whom is given power over the nations of the earth, to bring as many as will come to the church of the Firstborn."

Hugh Nibley wrote an article in *Nibley on the Timely and the Timeless* titled: "Zeal without Knowledge." That title was taken from Romans 10:2.[182] In that article he wrote: "We think it more commendable to get up at 5:00 a.m. to write a bad book than to get up at nine o'clock to write a good one. That is pure zeal that tends to breed a race of insufferable, self-righteous prigs and barren minds." Nibley could be so hard on us at times. But then again, he also hit the nail on the head.

For some particularly unsuited people to talk expectantly about Zion when they are utterly unprepared to understand the subject is beyond irony. For them to be stirred to anger about the subject because they disagree with another's view about Zion must provoke both bemusement and despair for the gods.

Why the Second Comforter?

I was asked why my list of essential books included *The Second Comforter: Conversing With the Lord Through the Veil,* but omitted my other books. I responded:

If someone understands the message of *The Second Comforter,* they will be able to get for themselves everything else contained in all the other books. *The Second Comforter* is not about me, it is about the reader. You should apply that book to yourself, which will lead you inevitably back to the presence of the Lord. The Lord will then instruct you in all things needed to be prepared to be presented to the Father.

Beloved Enos is a description of the results of that audience. If you understand and apply *The Second Comforter* you will receive those results.

Come, Let Us Adore Him is my testimony of Christ. But my testimony is not as important as your own. It may help you to develop

---

[182] Romans 10:2 "For I bear them record that they have a zeal of God, but not according to knowledge."

your own, but without your own testimony borrowing from another can never be the end of the journey.

I wouldn't write a book unless I believed it to be important and to contain truth coming from a higher source. Nevertheless, it is what you know, not what I as an author may know, that will save you. It is the salvation of others, not the attention of others, that concerns me. If I can help point them to the Lord, then I have some limited use. Beyond that, I have no purpose.

Since all that we hope to receive from the Lord flows from the discussion in *The Second Comforter*, it is that book which I believe to be most important.

Lectures of Faith 6

This is an excerpt from the Sixth Lecture in the *Lectures on Faith*. This was at one point a part of the Doctrine & Covenants. They were prepared for the School of the Prophets and approved by Joseph Smith. Their presence in the scriptures was the reason for the change in the title from Book of Commandments to Doctrine and Covenants. The "Doctrine" portion of the book was comprised of these lectures. They were subsequently removed from the D&C. Below is an excerpt which I think is needed to be understood by anyone who would like to comprehend the faith restored through Joseph Smith:

> An actual knowledge to any person that the course of life which he pursues is according to the will of God, is essentially necessary to enable him to have that confidence in God, without which no person can obtain eternal life.

> It was this that enabled the ancient saints to endure all their afflictions and persecutions, and to take joyfully the spoiling

of their goods, knowing (not believing merely) that they had a more "enduring substance" (Hebrews 10:34).[183]

Having the assurance that they were pursuing a course which was agreeable to the will of God, they were enabled to take, not only the spoiling of their goods and the wasting of their substance joyfully, but also to suffer death in its most horrid forms; knowing (not merely believing) that when this earthly house of their tabernacle was dissolved, they had a building of God, a house "not made with hands, eternal in the heavens" (2 Corinthians 5:1).[184]

Such was, and always will be, the situation of the saints of God, that *unless they have an actual knowledge that the course that they are pursuing is according to the will of God, they will grow weary in their minds and faint;* for such has been, and always will be, the opposition in the hearts of unbelievers and those that know not God, against the pure and unadulterated religion of heaven (the only thing which ensures eternal life), that they will persecute to the uttermost all that worship God according to his revelations, receive the truth in the love of it, and submit themselves to be guided and directed by his will, and drive them to such extremities that nothing short of an actual knowledge of their being the favorites of heaven,and of their having embraced that order of things which God has established for the redemption of man, will enable them to exercise that confidence in him necessary for them to overcome the world, and obtain that crown of glory which is laid up for them that fear God.

For a man to lay down his all, his character and reputation, his honor and applause, his good name among men, his houses,

---

[183] Hebrews 10:34 "For ye had compassion of me in my bonds, and took joyfully the spoiling of your goods, knowing in yourselves that ye have in heaven a better and an enduring substance."

[184] 2 Corinthians 5:1 "For we know that if our earthly house of *this* tabernacle were dissolved, we have a building of God, an house not made with hands, eternal in the heavens."

his lands, his brothers and sisters, his wife and children, and even his own life also, counting all things but filth and dross for the excellency of the knowledge of Jesus Christ, requires more than mere belief or supposition that he is doing the will of God, but actual knowledge; realizing that when these sufferings are ended he will enter into eternal rest, and be a partaker of the glory of God.

For unless a person does know that he is walking according to the will of God, it would be offering an insult to the dignity of the Creator were he to say that he would be a partaker of his glory when he should be done with the things of this life.

But when he has this knowledge, and most assuredly knows that he is doing the will of God, his confidence can be equally strong that he will be a partaker of the glory of God.

Let us here observe, that a religion that does not require the sacrifice of all things, never has power sufficient to produce the faith necessary unto life and salvation; for from the first existence of man, the faith necessary unto the enjoyment of life and salvation never could be obtained without the sacrifice of all earthly things; it was through this sacrifice, and this only, that God has ordained that men should enjoy eternal life; and it is through the medium of the sacrifice of all earthly things, that men do actually know that they are doing the things that are well pleasing in the sight of God.

When a man has offered in sacrifice all that he has for the truth's sake, not even withholding his life, and believing before God that he has been called to make this sacrifice, because he seeks to do his will, he does know most assuredly that God does and will accept his sacrifice and offering, and that he has not nor will not seek his face in vain.

Under these circumstances then, he can obtain the faith necessary for him to lay hold on eternal life.

It is in vain for persons to fancy to themselves that they are heirs with those, or can be heirs with them, who have offered their all in sacrifice, and by this means obtained faith in God and favor with him so as to obtain eternal life, unless they in like manner offer unto him the same sacrifice, and through that offering obtain the knowledge that they are accepted of him.

It was in offering sacrifices that Abel, the first martyr, obtained knowledge that he was accepted of God.

And from the days of righteous Abel to the present time, the knowledge that men have that they are accepted in the sight of God, is obtained by offering sacrifice.

And in the last days, before the Lord comes, he is to gather together his saints who have made a covenant with him by sacrifice. Psalms 50:3–5, "Our God shall come, and shall not keep silence: a fire shall devour before him, and it shall be very tempestuous round about him. He shall call to the heavens from above, and to the earth, that he may judge his people. Gather my saints together unto me; those that have made a covenant unto me by sacrifice."

Those then who make the sacrifice will have the testimony that their course is pleasing in the sight of God, and those who have this testimony will have faith to lay hold on eternal life, and will be enabled through faith to endure unto the end, and receive the crown that is laid up for them that love the appearing of our Lord Jesus Christ.

But *those who do not make the sacrifice cannot enjoy this faith, because men are dependent upon this sacrifice in order to obtain this faith;* therefore, they cannot lay hold upon eternal life, because the revelations of God do not guarantee unto them the authority so to do; and without this guarantee faith could not exist.

All the saints of whom we have account in all the revelations of God which are extant, obtained the knowledge which they had of their acceptance in his sight, through the sacrifice which they offered unto him.

And through the knowledge thus obtained, their faith became sufficiently strong to lay hold upon the promise of eternal life, and to endure as seeing him who is invisible; and were enabled, through faith, to combat the powers of darkness, contend against the wiles of the adversary, overcome the world, and obtain the end of their faith, even the salvation of their souls.

But those who have not made this sacrifice to God, do not know that the course which they pursue is well pleasing in his sight; for whatever may be their belief or their opinion, it is a matter of doubt and uncertainty in their minds; and where doubt and uncertainty are, there faith is not, nor can it be.

For doubt and faith do not exist in the same person at the same time.

So that persons whose minds are under doubts and fears cannot have unshaken confidence; and where unshaken confidence is not, there faith is weak; and where faith is weak, the persons will not be able to contend against all the opposition, tribulations, and afflictions which they will have to encounter in order to be heirs of God, and joint heirs with Christ Jesus; and they will grow weary in their minds, and the adversary will have power over them and destroy them.

FYI

I have been surprised by the level of excitement which some of my posts have caused. My views are an extension of the faith I hold. It is not possible to take one issue and isolate it from the whole of what I know to be true. Therefore, if you want to understand the view, you need to take the time to read what I have written, which explains fully what I know, and why I know it.

To understand it will be necessary for you to study the faith as restored through Joseph Smith. I have explained what I believe and why I believe it in six books now. Rather than attempting to argue me into another position, it might be helpful to first understand what I have written.

However, I realize some people will not do that and therefore I attempt to respond piecemeal here to questions asked. But there are really two dialogues going on here. One is between those who have read what I have written and know why I am responding as I do. The other is between those who have no background from which to understand my answers and who make presumptions about them.

I appreciate the convictions of others, including those who disagree with me. I am thankful to the people who raise questions about what I have written. The level of excited rhetoric is something I do not find personally offensive, but I worry that those who use it will later regret doing so. I put up a quote from my father a little bit ago about never speaking a word in anger that he did not later regret. I would extend that to words spoken in haste, or in overwrought judgmentalism. Oftentimes at a later point a person regrets saying them. So I was extending to the authors of the comments a few days to reflect on whether they wanted them to be put up before them appearing here, as a courtesy to those who wrote them.

I am a trial lawyer. Everything I do for a living is opposed by someone who is paid to oppose my positions, my arguments, my reasoning. Therefore I do not get upset when someone holds a contrary view and expresses it. I live with that daily. My concern lies with those who express forcefully and judgmentally things which they may, upon second thought, realize reflects more about them than they would like.

In any event, I do want to note that there are at least two different dialogues going on here at any given time.

THE TRADITIONS OF MEN

I received this question in a comment:

"You often refer to incorrect traditions that you see members following. Can you give me a few specifics?"

This is a potentially sensitive question and I want to answer it with care. Before doing so, however, I want to clarify some initial matters: First, I sustain the church's leaders and I do not challenge their right to preside, make decisions, direct the affairs of the church, control tithing and call leadership. I "fall in line" behind them and do not question their right to lead. Second, I have a testimony of The Church of Jesus Christ of Latter-day Saints and of President Monson as the only one authorized to exercise all the keys within the church. Third, I do not think that observations about the church, even if they are critical of it, are proof that someone is misled, under Satan's influence, or on the road to apostasy. In fact, there are many active Latter-day Saints who have concerns, but who are content to remain active, faithful and supportive members of the church. *Concerns* are not the same thing as rebellion or rejection. Fourth, I do not either expect or advocate any changes being made. When or if changes are made they will happen as a result of someone else's actions, more than likely someone who would be in a position of authority within the church. I am not such a person.

Also, I want to be clear that I may personally make a value judgment about what has changed and mourn the loss, but another person may look at the same events and say they are good, developmental and preferred to what was there before. So these are **MY** opinions, and not necessarily the view you should adopt as your own view. You will have to decide such things for yourself. That having been clarified, here are some of the things which have changed dramatically and are the product of accepted tradition now, but were entirely innovative when they happened.

The discarding of the Presiding Patriarch of The Church of Jesus Christ of Latter-day Saints. There is no scriptural authority for this change and there was nothing in the original order which suggested that a change would be made. Now the current state of things is equivocal. We actually have still a Presiding Patriarch who is still living. He is emeritus. Whether the church intends to terminate the office upon his death is unclear. If they do, that will be an innovation and (in my personal opinion) unfortunate.

The alteration of the Presiding High Priest's status from "President" to "Prophet." From the time of Joseph Smith until 1955 the term "Prophet" was used exclusively to refer to Joseph Smith. It was changed in 1955 to apply to the living President, David O. McKay. Before then no living man was ever referred to as "Prophet" within the church, other than Joseph Smith. When the word "Prophet" was used after Joseph's death, it was understood the term meant Joseph Smith.

The result of this change was to create a "cult of personality" around the church president in much the same way that the Catholic Church has created a "cult of personality" around Mother Mary. You need to understand that whole subject before you get too excited by my putting it that way. If you do not understand this technical description then you need to become acquainted with it to be able to comprehend what I am saying here. To briefly touch upon the subject, the Catholic view of the "cult of personality" around Mother Mary is positive. It does not get viewed by them as a defect or some terrible aberration. Pope John Paul II considered himself a part of that "cult" involving Mary.

In our context, what has happened as a result of this alteration is that the former significance of the church's president was administrative, and priestly. He was a final arbitrator and judge, a presiding authority and a leader whose words were to be considered carefully. He was NOT considered infallible or to be invariably inspired. In fact, during the presidencies of the Prophet Joseph Smith, President Brigham Young and President John Taylor, they all spoke against any notion of infallibility of the church's president. President Young was particularly cautionary about trusting church leaders instead of the Holy Spirit as your guide. President Young said too much trust of a church leader would bring the saints to hell.

President Woodruff was so criticized by members for the Manifesto that he defended himself by claiming that the Lord wouldn't let him make a mistake on that order. He said that the Lord just wouldn't let the church's president lead the saints astray. That comment was what would later be used to buttress the notion popularly believed today that the "prophet is infallible."

President Heber J. Grant was an unpopular church president. One of the problems with getting the saints to respond to the church president's counsel was solved when the president of the church became the living "Prophet." You can reject or question counsel from an administrative authority. But to question a "Prophet of God" was to invite the damnation of hell. So the change in nomenclature worked a mighty change in the perceptions of the Latter-day Saints.

The "cult of personality" was an inevitable result. Everything the president did would be done as "God's Living Prophet." No matter what decisions were made, no matter their wisdom, goodness or undesirability, the result was the same: "They MUST be inspired. We may not have the human capacity to see it, but God's ways are higher than man's after all. To question is to lack in faith."

The change put the president into a league in which at a minimum criticism was disrespectful. Worse, if you were convinced that he made a mistake, it followed almost as an inevitability that you were absolutely forbidden from saying so because to do so revealed a "weakness in the faith." In fact, there are General Conference talks which speak about criticizing the church president (or "Living Prophet") claiming that the criticism was due to a weak faith, and it would lead to apostasy unless a person repented.

This cult of personality has grown as a result of internal structural changes, including correlation. The outcome is particularly dramatic with respect to the tolerance of women's inspiration. Whereas, in the early years a woman could be regarded as a "prophetess" (Eliza R. Snow, for example), today that recognition would be offensive to correlation, where all functions are combined under priesthood, and all priesthood is subject to the president alone as final authority.

The changes have been evolutionary, and over a single person's lifetime not all that dramatic. However the cumulative effect from the start to now is dramatic. Right now the church views any revelation or miraculous event originating with a woman as suspicious. It was so markedly contrary to this trend when a mission president's wife foretold the Chilean earthquake, and the *Meridian Magazine* covered the event without any notice that the message came through the wife, that I linked to that article on this blog. The article presumed the propriety of the inspiration. But the message came to the wife, not the mission president. That would be an un-correlated event to-day, and there is an existing infrastructure that would frown on that. Happily the event was not questioned, but instead celebrated.

The "cult of personality" has been extended to cover everything. You name it it is now covered. Take any complaint at all: The chapel paint is hideous! Well, there are those who will argue that the chapel's paint is chosen by the regular authorities of the church, who are cho-sen by the prophet, and your complaint about the paint color is really questioning the Prophet of God's authority. Therefore you are on the road to apostasy . . .

It doesn't matter the subject. The argument works by extension to everything. The Bishop cheated his business partner: You shouldn't question that because . . . yada, yada . . . you're questioning the Prophet of God. Therefore you are on the road to apostasy.

Try: My child was molested by her primary teacher. Oddly enough it even works there, too. At least there are many people will-ing to apply that by extension to every ridiculous proposition ad-vanced. So the cult of personality has now assumed a front and cen-ter position to curtail discussion, debate or consideration of even healthy alternatives to the way things are. EVERYTHING is in-spired. EVERYTHING, by extension, is happening because a "Prophet of God" has made it so. Therefore unless you concede that "All is Well in Zion" you are questioning the "Prophet of God" and on the road to apostasy.

The stifling effect of this is pernicious. It is not a view shared at the top. In fact, the brethren preach against this notion, but to no avail. I have coined the term "Brethrenites" to describe the result of this cult of personality in my book *Eighteen Verses*. There's a chapter in there that discusses this problem.

The Traditions of Men, Part 2

Originally, the view of personal revelation or any visionary experiences was quite different than what many believe today. In fact there are those who claim that ANY vision, visitation or revelation not received by the Prophet (meaning the president of the church alone) should be viewed as false. God speaks to the Prophet, and only to the Prophet, and we are to wait to hear what God wants us to know from the Prophet. This is an extension of the adoption of the term "Prophet" and the resulting cult of personality.

During Joseph Smith's time, he welcomed the revelatory experiences of others. He neither discouraged them nor felt threatened by them. His enthusiasm for what others told him of their revelations, and the acceptance of others' revelations is readily apparent in the first volume of the *Joseph Smith Papers*. Today the tradition is quite the contrary. Today, if anyone has a revelation they are advised to keep it to themselves. When others hear about them the cautionary attitude adopted is—'if it were something important then the Prophet of God would have told you about it.'

The effect of the adoption of the term "Prophet" for the living church president has been far ranging and dramatic. There has been a dramatic change in people's expectation of personal revelation, as a result of this title shift. The result is, of course, if you do not expect revelation you are not going to receive it. The expected charismatic gifts of the Spirit during the early church is now replaced by the assumption that charismatic gifts are driven by office and position. Bishops get revelation for wards (and by extension no one else does or can). Stake presidents get revelation for stakes (and by extension no one else does or can). Mission presidents get revelation for missions (and by extension no one else can or does—except in the notable case of the recent earthquake in Chile, as I mentioned before). What has always been true is that presiding authorities alone are the final say on revelation or guidance for their calling. What is not true is that no one else can, has or does get revelation. Revelation comes to those who are prepared. It comes in response to seeking, asking, knocking, and not automatically as a result of a new office or position. Now someone called to office may humble themselves, begin seeking, asking and knocking and then get revelation. But the revelation was always available, and the same information is available to all, "even the least of the Saints" as Joseph Smith put it. The proposition that there is a control over available revelation is one of the results of the post-1955 development of the cult of personality centered on the President as the Living Prophet of God.

Another change now firmly in place is the administration of temporal affairs within the church. For example, the Presiding Bishop's office controlled the operations involving all the church's construction projects until the David O. McKay presidency. As a result of some problems (beyond the scope of this), the *First Presidency* decided to take construction over as part of their duties. One of the members of the First Presidency got involved in some difficulties (again beyond the scope of this), and to placate the Quorum of the Twelve, the responsibilities were shared. The result was that the First Presidency and Quorum of Twelve now have budgetary involvement with the church's building program. This is a massive undertaking. It involves worldwide construction of church facilities. It is a major duty devolving upon these men. However, it was one time an Aaronic Priesthood assignment, and the duty of the Presiding Bishop's office. Temporal concerns are associated with that order of Priesthood. On the other hand, the higher Priesthood is involved primarily with the spiritual concerns of the church. It's all in the D&C. But the shift of Aaronic/temporal concerns onto the shoulders of the Melchizedek Priesthood leaders has its effect. The extent of that effect has been reflected in comments made by those who serve in the Twelve or

First Presidency. They hardly have time to do more than move from one meeting to another. One said he never had time to reflect or meditate.

The original Twelve Apostles of this dispensation were given a charge by Oliver Cowdery that their ordination was not complete until they had received an audience with Christ. That audience was what would entitle them to be a witness of the resurrection. The charge was given to newly ordained Apostles from the time of the first called Twelve until 1911, when the charge was discontinued. It was discontinued because so few of them had ever received an audience with Christ. Since then the Apostles have been encouraged to bear a witness of Christ based upon their spiritual conviction that He lived, died and rose from the dead. The manner in which this is done is to suggest an actual witness of His resurrection. But the words are carefully chosen.

When he was put under oath by the Senate Confirmation Committee, President Joseph F. Smith was asked directly if he was a "prophet of God." His response was, "my people sustain me as such." The senator asking the question didn't understand the answer, and asked again. After some back and forth, President Joseph F. Smith was asked directly if he had ever had a revelation; to which he responded that he had not. He added a bit later that he, like all other members of The Church of Jesus Christ of Latter-day Saints had a testimony that Joseph Smith was a Prophet and Jesus Christ had appeared to him.

[Now as an aside, this testimony was in 1905. Later, in 1918 President Joseph F. Smith received the vision now published as Section 138 of the Doctrine and Covenants; the Vision of the Redemption of the Dead.]

The church holds the tradition that the First Presidency and Twelve are sustained as "Prophets, Seers and Revelators" and as a result of that sustaining vote they must necessarily have all seen Christ. This idea/tradition is so widespread that even when the brethren clarify what their testimony consists of most members of the church won't listen to, or accept what they say. I've posted about President Packer's talk on his own testimony a little while ago in another post. There are those who don't believe him, and insist he is holding back because such things are just "too sacred to be revealed." However, the calling of an Apostle, as set out in Section 107, is *to bear witness of Jesus Christ.* There isn't anything "too sacred" about bearing testimony of Him that would prevent an Apostle from stating without equivocation they are a witness by having seen the Risen Lord. President Packer has been truthful, forthcoming and honest. I accept what he says at face value and I respect and sustain him all the more because of it. He is indeed an Apostle of Jesus Christ. And he is also an honest witness of Him. However, he has essentially explained what his testimony consists of honestly, truthfully and fully in General Conference. People continue to ignore his words and substitute the myth for the reality.

The terms "prophet, seer, and revelator" come from scripture where the president of the church is to "be a seer, a revelator, a translator, and a prophet, having all the gifts of God" (D&C 107:92). The way this is read in the church today is that any person who holds the office of President of the High Priesthood is *ipso facto* a "seer, a revelator, a translator, and a prophet." Meaning the office defines the gifts. What if that is not the intent of the scripture? What if the scripture means, instead, that a person who is these things is the only one to be called to the office? That is, unless the person "be" such a person possessing these gifts, he is not and cannot be the President? Such questions are not even possible to be asked today. They are, according to the current reading of that verse, evidence of weak faith and evidence someone is headed for apostasy. Therefore a dis-

cussion about this verse's meaning and possible differences of meaning are excluded and no other view is possible to be discussed.

President David O. McKay did not get a testimony of the church
until sometime after he had been called as an Apostle. President
Gordon B. Hinckley, when asked about revelation, said "I don't
know that we need much revelation anymore." President Packer has
defined revelation as when the presiding authorities reach an agreement. President Nibley (a counselor in the First Presidency and
Hugh Nibley's grandfather) said if an angel were to appear to him he
would jump out the window. There are other examples, but the point
is that there are many statements which have been made by the highest authorities in the church which contradict the popular myth that
the Lord has and does regularly appear to, meet with, and speak face
to face with the presiding authorities. Despite this, there are people
who presume the Lord is in the weekly meeting in the Temple, every
Thursday, telling them how to run His church. In contrast, President
Young said when he asks the Lord for guidance and then he receives
nothing, he will make his best judgment and proceed. And the Lord
is bound to sustain him in his decision, since he asked for guidance.
That approach is healthy, and allowed President Young and others to
move forward. However, it is one thing for men of good faith and
decency, who are making honest and worthwhile efforts to manage
the church to have our prayers, faith and confidence; and quite another to assume these men quote the Lord with their every breath.
As a church this subject is just not discussed. As a result those who
suspect that the brethren are making great efforts and are good men,
but who may not have had an audience with the Lord are kept from
asking the question. When a Gentile reporter has the impertinence to
ask such a question, they are rebuked and told things like that are
sacred.

A Prophet of God is not required to have seen Him. A prophet can and has been inspired to speak for the Lord by the inspiration of the Spirit. But when the scriptures use this phrase "and the word of the Lord came unto me, saying..." This formula assures the listener that the words which follow originate from the Lord and not a good and honest man's best advice. All this has happened in the past and therefore you cannot discount a prophet's calling because the word of the Lord comes by the Spirit, rather than from a personal visitation. Visitations are rare. However, the calling of a prophet in scripture was not institutional. The Lord was directly, personally and individually involved. Moses was told by the Lord, directly, as the Lord stood in a pillar-cloud at the door of the tabernacle:

> "Hear now my words: If there be a prophet among you, I the Lord will make myself known unto him in a vision, and will speak unto him in a dream." (Numbers 12:5–6)

When the Church was led by a president (from the death of Joseph Smith until 1955) there was no cult of personality around the church president. He was the presiding High Priest over the High Priesthood. When the title shifted, things began to change. Today a discussion about this process is not possible because the subject matter is too charged.

The difference between good men doing good things in good faith, who are entitled to our support in their calling and efforts on the one hand, and a prophet of God whose words are questioned at the peril of eternal damnation on the other hand is the overwhelming difference which now plagues the church. We cannot have a discussion that questions the wisdom of church policies, procedures or decisions. When even obvious mistakes are made, people who notice are not to speak of it, and if they do they are told that they are weak in the faith and on the road to apostasy. Criticism is essential to a healthy mental state. Without feedback and criticism you cannot raise a normal, healthy child. Try raising a child to whom you lavish only praise, and to whom you say, without regard to how bad, poorly or evil an act they commit: "You are inspired! You are right! It was good of you to have done that! God Himself inspired that act!" What you would raise up would be a monster. Without criticism and challenges to decisions made, no-one can ultimately become anything worthwhile.

We have a church in which those who love it the most, and whose perceptions may be the keenest, are required to take a host of questions, suggestions or criticisms and never give them voice. The only negative feed-back must originate from either outside the church, or if inside they are cast out because they are weak in the faith and on the road to apostasy. This was the inevitable evolution from the cult of personality. It is still unfolding. It will progress in a funnel which narrows over time until, at last, when the work has been fully completed, we will have a Pope who is infallible. Not because he is always inspired, but instead because he holds the keys to bind on earth and in heaven, and as a result God is bound by whatever he does. History assures us this will be the case. UNLESS, of course, we open things up to a more healthy way of going about our Father's business.

The Traditions of Men, Part 3

This subject causes a great deal of anxiety for saints. The fact it causes anxiety is proof that the saints have become conditioned to a mythology which requires everything to be good, all to be well, our current path a direct line to Zion itself, and all questions concerning the current state of affairs to be wrong. More than "wrong," questions are evidence of weak faith and the road to apostasy.

From the questions which started as soon as this subject began, I see I need to reiterate what I said at the first. I have a testimony, I am active in the church, and I am not in a position to change things. I support the brethren, pay tithing, serve where called and do not challenge the right of the regularly constituted authorities to manage the affairs of the church. I rise when President Monson enters a room I am in, I sustain him with my vote, my prayers and my confidence. I admire him. I posted about him a few days back. I meant what I said. I do not envy him nor aspire to church leadership. I am not called and do not anticipate I would ever even be considered; in part because of things like this subject appearing on this blog and concerns raised in books I have written.

I love the church and I am content as a Latter-day Saint. I love my ward and serve gladly wherever I am called.

The fact that those clarifications need to be added again, although it should have been apparent from the beginning remarks, is again revealing how shaky the saints are today. We do not have a foundation that allows us to consider alternatives. We have a single "on/off" switch for all subjects and for our testimonies. That is NOT as it should be. We should be able to confront dilemmas, difficulties, troubling news and failures by leaders while we suspend judgment and tolerate dissonance. We want instant messages, instead of having the patience to see the Hand of the Lord work over decades to bring good things from bad.

An open, candid and critical look at ourselves is not possible with people who are so insecure that they feel threatened. The progression of these insecurities will be disastrous unless at some point it is reversed. When those who raise questions are excluded, told they are weak in the faith and are on the road to apostasy, eventually everyone who is thoughtful is chased away from the church. Instead of celebrating their critical thinking and working to understand issues better, we chase some of the best minds out of the church. I wish all our critics were active members. I wish all our discussions were open enough to allow the marketplace of ideas inside the church to air everything. As I have said before, I believe the truth will prevail. You can knock it down, burn it, pave it over, kill it and threaten it, but it will prevail. A whisper of truth will overcome a hurricane of opposition. It endures. It will triumph.

I've only touched on a few matters here. I'm not going to go further at this point. However, the greater mischief we face at present is the de-emphasis of doctrine. We are raising a new breed of Latter-day Saint today whose familiarity with doctrine is negligible. They understand only a fraction of what has been restored, and for many of the doctrines, their understanding is incomplete, or so skewed that they are incorrect. Doctrine has become less important. We feed upon "inspirational stories" that salve the emotions, but do not edify the soul or bring the personal changes necessary to return to God's presence. More and more of the saints grow up inside this new environment and have never even gained a fundamental command of the doctrines which Joseph Smith restored. Gospel Doctrine classes rehash the same material every four years, which is quite challenging to those who have a memory which goes back decades. The format adopted for teaching involves group discussions, and the teacher becomes a "discussion leader." Little is learned. The group is made to share fellowship, and feel better for having attended, without any forward momentum in understanding the doctrines of salvation and exaltation.

When, over time, the leadership is replaced at all levels by those who are raised in the current milieu, the church will have completed a transformation back into a Protestant, powerless body of good people who want to do right and feel good about themselves. But the power of godliness will have fled them.

President Packer again sounded the alarm in General Conference. It was a brilliant talk. I use the term "brilliant" to describe the light within it. He said we had done a "good job of correlating" the priesthood "authority" but we had failed to disburse any "power" in the priesthood. I think it was a wonderful talk. What I would like to see discussed is whether there is a cause-and-effect between the correlation process on the one hand, and the admitted failure of priesthood power on the other hand. That discussion, however, cannot happen in the current environment. To ask the question about the underlying wisdom of the correlation process would be to directly challenge the "inspiration" of the prophet Harold B. Lee, who created this process. Therefore, any questions about correlation demonstrates that the one asking questions is weak in the faith and on the road to apostasy. So the discussion cannot occur. That is until we become a little more secure in our faith and are willing to de-mythologize the cult of personality and recognize that questions are the first step to getting answers.

I love the church, and my fellow saints. I mourn many of the changes. However, I also celebrate the fact that the fullness of the Gospel of Jesus Christ, with all its gifts, privileges, opportunities and power remains still on the earth. The Church of Jesus Christ of Latter-day Saints administers the fundamental ordinances of that Gospel. How far you take it is up to you.

There was a talk in General Conference given by a Seventy named Elder Ronald Poelman, in which he distinguished between the church and the gospel.[185] The talk is still available on-line in its original form.[186] However, he was required to re-record the talk to conform to the correlation department's challenge to any statement which distinguished between the church and the gospel. Right now

---

[185] Poelman, "The Gospel & The Church", October 1984.

[186] http://loydo38.blogspot.com/2006/04/1984.html

testimonies within the church recite the mantra "I know the church is true." The correlation process has made the church into god. People's testimonies of the "church" have supplanted their testimonies of Christ. Read any *Ensign* issue of any Conference held within ten years after the triumph of the correlation process, and consider how many of the talks focus upon the church and the church's processes and goodness, in contrast to how many of the talks focus upon Jesus Christ and His doctrines. Christ's role has been diminished by the emphasis upon the correlated church.

These are trends and traditions. They are at their incipient stages. We are a 180 year old church. Barely out of the cradle, so to speak. But trends endure. Add another 200 years of progression of these trends and you will vindicate the fellow who said: "When Mormons have been Mormons as long as Catholics have been Catholics, the Mormons will be more Catholic than the Catholics." If you want to see the future of the church in its present course, attend Mass this Saturday evening (held on Saturday so as to keep your Sunday open for basketball playoffs and MLB play now starting).

Ultimate Source

I really appreciate my status as a lay member of The Church of Jesus Christ of Latter-day Saints. I'm no-one who any of you should think important. I'm just like you. I offer my opinions and they are yours to consider as you try and sort out the challenges of this life. The ultimate source for light, truth and salvation is the Lord. Not me. Not even an institution. Not some other man. You should be dependent upon the Lord for your knowledge and Him alone. The Spirit brings you words from Him.

As you listen to any man speak, measure what he has to say against the standard found in the scriptures and against the whisperings of the Spirit to you. Any man who tries to come between you and the Lord is seeking to make themselves an idol and they will lead you astray. There is no-one who can stand between you and the Lord. He alone is the keeper of the gate, and He does not now and never has employed a servant there.[187]

You should obtain your own independent knowledge of everything another man tells you. If you don't then you are surrendering what should never be surrendered: your own agency and responsibility.

" . . . for it shall be sweet unto them."

I received another inquiry (in the form of a comment on the "Violence and the Violent" post) about the subject of self-defense, citing various scriptures from the Book of Mormon as proof I have a flawed view. This is the comment:

> I have thought it would be so nice and easy to just let them kill me and go to the spirit world scot free as it were! Clasped in the arms of Jesus again! No blood on MY hands . . . But then I read in the Book of Mormon, the commandment of Jesus: "And again, the Lord has said that: 'Ye shall defend your families even unto bloodshed.' (Alma 43:47)

> Very clear. So I do not think I am obedient to Him if I refuse to take up arms. How do you reconcile this, Denver?

> There is a further warning from this marvelous Book for our day that is apropos: "they could not suffer to lay down their lives, that their wives and their children should be massacred by . . . barbarous cruelty" (Alma 48:24)

---

[187] 2 Nephi 9:41 "O then, my beloved brethren, come unto the Lord, the Holy One. Remember that his paths are righteous. Behold, the way for man is narrow, but it lieth in a straight course before him, and the keeper of the gate is the Holy One of Israel; and he employeth no servant there; and there is none other way save it be by the gate; for he cannot be deceived, for the Lord God is his name."

You see, I cannot ignore the high probability that I will need to defend my wife and children from "massacre by barbarous cruelty" in the Last Days. I plead with you NOT to suffer to just lay down your life and watch as you see them massacred."

I debated over whether to let the subject die or to respond. I decided I'd give the following reply:

The Book of Mormon history of an escalating arms race between the smaller Nephite people, against the greater Lamanite people, teaches us many things. First, technology can level the playing field. The Nephite technological adaptations kept them safe from Lamanite aggression. Second, an arms race continues after each encounter. The Nephites began using armor. The Lamanites adopted the use of armor. Later wars included this technical advance on both sides of the battlefield. The result was still more innovation by the Nephites, with controlled fortifications, limited points of entry, and kill-zones with cross fire from towers aimed at the aggressive Lamanites. All of this reads like the modern Military-Industrial Complex (to use Pres. Eisenhower's term). It ended badly, however.

Ultimately, it was not the force of arms that brought about peace. It was conversion of the Lamanites, and the Divine power in judgment to destroy the wicked. Conversion allowed some Lamanites to survive the destruction. But the hand of the Lord was what ended the widespread wickedness, killing and disorder.

The conversion of the Lamanites was greatly accelerated when the group converted by Ammon determined to lay down their arms, even at the cost of their lives. Over a thousand of them were killed before the killing stopped. When it stopped, however, more were converted than had been killed.

When the Lord visited them and they experienced a two century long hiatus from warfare, their Zion did not have arms, killing or war. When they divided again, they set in motion a return to the earlier cycles, ultimately ending in the complete destruction of the Nephites. They left a record. Their advice cannot be divided from their history. Their history was filled with violence. It ended in the genocide of the "good guys." The end of the record is referred to by Mormon all throughout his abridgment of the records. We should not miss the end of his story as we read the unfolding story.

Death is not the end. John the Baptist was arrested and beheaded. He suffered no loss. He returned to minister to Joseph and Oliver and bestowed upon us a lost priesthood. Peter and James were martyrs. They suffered no loss either. Stephen was stoned to death, and had the heavens open to him and a visit with the Father before his death. He died forgiving those who stoned him, as he was at that moment filled with grace and charity toward others. Stephen suffered no loss. Joseph Smith was killed by a mob. He suffered no loss. He moved to his inheritance. Isaiah was put inside a hollow log and sawed in two. He suffered no loss.

Killing is not as easy as the theoretically-macho may think. It changes a person. My father landed on Omaha Beach on the morning of June 6, 1944. On the morning of June 7, 1944 he was the only one of his company who was able to continue fighting. He was there at the liberation of Paris. He fought in the Battle of the Bulge. He killed men. It affected him. He could hardly speak about it. What few comments he made were separated by years in between. A sentence here, a comment there. Even when asked directly, he wouldn't offer more than a paragraph. It wasn't a memory he could either forget or bring himself to discuss openly. It is a great and terrible thing to kill another.

Using popular culture to illustrate the point, there is a younger partner of Clint Eastwood's character in *Unforgiven*. He talked about how much he wanted to kill someone. After he had finally killed a man, he said to Eastwood's character, "I'm not like you." Meaning that he couldn't reconcile himself to having taken a man's life. That is only a movie and Hollywood and perhaps overwrought. But it nevertheless touches upon something absolutely true—killing is irrevocable. There is no repair for having taken another's life. Those who do carry that to the grave.

You can toss about quotes from anyone you please. But when you cause another's life to end you have done something irrevocable. You have crossed a line which, even with all your prayers and regrets, you cannot reclaim.

Given the choice between killing and being killed, I think a perfectly rational person can decide they would rather be killed than kill. And I think the Lord could respect a decision of that kind, as well. Death can be sweet for those who are prepared.[188]

Who Will Save You?

I was asked if some mortals, like Jesus Christ, are inerrant, perfect and without sin. Actually, the question was phrased differently. The question asked if I thought the church president could make mistakes. [I suppose my rephrase gives my view.] But to clarify:

I do not think any person should trust ANY other person to save them. Don't trust another man, for all have sinned and fallen short of the glory of God. Don't trust me. Don't rely upon those who are gifted, those who lead you, or any man.

"I am more afraid that this people have so much confidence in their leaders that they will not inquire for themselves of God whether they are led by him. I am fearful they settle down in a state of blind self-security, trusting their eternal destiny in the hands of their leaders with a reckless confidence that in itself would thwart the purposes of God in their

---

[188] D&C 42:46 "And it shall come to pass that those that die in me shall not taste of death, for it shall be sweet unto them;"

salvation, and weaken that influence they could give to their leaders, did they know for themselves, by the revelations of Jesus, that they are led in the right way" (*Discourses of Brigham Young*, 135).

If a man is a leader and he has the Spirit of God upon him, and speaks by the Spirit of God words of eternal life, then I follow the Spirit of God, not the man. I trust no one. And I look to find the Spirit of God, wherever it speaks, without regard to who possess it.

Faithful to the Gospel of Jesus Christ

I've been asked why I remain faithful if I think things are off track. (That's an abbreviated way of stating a long question.)

I believe in the Book of Mormon. Therefore I expect that the Latter-days will be filled with trouble, difficulties, and the church will be struggling with perplexities. If we didn't have problems we wouldn't fit the pattern Nephi, Mormon and Moroni warned about. So when I see problems I do not get anxious, I accept what is and deal with it.

I don't blame anyone. We didn't get here by some single person's failings. We have proceeded carefully, and with the best of intentions. But we still have challenges. That is part of being here in the Telestial Kingdom.

Doing a little good, conferring a little hope, and bringing a little light into the world each day is as much as a person can hope for. I can do that. I am grateful for the limited sphere inside of which I serve. I fight on that small bit of ground and leave the bigger picture for those who are responsible for the bigger picture.

I have a great deal of sympathy for those who are required to lead in this troubled world. I doubt I could have done any better, and fear I may have done a lot worse. So I temper any shortcomings I see with the recognition that things aren't as easy as we sometimes think they are. I'm grateful for what I have been given and am content with life.

What Can They Share?

I was asked:

"For those among us who have had a personal visit with the Lord... what can they share with us that have not ? Can they share what our Lord looked like? His eye color? hair? height? how was he dressed? Is he among us now? How did he sound? Is this too sacred to be discussed openly?"

From the beginning, mankind was told not to make idols and displace their reverence for God by a physical image or talisman. It has been enshrined in the Ten Commandments.[189] The commandment extends to the "likeness of anything that is in heaven" and would include the Lord.

The images I have seen of Him are for the most part inaccurate. The reason we don't have accurate pictures is in all likelihood related to the fact that those who come to see Him would understand the importance of avoiding idols and would question the wisdom of recreating an image of Him that might be used by others to displace their attention and worship.

What is appropriate is to affirm that He is real, that He lives, that He has been resurrected from the dead, and that He came, sacrificed and rose because of His role as the Savior and Redeemer of mankind. I've written as much as I've been asked to write about Him by way of testimony in the Appendix to *Eighteen Verses*, in *Come, Let Us Adore Him*, and a brief physical description in *Nephi's Isaiah*. However, the brief physical description is not enough from which to

---

[189] Exodus 20:4–5 ""Thou shalt not make unto thee any graven image, or any likeness *of any thing* that *is* in heaven above, or that *is* in the earth beneath, or that *is* in the water under the earth: Thou shalt not bow down thyself to them, nor serve them:"

reconstruct an image. It merely refers to some of His physical attributes and then tie them to the scriptural accounts to show why the narrative in the New Testament would read as it does.

The most important understanding of Christ is tied to what He suffered in Gethsemane. D&C 19:16–20 and my testimony about Gethsemane are both useful in understanding what He went through and what role our own actions will play in obtaining the benefits of His Atonement.[190]

To Possess Your Soul

I was asked this question:

"In one scripture the Lord connects patience to possessing your soul. What does it mean to possess your soul? And its connection to patience? This is a very new connection for me."

My answer:

That's a great question. The verse reads: "And seek the face of the Lord always, that in patience ye may possess your souls, and ye shall have eternal life" (D&C 101:38). To possess your soul is to have body and spirit inseparably connected, in a resurrected and immortal state. D&C 88:14–16 explains:

"Now, verily I say unto you, that through the redemption which is made for you is brought to pass the resurrection from the dead. And the spirit and the body are the soul of

---

[190] D&C 19:16–20 "For behold, I, God, have suffered these things for all, that they might not suffer if they would repent; But if they would not repent they must suffer even as I; Which suffering caused myself, even God, the greatest of all, to tremble because of pain, and to bleed at every pore, and to suffer both body and spirit—and would that I might not drink the bitter cup, and shrink— Nevertheless, glory be to the Father, and I partook and finished my preparations unto the children of men. Wherefore, I command you again to repent, lest I humble you with my almighty power; and that you confess your sins, lest you suffer these punishments of which I have spoken, of which in the smallest, yea, even in the least degree you have tasted at the time I withdrew my Spirit."

man. And the resurrection from the dead is the redemption of the soul."

To possess your soul, therefore, is to have the resurrection.

In the context of 101:38, it is also saying that while in that resurrected state you will "inherit eternal life." This means to receive exaltation. So the concept that these words are covering is the concept of exaltation and receiving, in the resurrection, a Celestial inheritance.

Patience is tied directly to this. Indeed, patience is required for this. No person arrives in this state without offering sacrifice sufficient to develop the faith to lay hold on eternal life. That is explained in the post a day or so ago about *Lecture on Faith* Number 6. This kind of sacrifice is very rarely done in a single act, but over a number of years by faithful obedience to the Lord's plan for your own life. It is developed by learning the Lord's will for your life and then following that will.

The whole concept begins by framing the issue around, "seeking the face of the Lord always." That is, possessing your soul, eternal life, and exaltation are all tied to the quest to return to God's presence here in mortality. It is tied to the path of seeking the Second Comforter. As you know, I've written about that process and it takes more room than this blog can accommodate. But this verse it speaking about that process.

It's a beautiful verse. It is another affirmation that the Second Comforter is intended to be a regular minister to mankind. Not some distant, unattainable visit, limited to a select few because of its difficulty.

Awake and Arise

From time to time I am constrained to say something that is beyond what I feel comfortable saying in a public venue. This is one of those times.

The content of this may not be for everyone. In fact, I think there can be a lot of mischief done by reading this if you are unprepared. Nevertheless, I'm constrained to cover this by Him who knows much better than I do—I readily recognize I am a fool. When something like this happens, I bury my own feelings and do what I'm told.

I pointed out a bit ago that Joseph Smith received the sealing authority in a revelation to him sometime between 1829 and 1843, the exact date is not known. The way in which he received this authority was by a direct revelation to him from heaven. The "voice of the Lord" came to Joseph making the declaration. At the same time Joseph's calling and election were made sure. Here are the verses from Section 132:

> For I have conferred upon you the keys and *power of the priesthood*, wherein I restore all things, and make known unto you all things in due time.

> And verily, verily, I say unto you, that whatsoever you seal on earth shall be sealed in heaven; and whatsoever you bind on

earth, in my name and by my word, saith the Lord, it shall be
eternally bound in the heavens; and whosesoever sins you
remit on earth shall be remitted eternally in the heavens; and
whosesoever sins you retain on earth shall be retained in
heaven.

And again, verily I say, whomsoever you bless I will bless, and
whomsoever you curse I will curse, saith the Lord; for I, the
Lord, am thy God.

And again, verily I say unto you, my servant Joseph, that
whatsoever you give on earth, and to whomsoever you give
any one on earth, by my word and according to my law, it shall
be visited with blessings and not cursings, and with *my power*,
saith the Lord, and shall be without condemnation on earth
and in heaven.

For I am the Lord thy God, and will be with thee even unto
the end of the world, and through all eternity; for verily I seal
upon you your exaltation, and prepare a throne for you in the
kingdom of my Father, with Abraham your father.

Behold, I have seen your sacrifices, and will forgive all your
sins; I have seen your sacrifices in obedience to that which I
have told you. Go, therefore, and I make a way for your escape, as I accepted the offering of Abraham of his son Isaac.
(D&C 132:45–50)

No one noticed this when I put it up, and no one has asked any
questions about this. Therefore it is apparent that none of you have
been prepared to receive what this is talking about. I am going to try
to help you to see things by asking questions. I will not be answering
them. I just offer them to you to ponder:

Did you notice this is referring to "power" and not authority?

Do you see any connection between this "power" and President
Packer's talk in General Conference about the church's inability to

disseminate "power" among the saints in the same way the church has been able to disseminate authority?

Does sealing authority and calling and election necessarily go together?

Can a man hold sealing authority if his calling and election have not been made sure?

How does this authority come to a man?

Must it come from the word of the Lord, declaring it from heaven, or can it come by some other kind of laying on of hands from another man?

Since Joseph received it from the declaration of God from heaven, and Nephi received it the very same way,[191] is this the only way to receive it?

If it comes from heaven alone, can any institution ever control this "power" generation after generation by handing it down from man to man?

Why did Joseph receive this power by the declaration of God from heaven, perhaps as early as 1829, outside the Temple and apart from the vision in Section 110?

---

[191] Helaman 10:6–11 "Behold, thou art Nephi, and I am God. Behold, I declare it unto thee in the presence of mine angels, that ye shall have power over this people, and shall smite the earth with famine, and with pestilence, and destruction, according to the wickedness of this people. Behold, I give unto you power, that whatsoever ye shall seal on earth shall be sealed in heaven; and whatsoever ye shall loose on earth shall be loosed in heaven; and thus shall ye have power among this people. And thus, if ye shall say unto this temple it shall be rent in twain, it shall be done. And if ye shall say unto this mountain, Be thou cast down and become smooth, it shall be done. And behold, if ye shall say that God shall smite this people, it shall come to pass. And now behold, I command you, that ye shall go and declare unto this people, that thus saith the Lord God, who is the Almighty: Except ye repent ye shall be smitten, even unto destruction."

Since Elijah's words in Section 110:13–16 do not mention the "power to seal" did Joseph really get the sealing "power" from the vision in the Kirtland Temple?[192]

Does Elijah only confirm the process of restoring keys has completed, but sealing "power" came from somewhere else?

Is it possible that the institutional church has one understanding, but the truth and the scriptures teach another understanding?

If that is possible, then why have you not been studying things out for yourself to decide what the truth is concerning where this kind of "power" comes from?

Is this related to the "sealing" which is done, not by the church, but by the angels as revealed in D&C 77:11?[193]

Should you get a testimony of Christ, rather than recite merely that you "know the church is true?"

Can the church be true, and yet your soul not saved?

Do the ordinances of salvation, including sealing you up to eternal life, require you to have "power" given to you from heaven?

With respect to the words in Section 121:

"That the rights of the priesthood are inseparably connected with the powers of heaven, and that the powers of heaven cannot be controlled nor handled only upon the principles of righteousness." (D&C 121:36)

Do these words relate to this same subject?

---

[192] D&C 110:13–16 "After this vision had closed, another great and glorious vision burst upon us; for Elijah the prophet, who was taken to heaven without tasting death, stood before us, and said: Behold, the time has fully come, which was spoken of by the mouth of Malachi—testifying that he [Elijah] should be sent, before the great and dreadful day of the Lord come— To turn the hearts of the fathers to the children, and the children to the fathers, lest the whole earth be smitten with a curse— Therefore, the keys of this dispensation are committed into your hands; and by this ye may know that the great and dreadful day of the Lord is near, even at the doors."

[193] D&C 77:11 "

Do these words confirm that if priesthood "power" has been lost that the remaining priesthood "authority" cannot bind or seal?

Do the words "that they may be conferred upon us, it is true"[194] confirm the very real distinction between "authority" and "power"?

Is President Packer trying to alert us to something very important missing in the current state of the church?

The questions are not intended to suggest any answer. They are food for thought. The Gospel of Jesus Christ is so important a subject that you ought to be thinking deeply about it. Joseph Smith said:

> "[T]he things of God are of deep import; and time, and experience, and careful and ponderous and solemn thoughts can only find them out. Thy mind, O man! if thou wilt lead a soul unto salvation, must stretch as high as the utmost heavens, and search into and contemplate the darkest abyss, and the broad expanse of eternity-thou must commune with God. How much more dignified and noble are the thoughts of God, than the vain imaginations of the human heart! None but fools will trifle with the souls of men." (*DHC* 3:295)

We should not be dealing with the Gospel at a superficial level. We should be ashamed of how we have been treating it. Again, Joseph said:

> "How vain and trifling have been our spirits, our conferences, our councils, our meetings, our private as well as public conversations—too low, too mean, too vulgar, too condescending for the dignified characters of the called and chosen of God, according to the purposes of His will, from before the foundation of the world! We are called to hold the keys of the

---

[194] D&C 121:37 "That they may be conferred upon us, it is true; but when we undertake to cover our sins, or to gratify our pride, our vain ambition, or to exercise control or dominion or compulsion upon the souls of the children of men, in any degree of unrighteousness, behold, the heavens withdraw themselves; the Spirit of the Lord is grieved; and when it is withdrawn, Amen to the priesthood or the authority of that man."

mysteries of those things that have been kept hid from the foundation of the world until now." (Ibid.

A religion that allows you to foolishly waste the days of your probation will not save you. That religion is NOT the faith that Abraham followed or that Jesus Christ taught. If you are attending "vain and trifling" meetings that are "low, mean, vulgar and condescending" then you must do something about your own education in the faith to obtain exaltation.

The path trod by the ancients is exactly the same path every saved soul must walk. Read "Lectures on Faith No. 6" post again.

I testify that you can know for a certainty the answer to these questions. Anyone can. Even the least of the Saints.

I wish all mankind might be saved. Neglect and indifference seem to be such prevailing impediments to the salvation of the souls of men that Satan must rejoice, look up at heaven with a great chain in his hands, and declare that he has bound all mankind! How little the world has changed since the time of Enoch.

Awake.

Arise.

Your soul is in jeopardy.

Get Busy!

Another statement from Joseph Smith worth considering as part of deciding how seriously you would like to be a disciple of Christ's:

"All men know that they must die. And it is important that we should understand the reasons and causes of our exposure to the vicissitudes of life and of death, and the designs and purposes of God in our coming into the world, our sufferings here, and our departure hence. What is the object of our coming into existence, then dying and falling away, to be here no more? It is but reasonable to suppose that God would reveal something in reference to the matter, and it is a subject we ought to study more than any other. We ought to study it day and night, for the world is ignorant in reference to their true condition and relation. If we have any claim on our Heavenly Father for anything, it is for knowledge on this important subject. Could we read and comprehend all that has been written from the days of Adam, on the relation of man to God and angels in a future state, we should know very little about it. Reading the experience of others, or the revelation given to them, can never give us a comprehensive view of our condition and true relation to God. Knowledge of these things can only be obtained by experience through the ordinances of God set forth for that purpose. Could you gaze into heaven five minutes, you would know more than you would by reading all that ever was written on the subject." (DHC 6:50)

The definition of "ordinances of God" are not all contained in a formal church setting. Read again the experiences of others in scripture and you will find that a great deal takes place between the Lord and those who follow Him. When He appears He also ministers. There is also the description of the "sealing" which will qualify those living in our day to become a member of the Church of the First-born, which involves an ordinance performed by "angels to whom is given power" and to whom this ministry belongs.[195]

Search the scriptures. They testify of all things. The Church of Jesus Christ of Latter-day Saints administers the ordinances of salvation and prepares you to receive further light and knowledge directly from the Lord. If you have received what the Lord offers through

---

[195] D&C 77:11 "Q. What are we to understand by sealing the one hundred and forty-four thousand, out of all the tribes of Israel—twelve thousand out of every tribe?
A. We are to understand that those who are sealed are high priests, ordained unto the holy order of God, to administer the everlasting gospel; for they are they who are ordained out of every nation, kindred, tongue, and people, by the angels to whom is given power over the nations of the earth, to bring as many as will come to the church of the Firstborn."

the church, but have failed to take the final admonition to receive further light and knowledge by conversing directly with Him, then your salvation has not been perfected. You still have work left before you.

Get busy.

God Is No Respecter of Persons

I am surprised by how people regard me as something special. I have been blessed by the Lord to be able to write some books and put some information on this blog. However, if you were raised LDS and put forth some nominal effort to living your religion, you have lived a better life than I have. I wasn't raised LDS and had no understanding of the Gospel, or the underlying reasons for the commandments. Therefore, I never obeyed even a fraction of the commandments that you have grown up following.

I am absolutely convinced that any one of you is a better candidate than I was to receive an audience with the Lord. The wonder of this process is not that someone has done it, but that so few have. Given that I am probably the least qualified, the point should not be lost on you. If it has happened to me, then it absolutely can and should happen to you.

God is no respecter of persons. All are alike to Him. Qualifications are based upon the behavior and faith of the person, not on their status or past mistakes.

You probably think your errors are more serious an impediment to God accepting you than He ever has. He doesn't want to judge you, He wants to heal you. He wants to give you what you lack, teach you to be better and to bless you. He doesn't want to belittle, demean or punish you. Ask Him to forgive and He forgives. Even very serious sins. He does not want you burdened with them. He wants you to leave them behind.

His willingness to leave those errors in the past and remember them no more is greater than you can imagine. It is a guiding principle for the Atonement. Asking for forgiveness is almost all that is required to be forgiven.

What alienates us from Him is not our sins. He will forgive them. What we lack is the confidence to ask in faith, nothing doubting, for His help. He can and will help when you do so.

The sins that offend Him are not the errors, weaknesses and foolishness of the past. He is offended when we are forgiven by Him, and then return to the same sin. That shows a lack of gratitude for His forgiveness. Even then, however, there are addictions, compulsions and weaknesses that we sometimes struggle with for years, even decades. When the sin is due to some difficulty based on biology, physiology or an inherent weakness that we fight for years to overcome, then His patience with us is far greater than our own. He will help in the fight. He will walk along side you as you fight. He does not expect you to run faster than you have strength. When, at last, because of age or infirmity, a troubling weakness is at last overcome, He will readily accept your repentance and let you move forward clean, whole and forgiven. That is His ministry—to forgive and make whole.

I know all my mistakes. They are greater than most of yours. I am in awe of His mercy and forgiveness. I am not at all impressed by my worthiness. It is nothing. It consists of borrowed finery from Him who has let me use His great worthiness to cover my own failings. To the extent that I have any merit, it comes from Him. I remain astonished that He would condescend for someone like me.

It is a wonder some think I have an advantage. I assure you that the promised blessings are available to ALL. If that were not true then someone as weak, simple and flawed as I am would never have had the hope that I now have in Christ.

Opposing Wickedness through Violence

There is a continuing unease about the subject of opposing wickedness through violence. So I thought I would add this additional explanation:

I do not foresee that a gun will be effective against radioactivity; nor against weaponized anthrax. I read the plagues that are coming and the descriptions in D&C 29:15–21 and I do not foresee a handgun doing me any good under those circumstances.[196] I see wicked being killed, but no role for me and a sidearm to join in the fray.

I do not foresee any need for Zion to be protected by armed machine-gun nests around a perimeter when a pillar of smoke by day and fire by night hangs over them.[197] In the description, it does not say they go up with songs of joy, interrupted by occasional gunfire

---

[196] D&C 29:15–21 "And there shall be weeping and wailing among the hosts of men; And there shall be a great hailstorm sent forth to destroy the crops of the earth. And it shall come to pass, because of the wickedness of the world, that I will take vengeance upon the wicked, for they will not repent; for the cup of mine indignation is full; for behold, my blood shall not cleanse them if they hear me not. Wherefore, I the Lord God will send forth flies upon the face of the earth, which shall take hold of the inhabitants thereof, and shall eat their flesh, and shall cause maggots to come in upon them; And their tongues shall be stayed that they shall not utter against me; and their flesh shall fall from off their bones, and their eyes from their sockets; And it shall come to pass that the beasts of the forest and the fowls of the air shall devour them up. And the great and abominable church, which is the whore of all the earth, shall be cast down by devouring fire, according as it is spoken by the mouth of Ezekiel the prophet, who spoke of these things, which have not come to pass but surely must, as I live, for abominations shall not reign."

[197] D&C 45:65–71 "And with one heart and with one mind, gather up your riches that ye may purchase an inheritance which shall hereafter be appointed unto you. And it shall be called the New Jerusalem, a land of peace, a city of refuge, a place of safety for the saints of the Most High God; And the glory of the Lord shall be there, and the terror of the Lord also shall be there, insomuch that the wicked will not come unto it, and it shall be called Zion. And it shall come to pass among the wicked, that every man that will not take his sword against his neighbor must needs flee unto Zion for safety. And there shall be gathered unto it out of every nation under heaven; and it shall be the only people that shall not be at war one with another. And it shall be said among the wicked: Let us not go up to battle against Zion, for the inhabitants of Zion are terrible; wherefore we cannot stand. And it shall come to pass that the righteous shall be gathered out from among all nations, and shall come to Zion, singing with songs of everlasting joy."

and all hell breaking loose. It says they proceed quite peacefully, singing songs of everlasting joy.[198]

When sickness and scourge are poured out, there will be widespread death and destruction. But there is no need for me to join in the killing. In fact, all those who take up the sword are included within the ranks of the wicked scheduled to die.[199]

I think the "power" we need in the Priesthood of God will be necessary to protect us from plagues. To stay the disease which will be poured out. To keep at bay the effects of the illnesses caused by the wickedness and evil of men who, killing one another and leaving the unburied dead to rot, will spread cholera, diphtheria and other illness.

I do not foresee the need to take up arms. The violence of nature will be responsible for killing many. In fact, the depopulation of the earth will be as a result of the following, as I understand it:

- War
- Pestilence incident to war
- Famine (incident to war and pestilence)
- Drought (incident to wickedness)
- Hail (to destroy what few crops remain)
- Earthquakes and Tempests (targeting those who remain alive but who are wicked and threaten Zion)

Nowhere on *my* list is there an entry for a Zion-based sniper unit. (I'm just trying to let a little humor into this, not mocking this idea. It is a serious idea to be sure, deserving serious thought and pondering.)

---

[198] Ibid, verse 71.

[199] D&C 45:30–33 "And in that generation shall the times of the Gentiles be fulfilled. And there shall be men standing in that generation, that shall not pass until they shall see an overflowing scourge; for a desolating sickness shall cover the land. But my disciples shall stand in holy places, and shall not be moved; but among the wicked, men shall lift up their voices and curse God and die. And there shall be earthquakes also in divers places, and many desolations; yet men will harden their hearts against me, and they will take up the sword, one against another, and they will kill one another."

What we are going to face is global genocide. A handgun won't do much good against the things that are prophesied. There may be isolated opportunities to shoot a bad guy. But there may also be the same isolated bad guy who, in his fear and cowardice, may be vulnerable to conversion to the Gospel if we don't shoot him. What is coming will intimidate mankind so fearfully that men's hearts will fail them. I think preaching to them while they are in such a stupor rather than shooting them may work. And if not, well then I haven't taken my brother's life.

Holy Ghost vs. The Holy Spirit

I was asked this question:

Can you comment on the Holy Ghost vs. The Holy Spirit and who Jesus is and who the Father is, etc... Also, is it possible that Jesus is the same Spirit as the Holy Ghost?[200]

This is fraught with debatable language in the scriptures. There are those who will absolutely disagree with what I have to say. I can explain how I have sorted it out to my understanding, but you should recognize that there are others who would take a different view of the scriptures and of the definition of these roles of the Godhead.

First the clarification:

The Holy Ghost is a personage. It is an individual. It is a Spirit that will dwell inside you.[201]

---

[200] Moses 5:9 "And in that day the Holy Ghost fell upon Adam, which beareth record of the Father and the Son, saying: I am the Only Begotten of the Father from the beginning, henceforth and forever, that as thou hast fallen thou mayest be redeemed, and all mankind, even as many as will."

[201] D&C 130:22 "The Father has a body of flesh and bones as tangible as man's; the Son also; but the Holy Ghost has not a body of flesh and bones, but is a personage of Spirit. Were it not so, the Holy Ghost could not dwell in us."

The Holy Spirit is the power of God which fills the immensity of space.[202]

Now the problem:

Sometimes the Holy Spirit is called the "Light of Christ" rather than the Holy Spirit.[203]

Sometimes the Holy Ghost is called the Holy Spirit.[204]

Whether you are reading something about the Holy Spirit or Holy Ghost is something that must be determined by the context, not the language used.

The relationship between the Holy Spirit or Light of Christ and every living thing, whether a planet, plant, animal, human or ecosystem is direct, immediate and continual. They are all borrowing power from the Holy Spirit to live, move breath, remain organized, and do

---

[202] D&C 88:12–13 "Which light proceedeth forth from the presence of God to fill the immensity of space—The light which is in all things, which giveth life to all things, which is the law by which all things are governed, even the power of God who sitteth upon his throne, who is in the bosom of eternity, who is in the midst of all things."

[203] D&C 88:7–11 "Which truth shineth. This is the light of Christ. As also he is in the sun, and the light of the sun, and the power thereof by which it was made. As also he is in the moon, and is the light of the moon, and the power thereof by which it was made; As also the light of the stars, and the power thereof by which they were made; And the earth also, and the power thereof, even the earth upon which you stand. And the light which shineth, which giveth you light, is through him who enlighteneth your eyes, which is the same light that quickeneth your understandings;"

[204] Luke 11:13 "If ye then, being evil, know how to give good gifts unto your children: how much more shall *your* heavenly Father give the Holy Spirit to them that ask him?"

according to their own wills.[205] This is the means by which the Holy Ghost, which resides inside of you, receives intelligence from Christ.

The Holy Ghost is the "record of heaven" which lives inside you and that you have lost contact with because of the veil. It is a personage of spirit who resides inside you, and you must "receive" it after baptism by finally listening to that inner "truth of all things" or "record of the Father and the Son."[206]

The Holy Ghost bears record of the Son. When the Son speaks to you through the Holy Ghost you hear the words in the first-person. Hence the Holy Ghost speaking that it "is the Son" in Moses 5:9.[207]

I'm keeping this short because the more I explain the more questions will arise. So clarity on this topic is almost invariably related to brevity.

---

[205] Mosiah 2:21–25 "I say unto you that if ye should serve him who has created you from the beginning, and is preserving you from day to day, by lending you breath, that ye may live and move and do according to your own will, and even supporting you from one moment to another—I say, if ye should serve him with all your whole souls yet ye would be unprofitable servants. And behold, all that he requires of you is to keep his commandments; and he has promised you that if ye would keep his commandments ye should prosper in the land; and he never doth vary from that which he hath said; therefore, if ye do keep his commandments he doth bless you and prosper you. And now, in the first place, he hath created you, and granted unto you your lives, for which ye are indebted unto him. And secondly, he doth require that ye should do as he hath commanded you; for which if ye do, he doth immediately bless you; and therefore he hath paid you. And ye are still indebted unto him, and are, and will be, forever and ever; therefore, of what have ye to boast? And now I ask, can ye say aught of yourselves? I answer you, Nay. Ye cannot say that ye are even as much as the dust of the earth; yet ye were created of the dust of the earth; but behold, it belongeth to him who created you."

[206] Moses 6:61, 66 "Therefore it is given to abide in you; the record of heaven; the Comforter; the peaceable things of immortal glory; the truth of all things; that which quickeneth all things, which maketh alive all things; that which knoweth all things, and hath all power according to wisdom, mercy, truth, justice, and judgment. And he heard a voice out of heaven, saying: Thou art baptized with fire, and with the Holy Ghost. This is the record of the Father, and the Son, from henceforth and forever;"

[207] Moses 5:9 "And in that day the Holy Ghost fell upon Adam, which beareth record of the Father and the Son, saying: I am the Only Begotten of the Father from the beginning, henceforth and forever, that as thou hast fallen thou mayest be redeemed, and all mankind, even as many as will."

A "Friend" of God

Here's a concept to ponder . . .

In the beginning, our relationship with God is rather primitive. We start out fearing Him and following His "commandments" in the hope of appeasing Him or avoiding punishment.

We later get some insight that allows us to see Him as a more loving God. As a result of that insight and growth, we begin to view the commandments as warnings and blessings that will benefit us if we heed them.

Developmentally there is a point somewhere far distant along this path where we become a "friend" of God. Abraham achieved this. When he did, the relationship was quite different than what it was in the beginning.

When the Lord requested Isaac be sacrificed, it wasn't a "commandment." The language in the KJV Bible is too coarse to really communicate the idea underlying what happened. It wasn't a "commandment" to Abraham. It was more of a polite suggestion. It was an expression of the Lord's preference. The suggestion was quite gentle. Abraham responded to this polite suggestion from the Lord by proceeding without question. He was willing to sacrifice his long awaited heir.

Now if you can get your hands around this idea, then you can begin to see the difference between where our relationship with God starts and where it should eventually end. At the beginning, our relationship with God is quite primitive. At the end it is a trusted, loving friend in whom absolute confidence resides in the one who has become His friend.

There is such a profound difference between one end of the spectrum and the other that it hinders our understanding of the examples we see in scripture. We distort things considerably when we view His relationships with others in the scriptures in the same context we relate to Him.

When a person has become a "friend" of God, they are introduced to another level of language and experience with Him. When they become a member of His family, they have yet another kind of relationship. The openness and love that exists, and the accompanying trust that goes with it, is something quite distinct from the coarse beginnings of the path.

The faiths which view our relationship to God as "slave to master" are only in the beginning of the process. From that end things which seem to be alright (and may even **be** alright) are different from what is found further along the progression.

Your end is to become part of the household of God, a member of the Church of the Firstborn, and a family member of God the Father. When that happens, the relationship is considerably more polite and respectful than it is when you are first experiencing awareness of God's existence and His commandments to bring us light and truth.

Abraham and Sarah

I have been thinking a lot lately about Abraham and Sarah and their relationship. Their story is one of the greatest in history.

Little details in the story are touching. The "ten years" that Sarah waited[208] before urging Abraham to father a child with Hagar is based upon a custom at the time. Abraham's willingness to follow the custom was because the Lord promised him children, Sarah could not conceive and Sarah urged him to do so. In fact, of the three, Sarah's urging was what seems to persuade Abraham. Her urging is tem-

---

[208] Genesis 16:3 "And Sarai Abram's wife took Hagar her maid the Egyptian, after Abram had dwelt ten years in the land of Canaan, and gave her to her husband Abram to be his wife."

pered by making it seem she is looking out for her own interests: "it may be that I (Sarah) may obtain children by her."[209] This softens the request, makes it a blessing for Sarah, and casts it in terms which do not belittle or dismiss Sarah. Then, as the account reads: "Abram hearkened to the voice of Sarai."[210]

Abraham was willing to wait on the Lord's promises of children. He was willing to forego the customs that allowed a man to take another wife. It was Sarah's gentle persuasion that convinced Abraham to take Hagar. Sarah was loved by Abraham with his whole heart. It was this great marriage relationship that allowed the Lord to preserve them as the parents of "all righteous." A new Adam for the Lord's covenant people. And, of course, there cannot be an Adam without an Eve. Sarah becomes the "Mother of All Righteous."

This is more critical than most people recognize. It was because of this important relationship that the tenth parable in *Ten Parables* begins with the marriage relationship. Without this, there was no reason to save the man.

Marriage is separate from its two parties. It has a life of its own. The husband and the wife may be parties to the marriage, but the marriage itself is a separate and living thing. It is distinct from the two partners in the relationship, and greater than either of them. It lives. It is real.

The only people whose right to eternal life has been secured, to my knowledge, came as a result of the marriage relationship and its worthiness to be preserved into eternity. Neither is the man without the woman nor the woman without the man in the Lord. Therefore,

---

[209] Genesis 16:2 "And Sarai said unto Abram, Behold now, the Lord hath restrained me from bearing: I pray thee, go in unto my maid; it may be that I may obtain children by her. And Abram hearkened to the voice of Sarai."

[210] Ibid.

if you are interested in eternal life, the very first place to begin is inside your marriage.

Repentance and Redemption

I was asked this question:

In D&C 138:57–59 it states: "the faithful elders from this dispensation, when they depart this life continue their labors by preaching to those who are in darkness and under bondage of sin, etc."

The scripture then says that the dead who *repent will be redeemed, through obedience to the ordinances of the house of the Lord*. I thought temple ordinances, including baptisms for the dead, were only necessary for those who are heirs to at least some degree in the Celestial Kingdom. (See *Doctrines of Salvation* 2:191.) If this is so, then why does the scripture go on to say "[a]nd after they have paid the penalty of their transgressions, and are washed clean, shall receive a reward according to their works, for they are heirs of salvation."

If they repent and are redeemed through the ordinances of the temple then why are they paying the penalty for their transgressions? I understood D&C 19:15–18 to mean if you repent then because of the atonement you do not suffer because Christ suffered for us. As I read this scripture it can only mean one of two things. First, some people who end up in he Celestial Kingdom must suffer for their own sins. Second it could mean that these people are not going to the Celestial Kingdom ("for they shall receive a reward according to their works"). So am I wrong that an "heir of salvation" (not "exaltation") can end up in the Celestial, Terrestrial, or Telestial Kingdom, as all are kingdoms of glory and the heirs of each of these kingdoms are saved with a "resurrection of endless life and happiness"? (Mosiah 16:11) And if so then why did they need the ordinances of the temple?

My response:

To enter into the Celestial Kingdom requires the ordinances of the Temple. As explained in D&C 131:1–4:

> In the celestial glory there are three heavens or degrees; And in order to obtain the highest, a man must enter into this order of the priesthood [meaning the new and everlasting covenant of marriage]; And if he does not, he cannot obtain it. He may enter into the other, but that is the end of his kingdom; he cannot have an increase.

This statement defines the "*highest*" as the only one involving the covenant of marriage. The other Celestial Kingdom residents would require all Temple ordinances, from washings, anointings through endowment to be able to enter and pass by the sentinels who stand guard there. Only the *highest* requires the new and everlasting covenant of marriage.

As to who will "suffer for their own sins" and yet enter into the Celestial Kingdom, there are at least two categories: First, those who have received their calling and election, but who return to sin, but not an unpardonable sin. Those are required to "pay the price" for this misconduct.[211] Second, those who are "sealed up" through the faithfulness of their parents, who claim them as children of promise as a matter of right because of the sealing upon the parents. Such children will need to either qualify in their own right, or if inheritors of the promise through the merit of their parents' sealing they will have to suffer to become clean in order to inherit what is sealed upon them by this right.

---

[211] D&C 132:26 "Verily, verily, I say unto you, if a man marry a wife according to my word, and they are sealed by the Holy Spirit of promise, according to mine appointment, and he or she shall commit any sin or transgression of the new and everlasting covenant whatever, and all manner of blasphemies, and if they commit no murder wherein they shed innocent blood, yet they shall come forth in the first resurrection, and enter into their exaltation; but they shall be destroyed in the flesh, and shall be delivered unto the buffetings of Satan unto the day of redemption, saith the Lord God."

It is a good question. It shows the order in heaven and the way in which things are governed by laws established before the foundation of the world.[212]

Communication from the Lord

I was asked how a witness of the Spirit is felt. Here are a variety of ways in which we receive communications from the Lord:

There was a talk I still recall where Elder LeGrand Richards used the expression "goose flesh." He was referring to the feeling he got upon hearing something he knew to be true as soon as it was spoken. He got "goose flesh" as he listened. That is not a bad way to describe how some people feel the witness from the Spirit. This form can also be replicated by stirring music, art or other performances. So if this is how one feels the Spirit, they must distinguish between an emotional outpouring and a manifestation from the Lord.

I believe that everyone's capacity to hear the Spirit bear testimony to them is more or less equal, as all have given to them the "light of Christ."[213]

How someone recognizes the witness to them is person-specific at the start. Whether it is Elder Richards' "goose flesh" or a burst of unmistakable insight coming from beyond, or a warmth in the heart

---

[212] D&C 130:20–21 "There is a law, irrevocably decreed in heaven before the foundations of this world, upon which all blessings are predicated— And when we obtain any blessing from God, it is by obedience to that law upon which it is predicated."

[213] D&C 84:46 "And the Spirit giveth light to every man that cometh into the world; and the Spirit enlighteneth every man through the world, that hearkeneth to the voice of the Spirit."
D&C 88:7 "Which truth shineth. This is the light of Christ. As also he is in the sun, and the light of the sun, and the power thereof by which it was made."
Moroni 7:19 "Wherefore, I beseech of you, brethren, that ye should search diligently in the light of Christ that ye may know good from evil; and if ye will lay hold upon every good thing, and condemn it not, ye certainly will be a child of Christ."

as D&C 9:8 describes, is based upon individual sensitivities.[214] How you feel this may differ from how I do.

When it has progressed from these initial stirrings to the "voice" which you hear within you, that assumes a more uniform experience. The "voice" is clearly not your own, and introduces ideas or concepts that are clearly not your own. You can have a dialogue with this "voice" in which your ideas are juxtaposed with those coming to you. It is not audible, but you hear it inside. It is clearly not your own voice, but that of another.

When you have proven yourself faithful and true to all required of you by the "voice" that comes into your mind and heart, then it becomes possible for angels to visit with you. Angels all come from this earth and have their mortality here.[215] If they appear as disembodied (not-resurrected) spirits, they may appear only as beings dressed in white. They will not make physical contact with you. Satan may attempt to appear as such a being, but since he invariably tries to deceive, if you attempt to make physical contact he will reciprocate as part of his deception. As a disembodied spirit, however, you can detect his lack of physical presence when such contact is attempted. A true messenger who lacks a body will not attempt physical contact, but will deliver his message to you. If a visitor is either resurrected or translated, they may appear without glory, in which case their physical appearance will be as any other person. The only difference you will likely note is that their countenance is pure and radiates a purity that other mortals rarely manifest. If resurrected and appearing in glory, they bear unmistakable signs of Celestial Glory.

---

[214] D&C 9:8 "But, behold, I say unto you, that you must study it out in your mind; then you must ask me if it be right, and if it is right I will cause that your bosom shall burn within you; therefore, you shall feel that it is right."

[215] D&C 130:5 "I answer, Yes. But there are no angels who minister to this earth but those who do belong or have belonged to it."

The closest image I have seen to the glory shown by a resurrected, glorified, celestial personage is the upper pattern, in gold, imprinted onto the Dome of the Rock Mosque. When I saw it for the first time a few months ago, I was startled by the pattern and its radiant glory. It is the closest earthly pattern I have seen to depicting a Celestial Glory. I do not know who fashioned the pattern, but they were depicting something that I recognized to be inspired by what lies beyond the veil and patterned after Celestial Glory itself.

Beings appearing in Celestial Glory do not show themselves, or in other words, cannot be seen, except by those only who are prepared to behold them. Others who may be present when they appear will feel a presence that often frightens them, as in the case of Daniel's companions in Daniel Chapter 10.

The final stage in development requires one to "see" the things that are being communicated. This happens when the "answer" to the inquiry is opened to view, but only inside the mind. You can actually "behold" something as if it were before you, without actually being there. Such a process is physically demanding, despite the fact it is so intangible a matter as to defy description. Seeing things by this process is not limited to time, place or location. A person exercising this gift, for example, may be able to behold Abraham as he receives the box containing the records from his father, who held the box in no particular regard because he could not open it.

When the person has developed the ability to "see," the answers to inquiries come almost entirely through the exercise of this gift. Although all these forms of messages and communication from the Lord and His messengers are still available to a seer when conditions or the circumstances warrant it.

There are seers among us. In fact, we "sustain," institutionally, fifteen men to be such every General Conference. The development of the gift, however, comes not by consequence of office alone but by the diligence of the individual. All are on equal footing before the Lord. Therefore, although it may be conferred upon you or them, the realization of these blessings depends upon their/your faithfulness. Elder Scott, for example, uses terms in some of his talks which intimate seership. The Vision of the Redemption of the Dead (D&C 138) has language I recognize as a seer's. So does D&C 76.

Sacred Things

I was asked this question:

What do you say to people who state: "I doubt people who've had an audience with Christ would be out writing books and blogs about it. We are counseled not to talk about sacred things. (Followed by several GA quotes.)"

I would say that they should accept counsel from whomever they trust and follow it. I might add that if they read *The Second Comforter: Conversing With the Lord Through the Veil* they will get an answer to the question. But, if they are hostile and offended and ask the question out of fear, I would not add the clarification.

It is not necessary for everyone to be stirred up by argument or persuasion to listen to something they do not want to hear. What is coming will stir up everyone who has not been already touched by the Spirit. Patience. We're headed somewhere. The Lord remains in charge and has a plan to cause every knee to bow and every tongue to confess the truth of who He is, what He has done, and what He has been doing. We shouldn't rush people forward.

There is more mischief in introducing people to truth before they are ready to comprehend and welcome it than there is in remaining silent. It is uncharitable to tell someone a great truth which they are unprepared to accept.

Eternal Life and the Covenant Marriage

"Eternal life" requires a couple who can have increase, or bear children. The requirement is that through the continuation of the marriage covenant men and women become exalted. And without that, they remain separate and single, saved, but not exalted. D&C 132 explains:

> Therefore, if a man marry him a wife in the world, and he marry her not by me nor by my word, and he covenant with her so long as he is in the world and she with him, their covenant and marriage are not of force when they are dead, and when they are out of the world; therefore, they are not bound by any law when they are out of the world.

> Therefore, when they are out of the world they neither marry nor are given in marriage; but are appointed angels in heaven, which angels are ministering servants, to minister for those who are worthy of a far more, and an exceeding, and an eternal weight of glory.

> For these angels did not abide my law; therefore, they cannot be enlarged, but remain separately and singly, without exaltation, in their saved condition, to all eternity; and from henceforth are not gods, but are angels of God forever and ever.

> And again, verily I say unto you, if a man marry a wife, and make a covenant with her for time and for all eternity, if that covenant is not by me or by my word, which is my law, and is not sealed by the Holy Spirit of promise, through him whom I have anointed and appointed unto this power, then it is not valid neither of force when they are out of the world, because they are not joined by me, saith the Lord, neither by my word; when they are out of the world it cannot be received there, because the angels and the gods are appointed there, by whom they cannot pass; they cannot, therefore, inherit my

glory; for my house is a house of order, saith the Lord God. (D&C 132:15–18)

The Celestial Kingdom has three heavens or degrees within it. To attain the highest, which is the only one in which the marriage covenant exists and continues, a person must have entered into a marriage and been sealed by the holy spirit of promise. As D&C 131 explains:

> In the celestial glory there are three heavens or degrees; And in order to obtain the highest, a man must enter into this order of the priesthood [meaning the new and everlasting covenant of marriage]; And if he does not, he cannot obtain it. He may enter into the other, but that is the end of his kingdom; he cannot have an increase. (D&C 131:1–4)

Exaltation is tied to the marriage covenant and without an eternal marriage there cannot be exaltation.

However, (I point out hesitantly) that all these verses are phrased in the masculine. In most cases the masculine does not matter because the commandment applies to both the man and woman. That is, when mankind is referred to collectively, it is referred to in the masculine. For example, the first couple are sometimes referred to collectively as "Adam" when what is meant is Adam *and* Eve. Therefore, what I'm going to say is not a universal truism and cannot be applied without regard to context. Here, however, it can be applied. Because in this instance, the male's right to exaltation is utterly dependent upon his successful completion of this requirement as part of this probation.

Women, on the other hand, who would be otherwise worthy (and that involves a great number beyond those who are parties to sealed and worthy marriage), are among those who D&C 137 describes:

. . . All who have died without a knowledge of this gospel, who would have received it if they had been permitted to tarry, shall be heirs of the celestial kingdom of God; Also all that shall die henceforth without a knowledge of it, who would have received it with all their hearts, shall be heirs of that kingdom; For I, the Lord, will judge all men according to their works, according to the desires of their hearts. (D&C 137:7–9)

Women have, throughout history, borne their obligation of motherhood and submission to husbands with considerable success. It is rare, however, when men have been able to retain priesthood. Apostasy is a male failing, not a female failing. Nor are the women of the Church responsible for the lack of "power" within the priesthood discussed by Elder Packer in the last General Conference.[216] This is a male failing.

Therefore, when the first two quotes are read above, the significance of the masculine phrasing ought not be overlooked. The whole subject is tied to a man's completion of a task required of him in mortality.

Women who are good mothers, worthy wives and who keep the faith will suffer no loss because of a failing husband. *However,* women are required to minister in love and righteousness even to a difficult husband, as did Abigail. Marriage to a "churlish" man did not stop her from showing her own nobility. Therefore, it is not enough for a woman to determine her husband is not likely to survive the judgment, give up on him, and await the next life to learn to serve in love and patience. She has an obligation to begin that service here and now. Indeed, the worse the man, the greater the opportunity to show Christ-like devotion. There is no man whose behavior is more offensive than those for whom Christ suffered. To be like Him, and

---

[216] Packer, "The Power of the Priesthood", General Conference, April 2010.

to live where He lives requires a similar capacity to forgive, love, bless, serve and elevate.

This isn't easy. Wasn't meant to be. Do you really think any of us are worthy to be called "gods" without first descending below all things so as to be qualified to rise above all things? Christ is not merely our Savior, He is our example. We must "follow Him" if we want to be where He is.

Two Ships Pass in the Night

Dialogue between two ships passing in the night. [Intended as humor, because so far as I know ships do not speak with one another]:

USS Saint: "I know the Church is true."

HMS Midevil: "Beg pardon, how's that?"

USS Saint: "I know the Church is true."

HMS Midevil: "Which? .. or is it all?"

USS Saint: "The Latter-day Saints, of course."

HMS: "By that do you mean to suggest that the Printing Services Division of the Materials Management Department is somehow 'true' as you say?"

USS: "Um, well, yes I suppose."

HMS: "In what sense. 'True' meaning that it exists? or 'True" in some other meaning of the word?"

USS: "I mean led by a Prophet of God, therefore imbued with the will of God Almighty in all respects."

HMS: "So not that it is 'True' in a metaphysical sense of existence on a higher plane, or bearing some corporeality, but somehow inerrant. Is that what you are saying? And, if so, does that preclude printing errors? Because if it means avoidance of printing errors well, then they ought to take a larger role in the publishing industry than simply providing grist for the Materials Management Department."

USS: "Since a prophet is only a prophet when acting as such, I would not attribute inerrancy to the truthfulness of the Printing Services Division of the Materials Management Department; but I would rather say that what they do is Inspired. I do suspect, however, there may be occasional printing errors."

HMS: "Inspired in the sense of the word meaning that it's output is somehow delightful and uplifting? Or in the sense of 'perfection itself'? But, then again, you've conceded the possibility of printing errors, so 'perfection itself' seems not to be included then. So I presume that you mean when you read the output of the printing of this Division of that Department it somehow inspires you to be a better ship, then? Perhaps somewhat of a worShip?"

USS: "I can see that you are not prepared to grasp the truth of my testimony as yet. So let me just warn you that you're going to hell."

HMS: "Atlantic City, rather."

USS: "What?"

HMS: "I'm sailing to Atlantic City. Though it might be called 'hell' with some validity I suppose."

Purpose of Teaching

I must clarify something very important for readers:

Giving answers to people apart from teaching how to get answers is wrong. Wrong because just giving an answer alone creates dependence upon the one answering. That is not the way in which I have tried to proceed. Instead, I have tried to teach *how to obtain your own answers*. The whole purpose of teaching is NOT to create dependence. It is to make you independent from me, establish your own capacity to relate to and get answers from God.

I've tried to give answers and illustrations inside the greater context of teaching "*how.*" The answer is nothing. It is the "*how*" that matters.

Some readers on this blog have not read *The Second Comforter* and presume incorrectly that it is a book about me. It is not. It is a book about the reader. It is an explanation of how the reader can grow into the greater relationship which Christ promised to them. All the illustrations from my personal experience, with the exception of nine words only, are taken from my mistakes, errors, or setbacks. The personal accounts of mistakes then are followed by chapters which explain how you can do it right. That is a teacher's role: to make the listener understand how they can do something.

It has become apparent that there are questions coming in from people who want answers completely separated from learning "how" to get an understanding of the basic process by which they can do it themselves. That was never my intention, never asked of me, and not something that I want to start.

Your development is your responsibility. I am trying to teach from my own experience how to grow. Some of you have demonstrated a remarkable capacity to grow, and have been directly benefited from my efforts. I view those people as such a triumph that I will always hold them dear. I look forward to eternal joy with these people. There are clearly others who have never realized what it means to be taught or how a true teacher is to proceed. I can help. But I cannot properly go beyond helping. I cannot be your guru, your answer-man, or your leader. Nor have I been called to preside. I teach. You must decide if you want to learn "how" to engage the Gospel of Jesus Christ and its associated blessings. You must avoid at all hazards becoming dependent upon me, or any man, as your guide. I am only here to help you in your own growth and development, and I am not here to tell you secrets, or amaze you with recitations of my personal experiences. That would be wrong for two reasons: First, it would do you no good, nor equip you with what you need. Second, it would be both prideful and arrogant, setting myself up as a light instead of pointing you to the True Light.

Questions that change the focus and which prevent me from teaching as a disciple of Jesus Christ cannot be answered. Therefore, if I cannot change the *"question"* into something I can use to teach, I will not answer the question.

The Same Is Required of All

I was asked this question:

"I am at a point where I do not know how to get past the fear to move on to faith. In my being I know that if I can get past this I can do all God asks of me, and I want to. Do you have any suggestions as to how I can accomplish to get over the hump? If you have any it would be greatly appreciated. I have always wanted to see my Savior from the time I was very small, but I know that I need faith to do it. Please help, if you can."

Everyone faces the identical challenge. It seems different only because of our individual strengths and weaknesses. The challenge is adapted to our own personality, capacity and life's history. Therefore, when you are asked to overcome something, it will fit in the framework of your life.

All are asked to make a sacrifice that shows they will not withhold anything from the Lord. It will come to each person based on what they value and would regret to their core surrendering. Whatever that is, you will be asked by the Lord to give it to Him. You must decide to do that when asked.

All are asked to do something that they view as wrong, evil or inappropriate and will seem to be inconsistent with the Lord's mercy, righteousness and perfection. The request will unmistakably come from Him. You cannot evade the request because you doubt He is asking. You will clearly know it is Him who asks, and that to all your understanding it will be wrong to do. You must do it anyway.

All are asked to take a step in faith beyond where they are at the time. Trust in Him, and only Him, as you take that step. You will be certain that if it were something you were undertaking on your own, it could not be accomplished. But because you are doing as He has asked, you know you will have the strength or support to do as He bids.

All are asked to come to Him without guilt or shame, knowing you have done everything you understand Him to have asked of you. Without this knowledge, you will not be able to endure what He asks.

All are able to develop the faith to lay hold on eternal life only because they have been led by Him through this process. When they have the faith sufficient to lay hold on these things, the Lord will declare to them by His own voice, that they have been begotten of Him and have a place with Him in eternity.

This is universally the process. The specific form each of these will take will vary from person to person because of individual traits.

Blessed Are the Peacemakers

Christ's disciples were ever willing to use both priesthood and the sword to vanquish their opponents. Christ taught them restraint. There is this incident in Luke:

> And it came to pass, when the time was come that he should be received up, he stedfastly set his face to go to Jerusalem, And sent messengers before his face: and they went, and entered into a village of the Samaritans, to make ready for him. And they did not receive him, because his face was as though he would go to Jerusalem. And when his disciples James and John saw this, they said, Lord, wilt thou that we command fire to come down from heaven, and consume them, even as Elias did? But he turned, and rebuked them, and said, Ye know not

what manner of spirit ye are of. For the Son of man is not come to destroy men's lives, but to save them. (Luke 9:51–56)

There is this incident in Gethsemane, a portion taken from John 18:

Then Simon Peter having a sword drew it, and smote the high priest's servant, and cut off his right ear. The servant's name was Malchus. Then said Jesus unto Peter, Put up thy sword into the sheath: the cup which my Father hath given me, shall I not drink it? Then the band and the captain and officers of the Jews took Jesus, and bound him (John 18:10–12)

The balance of the account is found in Luke 22:

And one of them smote the servant of the high priest, and cut off his right ear. And Jesus answered and said, Suffer ye thus far. And he touched his ear, and healed him. Then Jesus said unto the chief priests, and captains of the temple, and the elders, which were come to him, Be ye come out, as against a thief, with swords and staves? When I was daily with you in the temple, ye stretched forth no hands against me: but this is your hour, and the power of darkness. Then took they him, and led him, and brought him into the high priest's house. And Peter followed afar off. (Luke 22:50–54)

Christ taught and lived this:

"Blessed are the peacemakers: for they shall be called the children of God." (Matthew 5:9)

There are too many willing to cry for revenge or justice in the world. Eventually the spirit of revenge and justice will be set free, and the earth will be filled with violence. As it was in the days of

Noah—those days will return again.[217] Those who want to see *justi-fied* and *unjustified* killing will have their fill.

In the days before the flood the earth was filled with violence. There was also a corresponding return of Zion. It would not be as it was in the days of Noah if Zion were not to return. For that, the pattern is set out in Moses 7:

> And so great was the faith of Enoch that he led the people of God, and their enemies came to battle against them; and he spake the word of the Lord, and the earth trembled, and the mountains fled, even according to his command; and the rivers of water were turned out of their course; and the roar of the lions was heard out of the wilderness; and all nations feared greatly, so powerful was the word of Enoch, and so great was the power of the language which God had given him.

> There also came up a land out of the depth of the sea, and so great was the fear of the enemies of the people of God, that they fled and stood afar off and went upon the land which came up out of the depth of the sea.

> And the giants of the land, also, stood afar off; and there went forth a curse upon all people that fought against God; And from that time forth there were wars and bloodshed among them; but the Lord came and dwelt with his people, and they dwelt in righteousness. The fear of the Lord was upon all nations, so great was the glory of the Lord, which was upon his people. And the Lord blessed the land, and they were blessed upon the mountains, and upon the high places, and did flourish.

---

[217] Genesis 6:11–13 "The earth also was corrupt before God, and the earth was filled with violence. And God looked upon the earth, and, behold, it was corrupt; for all flesh had corrupted his way upon the earth. And God said unto Noah, The end of all flesh is come before me; for the earth is filled with violence through them; and, behold, I will destroy them with the earth."

Moses 8:28–30 "The earth was corrupt before God, and it was filled with violence. And God looked upon the earth, and, behold, it was corrupt, for all flesh had corrupted its way upon the earth. And God said unto Noah: The end of all flesh is come before me, for the earth is filled with violence, and behold I will destroy all flesh from off the earth."

And the Lord called his people Zion, because they were of
one heart and one mind, and dwelt in righteousness; and there
was no poor among them. And Enoch continued his preaching in righteousness unto the people of God. And it came to
pass in his days, that he built a city that was called the City of
Holiness, even Zion. And it came to pass that Enoch talked
with the Lord; and he said unto the Lord: Surely Zion shall
dwell in safety forever. But the Lord said unto Enoch: Zion
have I blessed, but the residue of the people have I cursed.
(Moses 7:13–20)

Why was the fear of the Lord upon people who did not gather to
Zion? It was because their own guilt prevented them from drawing
near. It will be the same in the last days as it was then. Moroni explains it in Mormon 9:

Behold, will ye believe in the day of your visitation—behold,
when the Lord shall come, yea, even that great day when the
earth shall be rolled together as a scroll, and the elements shall
melt with fervent heat, yea, in that great day when ye shall be
brought to stand before the Lamb of God—then will ye say
that there is no God?

Then will ye longer deny the Christ, or can ye behold the
Lamb of God? Do ye suppose that ye shall dwell with him
under a consciousness of your guilt? Do ye suppose that ye
could be happy to dwell with that holy Being, when your souls
are racked with a consciousness of guilt that ye have ever
abused his laws? Behold, I say unto you that ye would be
more miserable to dwell with a holy and just God, under a
consciousness of your filthiness before him, than ye would to
dwell with the damned souls in hell.

For behold, when ye shall be brought to see your nakedness
before God, and also the glory of God, and the holiness of
Jesus Christ, it will kindle a flame of unquenchable fire upon
you. O then ye unbelieving, turn ye unto the Lord; cry might-

ily unto the Father in the name of Jesus, that perhaps ye may
be found spotless, pure, fair, and white, having been cleansed
by the blood of the Lamb, at that great and last day. (Mormon
9:2–6)

How much guilt we bring with us to that final day depends entirely upon the intent of our hearts, the actions of our hands, and the
words we speak. (Alma 12:14.) Becoming a peacemaker and meriting
the call as a child of God is measured by our acts, but includes as
Alma warns us, our thoughts and words as well.

Hope to Be a Part of Zion?

I was asked if I thought it was wrong to own a gun or kill in self-
defense. My response.

I don't think there is anything wrong with owning firearms, hunt-
ing, or self-defense. But I do think we are too quick to presume we
are authorized to take life. Therefore, I am reluctant to encourage
that kind of thinking. I encourage a non-violent, non-confrontational
way to solve a problem first, and violent action as a last resort. When
violence or self-defense is used as the final option, then it is rarely
needed. When it is viewed as justified and approved, it gets employed
with the kind of recklessness that will condemn a person.

The Mountain Meadows Massacre is a hallmark event wherein
aggressive "self defense" resulted in murder. No one in the local
church leadership involved thought of it as murder at the time. In
hindsight, everyone, even the church's Assistant-Historian, admits it
was murder and that the blame went far beyond John D. Lee. It is far
better to suffer than to react too quickly and to take life.

This is a separate subject from the creation of Zion. Currently, as a people, we don't possess enough basic understanding of doctrine to begin to organize Zion. Our current models would be warmed over
Babylon with new names associated with it. Rather like the Historic

Christian movement adopted "Christmas" to celebrate "Sol Invictus." Or the fertility rites of Spring renamed "Easter."

Our "Zion" would be a commercial enterprise, with private ownership and capitalist competition to form an economic basis from
which to build a strictly regimented and highly controlled people.
Something so foreign to what Zion was meant to be that I rather
think it would draw tornadoes in a proportion greater than trailer
parks currently do in Mississippi.

Zion will be cooperative, not competitive. They will be "one" in
every sense of the word. No one will need to say "know ye the
Lord" because everyone will know Him, from the greatest to the
least. He will be able to dwell among them because He will have *already* been known by them.

Collectivist efforts are never going to work. FIRST, we must become *individually* the kind of people whom the Lord can visit. Then,
after that, the gathering together of like-minded people will be a
gathering of equals. It will not be an hierarchical gathering of "leadership" and drones. There won't be a single drone in Zion. Everyone
will be equal and no one will mind mowing the grass or taking out
the garbage.

I envision this scene from Zion:

A man walks down the street early in the morning and notices
that the bakery is unmanned. Its door is open, because there is no
need for locks in Zion. So, on an impulse, he enters, looks about for
the instructions left by someone, and begins to prepare bread. As the
morning goes on, a few others join him. They make bread. Others
come and take the bread to their homes. At the end of the day, the
man goes home. This was his first time working in the bakery. He did
it because he saw it needed to be done.

He returns to the bakery, because he enjoyed it. Day by day he
works in the bakery for months, perhaps years. One day on his way,

he notices that the grass needs to be cut and the mower has been carefully left beside a tree along the parkway. So he starts to cut the grass. He finds he likes it, and this is now what he does this day. And the next. And within a month he has cut all the grass needing cutting in his immediate neighborhood and starts over again where he began. He enjoys it.

Eventually he is asked by someone to help to move clothing and journals from one home to another. A couple whose children have all moved out no longer have need of the larger home they occupy, and are moving across town. So he puts the mower carefully beside a tree and begins to help move. Homes are occupied based upon need, and these people no longer have need of the larger space they once occupied.

Across town he notices that there is a new neighborhood being built. He decides, after finishing the move for the couple, that he will assist at the site. He returns there for over a year as he provides help with stocking and distributing materials, framing, installing shingles, painting and clean-up.

He has no job. He is never without work. He asks for no pay, because some labor to feed others. He has no need for housing, because what is available is shared.

Before I go on, I feel the need to interrupt:

How on earth is something like this going to work?

What about zoning laws and business licenses?

What about getting a building permit before commencing construction?

What quality control and food-handler's permits exist which will guarantee the bread the man makes won't make people sick?

This is chaos. Disorder. Anarchy. In short, how the hell will something like this WORK??!!??

Well, the answer is, of course, it won't. Can't. Not with the folks we have at present. We'll sit around arguing about the rules for establishing Zion and simply never get around to being Zion. Zion IS. It can't be organized, because it requires no organization. It can't be controlled because there is no need for control. It can't be governed because it is entirely voluntary and self-governing.

So for us, we imagine Zion to have a completely restrictive set of covenants on housing which will keep out those garish, bright colored stucco houses we see on the "west-side" in oh so many crowded cities. Right? We can't have that. And we need a code to mandate a common language. We can't put up with a polyglot society where we can't make out what someone is saying, now can we? And we ought to make sure zoning keeps the commercial stuff on one side and not scattered throughout the neighborhoods. Crap like that attracts crime. And crime should require immediate expulsion, right? Can't tolerate crime in Zion. We'll need law enforcement to make that work, and a fence so the criminals don't creep back in after dark. And street lights, so we can see what people are up to after dark when they're lurking about. And taxes to pay for the public improvements. And a cap on taxes. We can't let taxation become punitive.

Wait—we're right back in Babylon . . .

But you say you want to start Zion? Ok. Go help your neighbor. This is where our hearts will need to be before the foundation will ever be laid. Studying so you can justify using violence if the need arises will not get you any closer to Zion. Nor will developing a street plan for Zion ahead of a heart plan for changing mankind. Men's hearts have failed them.[218]

---

[218] D&C 45:26 "And in that day shall be heard of wars and rumors of wars, and the whole earth shall be in commotion, and men's hearts shall fail them, and they shall say that Christ delayeth his coming until the end of the earth."

I Am a Fool

Joseph Smith once said about himself that if *"he hadn't lived it, he wouldn't believe it."* What insight that provides.

I believe in the complete equality of all of us. God did not love Joseph Smith more than He loved Sidney Rigdon. Joseph remained true to the end, and Sidney fell away. That had nothing to do with God's love for them. It had to do with their love of God and willingness to sacrifice to have the faith to trust in God.

I do not blame anyone who questions my right to give answers. I renounce any authority over anyone. Even those over whom I have a position as father are treated with respect and urging, not by demanding they see or do things to please me.

If, however, I have the power to answer a question by the power of Spirit, and the answer seems to you to be filled with light and truth, then it is the Spirit you should thank—not me. Such an ability will flee the moment I leave the path, seek to control others or become prideful. You can mark it down as true: No man who has his own self as his concern will be able to declare the truth in purity and with the approval of the Spirit.

I have said before and I repeat it again—I am a fool. You mustn't trust me. If the Spirit does not ratify what I have to say, then I'm not worth the time to even consider.

This blog is an attempt to explain what I believe to be true. It is for those who are trying to find truth for themselves. Hopefully you will become acquainted with enough to begin to trust that God does exist, and that He will answer questions, and that He is no respecter of persons. Hopefully you will venture into asking and getting answers from Him directly. Then, when you have begun that process, I hope to encourage you to follow through and receive from Him what He alone can provide to us. For salvation lies in "knowing the only true God, and Jesus Christ whom He has sent" (John 17:3). It does not lie in following other men. Rather it is to be found as a result of you drawing near to Him. This will in turn cause Him to draw near to you.

He lives! He answers prayer! He cares about and loves you as much as He has loved any person who has ever lived on this earth.

The Process Is Everything—The Answer Is Nothing

Process is everything. Answers are nothing.

If you learn the process, you can develop godlike traits. That is, the very tools that are required for us to develop as disciples of Jesus Christ are, in fact, the tools used by God Himself.

Faith in God is necessary for us to develop. God extends His kingdom by His faith. Therefore, as we develop faith we are developing a characteristic that is godlike in its form and function. He knows we are unable to have faith in ourselves right now. Therefore, it is required for us to have faith in Him. Indeed at this stage of development it is necessary for us to concentrate all faith in Him because this whole creation belongs to Him. We are not self-existent yet. Our organization and continuation is dependent upon Him.[219]

---

[219] Mosiah 2:20–25 "I say unto you, my brethren, that if you should render all the thanks and praise which your whole soul has power to possess, to that God who has created you, and has kept and preserved you, and has caused that ye should rejoice, and has granted that ye should live in peace one with another— I say unto you that if ye should serve him who has created you from the beginning, and is preserving you from day to day, by lending you breath, that ye may live and move and do according to your own will, and even supporting you from one moment to another—I say, if ye should serve him with all your whole souls yet ye would be unprofitable servants. And behold, all that he requires of you is to keep his commandments; and he has promised you that if ye would keep his commandments ye should prosper in the land; and he never doth vary from that which he hath said; therefore, if ye do keep his commandments he doth bless you and prosper you. And now, in the first place, he hath created you, and granted unto you your lives, for which ye are indebted unto him. And secondly, he doth require that ye should do as he hath commanded you; for which if ye do, he doth immediately bless you; and therefore he hath paid you. And ye are still indebted unto him, and are, and will be, forever and ever; therefore, of what have ye to boast? And now I ask, can ye say aught of yourselves? I answer you, Nay. Ye cannot say that ye are even as much as the dust of the earth; yet ye were created of the dust of the earth; but behold, it belongeth to him who created you."

Christ is our great example, and in this He showed the way as well. While here, mortal, and before finishing the course, He declared: "I can of my own self do nothing" (John 5:30). When resurrected, however, He declared "all power is given unto me in earth and in heaven" (Matthew 28:18).

The rules of Celestial glory are the rules of the Temple. Obedience, sacrifice, Gospel, chastity and consecration are all the hallmarks of citizenship there. This is why peace, order, kindness and love prevail in that society. There is nothing to harm, threaten or break up families.

Why would an answer to a deep doctrinal question help someone who is not prepared to live in conformity with the Celestial standards? And contrariwise, if they live Celestial standards, how can you keep them from understanding the doctrine?[220]

Process is everything. A mere answer will not fill the empty soul. Those who have read my books should understand this. This blog is for them. Those who do not have a doctrinal basis to understand what is going on here will not be satisfied by this blog. It is not meant as a substitute for understanding what I've written. It is only a supplement to it.

That does not mean that you must read what I've written to understand the Gospel. There are many ways to obtain that understanding, the primary one being to *study* the scriptures. In my opinion the quality of what we teach now is so diluted, so basic and simplistic. It leaves by the wayside so much of what the Prophet Joseph Smith taught that you either have to read early church materials or else read what I've gathered (based primarily on the scriptures and secondarily on what Joseph Smith taught). If you have been a Latter-day Saint for longer than about 4 years, today's curriculum, in my view, is

---

[220] John 7:17 "If any man will do his will, he shall know of the doctrine, whether it be of God, or *whether* I speak of myself."

not adequate to inform you about the obligations devolving upon you as a disciple of Christ.

I labor to teach process. I want you independent of me and every other teacher, able to get answers for yourself directly from heaven itself. I want to avoid today what Joseph cautioned us against in Nauvoo:

> "[I]f the people departed from the Lord, they must fall—that they were depending on the Prophet, hence were darkened in their minds, in consequence of neglecting the duties devolving on themselves[.]" (*TPJS*, 237)

Joseph did NOT want you dependent upon him for answers. He wanted to teach you correct principles and let you govern yourself.

Any man who tries to put himself between you and heaven, claiming that he alone should be the source of your religious beliefs and education, is practicing priestcraft and will in the end lead both himself and you to damnation.

Belief Becomes Knowledge

The post I put up with an excerpt from Lecture 6 a bit ago was deliberately chosen as a foundation for what was put up a few days ago. That Lecture included the fact that you "*know*" not merely "*believe*" that what you are doing is in conformity with God's will. A person obtains "*actual knowledge*" that they are acting in conformity with God's will.

Kisi asked a question regarding the idea of being asked to do something you regard as "wrong" or perhaps even "evil," and how can a person avoid deception with such an idea. The answer lies within the doctrine taught in Lecture 6. You simply cannot proceed without knowing. You cannot know without following the correct course. You must make an acceptable sacrifice to obtain the knowledge. Without making that sacrifice you cannot obtain that knowledge. However, once you have possession of the actual knowledge, then it is not a matter of conjecture, or speculation, or desire, or "hope" as the world uses that term. Rather it is an act in utter righteousness, in strict conformity with the will of God, whose will is known to the person because they have proceeded correctly in obtaining this knowledge.

To gain that knowledge a person keeps the commandments, pays their tithes, does everything they are asked to do to follow the will of God as understood by them. Such a person will be "firm in their minds" and not weak minded or given to flights of fancy.[221] They will have been qualified by the things which they have done in following God to possess this kind of knowledge.

The idea that a person would do something which they regard as "wrong" or to be "evil" is typified in the experience of Abraham[222] and Nephi.[223] This is what the Lecture is talking about when it says:

> "a religion that does not require the sacrifice of all things, never has power sufficient to produce the faith necessary unto life and salvation; for from the first existence of man, the faith necessary unto the enjoyment of life and salvation never could be obtained without the sacrifice of all earthly things; it was through this sacrifice, and this only, that God has ordained that men should enjoy eternal life; and it is through the medium of the sacrifice of all earthly things, that men do actually know that they are doing the things that are well pleasing in the sight of God." (*Lectures on Faith* 6:7).

---

[221] Moroni 7:30 "For behold, they are subject unto him, to minister according to the word of his command, showing themselves unto them of strong faith and a firm mind in every form of godliness."

[222] Genesis 22:2 "And he said, Take now thy son, thine only *son* Isaac, whom thou lovest, and get thee into the land of Moriah; and offer him there for a burnt offering upon one of the mountains which I will tell thee of."

[223] 1 Nephi 4:10 "And it came to pass that I was constrained by the Spirit that I should kill Laban; but I said in my heart: Never at any time have I shed the blood of man. And I shrunk and would that I might not slay him."

Now I do not expect anyone to be asked to sacrifice their only child. Nor to be told to kill someone and take their possession. What I expect is that in the context of the life someone has lived or is living, they will be asked to do or not do something which is so specific to them that they alone will understand why it is a sacrifice to them. If asked of another, it may be completely insignificant. But when asked of them, it will be exactly what the person will struggle to lay upon the Lord's altar. Hence the term "sacrifice" with its partial meaning of parting with something involving great value to them. However, it is not possible to rule anything in or out—the Lord alone will know you and what is required for you to obtain this faith.

The terms for obtaining this kind of faith are the same for every man or woman who has ever lived. Without making the sacrifice it is not possible to obtain the faith.

Qualifying for Blessings under Adverse Circumstances

I was asked about someone who is an active, faithful man married to a non-member wife. The issue is their chances to receive all the blessings associated with an eternal family, despite the spouse's lack of faith.

From the question it is apparent that the person has first, has accepted and believes in the Gospel of Jesus Christ. Second, is living everything they can at present. Third, would gladly take the spouse to the temple if the spouse were willing to go and enter into the covenants there.

This, once again, is a Section 137 issue in which the person qualifies for everything which they would have gladly received, had the circumstances permitted it:

> And marveled how it was that he had obtained an inheritance in that kingdom, seeing that he had departed this life before the Lord had set his hand to gather Israel the second time,

and had not been baptized for the remission of sins. Thus came the voice of the Lord unto me, saying: All who have died without a knowledge of this gospel, who would have received it if they had been permitted to tarry, shall be heirs of the celestial kingdom of God; Also all that shall die henceforth without a knowledge of it, who would have received it with all their hearts, shall be heirs of that kingdom; For I, the Lord, will judge all men according to their works, according to the desire of their hearts. (D&C 137:6–9)

By continuing to be loyal to, supportive of, and loving toward the non-believing spouse the husband is living an example which will, in the Day of Judgment, be credited him for righteousness. This is particularly true when the husband remains loyal and faithful to her when she does not share his faith. It reflects credit on his character to do so. I cannot help but believe the Lord is pleased with such a man.

Finally, who knows but what the spouse will, at the end, convert and all the blessings be sealed upon them while still here anyway. Life is not over yet. There is something compelling and convincing to even a skeptic of the Gospel when they see someone actually live it.

Go About Doing Good

You should not look directly into the sun. Whenever you do, your eyes are unable to adjust to the intensity of the light. It is possible to even do damage to your eyes by looking directly at the sun.

Everything in mortality is a type or symbol of eternal things. All things bear testimony of Christ and His great plan.[224] The sun bears testimony of the Son of God. It is a great symbol of Him.

---

[224] Moses 6:63 "And behold, all things have their likeness, and all things are created and made to bear record of me, both things which are temporal, and things which are spiritual; things which are in the heavens above, and things which are on the earth, and things which are in the earth, and things which are under the earth, both above and beneath: all things bear record of me."

Our approach to gaining a relationship with the *Son* should be like that of our enjoyment of the *sun*—indirect. That is, entering into His presence is a by-product. It is as a result of the way you live. It is not the "goal."

To approach Him, you must live as He did. You must "keep His commandments." You must love others. You must live the way He lived. When you are walking in the same path He walked, you will find that He is walking there still. He will come alongside you, as you are "in the way" and will open to your understanding all things which He would have you know.[225] I've written about this in the talk in the Appendix to *Eighteen Verses* and will not repeat it here. But I would remind you that the account of those two disciples is a type of how He appears to those to whom He will minister. He will see you as you are in the right way, and then join with you.

---

[225] Luke 24:13–32 "And, behold, two of them went that same day to a village called Emmaus, which was from Jerusalem *about* threescore furlongs. And they talked together of all these things which had happened. And it came to pass, that, while they communed *together* and reasoned, Jesus himself drew near, and went with them. But their eyes were holden that they should not know him. And he said unto them, What manner of communications *are* these that ye have one to another, as ye walk, and are sad? And the one of them, whose name was Cleopas, answering said unto him, Art thou only a stranger in Jerusalem, and hast not known the things which are come to pass there in these days? And he said unto them, What things? And they said unto him, Concerning Jesus of Nazareth, which was a prophet mighty in deed and word before God and all the people: And how the chief priests and our rulers delivered him to be condemned to death, and have crucified him. But we trusted that it had been he which should have redeemed Israel: and beside all this, to day is the third day since these things were done. Yea, and certain women also of our company made us astonished, which were early at the sepulchre; And when they found not his body, they came, saying, that they had also seen a vision of angels, which said that he was alive. And certain of them which were with us went to the sepulchre, and found *it* even so as the women had said: but him they saw not. Then he said unto them, O fools, and slow of heart to believe all that the prophets have spoken: Ought not Christ to have suffered these things, and to enter into his glory? And beginning at Moses and all the prophets, he expounded unto them in all the scriptures the things concerning himself. And they drew nigh unto the village, whither they went: and he made as though he would have gone further. But they constrained him, saying, Abide with us: for it is toward evening, and the day is far spent. And he went in to tarry with them. And it came to pass, as he sat at meat with them, he took bread, and blessed *it,* and brake, and gave to them. And their eyes were opened, and they knew him; and he vanished out of their sight. And they said one to another, Did not our heart burn within us, while he talked with us by the way, and while he opened to us the scriptures?"

Go about doing good. You will find Him as you do. Do not think you will be able to find Him without setting about to do the things which He bid you to do. There is a law irrevocably decreed which governs these things.

The Nephites were keeping the appointed times with the Lord in His year-end festivals. In that process, He came to them. Set about doing what He bids you to do and He will likewise come to you. (This is described in *The Second Comforter: Conversing With the Lord Through the Veil.*) Keep His ways. He will be able to walk with you as you walk with Him.

One clarification that I think needs to be understood by those who have not read what I have written. I have never revealed anything sacred that has been revealed to me. I have taught the path. It is not necessary nor desirable to reveal personal matters, and I have not. It is important to teach the right way. Read what I've written and you will find that nothing improper or even difficult is taught there. It is taken from the scriptures. The scriptures are sufficient to teach you the way to eternal life. I only teach what I find in them.

PHILOSOPHIES OF MEN

The Gospel of Jesus Christ is a great whole. It requires an overall harmony between all its parts to be understood. Without that overall harmony it is jarring and discordant.

The problem with apostasy is that it forfeits truths which are necessary in order to comprehend the majesty of Christ's teachings. Those truths which get retained are not kept in balance with the rest. Simple virtues are kept while overall righteousness is forfeited.

No one can argue with the virtue of tolerance. But it is constrained and governed inside a larger context that prevents permissiveness and sloth.

No one can argue with the virtue of obedience. Indeed, obedience is itself one of the bedrock requirements of the Gospel. But divorced from the other virtues inside of which it is regulated, obedience can become a terrible weapon used to separate people from God's Holy Spirit and drive them into submission to "Popes and Priests." (Any man believed to be incapable of leading you into error is a "Pope.")

No one can argue against the virtue of patience. But when it is urged to prevent necessary action to develop a god-like people, then it has become a tool for deception and error and not a virtue at all.

Take any virtue and remove it from its overall context within the great Gospel whole and you see how apostasy can warp a people. They retain the conviction that they are still God's chosen disciples, because the virtues they practice are in fact, godly. However, they have become distorted, bloated and swollen. They are without harmony, capable of great evil or neglect, all the while celebrating their fidelity to the "truth" as they understand it.

You MUST understand doctrine. You MUST study the scriptures. But more important than anything else, you MUST seek to gain further light and knowledge by conversing with the Lord directly. Harmony of the whole is dependent upon His direct guidance and blessings. You simply cannot move forward a piece here and a bit there, while neglecting the whole composite picture of the Gospel. He will open it to your view. He will show you how one part is related to another, and that to another still, so that it all moves forward together. It is not to all be comprehended at once. It is to be gained a little bit of the whole here, a further harmony of things there, until the whole moves forward together. Always moving in balance, in harmony and as a complete magisterial revelation of God's will.

Latter-day Saints are not immune from this problem of disharmony. Indeed, it is the great challenge which we have faced since the time of the First Vision. Joseph's recalibrating of his own life was constant. He wanted to reward Martin Harris for his support, petitioned for permission to let him take the 116 pages of manuscript, and when he was told "no" he persisted. When he finally got the Lord's reluctant permission it was not for Martin Harris' benefit, but for Joseph's. Joseph was to learn a hard lesson about disregarding good advice from a superior Guide.[226] This comprehension of the harmony of the whole is what provoked Joseph to teach:

> "the nearer man approaches perfection, the clearer are his views, and the greater his enjoyments, till he has overcome the evils of his life and lost every desire for sin; and like the ancients, arrives at that point of faith where he is wrapped in the power and glory of his Maker, and is caught up to dwell with Him." (*DHC* 2:8)

Choose your teachers carefully. None of them will neglect to emphasize a virtue. However, without the whole of the Gospel in harmony in their own lives, they cannot bring it into harmony for you. Finding that harmony IS the great challenge in this lone and dreary world, filled as it is, with the philosophies of men mingled with scripture.

Why I Didn't Like It

I was asked by someone who liked the book *Odds Are You're Going To Be Exalted*, why I disliked it. My response is as follows:

I suppose first because it is filled with false doctrine and sentimental rubbish. It is unanchored in anything other than pure senti-

---

[226] D&C 3:1–8 "THE works, and the designs, and the purposes of God cannot be frustrated, neither can they come to naught. For God doth not walk in crooked paths, neither doth he turn to the right hand nor to the left, neither doth he vary from that which he hath said, therefore his paths are straight, and his course is one eternal round. Remember, remember that it is not the work of God that is frustrated, but the work of men; For although a man may have many revelations, and have power to do many mighty works, yet if he boasts in his own strength, and sets at naught the counsels of God, and follows after the dictates of his own will and carnal desires, he must fall and incur the vengeance of a just God upon him. Behold, you have been entrusted with these things, but how strict were your commandments; and remember also the promises which were made to you, if you did not transgress them. And behold, how oft you have transgressed the commandments and the laws of God, and have gone on in the persuasions of men. For, behold, you should not have feared man more than God. Although men set at naught the counsels of God, and despise his words— Yet you should have been faithful; and he would have extended his arm and supported you against all the fiery darts of the adversary; and he would have been with you in every time of trouble."

ment, contradicts the scriptures, and attributes motives to Heavenly Parents which are held by the author. It is worse than useless, it is misleading.

The numerosity argument takes groups who could not possibly be the audience for his book and makes them the statistical weight from which he reaches his conclusion. He takes folks who lived during the Nephite centuries of peace, the City of Enoch, and those who will live during the Millennium (whose numbers he speculates to be in the billions), then adds to those numbers all who die before the age of 8 (also a speculative but big number), then, after claiming the speculative total of all these will be far, far greater than those who merely slog along in mortality like us, he concludes that the odds are you're going to be exalted. Here's the logical fallacy of that whopper: First, the Nephites in ancient history didn't read the book. They're NOT in his audience. Neither was the City of Enoch's hosts; nor are the Millennial folk; nor are any of those who die before age 8. Meaning that the argument, IF it had validity, is an argument that THEY are going to be exalted. Not YOU. That is, the speculative total of those hosts are the ones who will benefit from their lives' condition. But none of them are readers of the book. So if the argument fits, then the title should have been: "*Odds Are They're Going To Be Exalted.*"

Second, the argument for the numbers is wholly speculative. We don't have a census for any of the prior Nephite, Enoch, City of Melchizedek, etc. populations. So without an actual number, we can't even make the argument. His conjecture for the Millennium is based upon Elder Bruce R. McConkie's speculation about the numerosity of that group. Repeating what Elder McConkie admits is his conjecture does not reduce it to fact. We simply can't say what the final numbers will be for these other groups.

Third, he conflates the promise of "salvation" with "exaltation." So far as I know there are no children under age 8 who have been sealed in marriage—a condition required for exaltation. Without an eternal marriage they are separate, single and angels; NOT exalted.[227] It is a quantum leap unsupported by scripture to conflate the promise of salvation for those who die before age 8, or who were not sealed in marriage from any of the other populations about which he speculates, with the promise of exaltation.

Fourth, he gives one bit of caution in his *Introduction* which the average reader will not catch. That caution is: "What follows is my perception of God's nature . . . " (p. xiv). That caution should be in **BOLD** and capitalized. In other words, the whole book is based upon his sentiments about God. These unanchored sentiments are NOT and never will be doctrine. They are just some guy's effeminate effort to avoid the rigors of confronting the narrowness, straitness and fewness of the Gospel's takers.

Going then to his sentiments about God, he writes: "The thought that God would promote something that would ensure that the vast majority of His children would never again be able to dwell in His presence is incomprehensible. And the assumption that our mother in heaven would idly sit back and allow such a guaranteed flop to eternally strip her of any interaction with her spirit offspring is equally unfathomable. Such could not—and did not—happen!"

There's not a stitch of support for this awesome conclusion. How does he know that? How does he presume to speak about a "mother in heaven" about whom nothing has been revealed? How does he know that she is not the champion of the plan? How does he know that she isn't absolutely persuaded that obedience to the

---

[227] D&C 132:16–17 "Therefore, when they are out of the world they neither marry nor are given in marriage; but are appointed angels in heaven, which angels are ministering servants, to minister for those who are worthy of a far more, and an exceeding, and an eternal weight of glory. For these angels did not abide my law; therefore, they cannot be enlarged, but remain separately and singly, without exaltation, in their saved condition, to all eternity; and from henceforth are not gods, but are angels of God forever and ever."

laws of perfection are the only protection of her children who do obey? How does he not recognize that to dwell with someone living a higher law, when the person refuses to obey that higher law, is more miserable than being cast out?[228] How does he fail to recognize that throughout nature from the hosts of animals born, relatively few ever reach adulthood and reproduce? Again, this natural process is a symbol of God's own great plan, is it not?[229] If so, why, if God cares with sentimentality about all His creations (i.e., that they fill the measure of their creation and have joy in their posterity), then why not let all them reproduce as adults? After all it takes about 10,000 sea turtles before you get a successful reproducing adult. Pretty much the case with frogs, sea life generally, and wildebeests—well, their young are essentially the roving McDonald's menu for all the African meat-eaters.

When he doesn't like a parable told by CHRIST, he attributes it to Matthew and dismisses it as Matthew's conjecture about numbers. (See footnote 2 on the top of page 133 of *Odds Are You're Going To Be Exalted*)

He absolutely contradicts Christ when he claims, without any support other than his own sentiment, "God does not require perfection of us in order for us to gain exaltation" (page 13). But Christ commanded:

"Therefore I would that ye should be perfect even as I, or your Father who is in heaven is perfect." (3 Nephi 12:48)

---

[228] Mormon 9:4 "Behold, I say unto you that ye would be more miserable to dwell with a holy and just God, under a consciousness of your filthiness before him, than ye would to dwell with the damned souls in hell."

[229] Moses 6:63 "And behold, all things have their likeness, and all things are created and made to bear record of me, both things which are temporal, and things which are spiritual; things which are in the heavens above, and things which are on the earth, and things which are in the earth, and things which are under the earth, both above and beneath: all things bear record of me."

He is a PhD in Theology. That education has done violence to his ability to see what the scriptures teach. Instead of using that education properly (i.e., to understand the fallacies of man's reasoning as they apply their philosophy), he has instead become persuaded by it and decided to measure truth by this damaging set of errors.

He thinks that if "most" people are lost then the plan is a failure. The measure of the Gospel's success does not lie in numerosity. It lies in the fact that if the whole of creation produces but one successful couple, then it will have all been worth it. Even then, if only one couple were exalted, then you still have an infinite number to follow, because they are by definition infinite and eternal as long as they produce seed.

I have marked up my copy for the first couple of chapters, then just relented and read it without a running commentary in the margins. But the book was an insult to my understanding of the truth. It attempts to urge the Calvinist notion of "irresistible grace" in new clothes. It attempts to give life to "grace" as Martin Luther championed the concept in LDS garb. It is a litany of Evangelical/Protestant philosophy mingled with scripture. And most astonishing of all, this cacophony of error is published by the good people at Deseret Book, as if its creeds were not included among those denounced by the Savior in His first visit with Joseph in the Grove.

I keep running in my mind: "Perhaps you do not believe in this great being Alonzo Gaskill proposes, who is surrounded by myriads of beings who have been saved, not for any act of theirs, but by His good pleasure?"

And the response thunders back: "I do not! I cannot comprehend such a being!"

I cannot recall where that dialogue, which is now simply part of my consciousness, came from. But it seems somehow sacred to me, coming from some source I trusted. Something which goes back long before 1990. But, alas, when I try to pin it down it eludes me.

I could go on, but I think it would degenerate into incautious words which will offend the average reader. Given my upbringing in Idaho, I will soon be making scatological references to bovine feces, reverting back to the lexicon of my pre-conversion youth. So I will meekly stop and settle back into the day's work.

I hope that answers the question.

Constantine and Correlation

I was asked in several ways how I reconcile some modern trends in the Church. One question was phrased this way:

> "Hearkening back to Elder Poleman's talk on the differences between the Church and the Gospel. It's often stated (over-stated?) that the church is the Kingdom of God in various meetings and most members conflate the Church with the Gospel (i.e., they are synonymous terms these days). Could you discuss the original differences (as intended in the scriptures) between "church" and "gospel"? Is church, as we currently know it (big meetinghouses, 3 hour blocks, weekly attendance, etc.), the same thing as "church" in the times of the Old and New Testaments?"

Here's how I reconcile it all: I don't. What I do is reflect upon history. Here are a few of my ruminations:

Christianity became diverse quite early on. Almost immediately after the closing of the New Testament, the diversity began to metastasize.

There were those who viewed Christ as a normal man, who had been "adopted" by the Father at the time of His baptism. These were called "Adoptionists."

There were those who believed that Christ was just a normal man, but that He had a divine spirit inhabit Him temporarily from the time of His baptism until the time of His crucifixion, at which time the divine spirit left. It was incomprehensible to them that God would suffer and die. Therefore, they developed a theory in which He did not.

There were those who believed that Christ was a transcendent spirit, and never corporeal as other men were. They believed that He manifested Himself as if he were a mortal, but never truly was mortal. They did not believe it possible for God to become incarnate.

There were those who believed that Christ taught a secret Gospel to His insiders, and that the public teachings were misleading. It was the private "gnosis" that would save you.

There were those who believed that Christ was a separate and distinct being from God the Father, and that the result was that there were two gods and not one.

There were those who argued that if they were separate then it violated the idea of "monotheism" and therefore, God the Father, Christ and the Holy Ghost had to be one, single person. However incomprehensible that may be, there was only one being, manifesting itself in three forms.

There were those who believed priesthood authority was immutable, and once conferred it could not be lost no matter what the conduct of the person ordained. That is, authority was not dependent at all upon righteous behavior, and even a thoroughly wicked man, once ordained, held priesthood authority no matter what he did.

There were those who believed that priesthood authority was entirely dependent upon faithful living, and that a failure to live according to God's will terminated the authority of that man. This movement was named after a North African priest named Arius who remained devoted during the persecutions and was blinded and crippled by those who were seeking to destroy the Christian faith.

Well, by 324 A.D. the whole thing had become riddled with controversies and sects. Therefore, when King Constantine, who had battled his way into sole ownership of the Roman Emperor's seat, determined to adopt a state religion (he chose Christianity as that state religion) he presumed he was taking a harmonious, consistent faith. Upon learning that there were strong internal Christian disputes, some of which led to violence between professors of the various beliefs, he decided that he needed to put down the disputations.

In a fit of practicality, King Constantine convened the great council at Nicea, and summoned all the Bishops of Christianity to a single gathering. At the gathering he demanded they come to an agreement on what the Christian faith believed. He could not tolerate disputes leading to violence in the newly adopted Roman state religion.

This council at Nicea was the first attempt at correlation. The result had little to do with the truth. It had to do with peace for the Roman state. Constantine himself did not believe in the doctrine. He believed in the effectiveness of the faith as a basis for political power, domestic security and ease of ruling a diverse population scattered about on three continents. When the results were achieved, he then exiled the handful of dissenters and 'voila, Historic Christianity began. That Historic Christianity remained correlated and of a singular view until the split between Constantinople and Rome at about 1000 A.D. It became further uncorrelated in the 1500's with Martin Luther.

Once you start letting doctrinal disputes develop you wind up with a split empire, and internal loss of government. The original effort was imposed at the tip of a sword. When there were dissenters, they were exiled, or eventually made "heretic." When the final step was taken, and the intellectual buttress supplied by Bishop Ambrose's arguments, it at last became possible for "heresy" or "here-

tics" to be snubbed out by murder. The persecuted became the persecutors. They were justified by the change, having a correlated
promise that the *faith* ratified the reasons that allowed you to persecute, torture and kill those who strayed from the "one true, Catholic
faith." After all, if you could reclaim them merely by torture of the
body, how much better than allowing them to lapse into eternal torment by being consigned to hell. An endless "Hell" also being an
invention of the Historic Christian faith. So it was really good to do
that burning, racking, thumb-dislocating, flaying, stuff after all. All in
a day's work to convert the wayward soul back to Christ.

Elder Lee, while still a member of the Twelve, began the correlation process in the LDS Church. It was his crowning achievement
when he became President. Now everything is in harmony. That
harmony has come at the price of developing the internal idea of
"apostasy" based upon the doctrine we believe in. A test which was
altogether alien to Joseph Smith. Joseph said, when a brother Brown
was being threatened with excommunication for his error in doctrine:

> "I did not like the old man being called up for erring in doc-
> trine. It looks too much like the Methodist, and not like the
> Latter-day Saints. Methodists have creeds which a man must
> believe or be asked out of their church. I want the liberty of
> thinking and believing as I please. It feels so good not to be
> trammeled. It does not prove that a man is not a good man
> because he errs in doctrine." (*DHC* 5:340)

The price we have paid to date for correlation is a fraction of
what will ultimately be paid, if history informs us of anything. It is
now possible to be a "Mormon heretic" for believing doctrine which
someone else has determined should be discarded—a thing which
was unimaginable at the time of Joseph Smith, even as a result of an
actual error in doctrine. For Joseph, the way to reclaim some errant
Saint was, well, confined to the means permitted by revelation:

"only by persuasion, by long—suffering, by gentleness and meekness, and by love unfeigned; By kindness, and pure knowledge, which shall greatly enlarge the soul without hypocrisy, and without guile" (D&C 121:41–42)

Today that has been expanded to excommunication for doctrinal errors. When such a thing takes place, years go by before such a person is re-welcomed into the church, and then only after receiving permission from the First Presidency. So the correlation of doctrine has slipped already into a coercive use of authority within the church. Instead of persuading using better doctrine to correct an error, we punish and silence them through a method that was alien to the original pattern.

History is an interesting thing to study. Particularly at the beginnings of any religious movement. It always progresses from movement to institution. Once it becomes an institution, as King Constantine realized, the institution itself must protect itself against disorder. That protection comes, as history shows, at the price of contradicting the original premise upon which the movement began.

The ironies of this are always astonishing. But somehow those who live through it never realize the irony while it is happening. Only later, as it has taken its full bloom in torture, killing, flaying, racking and destroying the lives of people does the original, root moments in which the errors began to creep in get recognized. Those making the errors in the first place are celebrated for centuries as "Saints" and "Popes."

The history of religion, generally, is a transition between the movement stage, where there is always a charismatic or gifted core from which it springs, to the institution stage. Unfortunately for the institution, gifted folks aren't usually good businessmen. (Joseph Smith, for example, had a pending petition for bankruptcy when he was killed.) Once the movement gets underway, it gets co-opted by businessmen, managers and captains of industry. Folks like Emperor Constantine, who if nothing else was a consummate manager.

Managers crave order. They dislike the chaos of the Spirit, which is always unstable, unpredictable, and uncorrelateable.[230] As a result, they change a movement into an institution. Institutions require order. The nature of an institution requires managers, bankers, businessmen and generals. They consider their "product" to be religion, and they manage and sell their product as if they were General Motors, or the Roman Empire. The kind of freedom that gave birth to the movement must be disciplined, marshaled and controlled.

Our faith is in a complete internal opposition at the moment. To become a Mormon, if you aren't born one, you must go through a conversion process which is grounded in the bedrock of revelation. You must pray and ask God if the Book of Mormon is true, and then you are to get an answer from God. We expect you to have a revelatory experience to join. But, once you have joined, then the scope of your revelatory experience is strictly limited. You must NOT question any leader, nor ever expect God to tell you something about any subject over which you do not preside, nor to ever realize through the inspiration of the Spirit that there are foolish, vain and wrong notions circulating about. You must NOT notice that Deseret Book has become a repository of false and foolish books parading sentimentality as if it were salvific. You should never consider God's revelations to you as something to be honored apart from what the institution says, does, does not do, or does poorly. Indeed, the voice of God will come to you solely and exclusively through the institution. If you need to know something, then the institution will tell you. Unless you hear your orders from it, then stay as you are.

---

[230] John 3:8 "The wind bloweth where it listeth, and thou hearest the sound thereof, but canst not tell whence it cometh, and whither it goeth: so is every one that is born of the Spirit."

We are at a cross-roads. At the moment the movement is ending. The institution is at its pinnacle of complete triumph. When the process concludes, it will not welcome converts who will challenge the basic assumptions that they, having received revelation to come on-board in the first place, must now quash the Spirit which raises so many questions about how things are proceeding. Then to be Mormon will mean to be correlated. Correlated body and soul. An institutional man. No longer distinct, unique, or creative. Disciplined, orderly, subservient, and under control. Then the institution will become a remarkably appealing tool for not only the captains of industry, but also the heads of state. It will become an almost irresistible tool to be employed as part of governing the world. And so history repeats itself.

Well, these direful lessons are ones which can be either relived or avoided. But to avoid them people who are inside the process must step outside their own times and context and to view everything within a larger picture. I don't think bankers, businessmen and lawyers do that often. Indeed, the well educated who lack inspiration are not qualified. Only the meek. Only the humble. As Nephi described:

> "they have all gone astray save it be a few, who are the humble followers of Christ; nevertheless, they are led, that in many instances they do err because they are taught by the precepts of men" (2 Nephi 28:14).

That was the group to whom I dedicated my book *The Second Comforter.*

Then I pull myself back into the present reality, and let it all wash over me like a wave. I take a deep breath and I realize how grateful I am for any bit of goodness I can find anywhere. And in The Church of Jesus Christ of Latter-day Saints I can find a lot of good. And I count my blessings and rise determined to remain a true, faithful, active Latter-day Saint throughout my life; and to die as an active and contributing fellow member. But reconciling everything, well, I'm told that's not my calling to do anyway. And I'm grateful to sustain other men to grapple with the management of this historic trend, fraught as it is with the damnation or exaltation of the souls of men. Particularly when they claim to speak in the Lord's name. For them there is only an "on/off" button. They can't have it any other way. Either they speak truthfully in the name of the Lord and with His authorization, or they use His name in vain. I certainly wouldn't want to be put into that spot. So I gratefully sustain those who rush to fill the offices when asked to do so. As one who is simply unfit to serve in such a call, I thank God for my disqualification.

Correlating the Chaos

Despite what I wrote yesterday about the process of correlation, there is of course another argument in favor of the process. That argument would be based on the exact same history of the transition from Primitive Christianity into Historic Christianity. That is, by the Fourth Century those claiming to be part of the original faith had become so divided that they were actually killing one another over doctrinal disputes. They had a riot in Antioch wherein competing congregations went to battle over possession of the synagogue where they met. An actual street fight, people getting killed and all.

So, rising from rancor of doctrinal dispute into a singular set of beliefs which could later become "orthodox" and all else be branded "heterodox" or, with time, "heretical" was essential just as Constantine knew it would be. Without there being a singular set of beliefs the faith which would eventually sweep the European Continent and beyond could not have brought any unity at all. So it was a good thing, right?

That is the argument for. It is quite compelling, actually. I do not underestimate its strength. However, it simply does not persuade me.

Admittedly the violence was foolish and wrong. But the violent sects were never Christ's anyway. They never got what He was teaching. Let them run their violent course and, in time, they will never attract a large audience anyway.

Additionally, the definition of "orthodoxy" was not based upon truth or revelation, it was based only upon what was practical. Constantine never concerned himself with the truth. The legacy of that error lives on. The descendants of that original council in Nicea all condemn us as "Non-Christian" because we reject their creeds, beginning with the Nicean Creed, which defined God.

Inside the Restoration there was an order which allowed tolerance (as Joseph originally envisioned it) of divergent views of doctrine. A consensus wasn't necessary. Only knowing that we were united as a people was necessary. How we viewed different subjects or doctrines was to be left to each individual. The way such people became "one" is something I've already explained in the "Becoming One" post.

We've had healthy and meaningful doctrinal disagreements inside the Church without any ill effects. President Brigham Young believed that God knew everything, was not progressing in knowledge, and that if he were progressing in knowledge it would make God's plans vulnerable to overthrow by something which He did not understand. Elder Orson Pratt thought God was progressing in every respect, including gaining knowledge. He thought the principle of "eternal progression" was the greatest joy and happiness and God enjoys the benefits of that great joy. For him it was a principle of joy. These two never agreed.

Widstoe was in disagreement with Joseph Fielding Smith. Publication of *Man, His Origin and Destiny* was nearly a seditious act by Joseph Fielding Smith and incurred the rancor of President McKay. President McKay shut the thing down at that point and wouldn't let either one publish further by adopting a rule that no-one who is a

General Authority is permitted to publish without permission of the First Presidency.

We survived. We tolerated. There wasn't a group of violent Widstoeites attacking the Smithites to overtake the Pioneer Ward building. We were civil. I do not think it did anything more than raise the blood pressure of the High Priests' Groups. Something I believe preferable to the somnambulism of that assortment we see today. Doctrinal differences sort themselves out by persuasion, pure knowledge and love. Eventually, when the problem or confusion becomes acute and we need an answer, then we can all unite and go to the Lord in prayer, seeking mercy from Him for the dispute we cannot ourselves solve. Then, through revelation, we can come to a consensus as we hear from Him. We don't use that model very often.

Right now the Correlation Department is actively polling to give updated information to the Brethren about what policies, programs and procedures are effective. I have a lengthy questionnaire at my home to fill out right now. I don't know if I'm going to do it. I've commented on that process and Elder Holland's reference to it before. I think it is more dangerous to use the polling and focus group approach to manage the diversity of opinions than it is to tolerate them.

What loss is it to us if the church simply refuses to take a position on the Gay Rights Ordinance; while some Saints believe it to be appropriate and others believe it to be the sinful prelude to Sodom and judgments of God. These opinions can be discussed, debated and people can make up their own minds. Joseph's position of tolerance worked, when we tried it. When we had keen and publicly expressed disagreements on doctrine between the First Presidency and members of the Twelve it did not harm us at all. It made us more interesting.

Now that we have chosen to establish "orthodoxy" we are risking the freedom to be individually accountable for our beliefs before God. We have also lost doctrinal adventurism. This is because of our critics.

You see one of the harms of tolerating divergent opinions about doctrine is the clamor of the critics. They take a quote here and juxtapose it with another quote there, and say that Mormonism is a bundle of confusion. We targeted that in the Correlation process and have attempted to entirely stamp out the divergent or disagreeing doctrinal statements or positions. We want "oneness" in a different way than Paul suggested it in the post I referenced above. In doing so, we have conceded the point to our critics, and now make unity of doctrine a greater virtue than freedom to progress and develop our own understanding by degrees.

Sometimes what you understand at one point is not what you understand at another. Hugh Nibley, for example, said nothing he wrote ten years earlier would be binding upon him because he continued to discover and learn. We would be benefited from a similar approach all the way from the top to the bottom. New converts will, by degrees, leave their earlier faith traditions behind them. Or they won't. Instead they will bring with them an understanding from those traditions which have a resonance with the Book of Mormon or something in the Doctrine and Covenants which had escaped all our notice before. And we will all be "added upon" by tolerating their view, even embracing their view. Freedom always pays dividends which control cannot.

Well, I'm not trying to solve the issue. I'm only trying to raise the issue. It is important.

Peoplehood

One of the very substantial differences in the way we are currently evolving is almost unnoticed. I've tried to capture the difference in what I've written by using the terms "movement" in contrast to "institution." Those terms help to explain the notion, but it is really something more than that. I'm going to use a different way to explain it in this post, and see if I can get a little closer to the real underlying process which is now underway.

The original development under Joseph Smith was something quite distinct from all existing faiths. It was not just a new religion. It was a wholesale resurrection of an ancient concept of "Peoplehood." It was radical. Its purpose was to change diverse assortments of people, from every culture and faith, with every kind of ethnic and racial composition, into a new kind of People. They were to be united under the banner of a New and Everlasting Covenant, resurrecting the ancient Hebraic notion of nationhood and Peoplehood. No matter what their former culture was, they were adopted inside a new family, a covenant family. Status was defined not be virtue of what you believed or confessed, but instead by what covenants you have assumed.

What returned through Joseph Smith was not a religion, nor an institution, nor merely a faith. It was instead the radical notion that an ancient covenant family was being regathered into a separate People. This return to ancient roots brought with it, as the hallmark of its source of power, the idea of renewed covenants that brought each individual into direct contract with God. It did not matter what they believed. It only mattered that they accepted and took upon them the covenant.

Once inside the new People, there was a new culture where ancient ties returned to bind the hearts together. There was a dietary regimen where the People were reminded at every meal that they were distinct and apart from the world. There was the gift of sacred clothing, in which they were reminded of their separateness by the things put upon their skin. There were financial sacrifice of tithes, gathered from the People to help the People. The fortunes of all were intertwined with each other by the gathering of tithes and offerings into the Bishop's storehouse to help the poor and needy among the People. It was NOT a religion. It was a People. It was to become The People. And The People were required to extend to all others the same equal opportunity to become also part of the covenant.

This is different from a religion. It was cultural, personal, and as distinct as a Jew views himself to be from a Christian. To a Jew, religion is a part of the equation. They share blood with other Jews, and therefore even if a Jew is not attending weekly synagogue meetings, they retain their status as one of the Jews.

Religion on the other hand is merely a brand name for a sentiment. One can be a Presbyterian or a Lutheran and still belong to the same Elks Lodge. There is nothing really distinct between the two, other than where they meet for an hour or two on Sundays. Apart from that, they identify culturally as "Protestants" and brothers. There is no great distinction, and the theological differences which separate them are so trivial that a doctrinal disagreement between them is unlikely.

Mormonism has taken a direct course-change where the original elements of separate Peoplehood are now viewed as an impediment to wider acceptance. The distinctions are being minimized in order to undo the conflicts that marred the relationship between Mormonism and the larger American society. The lessons learned from those conflicts have led to the idea that we must become more actively engaged in public relations. Our commitment to the public relations process has informed us that we have to become less distinct to get along with others. We need to drop our misunderstood and offensive claims to distinctions that claim superiority, and urge instead the things that we share with the Presbyterians and Lutherans. The ultimate end of that process is to make it just as meaningless and controversial a thing for a Mormon to belong to and fellowship with the Elks Lodge as it is for the Presbyterian and Lutheran. This is one of the great goals of the Correlation process and the public relations effort of The Church of Jesus Christ of Latter-day Saints.

The outreach at present is merely an attempt to get people to accept the church as another form of Historic Christianity, claiming equality among peers, without any desire to confront or cause conflict. The notion of Peoplehood is being suppressed. Any claims of superiority of the faith are suppressed.

Enthusiastic scholarship is working alongside the larger public relations effort. The work of Robinson at BYU, for example, in his reconciliatory book, (co-authored with a member of the Evangelical-based Denver Theological Seminary faculty) "How Wide the Divide," made an attempt to discuss Evangelical Protestant notions alongside Mormon notions and to minimize any differences. The underlying presumption is that we are both merely religions. As fellow religions we share an attempt to come to God through teachings we believe in and scriptural texts we share.

Reconciliation between what Joseph Smith restored and other religions should never have been a goal. Joseph's restoration was not a church. It was not a religion. It was not a bundle of beliefs. By trying to reach a common footing among other mainstream Christian faiths we have to first abandon the very different footing upon which Joseph established the Restoration.

The original Restoration could never be like any of "them." They were churches. Joseph restored Peoplehood. To go from what Joseph restored to a common footing requires us to first abandon the concept that we are neither a new form of Christianity, nor a return to

Jewish antecedents. We are something quite different from either. We are an Hebraic resurrection of God's People, clothed with a covenant, and engaged in a direct relationship with God that makes us distinct from all other people.

When we view ourselves as a Christian faith, we deconstruct the very foundation upon which we began. We aren't that. We can never be part of Historic Christianity. And yet that has been our front-and-center effort through the focus on public relations and the scientific study of what words we should use to advance our acceptance in the world.

Read the earliest of Mormon materials and you will be shocked by how differently they viewed themselves from how we now view ourselves. They were building a separate People. They invited all to come and partake of the covenant, renounce their prior errors, and return to living as one of God's New and Everlasting Covenant holders.

To rid ourselves of that tradition, we need to assume the elements of a typical religion. Rather than defining ourselves as a separate People, we turn to defining a set of beliefs. Establishing an orthodoxy and then insisting upon uniformity of belief to belong to the orthodox religion is the way of the Catholics and Protestants. They are bound together NOT by their peoplehood but instead by their confessions of faith. So as you de-emphasize our Peoplehood, you must then begin to emphasize and control an orthodox statement or confession of faith.

These dynamics are worth very careful thought. There is an actual consensus among church leaders that this is the right way to proceed. A discussion about it among Latter-day Saints has not even begun at the rank and file level. The transition takes place over decades, and unless someone first creates a vocabulary for the problem, we don't even have the capacity to discuss or notice what is happening and why.

This post has gone on too long. Not really a blog post subject. It's a book-length subject. I make fleeting comments about something that would take pages to develop. But I doubt I'll write the needed book. Instead I will try to bring the idea into the consciousness of you good people and let it percolate about. Surely some of you can do something about it.

Micah Chapter 3

O heads of Jacob, and ye princes of the house of Israel; Is it not for you to know judgment?

Who hate the good, and love the evil; who pluck off their skin from off them, and their flesh from off their bones; Who also eat the flesh of my people, and flay their skin from off them; and they break their bones, and chop them in pieces, as for the pot, and as flesh within the caldron.

Then shall they cry unto the Lord, but he will not hear them: he will even hide his face from them at that time, as they have behaved themselves ill in their doings.

Thus saith the Lord concerning the prophets that make my people err, that bite with their teeth, and cry, Peace; and he that putteth not into their mouths, they even prepare war against him.

Therefore night shall *be* unto you, that ye shall not have a vision; and it shall be dark unto you, that ye shall not divine; and the sun shall go down over the prophets, and the day shall be dark over them.

Then shall the seers be ashamed, and the diviners confounded: yea, they shall all cover their lips; for there is no answer of God.

But truly I am full of power by the spirit of the Lord, and of judgment, and of might, to declare unto Jacob his transgression, and to Israel his sin.

Hear this, I pray you, ye heads of the house of Jacob, and princes of the house of Israel, that abhor judgment, and pervert all equity.

They build up Zion with blood, and Jerusalem with iniquity.

The heads thereof judge for reward, and the priests thereof teach for hire, and the prophets thereof divine for money: yet will they lean upon the Lord, and say, Is not the Lord among us? none evil can come upon us.

Therefore shall Zion for your sake be plowed *as* a field, and Jerusalem shall become heaps, and the mountain of the house as the high places of the forest.

Mother's Day

Happy Mother's Day.

The single greatest institution is also the most successful one in all the earth's history. Mothers have kept civilization together from the beginning.

Fathers have been far less valiant in history than have mothers. Fathers have forsaken their responsibilities to bear priesthood and perpetuate the Gospel with such regularity that the history of mankind is predominately a history of apostasy. Mothers however, have continued to bear, raise, nurture and love their children.

God bless those who are our mothers or the mothers of our children. Today we should honor them in thought and deed.

(I'm doing all the cooking today. And all the dishes, too. I think I'll use TGIFridays to get them done . . .)

"of strong faith and a firm mind"

Consider this:

> "[N]either have angels ceased to minister unto the children of men. For behold, they are subject unto him, to minister according to the word of his command, showing themselves unto them of strong faith and a firm mind in every form of godliness. And the office of their ministry is to call men unto repentance, and to fulfil and to do the work of the covenants of the Father, which he hath made unto the children of men, to prepare the way among the children of men, by declaring the word of Christ unto the chosen vessels of the Lord, that they may bear testimony of him." (Moroni 7:29–31)

Note that angels show themselves to those "of strong faith and a firm mind." Also, that the visit will require them to whom such visits come to "bear testimony of [Christ]" as a result of those visitations.

From Joseph Smith:

> "A fanciful and flowery and heated imagination beware of; because the things of God are of deep import; and time, and experience, and careful and ponderous and solemn thoughts can only find them out. Thy mind, O man! if thou wilt lead a soul unto salvation, must stretch as high as the utmost heavens, and search into and contemplate the darkest abyss, and the broad expanse of eternity—thou must commune with God." (TPJS, 137)

Note that the "imagination" is not useful in gaining communion with God. Fanciful, flowery and heated imaginative thoughts will detract, not contribute, to knowing Him. The only way is to possess the same mental state as Moroni refers to—careful, sober, solemn, deep thoughts are required. The mind must reach into heaven as well as the darkest abyss. The opposition of things in this creation and the balance of those opposites will cause you to encounter the worst as you strive to enjoy the best. All is kept in balance throughout the process.

A person can't imagine they have salvation. They must "know" they possess it. The heavens should declare it to them. When the heavens bestow this knowledge upon a person, it is an anchor to their soul and they will never fall. But until then, a person needn't suppose they possess something which God has not declared by His own voice to be theirs.

True teachers will labor to help you understand how real, deliberate, attainable, and necessary this process is to engage in. They will not ask you to follow them. They will teach you how to follow God, and obtain from God knowledge of salvation. False teachers will distract you. They will tell you all is right, that there is enough good being done in your life to merit God's favor, and that it is not necessary for you to do more than belong to a privileged group.

You cannot possess the knowledge which will save you until you have learned for yourself that God lives, and that He has promised to you eternal life.

Why Wait?

The question was asked as to whether receiving the Second Comforter is necessary before you die, or if the afterlife supplies an adequate substitute. This requires the evaluation of two separate concepts.

First, the Second Comforter means a visit or personal appearance to someone by Christ. However, the *appearance* is not as important as the ministry of the Lord. He "comforts" those to whom He appears.

He will "not leave you comfortless, he will come to you."[231] Christ *and* His Father will "make their abode with you."[232] Meaning that the Son will bring you to the Father, and the Father will receive you as His son. This appearance is not merely "in the heart," but is an actual appearance or visit.[233]

However, the purpose of the ministry, the reason for the "abode" with you, the "comfort" that is promised by the Lord, involves the promise of eternal life. The promise of eternal life has been made an equivalency by the Lord in a revelation given in modern times. That is, the end or result of the ministry of Christ as the Second Comforter is to have the promise of eternal life. In a modern revelation the word of the Lord was given to a group of Latter-day Saints in which the promise of their exaltation was extended to them, and the Lord made this the equivalent to "another Comforter."

Here is what was said:

> "Wherefore, I now send upon you another Comforter, even upon you my friends, that it may abide in your hearts, even the Holy Spirit of promise; which other Comforter is the same that I promised unto my disciples, as is recorded in the testimony of John. This Comforter is the promise which I give unto you of eternal life, even the glory of the celestial kingdom; Which glory is that of the church of the Firstborn, even of God, the holiest of all, through Jesus Christ his Son—" (D&C 88:3–5)

---

[231] John 14:18 "I will not leave you comfortless: I will come to you."

[232] John 14:23 "Jesus answered and said unto him, If a man love me, he will keep my words: and my Father will love him, and we will come unto him, and make our abode with him."

[233] D&C 130:3 "John 14:23—The appearing of the Father and the Son, in that verse, is a personal appearance; and the idea that the Father and the Son dwell in a man's heart is an old sectarian notion, and is false."

Therefore, as a singular appearance, should the Lord appear to you, you have received the Second Comforter. However, His ministry is to bring you to the point at which you can receive the promise of eternal life, membership in the Church of the Firstborn, and the promise of the Celestial Kingdom as your eternal inheritance. In the fullest sense, therefore, the final promise of exaltation in the Celestial Kingdom can also be called the Second Comforter, since that is the result of His taking up His abode with you.

The second concept is really a question: Would it be preferable to have the promise of eternal life now than to die uncertain as to your eternal state? If so, then why would you waste your life now in hopes that some other opportunity may exist at some other stage?

If the answer to these questions are "yes" then the original question is simply unimportant. Why wait? The opportunity given to you now should not be forfeited, nor should the work be delayed. Don't dismiss the Lord's offered assistance for what you can achieve in mortality for the possibility of something in the after-life.

Charge to Twelve

This is really a "comment" in response to a question belonging to the earlier post on Elder Packer's Testimony. However, it was too long to put in there as a reply comment, so will be put up here as a blog entry. It is an interruption. Sorry. There is a fellow asking for it, and I delayed for so long that I feel I owe him a response. I am really writing this to him.

Taken from *Mormon Hierarchy: Extensions of Power.* (A good book by Quinn. He's written some bad ones, but this is not one of them. I think he was stinging from criticism and in this book proved he was still a good historian.)

"In 1835 Joseph Smith and Oliver Cowdery emphasized to the newly organized Quorum of the Twelve Apostles that their calling was charismatic, evangelical and also institutional. Of the three, the charismatic definition of the apostleship was the earliest, going back to 1829. Cowdery told the new apostles: 'It is necessary that you receive a testimony from heaven for yourselves; so that you can bear testimony to the truth of the Book of Mormon, and that you have seen the face of God.' Then he continued: 'That is more than the testimony of an angel . . . Never cease striving until you have seen God, face to face.' Cowdery acknowledged that most of the new apostles had depended on visions of others for their faith and suggested that some might even be skeptical of visions. Thus it was not necessary to see Jesus to be chosen as an apostle. However, once ordained each man had a lifelong obligation to seek this charismatic experience: a vision of deity. Some apostles from 1835 onward reported having had such visions before their ordination. Apostles in the nineteenth century referred publicly to their visionary witness.

" . . . some LDS apostles, including Orson Pratt and Heber J. Grant, felt inadequate because they had not had such encounters.

"In the twentieth century, charismatic apostleship changed in several ways. First, the 'charge' at ordination no longer obligated apostles to seek visions. Second, the Presidency and apostles began down-playing the importance of these experiences. Third, apostles began speaking of a non-visionary 'special witness of Christ' by the Holy Ghost in terms which allowed listeners to conclude that the apostles referred to an actual appearance of deity. Fourth, apostles were reluctant to discuss their visionary experiences publicly. Fifth, evidence indicates that a decreasing number of apostles experienced visions before or after ordination.

"The change in the apostolic 'charge' apparently began with the appointment of Reed Smoot as an apostle in 1900. General church authorities had long regarded him as 'reliable in business, but [he] has little or no faith.' President Lorenzo Snow blessed him to receive 'the light of the Holy Ghost' so that he could bear testimony of Jesus Christ and Joseph Smith. That was an extraordinary departure from the apostolic charge as given since 1835.

" . . . Twentieth-century apostles began applying this 'as if' approach to their spoken testimonies. Usually this involved wording their 'special witness' of Christ in a way that encouraged listeners to assume the leader has had a more dramatic encounter with the divine than actually claimed."

The full discussion ranges from pages 1–6 and would require too much typing to do it here. But the above, taken only from pages 1–2, gives you some more particulars than my brief reference before. The whole discussion is documented with references from the Church's archives where the writer reviewed the transcripts of the actual ordinations, etc. They are all set out in the footnotes, which are omitted from the quote I have excerpted above.

What Lack I Yet?

I was asked this question:

"Do you know with surety IN ADVANCE of doing some incredibly hard sacrifice that it is the Lord asking it of you, or do you come to know that it is His will AS you do it?"

My response:
You will know with absolute certainty that the request came from the Lord.
The request will be difficult, or a sacrifice.
HOWEVER, whether the person recognizes at the moment or only in hindsight that it was required for them to develop the faith necessary for redemption is not universal. Some know at the time,

some only know in hindsight. What is absolutely universal is that when the test has been passed, the faith exists. When it does, it will be enough for redemption and the promise of eternal life.

Joseph knew he had the promise of eternal life[234] before he went to Carthage to die. He knew he was going to die. Death was not his great challenge, but the physical ratification of the faith which already existed in him. The earlier trials had been enough to prove him and put that power within him. His death was an extension of existing faith and knowledge.

The order of things is established and can be known. The details of how it unfolds in individual lives will be specific to the individual. Whether the person realizes the final great test is underway or not will depend on the person. I did not. I only came to realize in hindsight what was underway.

One of the parables in *Ten Parables* shows how the heavens can interact with man, but man be unaware of the full agenda conducted. I have referred to that tenth parable several times. By the way, that parable is NOT a description of the test required to obtain the faith for redemption. It is just a parable about how heaven works to provide missing virtue or grace to a life that is lacking something, but still worthy of preservation.

Be Careful What You Ask For

It was weird, really. This guy went to visit with God in His House, but when he got there he couldn't see Him. I mean he couldn't "see" Him. God was there. They both were there. But God, as it turned out, the guy was unable to detect His presence.

---

[234] D&C 132:49 "For I am the Lord thy God, and will be with thee even unto the end of the world, and through all eternity; for verily I seal upon you your exaltation, and prepare a throne for you in the kingdom of my Father, with Abraham your father."

He went to the optometrist and got his vision checked. Everything worked. So he was left to wonder why it was he couldn't see God.

Some study later he concluded that although God was made of matter,[235] He must be more refined or pure, and therefore not detectable by normal eyesight.[236] Only "purer" eyes could see him. So he used Visine, returned to see Him, and still no luck.

Well, he decided to take up the matter in prayer and offered this supplication to the Almighty: "I'm beginning to doubt your love for me. Tell you what, you show yourself to me and I'll know you love me. But it you stay outside my field of vision then I know you're avoiding me and therefore don't love me." God loves everyone, see. And so the request was framed in a way to force God to make Himself visible. The man thought himself clever.

Well, God decided to take the fellow up on the request, as He always does. First the man's house burned down, then his business failed, then he got cancer. As he was in the hospital his family abandoned him, and his friends all thought he was cursed by God, and stayed away. So he waited out the final days of his mortality alone, in pain, and without possessions.

As a charity case the hospital treated him with some neglect, giving him many hours to suffer alone in his bed. Suffering brought about meditation and prayer.

It was during the last few hours of his life, as he lay fevered and in pain, that his burdens overwhelmed him and he sought in desperate humility for relief from God. His prayer was: "Oh Lord, I know I have done less than I should have with the things I have been given.

---

[235] Luke 24:39 "Behold my hands and my feet, that it is I myself: handle me, and see; for a spirit hath not flesh and bones, as ye see me have."

[236] D&C 131:7 "There is no such thing as immaterial matter. All spirit is matter, but it is more fine or pure, and can only be discerned by purer eyes;"

I long to part this life clean of my failings. Can you forgive me, a wretched sinner, for my many failings?" He expected little. Hoping only to salve his conscious by this prayer.

The Lord, who had been in the room for days, suddenly came into view. Startled by this appearance, the man asked: "Is it you, Lord?"

"Yes," came the reply.

"Can you forgive me?"

"Oh, I've done that long ago. Yes, you are certainly forgiven. I'm here for you to see I love you. You asked for that in your prayer a year ago and I've been working so that your eyes could become more refined. Now, at last they are."

Now the man could see what great love the Lord truly had for him. For in the extremity of his dying hour, he had a companion to comfort him.

He died in joy. The nurse thought it was the morphine.

ISAIAH 53

Isaiah 53:1

Isaiah 53:1 begins with the questions:

"Who hath believed our report? and to whom is the arm of the Lord revealed?"

These two questions remain as timely today as they were when asked 750 years before Christ's birth. As to the first question:

The report is Isaiah's testimony of the coming Messiah.

It is plural, although delivered by a lone prophet, because God Himself authorized the message to be delivered. Therefore it is not "my" but rather "our" report.

The question concerns the audience's "belief" in the report, because it contradicts the ideas held by them. It will tell them something remarkably different from what they though to be true.

As to the second question:

"The arm of the Lord" is a symbol of His strength or might.

To have the strength of the Lord revealed to someone is to have them come into knowledge of Him and His ways.

His ways are not what men presume they are. They are directed to much higher, much holier ends. The strength of the Lord as it will unfold in the chapter which follows is based upon the suffering He undertook for us.

The chapter that follows this opening verse is framed in the past tense. This is called the "prophetic perfect" tense. To the prophet, the events have been seen. To him, they are in the past. Therefore, future events are framed as if they already occurred. Prophets to whom things are shown will often frame their message in the past tense, even though they speak of things in the future. You find it throughout prophecy.

Isaiah 53:2

Isaiah 53:2 states this about the Messiah:

"For he shall grow up before him as a tender plant, and as a root out of a dry ground: he hath no form nor comeliness; and when we shall see him, there *is* no beauty that we should desire him."

The first "he" is a reference to the Messiah. The second "him" is either the Father in Heaven or Israel.

The Messiah will be a "tender plant" or a "root" that arises "out of a dry ground" because the barren, unproductive, rancorous people among whom He will be sent will not be producing redeemed souls when He comes. They will be racked with religious falsehoods; ambitious and controlling men who have obtained their leadership through political maneuvering, influence peddling and purchase.

The acquisition of religious status was so normal a thing in that day that the Apostles would later be asked by Simon if he could purchase the priesthood from them.[237] And yet the Messiah will find the way back to opening the heavens, receiving power from on high, and then go about preaching and leading other souls to redemption as well. For Him the barren, dry ground will be no impediment to salvation.

The Messiah will "have no form nor comeliness," and have "no beauty." Not because of His physical appearance, however. It will be due to the lack of position, absence of credentials, failure to hold a leadership position, and outsider status which makes Him undesirable. Those who recognize in His message the voice of the Lord will be required to overlook His obscurity and status. I've described this more fully in two chapters in *Come, Let Us Adore Him*.

This image contradicts the presumptions of the people who hear Isaiah's report. They imagine themselves as followers of the true faith. They presume they would hearken to the voice of God no matter when it came. But they look for it in barren ground. Therefore, when the Messiah should come, they will be unable to find anything desirable, beautiful or comely about Him. Rather they will shout "crucify Him!" because He will have merited the charge of blasphemy.

---

[237] Acts 8:13–24 "Then Simon himself believed also: and when he was baptized, he continued with Philip, and wondered, beholding the miracles and signs which were done. Now when the apostles which were at Jerusalem heard that Samaria had received the word of God, they sent unto them Peter and John: Who, when they were come down, prayed for them, that they might receive the Holy Ghost: (For as yet he was fallen upon none of them: only they were baptized in the name of the Lord Jesus.) Then laid they *their* hands on them, and they received the Holy Ghost. And when Simon saw that through laying on of the apostles' hands the Holy Ghost was given, he offered them money, Saying, Give me also this power, that on whomsoever I lay hands, he may receive the Holy Ghost. But Peter said unto him, Thy money perish with thee, because thou hast thought that the gift of God may be purchased with money. Thou hast neither part nor lot in this matter: for thy heart is not right in the sight of God. Repent therefore of this thy wickedness, and pray God, if perhaps the thought of thine heart may be forgiven thee. For I perceive that thou art in the gall of bitterness, and *in* the bond of iniquity. Then answered Simon, and said, Pray ye to the Lord for me, that none of these things which ye have spoken come upon me."

For those who heard Isaiah's report, this would seem altogether wrong. It is incomprehensible for the chosen people to fail to recognize the Lord's own Son. And yet they will kill Isaiah, as well. So when the message of the prophet Isaiah came to pass, the generation in which it was fulfilled was entirely oblivious to how his prophecy was unfolding before their eyes.

This is the Lord's doing, and it is marvelous in our eyes.

Isaiah 53:3

> "He is despised and rejected of men; a man of sorrows, and acquainted with grief: and we hid as it were our faces from him; he was despised, and we esteemed him not."

The Messiah would be both "despised" and "rejected" by the very people who claimed to follow Him. The astonishing report of Isaiah was unbelievable. It makes no sense that the people who looked forward to deliverance would reject their Deliverer. Why expect them to "despise" and "reject" the very one they rely upon for their hope? It is little wonder that Isaiah's report would not be believed.

Isaiah's Messiah would be "a man of sorrows, and acquainted with grief." He would mingle with the commonest of people, bearing with their infirmities, ministering to them. All the while, He will be a thorn to those who despised His ministry. Those in good society would "hide their faces from Him," and refuse to associate with Him. He had nothing to offer them. For them to acknowledge Him would require them to condescend. Better for them to hide their faces.

He warned them that if they were ashamed of Him, He would in turn be ashamed of them.[238] He also counseled them to be careful

---

[238] Mark 8:38 "Whosoever therefore shall be ashamed of me and of my words in this adulterous and sinful generation; of him also shall the Son of man be ashamed, when he cometh in the glory of his Father with the holy angels."

about their standard of judgment, because it would be applied to them.[239]

Despite the coming Messiah's teachings, and Isaiah's testimony of Him, the chosen people nevertheless "despise" Him, and "esteem Him not." It would simply be too difficult a task to confront Him in the flesh and find it possible to recognize Him for what He was.

We presume we could have recognized Him. However, the test He set up was one that He cautioned was coming. Our unflattering views of Christ's contemporaries may, in turn, leave us without excuse should He choose as He does so often, to send us a message from an obscure or un-credentialed source.

I wonder how many of us would recognize the truth, if it came only with the power of veracity behind it. Forgetting all the messenger is lacking, could we be starving ourselves from truth by again rejecting the open hand the Lord extends us? Whether by His own voice or by the voice of a servant, it will always be the same.[240]

Isaiah 53:4

"Surely he hath borne our griefs, and carried our sorrows: yet we did esteem him stricken, smitten of God, and afflicted."

This Messiah of whom Isaiah testifies will bear "grief" and "sorrow," but these will belong to us. They will be ours. In His suffering will be found our own shortcomings and failures. He will assume them for us.

---

[239] Matthew 7:2 "For with what judgment ye judge, ye shall be judged: and with what measure ye mete, it shall be measured to you again."

[240] D&C 1:38 "What I the Lord have spoken, I have spoken, and I excuse not myself; and though the heavens and the earth pass away, my word shall not pass away, but shall all be fulfilled, whether by mine own voice or by the voice of my servants, it is the same."

As He suffers, we will think it is His own deserved punishment. We will think it is God's doing. God will smite Him. God will afflict Him. After all, He was not truly God's Son.

We miss the point of Isaiah's message when we confine it to the Lord alone. His messengers will also come "as a thief in the night" to warn again before His coming. They, too, may fit the same pattern. If so, then we should be careful when we think another person's grief and sorrows are inflicted upon them by a God who has smitten them. Such an assessment may, like those who lived and rejected the Messiah, put you on the wrong side of the confrontation.

The Lord's doings are ever the same. The pattern simply does not change.

Isaiah 53:5

> "But he was wounded for our transgressions, he was bruised for our iniquities: the chastisement of our peace was upon him; and with his stripes we are healed."

Those wounds He suffered were not His, they were ours. Those iniquities which were laid upon Him were never His to bear. He volunteered to take them. We were relieved of them, and He took them. He purchased our peace by what He suffered to reconcile us to God. His infirmity was to heal us.

Our rejection of Him was the means by which He became fully acceptable to His Father. He bore our abuse to make His compassion perfect.

What we lacked we put on full display in our anger at Him.

What we held in our hearts we poured out upon Him, shouting to kill Him! Crucify Him! Away with Him!

He took it to allow our rejection to become His bridge back to the Father for us all.

When the outcast makes intercession for those who despised Him, there can be no crime which He cannot forgive. Having suffered the guilt of all, He holds the keys of death and hell. He suffered both. It was perfectly unjust for Him to have suffered anything. Yet He suffered it all.

How can the gates of hell be opened? It requires someone upon whom death and hell could have no claim to go there. When justice itself requires Him to be released, then death and hell are conquered. This is what He would do. He would suffer the wrath of the guilty and vile, fully assume their punishment and abuse, and bear their penalty of death itself. When the fury relented, and the wrath ended, He could reclaim life. His captivity ended the captivity for all. Having then returned to life, because it was just for Him to do so, He acquired the keys of death and hell. Now He can open those gates for any and all because it was unjust for Him to have been put through either. He can now advocate for others by virtue of what He suffered and the injustice of that suffering.[241]

Isaiah 53:6

"All we like sheep have gone astray; we have turned every one to his own way; and the Lord hath laid on him the iniquity of us all."

The Savior referred to those who would follow Him as His "sheep".[242] However, Isaiah's use of "sheep" here is not about those who would follow Him, but rather those who would scatter, find

---

[241] D&C 45:3–5 "Listen to him who is the advocate with the Father, who is pleading your cause before him— Saying: Father, behold the sufferings and death of him who did no sin, in whom thou wast well pleased; behold the blood of thy Son which was shed, the blood of him whom thou gavest that thyself might be glorified; Wherefore, Father, spare these my brethren that believe on my name, that they may come unto me and have everlasting life."

[242] John 10:27 "My sheep hear my voice, and I know them, and they follow me:"

other shepherds, or lose their way altogether. Isaiah's "sheep" are disorderly and have gone "astray."

The bookends of these two messages—Isaiah's sheep, who are astray, and Christ's, who "hear His voice"—are two sides of the same coin. Until "ALL" of us have been, or to some degree, have gone "astray," we are unprepared to "hear His voice" and be gathered by Him.

We have turned away from the True Shepherd and gone into our "own way." That errant "way" is appealing to the ego, the mind, the imagination, or the traditions we need to control us because they are safe, tested or handed to us by those whom we trust. Whatever the reason for choosing our own way, it is nevertheless ours. We must leave it, respond to the True Shepherd's "voice" and gather again to Him.

It is His "voice" whenever He sends a true messenger, empowered with a message from Him. It is not His "voice" when the messenger has not been sent or empowered with a message from Him.

The "iniquity of us all" in finding ourselves in these strange paths has been laid upon Him. He has found His way back from every error man can make. He has solved every dilemma, confronted every error, overcome every false and tempting doctrine the devil has thrown at you. He can solve your imponderable problems. He knows the answers. He has overcome the iniquities of every false, evil or prideful teaching ever given to any man or woman.

He can lead you back to the light, because He has remained true to the light throughout. Therefore look to Him.

Isaiah 53:7

> "He was oppressed, and he was afflicted, yet he opened not his mouth: he is brought as a lamb to the slaughter, and as a sheep before her shearers is dumb, so he openeth not his mouth."

These three references to Him refraining from "opening his mouth" and being "dumb" (meaning silent) are referring to more than His failure to respond to Herod's inquiries.[243] This is a reference to Christ's "Word," which if employed, could have moved mountains, held armies at defiance, and summoned "twelve legions of angels" to His defense.[244] Pilate was told that he may have been the Roman Procurator, but he had no power over Christ which Christ did not permit.[245]

Christ remained silent, choosing to exercise meekness in the face of the threat aimed at Him. ("Meekness" as explained in *Beloved Enos,* which is really a great power.) It was in this sense the Isaiah found His silence to be prophetically remarkable. One of the great signs of the Messiah. He would be the One whose words could have exercised power to defy armies, but who refrained from speaking those words. He would, instead, voluntarily submit to the abuse and scorn of those who hated Him.

---

[243] Luke 23:8–9 "And when Herod saw Jesus, he was exceeding glad: for he was desirous to see him of a long *season,* because he had heard many things of him; and he hoped to have seen some miracle done by him. Then he questioned with him in many words; but he answered him nothing."

[244] Matthew 26:52–53 "Then said Jesus unto him, Put up again thy sword into his place: for all they that take the sword shall perish with the sword. Thinkest thou that I cannot now pray to my Father, and he shall presently give me more than twelve legions of angels?"

[245] John 19:7–11 "The Jews answered him, We have a law, and by our law he ought to die, because he made himself the Son of God. When Pilate therefore heard that saying, he was the more afraid; And went again into the judgment hall, and saith unto Jesus, Whence art thou? But Jesus gave him no answer. Then saith Pilate unto him, Speakest thou not unto me? knowest thou not that I have power to crucify thee, and have power to release thee? Jesus answered, Thou couldest have no power *at all* against me, except it were given thee from above: therefore he that delivered me unto thee hath the greater sin."

As to our Lord being shorn, Isaiah also foretells His beard being plucked by those who would smite, abuse and strike Him.[246] Surely our Lord was indeed "shorn" as a "sheep" before His sacrifice.

Isaiah 53:8

"He was taken from prison and from judgment: and who shall declare his generation? for he was cut off out of the land of the living: for the transgression of my people was he stricken."

The idea of our Messiah emerging from "prison and from judgment" was a bit shocking to his listeners. There is little wonder at Isaiah's original question about who would believe the report. Should not the Messiah emerge from a palace? From a university (center of learning)? From a recognized hierarchy? From a notable family? From respectable circles? We would think so, wouldn't we?

Because of the presumptions, we do not look for Him as a prisoner, or one against whom judgment has been rendered. Nor do we expect His messengers to come, as they have so often in scriptures, from obscure places, bearing obscure names and having no credentials.

When Isaiah adds that the Messiah will be "cut off from the land of the living" he made a startling point. The Messiah will die! The Redeemer will not avoid death and the grave. He will lose His life. What follows adds to the wonder of it all: "For the transgression of my people" will the Messiah be cut off into death.

Now the focus has changed. Isaiah's message shifts from the suffering of the Messiah into the transgression of Israel. It is Israel's responsibility that their Messiah must suffer so. They will need a Messiah who will undertake this suffering, for they will not abandon

---

[246] Isaiah 50:6 "I gave my back to the smiters, and my cheeks to them that plucked off the hair: I hid not my face from shame and spitting."

their transgressions and will need a sacrifice made for them. They will need to confront love so great that it will die to redeem them. The proof of the Messiah's devotion to them will be shown by His humiliation, suffering and death. This is His proof. This is His credential. This is the record which will show for all mankind what great lengths God will go to reclaim His beloved people. They transgress, He atones. They sin and wander off as lost sheep, He pays to regather them with His blood.

His suffering may surprise them, but their surprise should be astonishment at the great love He holds for them.

Isaiah 53:9–10

"And he made his grave with the wicked, and with the rich in his death; because he had done no violence, neither was any deceit in his mouth." (Isaiah 53:9)

He died among two thieves, as a common criminal, along the road leading into Jerusalem. He would have been regarded as a criminal, worthy of the death He suffered, by any passer-by. His grave came as it would to any "wicked" and convicted criminal.

It was a rich man, member of the Sanhedrin, who begged for the body and buried it in a new tomb. His death was common, terrible, and worthy of the lowest member of society, but His burial would be in an honorable tomb worthy of the rich. His honorable burial was testament to the fact He had done no violence, nor had there been any deceit come from Him. Those wishing for a sign to confirm His honor will find it in the juxtaposition of the death He suffered and the burial He was given.

Isaiah 53:10 says:

"Yet it pleased the Lord to bruise him; he hath put him to grief: when thou shalt make his soul an offering for sin, he shall see his seed, he shall prolong his days, and the pleasure of the Lord shall prosper in his hand."

God will be "pleased" at the Messiah's suffering. His grief will be joyful to the courts of heaven. As odd as the comment may seem, it was nevertheless the case. We have a witness who was there, and saw the rejoicing for Christ's suffering. Enoch reported:

> "And it came to pass that Enoch looked; and from Noah, he beheld all the families of the earth; and he cried unto the Lord, saying: When shall the day of the Lord come? When shall the blood of the Righteous be shed, that all they that mourn may be sanctified and have eternal life? And the Lord said: It shall be in the meridian of time, in the days of wickedness and vengeance. And behold, Enoch saw the day of the coming of the Son of Man, even in the flesh; and *his soul rejoiced*, saying: The Righteous is lifted up, and the Lamb is slain from the foundation of the world; and through faith I am in the bosom of the Father, and behold, Zion is with me." (Moses 7:45–47)

Christ's death and suffering caused Enoch to "rejoice" at what He had accomplished. It was joyful. It was triumphant. It was the victory that would make it possible for Zion and Enoch to be redeemed. Therefore it did please God to bruise Christ, to put Him to grief. And the pleasure of God was in the fruits of that suffering. It was necessary to garner the victory over the fall of mankind. It was holy. It was cause for great joy.

His "seed" include all mankind. For in His triumph all who die have part. Victory over death means resurrection will come as the shared inheritance of all those who are descendants of Adam and Eve. As in Adam all die, even so in Christ are all made alive again.

Isaiah 53:11

"He shall see of the travail of his soul, and shall be satisfied: by his knowledge shall my righteous servant justify many; for he shall bear their iniquities."

The One who shall see the travail is the Father. The Father will be "satisfied" that the suffering of the Son, the payment made for mankind's debt of errors, has been sufficient to then inform the Son about salvation. Without descending below, the Son would have been unable to comprehend what mankind needs to overcome. Therefore Christ's suffering needed to be complete.

Upon receiving the full "wrath" of sin, Christ was then able to know how to overcome all that mankind must overcome to return to the presence of the Father. It is "by His knowledge" that Christ is able to "justify many." He possesses the knowledge, has the experience and suffered "for all" so that they might be instructed by Him.[247] He knows. He comprehends. By the things He suffered, He gained all that is needed to redeem, comfort and succor any man or woman in their extremity.[248]

This great burden was, however, merely His preparation; and not His completion.[249] He now uses His "knowledge" to "succor" and

---

[247] D&C 19:16–17 "For behold, I, God, have suffered these things for all, that they might not suffer if they would repent; But if they would not repent they must suffer even as I;"

[248] Hebrews 2:18 "For in that he himself hath suffered being tempted, he is able to succour them that are tempted."

[249] D&C 19:19 "Nevertheless, glory be to the Father, and I partook and finished my preparations unto the children of men."

tutor each soul who will permit Him to minister to them.[250] The most complete description of what He suffered and what He gained is set out in my testimony in *Come, Let Us Adore Him.*

Christ has gained "knowledge" which will save each of us, no matter what we are called to pass through, if we will come to Him, heed what He tells us, and follow His encouraging counsel. There is no depth we descend to which He does not already comprehend, having been there before us.[251]

To overcome all sin ourselves, we must accept His guidance and counsel. His comfort alone will rid us of our guilt. He knows how to shed the pains of sin, because He has first shed them, and therefore knows what must be done. Only in this way can we relieve ourselves of the suffering which is felt when an unclean person is exposed to

---

[250] Alma 7:11–12 "And he shall go forth, suffering pains and afflictions and temptations of every kind; and this that the word might be fulfilled which saith he will take upon him the pains and the sicknesses of his people. And he will take upon him death, that he may loose the bands of death which bind his people; and he will take upon him their infirmities, that his bowels may be filled with mercy, according to the flesh, that he may know according to the flesh how to succor his people according to their infirmities."

[251] D&C 122:7–8 "And if thou shouldst be cast into the pit, or into the hands of murderers, and the sentence of death passed upon thee; if thou be cast into the deep; if the billowing surge conspire against thee; if fierce winds become thine enemy; if the heavens gather blackness, and all the elements combine to hedge up the way; and above all, if the very jaws of hell shall gape open the mouth wide after thee, know thou, my son, that all these things shall give thee experience, and shall be for thy good. The Son of Man hath descended below them all. Art thou greater than he?"

God's presence.[252] He can lead you to cleansing, because He has been made completely filthy and covered with the wrath of God.[253]

His "preparations" are complete. He can "succor" you back to God's presence. But you must choose to allow Him to use this hard won "knowledge to justify you" before the Father. He has borne your infirmities before you bear them. He knows how to heal from them. There is nothing which you are called to pass through that He does not already comprehend. It is this great "knowledge" which renders Him the greatest, "most intelligent of them all."[254] He now has no perplexity from sin.

Isaiah 53:12

"Therefore will I divide him *a* portion with the great, and he shall divide the spoil with the strong; because he hath poured out his soul unto death: and he was numbered with the transgressors; and he bare the sin of many, and made intercession for the transgressors."

Isaiah's report ends with the Messiah's triumph. Hard won as it was to be, it will qualify Him to receive a "portion with the great." Although the Messiah may be greater than them all, He is only to

---

[252] Mormon 9:4–5 "Behold, I say unto you that ye would be more miserable to dwell with a holy and just God, under a consciousness of your filthiness before him, than ye would to dwell with the damned souls in hell. For behold, when ye shall be brought to see your nakedness before God, and also the glory of God, and the holiness of Jesus Christ, it will kindle a flame of unquenchable fire upon you."

[253] D&C 19:15–18 "Therefore I command you to repent—repent, lest I smite you by the rod of my mouth, and by my wrath, and by my anger, and your sufferings be sore—how sore you know not, how exquisite you know not, yea, how hard to bear you know not. For behold, I, God, have suffered these things for all, that they might not suffer if they would repent; But if they would not repent they must suffer even as I; Which suffering caused myself, even God, the greatest of all, to tremble because of pain, and to bleed at every pore, and to suffer both body and spirit—and would that I might not drink the bitter cup, and shrink—"

[254] Abraham 3:19 "And the Lord said unto me: These two facts do exist, that there are two spirits, one being more intelligent than the other; there shall be another more intelligent than they; I am the Lord thy God, I am more intelligent than they all."

receive "a portion." For the suffering He endures will be to redeem others and bring them back with Himself. There is to be no hoarding. There is to be no selfishness. Though He may earn it all, He will take only "a portion" and leave a "division" with others who may share in His joy. He abased Himself, and taught all others to do the same.[255]

This is nothing akin to the faithful son complaining about the Prodigal.[256] Christ will not only willingly share with His lesser brothers and sisters, but He will go further and "make intercession for the transgressors." He is neither jealous of their sharing in His triumph, nor resentful to "divide the spoil" of His great victory.

Here is a Messiah indeed! Here is a Redeemer indeed! "Truly, this Man was the Son of God!"[257]

Despise Him and His servants, He will still condescend to succor you so far as you permit Him to do.

Turn your face from Him and His servants, He will still plead for you to listen.

Forsake and abandon Him and His servants, they will still forgive and make intercession for your errors.

Those who follow Him will be misunderstood, reviled, persecuted. It is in the nature of things for this world. He anticipated that,

---

[255] Matthew 23:10–12 "Neither be ye called masters: for one is your Master, *even* Christ. But he that is greatest among you shall be your servant. And whosoever shall exalt himself shall be abased; and he that shall humble himself shall be exalted."

[256] Luke 15:29–30 "And he answering said to *his* father, Lo, these many years do I serve thee, neither transgressed I at any time thy commandment: and yet thou never gavest me a kid, that I might make merry with my friends: But as soon as this thy son was come, which hath devoured thy living with harlots, thou hast killed for him the fatted calf."

[257] Matthew 27:54 "Now when the centurion, and they that were with him, watching Jesus, saw the earthquake, and those things that were done, they feared greatly, saying, Truly this was the Son of God."

and gave instructions to you when you encounter it.[258] The entire prophecy in Isaiah 53 is a description not only of the Messiah, but also of the Messiah's children. They will not be welcome here, for the ruler of this world has nothing for either Him or His children.[259]

---

[258] Matthew 5:10–13 "Blessed *are* they which are persecuted for righteousness' sake: for theirs is the kingdom of heaven. Blessed are ye, when *men* shall revile you, and persecute *you,* and shall say all manner of evil against you falsely, for my sake. Rejoice, and be exceeding glad: for great *is* your reward in heaven: for so persecuted they the prophets which were before you. Ye are the salt of the earth: but if the salt have lost his savour, wherewith shall it be salted? it is thenceforth good for nothing, but to be cast out, and to be trodden under foot of men."

[259] John 14:30 "Hereafter I will not talk much with you: for the prince of this world cometh, and hath nothing in me."

THE SCRIPTURES HAVE ANSWERS

Patience

Christ was prepared eighteen years prior to the time His ministry would begin. He stood by ready, and "waited upon the Lord for the time of his ministry to come" (JST Matthew 3:24–26).

Prepared and waiting.

Patience. Even the Lord, who was "more intelligent than them all," waited.[260]

The Lord's counsel to all is that they must not "run faster than they have strength."[261]

---

[260] Abraham 3:19 "And the Lord said unto me: These two facts do exist, that there are two spirits, one being more intelligent than the other; there shall be another more intelligent than they; I am the Lord thy God, I am more intelligent than they all."

[261] Mosiah 4:27 "And see that all these things are done in wisdom and order; for it is not requisite that a man should run faster than he has strength. And again, it is expedient that he should be diligent, that thereby he might win the prize; therefore, all things must be done in order."
D&C 10:4 "Do not run faster or labor more than you have strength and means provided to enable you to translate; but be diligent unto the end."

There is no rush to receiving an audience with the Lord. When it happens it is always in His own time, His own way, and according to His own will.[262]

We must ask. Then we wait upon Him. If He waited, what makes you think you are entitled to rush ahead without paying a similar price to develop the necessary patience in waiting on the Lord.

Abraham was promised children, but waited decades to receive the promise. Anna and Simeon were promised they would behold the Lord's Messiah, but were both well stricken in age before He came.[263]

Patience. Recognize the Lord alone will determine the timing. Our responsibility is to trust in Him and await His will. We can ask, seek, and knock. He cannot respond *unless* we ask, seek, and knock. But having done so, then we trust in Him to decide when He will make Himself known to us.

Promise vs. Appearance

I was asked:

"I've wondered about this for a long time. In the blog post about 'Why wait?' there is a phrase that says '*This appearance is not merely "in the heart," but is an actual appearance or visit.*' The 'in the heart' is my question. Once in a while this concept doesn't contradict but at the moment it seems to. In D&C 88 it says: 'Wherefore, I now send upon you another Comforter, even upon you my friends, that it may abide in your hearts, even the

---

[262] D&C 88:68 "Therefore, sanctify yourselves that your minds become single to God, and the days will come that you shall see him; for he will unveil his face unto you, and it shall be in his own time, and in his own way, and according to his own will."

[263] Luke 2:25–28 "And, behold, there was a man in Jerusalem, whose name *was* Simeon; and the same man *was* just and devout, waiting for the consolation of Israel: and the Holy Ghost was upon him. And it was revealed unto him by the Holy Ghost, that he should not see death, before he had seen the Lord's Christ. And he came by the Spirit into the temple: and when the parents brought in the child Jesus, to do for him after the custom of the law, Then took he him up in his arms, and blessed God . . . "

Holy Spirit of promise.' So how can it be a false sectarian notion about God the Father and Jesus dwelling in a man's heart (D&C130:3) and yet a few sections later in the D&C when referring to the second comforter it says contrary. [Also Eph. 3:17 says: 'That Christ may *dwell* in your *hearts* by faith; that ye, being rooted and grounded in love.'] I at one point saw how this worked —but can't seem to at the moment. How do those two seemingly contradictory things work?"

My response: To have the promise "abide in your heart" is to keep inside your heart the knowledge there is a promise given by God, who cannot lie about such matters, that you have the promise of eternal life. This is referring to the promise, and keeping it dear to you, or in your heart. This, of course, is not the same thing as the appearance of the Son in the form of another Comforter, as promised by Christ in John 14:18, where Christ declares: "*I will not leave you comfortless: I will come to you.*" It is the promise that the Lord will come or appear or take up His abode with you which Joseph declared to be literal. He is saying those who believe or teach this to be merely a feeling "in the heart" are teaching an "old sectarian notion" because they deny its literal possibility.[264]

The culmination of the Lord's ministry is the promise of eternal life, as I explained in an earlier post. But the actuality of that ministry as an appearance to a person is not merely "in the heart." When His ministry does culminate in the promise, then the promise should "abide in the heart" of the person to whom the promise has been given. They ought never let it pass from within their hearts that they have obtained a promise from the Lord assuring them of life eternal.

These are two different subjects. But the question is quite a good one. Thanks for asking it.

---

[264] D&C 130:3 "John 14:23—The appearing of the Father and the Son, in that verse, is a personal appearance; and the idea that the Father and the Son dwell in a man's heart is an old sectarian notion, and is false."

Most Answers Are in the Scriptures

I've been reflecting upon a conversation I had with a self-described "tax protester" who has not paid income taxes and is now facing legal issues as a result. After a couple of days of reflection I had this considered response to this dilemma:

I use a particular method in determining what issues I need Divine direction to resolve and what issues I need no direction from the Lord to resolve. If there is an answer in the scriptures, contained in the teachings of Christ, then I simply do not ask the question. Instead I assume Christ's teachings are intended to govern my conduct and I comply. On the tax issue, for example, Christ did not resist paying taxes.[265] Nor did Christ teach anything other than to pay taxes.[266] Therefore, it would not occur to me to even ask the Lord about whether or not to pay taxes.

When it comes to asking the Lord about something on which His teachings are already clear, a person risks receiving permission to do what will ultimately instruct them by sad example that they ought to have followed His earlier teachings. The best example of this is when

---

[265] Matthew 17:24–27 "And when they were come to Capernaum, they that received tribute *money* came to Peter, and said, Doth not your master pay tribute? He saith, Yes. And when he was come into the house, Jesus prevented him, saying, What thinkest thou, Simon? of whom do the kings of the earth take custom or tribute? of their own children, or of strangers? Peter saith unto him, Of strangers. Jesus saith unto him, Then are the children free. Notwithstanding, lest we should offend them, go thou to the sea, and cast an hook, and take up the fish that first cometh up; and when thou hast opened his mouth, thou shalt find a piece of money: that take, and give unto them for me and thee."

[266] Matthew 22:15–22 "Then went the Pharisees, and took counsel how they might entangle him in *his* talk. And they sent out unto him their disciples with the Herodians, saying, Master, we know that thou art true, and teachest the way of God in truth, neither carest thou for any *man:* for thou regardest not the person of men. Tell us therefore, What thinkest thou? Is it lawful to give tribute unto Caesar, or not? But Jesus perceived their wickedness, and said, Why tempt ye me, *ye* hypocrites? Shew me the tribute money. And they brought unto him a penny. And he saith unto them, Whose *is* this image and superscription? They say unto him, Caesar's. Then saith he unto them, Render therefore unto Caesar the things which are Caesar's; and unto God the things that are God's. When they had heard *these words,* they marvelled, and left him, and went their way."

Joseph requested he be allowed to let Martin Harris take the 116 pages and was told "no." He persisted, and despite having been told "no," he asked again and was then told "yes." The "yes" was not because God had changed His mind, but because Joseph simply refused to learn by anything other than sad experience to respect God's counsel.[267]

Therefore, when there is already an instruction on point from the Lord, and we ignore it, the answer we receive may be for our benefit. We may need to learn by sad experience what we might have learned instead by precept and wisdom from the Lord.

It is this kind of experience men repeat by failing to follow God's counsel. Then, when they might have avoided the sting which follows, they choose instead to suffer. Oftentimes they will blame the Lord for the hardships they brought upon themselves, when, if they had hearkened to the Lord's counsel in the first place, they would never have had to suffer.

This is why it is so important to study the scriptures. If the answer is in there (and almost everything IS in there) and we do not choose to find it, but to inquire for a new revelation instead, we oftentimes doom ourselves to a sad experience. His counsel should be heeded. When we don't heed, and ask instead for new or different guidance, we may be given permission to do what He has already told us to avoid. This is one of the great lessons from the lost 116 pages.

Debate Is Not Necessary

I am not trying to make my mind up about Mormonism or The Church of Jesus Christ of Latter-day Saints. I have long ago sorted out my views. They are not going to change.

---

[267] See D&C 3 and D&C 10:1–30.

Although my views are explained in this blog, I do not debate them. You are welcome to have contrary views, to disagree and to think I am altogether incorrect. But you shouldn't waste the effort to try and persuade me to change my own view.

My testimony of Christ is informed both by what I have studied and what I have witnessed. It has taken decades of devotion in study and living to obtain a stable, firm view of the Lord and His role in my life. No one should expect to acquire an unchanging view of the Lord without paying a significant price in their time and effort. I can try to help, give advice and make suggestions. I can explain my views. But, in the end, every person must determine for themselves what Christ means and how they intend to relate to Him.

I believe the truth exists independent of your view or my view. Just because someone believes a false notion does not make it so. Eventually we will all come into agreement by the things which we experience. For most of the world, that will be some time after they are dead.

Debate is not necessary. And I am just a lay member of the Church, without any reason for you to consider what I have to say. Therefore, you ought to measure my views against the scriptures and the Spirit, and let the truth be the single standard for deciding to accept something.

I quoted a few ideas from Mark Twain in a post a while back. You ought to re-read them if you don't remember them. They were chosen with some care. They summarize ideas which I believe to be important.

Presiding Authority

When Joseph Smith died, the crisis in succession produced arguments from various contenders who claimed it their right to lead the Church. Although no one argued that Section 107:22–24 controlled the decision, ultimately the decision was that the Twelve Apostles held keys to lead the Church.[268] A few years later the verses in Section 107 just cited became the rationale for why the Twelve would lead.

This decision was further clarified by adoption of the rule that the senior (one who held office longest) Apostle would be the presiding authority and by virtue of that seniority would be the President. Initially he was President of the Twelve. Then when Brigham Young reformed the First Presidency after a few years, he became President of the Church. Then in 1955 he became the living "prophet" as well.

Since the system has now reached a stable, orderly manner of choosing and recognizing whose right it is to preside over the church, what happens if another, more senior Apostle happens along? Whose right is it to preside if *you* are required to choose between direction that comes from the presiding authority of the church or direction that comes from John (who tarries in the flesh),[269] or Peter, James and John?[270] Everyone presumes the messages from those

---

[268] D&C 107:22–24 "Of the Melchizedek Priesthood, three Presiding High Priests, chosen by the body, appointed and ordained to that office, and upheld by the confidence, faith, and prayer of the church, form a quorum of the Presidency of the Church. The twelve traveling councilors are called to be the Twelve Apostles, or special witnesses of the name of Christ in all the world—thus differing from other officers in the church in the duties of their calling. And they form a quorum, equal in authority and power to the three presidents previously mentioned."

[269] D&C 7:1–4 "AND the Lord said unto me: John, my beloved, what desirest thou? For if you shall ask what you will, it shall be granted unto you. And I said unto him: Lord, give unto me power over death, that I may live and bring souls unto thee. And the Lord said unto me: Verily, verily, I say unto thee, because thou desirest this thou shalt tarry until I come in my glory, and shalt prophesy before nations, kindreds, tongues and people. And for this cause the Lord said unto Peter: If I will that he tarry till I come, what is that to thee? For he desired of me that he might bring souls unto me, but thou desiredst that thou mightest speedily come unto me in my kingdom."

[270] D&C 27:12 "And also with Peter, and James, and John, whom I have sent unto you, by whom I have ordained you and confirmed you to be apostles, and especial witnesses of my name, and bear the keys of your ministry and of the same things which I revealed unto them;"

who preside over the church on the earth and those who "tarry in the flesh" will be congruent, and that there is no conflict between the messages. But query what choice should be made if there is at least some inconsistency? Upon whom does the seniority rest?

A simpler question is what choice should be made between the Lord and those who preside in The Church of Jesus Christ of Latter-day Saints. I think all would agree that all church authorities are inferior to the Lord. However, we also presume that there will be no conflict between the two. What if there is at least some inconsistency?

It is an interesting question to ponder. Not that I have anything to add to your reflection on the matter. Sometimes it is just interesting to consider a question. Like I've said elsewhere, answers are less important than a good question to ponder from time to time. In the pondering, new and important ideas can occur to you.

WWJD

Stopped shaving a few weeks ago, except for the neck. Now I've got a bit of face hair, which feels like spiders are crawling all over my face. I took a poll, figuring I'd get a vote to return to the orthodox visage. To my surprise all the kids said "keep it." Even my wife says to leave it for a while. So I'm going to keep the spiders for a while.

I've done this before, back when I made the annual trip to Sturgis. I know that eventually there isn't any feeling to a beard. In fact, when you shave it off then you can feel the air movement on your face and that's quite weird for a few days. But I haven't been to Sturgis for about 5 years or more, and so I hadn't grown a beard for that long.

As an aside, when you go to Sturgis you ought to look the part. The "brethren" there expect some effort to blend in. Consequently, I have managed a fairly true 'scooter-trash' look when I make the effort.

As long as I have the chin-hair I need to dust off the Harley, get it inspected and licensed, and start riding again this summer. It is, of course, the answer to the question: "WWJD?" (What would Jesus drive?) It's environmentally friendly, leaves a small carbon footprint, quick, high-mileage . . . fun as hell, and pretty badass, too. All the ingredients needed for transcendental transportation.

Steppenwolf sang the theme song to it all:

> *Get your motor runnin'*
> *Head out on the highway;*
> *look'in for adventure*
> *and whatever comes our way . . .*
> *I like smoke and lightning*
> *Heavy metal thunder*
> *Racin' with the wind*
> *And the feelin' that I'm under . . .*

It's a biker thing. Can't be explained. Can be shared, though. You start with face hair; ... then let it take you to its logical extreme.

Hmmmm . . . no wonder missionaries are clean-shaven.

Books for Sale—Used

A friend of mine brought to my attention that there are "used" copies of my books available on the web for sometimes hundreds of dollars. I was surprised. Let me give some warning to people so no-one takes advantage of you.

First, there is absolutely no reason to pay anything more than what the *Amazon.com* book charges are to anyone anywhere. The books are all still in print and you do not need to resort to buying them used. Buy them new from Amazon and you'll get a newly printed copy at the lowest price, other than shipping which they add on to the cost.

Second, if you live in Utah, you can buy copies at the same reasonable prices from either Benchmark Books on about 3300 South Main Street, or from a place called Confetti Books in Spanish Fork (whose address I do not have at the moment). Neither of these stores mark the books up, and they don't charge you shipping. But you have to drive there to buy them.

Third, I am not trying to make money from book sales. I work as an attorney for a living and writing is not a commercial endeavor. Whatever royalties I earn are donated to The Church of Jesus Christ of Latter-day Saints. So you buying a book I've written does nothing financial for me.

SPEAKING
PLAINLY

The Sealing Power

I've explained the sealing authority in the last three chapters of *Beloved Enos*. An example of the Lord and His servant Enoch conversing, and the Lord requiring the sealing authority to be used is found in Moses 7:6–7, which reads as follows:

> "And again the Lord said unto me: Look; and I looked towards the north, and I beheld the people of Canaan, which dwelt in tents. And the Lord said unto me: Prophesy; and I prophesied, saying: Behold the people of Canaan, which are numerous, shall go forth in battle array against the people of Shum, and shall slay them that they shall utterly be destroyed; and the people of Canaan shall divide themselves in the land, and the land shall be barren and unfruitful, and none other people shall dwell there but the people of Canaan;"

Enoch was shown the events, but the Lord required the voice of Enoch to speak and "prophesy" what was to happen. The voice of one holding this authority is the same as the Lord's own voice.[271] The "Word" needed to be employed, because it is by the "Word" that all things are established.

The "Word" comes through Christ, who has in Him all power and authority. It was and is through Him that others are called upon from heaven, given authority, and commissioned to speak and make the Word of God live again on the earth.

> "Therefore, in the beginning the Word was, for he was the Word, even the messenger of salvation— The light and the Redeemer of the world; the Spirit of truth, who came into the world, because the world was made by him, and in him was the life of men and the light of men." (D&C 93:8–9)

It was by employing the "Word" that the creation of this earth rolled into order at the direction of the "noble and great" souls who were the "Gods" or the "Elohim" in the beginning. Abraham recorded:

> "And they (the Gods) *said*: Let there be light; and there was light. And they (the Gods) comprehended the light, for it was bright; and they divided the light, or caused it to be divided, from the darkness. And the Gods called the light Day, and the darkness they called Night. And it came to pass that from the evening until morning they called night; and from the morning until the evening they called day; and this was the first, or the beginning, of that which they called day and night. And *the Gods also said* . . . " (Abraham 4:3–6.)

It is through the Word, or sealing authority, spoken by one sent from God, that salvation and exaltation are made available to mankind. It was intended that this authority to speak in His name might belong to every man in this dispensation:

---

[271] D&C 1:38 "What I the Lord have spoken, I have spoken, and I excuse not myself; and though the heavens and the earth pass away, my word shall not pass away, but shall all be fulfilled, whether by mine own voice or by the voice of my servants, it is the same."

"But that every man might speak in the name of God the Lord, even the Savior of the world; That faith also might increase in the earth; That mine everlasting covenant might be established;" (D&C 1:20–22)

This was not to be a time when there would be a famine in hearing the Word of the Lord.[272] Rather it was to be a time of great abundance, when every man would know the Lord.[273] This was to be the day when all would see visions and dream dreams, beholding the Lord.[274]

For some, this IS a day of great plenty. For others it remains a time of famine. The Lord spoke truly that in our day two shall be together, and the one taken but the other left.[275] Why are they not taken?

"Because their hearts are set so much upon the things of this world, and aspire to the honors of men, that they do not learn

---

[272] Amos 8:11 "Behold, the days come, saith the Lord God, that I will send a famine in the land, not a famine of bread, nor a thirst for water, but of hearing the words of the Lord:"

[273] Hebrews 8:11 "And they shall not teach every man his neighbour, and every man his brother, saying, Know the Lord: for all shall know me, from the least to the greatest."
D&C 84:98 "Until all shall know me, who remain, even from the least unto the greatest, and shall be filled with the knowledge of the Lord, and shall see eye to eye, and shall lift up their voice, and with the voice together sing this new song, saying:"

[274] JS–H 1:41 "He also quoted the second chapter of Joel, from the twenty-eighth verse to the last. He also said that this was not yet fulfilled, but was soon to be. And he further stated that the fulness of the Gentiles was soon to come in. He quoted many other passages of scripture, and offered many explanations which cannot be mentioned here."
Joel 2:28 "And it shall come to pass afterward, *that* I will pour out my spirit upon all flesh; and your sons and your daughters shall prophesy, your old men shall dream dreams, your young men shall see visions:"

[275] Luke 17:34–36 "I tell you, in that night there shall be two *men* in one bed; the one shall be taken, and the other shall be left. Two *women* shall be grinding together; the one shall be taken, and the other left. Two *men* shall be in the field; the one shall be taken, and the other left."
Matthew 24:40–41 "Then shall two be in the field; the one shall be taken, and the other left. Two *women shall be* grinding at the mill; the one shall be taken, and the other left."
JS–Matthew 1:44–45 "Then shall be fulfilled that which is written, that in the last days, two shall be in the field, the one shall be taken, and the other left; Two shall be grinding at the mill, the one shall be taken, and the other left;"

this one lesson— That the rights of the priesthood are inseparably connected with the powers of heaven, and that the powers of heaven cannot be controlled nor handled only upon the principles of righteousness. That they may be conferred upon us, it is true; but when we undertake to cover our sins, or to gratify our pride, our vain ambition, or to exercise control or dominion or compulsion upon the souls of the children of men, in any degree of unrighteousness, behold, the heavens withdraw themselves; the Spirit of the Lord is grieved; and when it is withdrawn, Amen to the priesthood or the authority of that man." (D&C 121:35–37)

Whenever men possess the "word" from God, they necessarily speak it in plainness. When men do not, history tells us they will assert the right to control, dominate and exercise authority over others to prevent the "word" from being spoken by anyone. This is the consistent pattern found among the Jews at the time of Christ; among the Catholics when they obtain political dominance; and it is the pattern that we must *not repeat* in our own dispensation. For we all share responsibility for how this turns out. Nephi's view of how we would perform was quite pessimistic.[276]

---

[276] 2 Nephi 28:20–29 "For behold, at that day shall he rage in the hearts of the children of men, and stir them up to anger against that which is good. And others will he pacify, and lull them away into carnal security, that they will say: All is well in Zion; yea, Zion prospereth, all is well—and thus the devil cheateth their souls, and leadeth them away carefully down to hell. And behold, others he flattereth away, and telleth them there is no hell; and he saith unto them: I am no devil, for there is none—and thus he whispereth in their ears, until he grasps them with his awful chains, from whence there is no deliverance. Yea, they are grasped with death, and hell; and death, and hell, and the devil, and all that have been seized therewith must stand before the throne of God, and be judged according to their works, from whence they must go into the place prepared for them, even a lake of fire and brimstone, which is endless torment. Therefore, wo be unto him that is at ease in Zion! Wo be unto him that crieth: All is well! Yea, wo be unto him that hearkeneth unto the precepts of men, and denieth the power of God, and the gift of the Holy Ghost! Yea, wo be unto him that saith: We have received, and we need no more! And in fine, wo unto all those who tremble, and are angry because of the truth of God! For behold, he that is built upon the rock receiveth it with gladness; and he that is built upon a sandy foundation trembleth lest he shall fall. Wo be unto him that shall say: We have received the word of God, and we need no more of the word of God, for we have enough!"

However, the group outcome needn't ever be the individual's outcome, even in Nephi's prophetic "word" about our day.[277]

Be of Good Cheer

In Luke 22:54–62 there is this account of the night when Christ was taken captive:

> "Then took they him, and led him, and brought him into the high priest's house. And Peter followed afar off. And when they had kindled a fire in the midst of the hall, and were set down together, Peter sat down among them. But a certain maid beheld him as he sat by the fire, and earnestly looked upon him, and said, This man was also with him. And he denied him, saying, Woman, I know him not. And after a little while another saw him, and said, Thou art also of them. And Peter said, Man, I am not. And about the space of one hour after another confidently affirmed, saying, Of a truth this fellow also was with him: for he is a Galilaean. And Peter said, Man, I know not what thou sayest. And immediately, while he yet spake, the cock crew. And the Lord turned, and looked upon Peter. And Peter remembered the word of the Lord, how he had said unto him, Before the cock crow, thou shalt deny me thrice. And Peter went out, and wept bitterly."

President Kimball cautioned about "judging" Peter's motives and even suggested that no cowardice was involved when he denied Christ three times.[278]

I'm not interested in judging Peter. But I am quite interested in this incident, the Lord's actions, and the implications for us.

---

[277] 2 Nephi 28:14 "They wear stiff necks and high heads; yea, and because of pride, and wickedness, and abominations, and whoredoms, they have all gone astray save it be a few, who are the humble followers of Christ; nevertheless, they are led, that in many instances they do err because they are taught by the precepts of men."

[278] http://emp.byui.edu/marrottr/GenlAuthorities/PeterMyBrother.pdf

The hall in which this took place was large enough to have separate groups and conversations in it. But it was still intimate enough that Peter's raised voice in the third denial could be heard across the hall where Jesus was being held. Matthew added that Peter not only denied Christ, but also cursed as he did so.[279] When, therefore, the Lord heard this loud outburst accompanying Peter's final cursing denial in that raised voice, "the Lord turned, and looked upon Peter."

It was that "look upon Peter" that provoked Peter's response. Peter did not remember the Lord's earlier comments until His "look upon" him. Then promptly "Peter went out, and wept bitterly."

Now consider this—Here you have Christ's chief apostle and leader whose entire demeanor changes from gruff, loud cursing and denial of the Lord into bitter weeping, because the Lord "looked upon" him.

If you can get this picture firmly in your mind, then you may understand this scripture:

"Then will ye longer deny the Christ, or can ye behold the Lamb of God? Do ye suppose that ye shall dwell with him under a consciousness of your guilt? Do ye suppose that ye could be happy to dwell with that holy Being, when your souls are racked with a consciousness of guilt that ye have ever abused his laws? Behold, I say unto you that ye would be more miserable to dwell with a holy and just God, under a consciousness of your filthiness before him, than ye would to dwell with the damned souls in hell. For behold, when ye shall be brought to see your nakedness before God, and also the glory of God, and the holiness of Jesus Christ, it will kindle a flame of unquenchable fire upon you." (Mormon 9:3–5)

---

[279] Matthew 26:74 "Then began he to curse and to swear, *saying,* I know not the man. And immediately the cock crew."
Mark 14:71 "But he began to curse and to swear, *saying,* I know not this man of whom ye speak."

Peter literally experienced the bitterness of hell in that disappointed glance from the Lord. It came from recognizing of how great a disappointment he was to the Lord. It was produced by a mere glance from Christ. He who loved all of us the most was the One whom Peter in return cursed and denied. When he saw himself through the Lord's disappointment, it made Peter bitter, filled with remorse, and caused him to retreat to weep alone.

We do not want to disappoint the Lord. None of us want to see that same look from the Lord that He showed Peter. We have opportunities to do what He asks us every day. All of us do. Little things, moment to moment, particularly if you look for them. They matter. Every thought, every word, every deed. They matter. Let them reflect credit upon your faith in Him.

I'm not saying be dour, long-faced or stoic. Quite the contrary. "Be of good cheer" was His oft repeated expression, even using it as a greeting on many occasions.[280] Cheerfully go about doing good,

---

[280] Matthew 14:27 "But straightway Jesus spake unto them, saying, Be of good cheer; it is I; be not afraid."

Mark 6:50 "For they all saw him, and were troubled. And immediately he talked with them, and saith unto them, Be of good cheer: it is I; be not afraid."

John 16:33 "These things I have spoken unto you, that in me ye might have peace. In the world ye shall have tribulation: but be of good cheer; I have overcome the world."

Acts 23:11 "And the night following the Lord stood by him, and said, Be of good cheer, Paul: for as thou hast testified of me in Jerusalem, so must thou bear witness also at Rome."

3 Nephi 1:13 "Lift up your head and be of good cheer; for behold, the time is at hand, and on this night shall the sign be given, and on the morrow come I into the world, to show unto the world that I will fulfil all that which I have caused to be spoken by the mouth of my holy prophets."

D&C 68:6 "Wherefore, be of good cheer, and do not fear, for I the Lord am with you, and will stand by you; and ye shall bear record of me, even Jesus Christ, that I am the Son of the living God, that I was, that I am, and that I am to come."

and trust in Him. He will guide you. He was happy. He was cheerful. So are those who know Him best.[281]

There isn't a single thing you do for His sake which He will forget or fail to credit to you. Nor is there a single mistake which He will remember and hold against you, if you repent.[282]

You should let your thoughts be such that you will be confident in His presence.[283] Be of good cheer.

Prophet, Seer, Revelator

I was asked this question:

"If the first presidency and the twelve really operate much like the lay members do, how then do you reconcile the MEAN-ING of the words: Prophet; Seer; and Revelator. Aren't these gifts unusual and set apart for the highest positions of the church? Wouldn't one necessarily receive visions and dreams to qualify as a Prophet, Seer, or Revelator? How else would one SEE into the past, or the future, let alone clearly understanding the present? How do you reconcile the current reve-

---

[281] JS–H 1:28 "During the space of time which intervened between the time I had the vision and the year eighteen hundred and twenty-three—having been forbidden to join any of the religious sects of the day, and being of very tender years, and persecuted by those who ought to have been my friends and to have treated me kindly, and if they supposed me to be deluded to have endeavored in a proper and affectionate manner to have reclaimed me—I was left to all kinds of temptations; and, mingling with all kinds of society, I frequently fell into many foolish errors, and displayed the weakness of youth, and the foibles of human nature; which, I am sorry to say, led me into divers temptations, offensive in the sight of God. In making this confession, no one need suppose me guilty of any great or malignant sins. A disposition to commit such was never in my nature. But I was guilty of levity, and sometimes associated with jovial company, etc., not consistent with that character which ought to be maintained by one who was called of God as I had been. But this will not seem very strange to any one who recollects my youth, and is acquainted with my native cheery temperament."

[282] D&C 58:42 "Behold, he who has repented of his sins, the same is forgiven, and I, the Lord, remember them no more."

[283] D&C 121:45 "Let thy bowels also be full of charity towards all men, and to the household of faith, and let virtue garnish thy thoughts unceasingly; then shall thy confidence wax strong in the presence of God; and the doctrine of the priesthood shall distil upon thy soul as the dews from heaven."

latory state of the leadership with the meaning of the words, prophet, seer, and revelator?"

Inside the Church the current interpretation is that the "office" has associated with it a "title" set out in scripture. The "office" of the President of the High Priesthood,[284] who is the President of the Church, also bears the "title" of "prophet, seer and revelator".[285] The current interpretation of these verses is that the possessor of the office is entitled to the title of "prophet, seer and revelator" by virtue of office alone. Therefore, nothing more is needed in current church usage other than possession of the office, which alone gives the possessor of the office the title accorded to the office. So, no, our current terminology does not require something other than office.

It is possible to read the words of the verses differently, of course. First, the words we have adopted as they appear in scripture are not actually "prophet, seer and revelator" but are instead: "a seer, a revelator, a translator, and a prophet." Those are different words and include in the phrase "a translator" in addition to "seer, revelator and a prophet." We have dropped the word "translator" from the title we now use.

Second, it is possible that the following words may be viewed to mean something different than the way we currently read them, "to be like unto Moses—Behold, here is wisdom; yea, to be a seer, a revelator, a translator, and a prophet".[286] They could be read to mean that before you fill the office of President of the High Priesthood

---

[284] D&C 107:65–66 "Wherefore, it must needs be that one be appointed of the High Priesthood to preside over the priesthood, and he shall be called President of the High Priesthood of the Church; Or, in other words, the Presiding High Priest over the High Priesthood of the Church."

[285] D&C 107:91–92 "And again, the duty of the President of the office of the High Priesthood is to preside over the whole church, and to be like unto Moses— Behold, here is wisdom; yea, to be a seer, a revelator, a translator, and a prophet, having all the gifts of God which he bestows upon the head of the church."

[286] Ibid.

you must first locate "a seer" who is also, by definition, "a revelator" and "a translator" who is undoubtedly therefore "a prophet" and, having found such a person, you are to sustain him into the office. The office doesn't make the man, but the Lord makes a man into such an instrument, and having done so then the church is to put him into the office. There are of course those who have these gifts. Many of them have no church office involving priesthood, because they are female. They may possess gifts, but they are disqualified for office. Then there are men who possess such gifts, but they may be living in South America, serving in a small branch, and completely unnoticed by the leadership, and therefore, never called.

The problem with the second point is that it invites near chaos. You would have dozens, hundreds or perhaps thousands of people who would step forward and make the claim that they are entitled to the office. Ambitious men who are either deceived or, worse still, cunning and dishonest, would seek to gain the office to further their ambitions. Such a parade of the deluded or the dishonest would be foisted upon the Saints every time the President died. Therefore, no matter how much merit you may think the second interpretation holds, it would be far more problematic to implement than the current interpretation and method.

The advantage of the current system is that the man who fills the vacancy is distinguished by how long he has held the church's office of Apostle. Generally that means an elderly man, often suffering from the decline of advanced years and poor health. That means you are likely to have a man whose ambitions and exuberance are tempered by the maturity of age and the wisdom that comes from long life's experience. It gives stability to the decision, as well as the person chosen.

If the second approach were to be adopted, then the choice would need to be made by the serving President before he left office (died), by making the choice of his successor as part of his official service. This is the method that the Lord revealed to Joseph Smith.[287] Joseph attempted this, but the one he chose to succeed him died with him (his brother Hyrum). So the office was left vacant and we had to sort it out.

There is another method that we haven't tried, so far as I know. That would be to use "lots" to choose from every male in the church. This method was used to fill Judas' vacancy in the original Twelve in Jerusalem.[288] The description there is ambiguous, but was intended to be random, unpredictable and not just a vote. It was a recognized way to choose someone.[289] It has been used to sort through the entire nation of Israel when all twelve tribes were assembled. Someone had stolen an idol, resulting in the withdrawal of the Lord's Spirit from them in battle. The result was defeat for Israel and the death of many men. They needed to find the one who committed the offense. So they had to choose from the entire gathering of all twelve tribes. Beginning at the tribe level, they sorted through to find the right tribe (Judah). Then proceeded to sort through the tribe to locate the larger family involved (Zarhites). Then went through the family

---

[287] D&C 43:3–4 "And this ye shall know assuredly—that there is none other appointed unto you to receive commandments and revelations until he be taken, if he abide in me. But verily, verily, I say unto you, that none else shall be appointed unto this gift except it be through him; for if it be taken from him he shall not have power except to appoint another in his stead."

[288] Acts 1:21–26 "Wherefore of these men which have companied with us all the time that the Lord Jesus went in and out among us, Beginning from the baptism of John, unto that same day that he was taken up from us, must one be ordained to be a witness with us of his resurrection. And they appointed two, Joseph called Barsabas, who was surnamed Justus, and Matthias. And they prayed, and said, Thou, Lord, which knowest the hearts of all *men,* shew whether of these two thou hast chosen, That he may take part of this ministry and apostleship, from which Judas by transgression fell, that he might go to his own place. And they gave forth their lots; and the lot fell upon Matthias; and he was numbered with the eleven apostles."

[289] 1 Nephi 3:11 "And we cast lots—who of us should go in unto the house of Laban. And it came to pass that the lot fell upon Laman; and Laman went in unto the house of Laban, and he talked with him as he sat in his house."

to find the individual involved (Achan). The whole thing is in the scriptures.[290]

Such a system was uncontrolled by man, done by lot, completely random, but produced the right person. Left to God, it obtained God's answer. Did with the sons of Lehi, and with the vacancy in the Twelve in the Book of Acts, too. There is no reason why such a system wouldn't generate the Lord's choice today.

If the President died without a successor having been designated, then random choosing using a lot system would put the choice in the Lord's hands. But I suppose we don't have the stomach to try it, particularly when we already have a system that seems to work for us.

Your question raises the issue of "authority" or office on the one hand, and "power" or gifts of the Spirit on the other hand. You should read President Packer's talk in last General Conference for a recent statement by a respected church leader on that subject. I think I've commented on that talk enough already. As I re-read it this week

---

[290] Joshua 7:13–23 "Up, sanctify the people, and say, Sanctify yourselves against to morrow: for thus saith the Lord God of Israel, *There is* an accursed thing in the midst of thee, O Israel: thou canst not stand before thine enemies, until ye take away the accursed thing from among you. In the morning therefore ye shall be brought according to your tribes: and it shall be, *that* the tribe which the Lord taketh shall come according to the families *thereof;* and the family which the Lord shall take shall come by households; and the household which the Lord shall take shall come man by man. And it shall be, *that* he that is taken with the accursed thing shall be burnt with fire, he and all that he hath: because he hath transgressed the covenant of the Lord, and because he hath wrought folly in Israel. So Joshua rose up early in the morning, and brought Israel by their tribes; and the tribe of Judah was taken: And he brought the family of Judah; and he took the family of the Zarhites: and he brought the family of the Zarhites man by man; and Zabdi was taken: And he brought his household man by man; and Achan, the son of Carmi, the son of Zabdi, the son of Zerah, of the tribe of Judah, was taken. And Joshua said unto Achan, My son, give, I pray thee, glory to the Lord God of Israel, and make confession unto him; and tell me now what thou hast done; hide *it* not from me. And Achan answered Joshua, and said, Indeed I have sinned against the Lord God of Israel, and thus and thus have I done: When I saw among the spoils a goodly Babylonish garment, and two hundred shekels of silver, and a wedge of gold of fifty shekels weight, then I coveted them, and took them; and, behold, they *are* hid in the earth in the midst of my tent, and the silver under it. So Joshua sent messengers, and they ran unto the tent; and, behold, *it was* hid in his tent, and the silver under it. And they took them out of the midst of the tent, and brought them unto Joshua, and unto all the children of Israel, and laid them out before the Lord."

I was again stirred by President Packer's sagacity. I believe he is being candid, honest and giving the Saints the absolute best advice and counsel he can at this time.

Interesting subject. Something worth contemplating. Perhaps there will come a time when we are able to implement the system in D&C 43. Or when we put the Lord's hand to work by using lots to choose a President. Though I do not expect to see any change made during my life.

Infallibility's One-Way Street

[This is about foundational, indispensable, bed-rock doctrines involved in salvation. It is not about trifling changes which can come and go at any time. I'm talking about the big stuff, in the big picture, which will make-or-break salvation itself.]

Here's the destructive course that inevitably follows from the notion that the President of the church cannot lead us astray when foundational changes are made to the doctrine—we can only subtract from our body of principles. We never can add back what we have subtracted.

To illustrate the one-way street problem you need only look at the changes to the endowment. The endowment is considered indispensable for exaltation and therefore part of the required, correct, bed-rock doctrines. In 1990 it was changed to drop a character, eliminate dialogue, alter the manner of covenant-making and delete things considered distasteful. I will not discuss details, although others have and you can find them if you look. That isn't important to understanding the problem. It is only necessary to know some things were deleted.

Suppose that in 2015 there was a consensus that the deletions were wrong and should be returned. If you were to attempt to return them into the endowment, you would immediately raise these questions:

- Do all church members who received their endowment between 1990 and 2015 have to do them over again?
- Do all the vicarious ordinances performed on behalf of the dead between 1990 and 2015 have to be redone?
- If not, then why would a change be made, since it isn't necessary to redo the work already done?

Now suppose that you reach a satisfactory resolution to these questions, and as a result you change back and redo ordinances -immediately critics and others then raise these questions:

- Why did they change them if it was wrong to do so?
- How could they have been "inspired" if they made a mistake?
- Does this mean that the President wasn't a prophet; or, worse, a false prophet when he made this mistake?
- How can we ever trust the President again?

So, even if there were a consensus, a change that returns what was subtracted would be such a set-back to the institution that it could never be seriously entertained. It could not happen without shaking the very foundation of the premise (inerrancy of the President) upon which correlation relies to control the church.

It would take a very different group of people, having a much higher tolerance for changes, and a greater capacity to tolerate human failings, before it would be possible to add back what has once been deliberately subtracted. Such a radically different kind of Saint is unlikely to be produced without some rather dramatic changes to the population. Of course, dramatic changes are what the Lord has always told us will come as a part of preparing the earth for His return. (He calls it "calamity" in D&C 1:17.)[291]

Now I've used the endowment to illustrate the point, but the same principle works across the board with any bedrock policy, ordinance or teaching which has been deliberately discarded or adopted in place of something else by the church. Once it has been set into place by the correlation process, it is put into concrete and cannot be moved without demolition. Therefore, if we have made any mistake, discarded anything we should have retained, or neglected or opposed any teaching which the Lord wanted us to keep, He will use demolition to prepare us to receive it back again. We can only subtract. Fortunately for us, a caring God can (and will) add upon us still. 'Gotta break some concrete first, of course. But He cares enough to do that.[292] He's determined that we are to be added upon.[293] Even when we prefer subtraction to addition.

Obeying God, Not Fearing Man

As the voice of the Lord conferred the sealing power upon Nephi, this statement was made:

> "And now, because thou hast done this with such unwearyingness, behold, I will bless thee forever; and I will make thee mighty in word and in deed, in faith and in works; yea, even that all things shall be done unto thee according to thy word,

---

[291] D&C 1:17 "Wherefore, I the Lord, knowing the calamity which should come upon the inhabitants of the earth, called upon my servant Joseph Smith, Jun., and spake unto him from heaven, and gave him commandments;"

[292] Psalms 94:14 "For the Lord will not cast off his people, neither will he forsake his inheritance."

[293] Abraham 3:26 "And they who keep their first estate shall be added upon; and they who keep not their first estate shall not have glory in the same kingdom with those who keep their first estate; and they who keep their second estate shall have glory added upon their heads for ever and ever."

for thou shalt not ask that which is contrary to my will." (Helaman 10:5)

This is not a commandment, but a statement. It is a description
of what kind of person Nephi was. The Lord knew that even en-
dowed with that power he "shall not ask that which is contrary to
[the Lord's own] will."

How did the Lord know this about Nephi? Because of what
Nephi had done with such unwearyingness:

"for I have beheld how thou hast with unwearyingness declared the word, which I have given unto thee, unto this people. And thou hast not feared them, and hast not sought thine
own life, but hast sought my will, and to keep my commandments." (Helaman 10:4)

Nephi's prior assignments from the Lord had been done consis-
tently, without letting criticism or threats deter him. He said what the
Lord asked him to say, without fear of those who opposed, threatened, or belittled him. He had been "proven" and found worthy.[294]
Therefore, even though he may have been misunderstood or re-
sented by his peers, he was approved and trusted by the Lord.

How much better is it to be trusted by the Lord than to be popular with mankind?[295] What a remarkable relationship this man Nephi
must have had. It makes one think that such a thing can only happen
when a person is willing to follow in those exact steps.[296]

---

[294] Abraham 3:25 "And we will prove them herewith, to see if they will do all things
whatsoever the Lord their God shall command them;"

[295] Proverbs 29:25 "The fear of man bringeth a snare: but whoso putteth his trust in
the Lord shall be safe."

[296] D&C 121:20–21 "Their basket shall not be full, their houses and their barns shall
perish, and they themselves shall be despised by those that flattered them. They shall
not have right to the priesthood, nor their posterity after them from generation to
generation."

Obeying God and not fearing man is so rare a thing that when we do encounter it, we're likely to either misunderstand such a person or be offended by him.

Schism

Right now there is such a diversity of views among the political groups in the United States that there is potential for a national breakup. States are talking about seceding from the Union. Texas, which was an independent nation before it joined the United States, has always retained the right to secede. Other states have discussed departing, and the reasons are diverse. Taxation and profligate Federal spending motivate some. Liberal issues motivate others, like Vermont, to want to leave in order to avoid conservative backlash. Conservative issues motivate others, who believe the Federal agenda is just too reckless.

The problem of national politics is its "one-size-fits-all" approach to governing. There is no room for diverse local populations to make independent decisions about their course of political development. Originally the nation was intended to be loosely governed from the national level, where such minimal governance as was necessary would be provided. National defense and interstate commerce were to be controlled to prevent invasion and internal warfare between the states. But the states were to govern their populations as independently sovereign states whose authority sprang from their people.

When you move power to the national level alone, you then create a distant and oftentimes disconnected government which will take so much upon themselves in taxation and regulation that they alienate local populations throughout the country. Taxes which would never be assessed at the local level are levied to impose policy decisions and programs which are not wanted by the local populations. That continues until, as we see now, there is resistance from both sides of the political spectrum and talk about how oppressive the national government has become.

There's a lesson there about how humanity will react when they are forced to accept a one-size approach to a divergent local circumstance. When there is only one approach tolerated, and others suppressed and controlled, then people will eventually rebel. They will simply walk away from the benefits of national programs in order to pursue their own course freely.

It is always better to leave room for divergent approaches to divergent problems. That was what the separate states were originally intended to accomplish. A problem could be experimented with at the state level. Kentucky could try one approach, Florida another, and Maine yet another. If Kentucky's worked better, and Florida's was a disaster, and Maine's somewhat of a success but nothing like Kentucky's; then the populations of the various states could learn from what worked and what didn't. They could debate based upon the outcome of various experiments they conducted in their sovereign territories. Every one of them would benefit from the conduct of the other. Now, with only a national approach to social issues, tax issues, educational issues, and health issues, failure is not acceptable. When there is failure, the failed program is given more money, more personnel and more rhetoric to justify it. It becomes a matter of politically-correct thinking and speaking; because if you don't believe in supporting some failed program then you are uncharitable, or racist, or bigoted, or ignorant, or worse. Experimentation is not permitted and therefore failure is national in scope and expensive to endure.

It is always best to "control" as little as possible and to interfere with development of separate ideas as little as necessary. This is true of government, and it is true of rearing children [after you have instructed them in the foundational truths], as well. It is also true of churches, civic organizations and any cooperative human endeavor.

Cooperation through persuasion, meekness, kindness, pure knowledge and love unfeigned works, whenever it is tried.[297]

Be Firm and Steadfast!

I've said *several* times in *several* ways that we have an obligation to support the church's leaders and the programs of the church. I believe that with all my heart. The Lord is going to hold us all accountable. No one is going to be relieved from their respective responsibilities.

Pay tithes, attend your meetings. Keep a current temple recommend and use it. Serve when asked to do so. You will have a great influence on others for the good when you provide service. Not merely by what you say, but by the example you provide.

There is a great deal of unrest in the church. Oftentimes the result is inactivity. I believe that is a mistake. If all those who continued to care about the Gospel persisted in attending meetings and serving, it would do more to help the church than drifting into inactivity. Those who are sensitive to the troubles which beset the church need to be there, faithfully serving. If only those who are blinded to the troubles remain active, then the organization becomes narrower and narrower, less and less aware of its situation, and prone to continue in a course that will discard yet more of what matters most.

I wish I could inspire thousands of inactive Saints to return to activity. I know I have helped hundreds to return. Those who are most troubled are the ones who the church can use right now. Those who keenly sense that all is not well with Zion are the ones who need

---

[297] D&C 121:39–42 "We have learned by sad experience that it is the nature and disposition of almost all men, as soon as they get a little authority, as they suppose, they will immediately begin to exercise unrighteous dominion. Hence many are called, but few are chosen. No power or influence can or ought to be maintained by virtue of the priesthood, only by persuasion, by long-suffering, by gentleness and meekness, and by love unfeigned; By kindness, and pure knowledge, which shall greatly enlarge the soul without hypocrisy, and without guile—"

to be filling the pews. Until they fill the pews they won't be filling the leadership positions. And until they fill the leadership positions, there won't be any changes made to the course we are on at present.

If you love Zion and want her redemption, then serve her cause. Faithfully serve her cause. Don't sever yourself from her.

There is no question the Lord will hold accountable those who are in leadership positions for every word, every thought, and every deed.[298] They aren't spared. This is why we should pray for them, uphold them, and do what we can to relieve them of the terrible burdens and consequences of being accountable for their callings.[299]

When you withdraw from the church you cut yourself off from necessary ordinances, including the sacrament. You imperil your capacity to keep the Sabbath day holy. You limit your capacity to serve others. Even a bad lesson makes you consider what the teacher and manual is ignoring, misstating or mangling. You needn't be argumentative or unpleasant. But by being there you have a time to reflect upon the subject being addressed by the class and to contemplate what that subject means to you. Use it meditatively and gratefully. It is a gift. If you see more clearly than others, then thank the Lord for that and stop being impatient with your fellow Saint.

You are a gift to the church. Your talents and your abilities belong to and were intended to be a part of the church. Serve there. Patiently and kindly. You needn't start an argument in every class to make a difference. Quietly going about serving and occasionally providing a carefully chosen insight is important and will garner you far more blessings than withdrawing and letting your light grow dim.

---

[298] Alma 12:14 "For our words will condemn us, yea, all our works will condemn us; we shall not be found spotless; and our thoughts will also condemn us; and in this awful state we shall not dare to look up to our God; and we would fain be glad if we could command the rocks and the mountains to fall upon us to hide us from his presence."

[299] D&C 107:22 "Of the Melchizedek Priesthood, three Presiding High Priests, chosen by the body, appointed and ordained to that office, and upheld by the confidence, faith, and prayer of the church, form a quorum of the Presidency of the Church."

We're all in this together. This is our dispensation. You are responsible for helping it be preserved and passed along to the rising generation. Do not grow weary in this fight. We share a common enemy, and *it is not* the leadership of the church. It is the one who stirs people up to anger.[300]

I'd like to open people's eyes only so as to permit them to save their own souls and those of others. I would never want anyone to walk away from the church as a result of seeing its weaknesses. Be wise, but harmless.[301] Be patient with anyone's shortcomings, no matter whether they serve in the nursery or in the presidency of an organization.

Blood Crying for Vengeance

I was asked about blood crying for vengeance from the ground. The question was how this reconciled with charity or forgiveness.

Blood "crying from the ground" is not the same thing as a person crying out for vengeance. Keep the context in mind: It is the blood which was shed upon the earth which cries out for vengeance or fairness or retribution. Something unfair has occurred, and the cry of the blood "upon the ground" is a reminder of the injustice of it all.

The ground is a reference to the earth, which has a spirit, intelligence, and is able to communicate if a person were capable of listening. It is a female spirit, and she regards herself as "the mother of men." This earth is offended when the men who are upon her kill one another or engage in any form of wickedness upon her surface. Below is her lament as she beheld the disorder and murder caused by that generation upon whom the flood was unleashed:

---

[300] 2 Nephi 28:20 "For behold, at that day shall he rage in the hearts of the children of men, and stir them up to anger against that which is good."

[301] Matthew 10:16 "Behold, I send you forth as sheep in the midst of wolves: be ye therefore wise as serpents, and harmless as doves."

"And it came to pass that Enoch looked upon the earth; and he heard a voice from the bowels thereof, saying: Wo, wo is me, the mother of men; I am pained, I am weary, because of the wickedness of my children. When shall I rest, and be cleansed from the filthiness which is gone forth out of me? When will my Creator sanctify me, that I may rest, and righteousness for a season abide upon my face?" (Moses 7:48)

Even if the person whose blood was shed departed this earth forgiving those who made offense against him, yet would "the ground" cry out for vengeance because the earth has become filthy by reason of the killing which took place upon her. She, as the "mother of men," regards the killing of men upon her as an abomination. She cries out. She is offended. She wants righteousness to appear on her, as has happened before. She longs that it be brought about again. When, instead of Zion, she has the murder of men upon her face, it is so great a lamentation by her spirit that "the ground cries out for vengeance" because of the atrocity.

Men's Hearts Will Fail Them

Luke records Christ's first public sermon that occurred after His baptism, temptation, wedding and commencement of the public ministry. He read from Isaiah about the commission He had received from God to preach.[302] After reading the verses, He proclaimed that *He* was the fulfillment of those verses.[303]

---

[302] Luke 4:17–19 "And there was delivered unto him the book of the prophet Esaias. And when he had opened the book, he found the place where it was written, The Spirit of the Lord *is* upon me, because he hath anointed me to preach the gospel to the poor; he hath sent me to heal the brokenhearted, to preach deliverance to the captives, and recovering of sight to the blind, to set at liberty them that are bruised, To preach the acceptable year of the Lord."

[303] Luke 4:20–21 "And he closed the book, and he gave *it* again to the minister, and sat down. And the eyes of all them that were in the synagogue were fastened on him. And he began to say unto them, This day is this scripture fulfilled in your ears."

He expounded on the verses adding that not only were they fulfilled, but He pressed on to explain how He would fulfill them in comments that were unrecorded. However, those who heard could not help but be persuaded at His gracious words.[304]

He moved from these verses in Isaiah to add His own prophecy about what they would eventually do to Him. You will tell me: "Physician, heal thyself," He added.[305] He will be asked by them to do miracles among them as He will do in Capernaum, but they will not be given such a witness. He explains that not all of a prophet's works will be put to display before all people. That some will see Him, but only have the testimony of others to learn of His works.[306]

They were indignant at His comments. It filled them with wrath. They thought they should be given the same signs, the same proof, of His claim to Messiahship as He would put before others.[307] However, He explained to them that He would be without honor among those closest to Him.[308] The attempt of the congregation to kill Him failed. He departed and went among more believing people, who heard Him speak with power from heaven.[309]

---

[304] Luke 4:22 "And all bare him witness, and wondered at the gracious words which proceeded out of his mouth. And they said, Is not this Joseph's son?"

[305] Luke 4:23 "And he said unto them, Ye will surely say unto me this proverb, Physician, heal thyself: whatsoever we have heard done in Capernaum, do also here in thy country."

[306] Luke 4:24–27 "And he said, Verily I say unto you, No prophet is accepted in his own country. But I tell you of a truth, many widows were in Israel in the days of Elias, when the heaven was shut up three years and six months, when great famine was throughout all the land; But unto none of them was Elias sent, save unto Sarepta, *a city* of Sidon, unto a woman *that was* a widow. And many lepers were in Israel in the time of Eliseus the prophet; and none of them was cleansed, saving Naaman the Syrian."

[307] Luke 4:28–29 "And all they in the synagogue, when they heard these things, were filled with wrath, And rose up, and thrust him out of the city, and led him unto the brow of the hill whereon their city was built, that they might cast him down headlong."

[308] Luke 4:24 ". . . Verily I say unto you, No prophet is accepted in his own country."

[309] Luke 4:30–32 "But he passing through the midst of them went his way, And came down to Capernaum, a city of Galilee, and taught them on the sabbath days. And they were astonished at his doctrine: for his word was with power."

What an interesting commencement of His public ministry. Telling the truth among those unprepared to welcome Him did them no good, persuaded no-one of the truth, and resulted in His forced departure.

What can be said of those who would cast out of their congregation He who was greater than them all? They thought they were making a bold statement about their fidelity to their religious traditions, and holding fast to the truth. Instead, they were cutting themselves off from the lifeline sent to save them.

Irony is not a strong enough word to describe this singular scene. It would be repeated throughout Christ's ministry among the hierarchy and leadership of His day, ultimately culminating in His death at their hands. These were the only people who would kill their God.[310] They were devout. They were misinformed. They were very religious, but entirely mistaken.

What happened on that first day of teaching was a microcosm of His entire ministry. It is often the case that those who regard themselves as the "most religious" and "most correct" are capable of missing the truth sent to them by the Lord. They prefer the Lord package the truth in one way, coupled with a written guarantee that the package will never fail them, while the Lord is always sending it in another, and requiring them to receive it when only their hearts can guide them into recognizing it. It is little wonder, then, that our day is when "men's hearts will fail them" because they fear, and trust not the things sent to them.[311]

---

[310] 2 Nephi 10:3 "Wherefore, as I said unto you, it must needs be expedient that Christ—for in the last night the angel spake unto me that this should be his name—should come among the Jews, among those who are the more wicked part of the world; and they shall crucify him—for thus it behooveth our God, and there is none other nation on earth that would crucify their God."

[311] Luke 21:26 "Men's hearts failing them for fear, and for looking after those things which are coming on the earth: for the powers of heaven shall be shaken."

Broken Souls

I'm hoping to solve Ben's perplexity (raised in a recent comment), and give all those who come here something to reflect on at the same time.

There are those who are kept from active church attendance because they have read something about history or doctrine which has alarmed and/or discouraged them. There are those who, because of their circumstances, are embarrassed to come to church. There are those who are poor and ashamed, or they are living with the heavy burden of sin and choose to stay away from our meetings. Perhaps they suffer from depression or anxiety, have addictions and feel unclean and unworthy.

I have home taught or spent time with people with all of these issues, concerns and experiences, and more. They stay away because they do not feel welcome among us. Many feel judged, some feel like they just can't abide hypocrisy, some are hurting and the church makes their hurt worse.

From the time I joined the church until today, I look for these people. I volunteer to go and visit with them in every ward I have attended, in every stake where I have served, and across the Mission when missionaries have asked me to come help teach. I was honored just a few days ago to meet with a man and his wife who are inactive, but who have a towering understanding of the church, gospel, its history, the scriptures and doctrine. They have figured out a great deal more than either their bishop or stake president. As a result, I think the local church authorities are somewhat intimidated by their understanding, and the leaders cannot answer their questions. It was, for me, a joyful visit and I hope to return again and talk with this wonderful Latter-day Saint couple soon.

I have met with people whose son committed suicide while attending a church-owned university because he was so lonely and isolated that his last desperate act was intended to end his life and re-buke those who had dismissed his pain. I loved these people who spoke with me about their son's life and death. They possessed a sensitivity to the feelings of others which can only be purchased at the price of enduring great personal pain.

I have close friends who struggle with addictions. Some of these people struggle with things so haunting, so terrible a force in their lives that rising each day to face the coming fight takes greater courage than I can even imagine. They are acting in faith at every waking breath, as they fight against a foe I do not comprehend and could not face.

I have helped women whose husbands are esteemed as church leaders, but the husbands' private actions are hellish and abusive. Women who have nowhere to turn, because their husband IS the leader with jurisdiction over them. No one will believe them because their "righteous" husband says they have mental or emotional ill-nesses. These women somehow manage to continue to serve their children and remain steadfast despite the hell they find themselves in.

It is not possible to set out all the different ways wherein the men and women I have met struggle. It is a great privilege to know these people. People whose insight into life and difficulties is far greater than I can begin to comprehend. People whose strength is not even recognized, because others are too busy dismissing, belittling or judg-ing them as "a thing of naught."[312]

I have marveled at how very much these broken souls, these dis-couraged people, these victims of our judgments who we have dis-carded or neglected are the very ones with whom I feel the Lord's presence and love as I have the honor of meeting and talking with

---

[312] 2 Nephi 28:16 "Wo unto them that turn aside the just for a thing of naught and revile against that which is good, and say that it is of no worth! For the day shall come that the Lord God will speedily visit the inhabitants of the earth; and in that day that they are fully ripe in iniquity they shall perish."

them about the Gospel. These are the ones He loves the most. These are the ones with whom He associated during His ministry. He associates there, still.

We have driven many of them away from activity in the church because of how *we* behave. In turn, the Spirit does not dwell with many of the "righteous" and proud active Latter-day Saints because hearts have not been broken nor spirits made contrite. We are made to think God favors us because we have worldly successes. We prosper. It is the successful, the financially well-to-do, the educated, the bank president, the lawyer and doctor whom we hold up as the model of a true Saint. Read the resumes of those who are called to lead the stakes and missions of the church in each week's *Church News*. We draw from a very narrow social gene-pool to find those who serve. They come from among those who have the financial resources in place to spare the time it takes to serve. In the process we get a 'Gospel of Success' mentality, right out of one segment of the Evangelical movement.

I am NOT saying that nothing good can come from the Stanford Business School. I am NOT saying bankers are damned (though they are in truth damnable). I am not talking about them. I am talking instead about those broken souls whom I know the Lord loves, but who are not among us because of our own pride and haughty attitudes.

If we were to flood the wards of Zion with those whose hearts are broken, who mourn because of issues that weigh heavy upon them, and who feel that there is nothing in the church for them, but who look to Christ to lift them from their torment, we would be enriched by their homecoming. In much the same way as the Prodigal was worthy of a feast, but the resentful but faithful son who stayed behind was not, so also are the riches of eternity reserved for the poor, downtrodden and broken hearted.

We are the poorer because of their absence. Our wards are not informed by hearing of their dilemmas and struggles. We are not what we could be if we were to make such people welcome—throwing our arms open to greet them. We do not hear their struggle to keep a testimony after learning about some serious failing of a past leader. We are not informed, as we should be, in our meetings and discussions.

This is a lamentation, and not an explanation. This is not the fullness of the subject, but merely a hint of what I know displeases the Lord about us. It is not my responsibility to define fully the Lord's displeasure with us at the moment. I can, however, assure you He is not pleased. Some of what we think ourselves best for doing is not what He would want us to take pride in. Our Lord's heart is broken still. His ways are higher than ours because He values the least more than do we.

I cannot say more. But I am left amazed at the hardness of the hearts of this generation who claim they are the Lord's. Many, many will be told by Him to depart from His presence at the time of Judgment because they never knew Him. They speak today in His name, yet they know Him not. It would be better for them to not speak at all, than to toss about His name as the author of foolish, vain, proud and evil notions while claiming He agrees with such things.

Reminder

I can see my wife put up another reminder about the stuff I've written previously. I can tell you why she did that.

Some folks presume that a brief post contains all of an idea that I have spent many pages setting out a full explanation for elsewhere. They comment, challenge, criticize or contradict in a reply comment as if the whole of what I have to say about some topic is contained in the briefest of posts. It is apparent that if the person had read what I've written elsewhere they wouldn't be making the comment they make here.

An example is the plural marriage notion. I've spent pages and given both history and scripture to explain what my explanation is for the position I take in the book *Beloved Enos*. There are persons who are obsessed with the whole plural marriage subject, and very well may be practicing plural marriage. My comments and views probably threaten them, because I do not believe it appropriate to practice plural marriage now that it has been banned by both the law of Utah, law of the United States, confirmed by the United States to be prohibited, and abandoned by the church as a practice.

The keys which allowed the practice are addressed at length in *Beloved Enos*, and it would be too long a discussion to take the subject up here. I anticipated that there would be those who practice plural marriage who would read what I have to say, and so I addressed their concerns in that book. So when they want to have a discussion about the topic, this isn't the forum for that. I've written my understanding before and it becomes apparent that the person(s) replying do not understand my position because they haven't read it.

I think my wife as Moderator gets somewhat exasperated with these comments, because they are something which she necessarily has to read before putting up and seem so contrary to the intent of doing this blog. I get vicariously frustrated as well as we discuss it.

I worry that some very good folks, with great comments, are thinking that their comments are not welcomed. That isn't true, of course. What is true is that it is unfair and inaccurate to reach a conclusion about what I think or understand based upon the briefest of comments made on this blog. The comments would need to be read in light of lengthy explanations provided elsewhere and fit into the context of what I've already explained, before it is fair to react as if you understand my position. Some of you have taken the trouble to read what I've written and do understand a comment made here. Some clearly have not. Everyone is welcome to put a comment up in response to a post, but I'm not going to respond to all of them when the explanation is already provided elsewhere.

I hope that clarifies again the reasons behind the periodic reminders put up here.

A MESSAGE OF WARNING

A Message of Warning

The Jews thought themselves favored of God. They trusted that the land they occupied had been promised to Abraham, Isaac and Jacob. They were the descendants of these patriarchs. The land had been promised to them. They had the priesthood, the temple, God's promise and a true religion. They knew nothing could molest their peace.

The Lord commissioned Zechariah to deliver this warning to them:

"Thus speaketh the Lord of hosts, saying, Execute true judgment, and shew mercy and compassions every man to his brother: And oppress not the widow, nor the fatherless, the stranger, nor the poor; and let none of you imagine evil against his brother in your heart. But they refused to hearken, and pulled away the shoulder, and stopped their ears, that they should not hear. Yea, they made their hearts as an adamant stone, lest they should hear the law, and the words which the Lord of hosts hath sent in his spirit by the former prophets: therefore came a great wrath from the Lord of hosts. Therefore it is come to pass, that as he cried, and they would not hear; so they cried, and I would not hear, saith the Lord of hosts: But I scattered them with a whirlwind among all the nations whom they knew not. Thus the land was desolate after them, that no man passed through nor returned: for they laid the pleasant land desolate." (Zechariah 7:9–4)

We can look at the Jews to whom this prophecy was delivered and see with clarity how they failed. We can see through their false presumptions, foolish beliefs and evil ways. We know how to correctly weigh them in the balance.

Imagine, however, if you lived among those people and shared their false presumptions. Imagine that you believed, as they did, that they were chosen, promised that nothing would molest them. Imagine you possessed a temple of God, true priesthood, and descended from prophets. How would you react when a prophet came among you crying that you were wicked, oppressed the poor, the fatherless and the stranger? Wouldn't you think Zechariah was wrong while all of you were right? How can a message from a single person hold an entire nation of people accountable for how they respond?

I suspect it wouldn't be any easier for us to see our plight as it was for the Jews to see theirs. I suspect our own harsh assessment of the failure of the Jews will be the very standard against which we will be measured in how we react to truth when it is declared among us. I doubt we can distinguish between truth and error any better than they did. But we pride ourselves on condemning them, and justifying ourselves.

The irony in all this is so thick you can hardly move.

How grateful I am to live at a time when there are messages received again from the Lord which can lead us to salvation, despite earth and hell, false messengers and fools, pretenders and charlatans.

Yet will the Lord keep His promise that before He does anything, He will commission a message of warning.[313]

The Arm of Flesh

When the church commissions an opinion poll and then, as a result of that poll, concludes that some program or position is popular, or would be accepted by the Saints without complaint—and then adopt that position in a public statement—has a "revelation" been received? I do not think so. I think an opinion has been obtained, and a policy or statement has been adopted. Therefore, I do not think there is one thing wrong with disagreeing with the policy or statement.

When the church endorses something or some position, I do not think it is right to simply "fall in line" behind the statement without also thinking the same issue through and reaching my own conclusion. The first question I ask myself is what the statement is, and does it imply a revelation from the Lord.

I can think of two examples. One was a public announcement that was heralded in the press. The other was the subject of a letter from the First Presidency read in sacrament meetings.

The public announcement was regarding the housing and employment of homosexuals in Salt Lake City, using the force of government sanction to prevent an employer or owner of property from refusing to grant equal access or rights to homosexuals. I've previously commented here in a critical way about that announcement. This is an example of how I view things.

Since the church's position on the matter had absolutely nothing to do with revelation, and the church did not make any attempt to claim the position came through revelation, I do not believe it is im-

---

[313] Amos 3:7 "Surely the Lord God will do nothing, but he revealeth his secret unto his servants the prophets."

mune from question or criticism. Indeed, the defense of the policy to the press involved a public relations/opinion poll driven justification. It was expected to "resonate on the basis of fairness" with all those in the middle, and only offend those at the two ends of the spectrum. This is opinion gathering to inform a position, then announcing the position because of the results of opinion gathering. It is what a politician or a marketing firm would do. It is not at all akin to a revelation, and should not command my respect. I am under no obligation to alter my view based on what the church's opinion gathering has concluded. If that were the case, then the church's ability to control everyone's thinking would be based only upon prevailing opinion at the moment. This is the "tossed about by every wind" concern which Paul addressed in one of his letters.[314] (Eph. 4:14.) Shifting opinion is not revelation. I am free to point it out, disagree with it, and explain my contrary view.

Another example is the letter from the First Presidency asking speakers in sacrament meetings to no longer ask those in attendance to open their scriptures. No explanation was provided in the letter. It was just an instruction to the Saints to no longer let sacrament meeting speakers tell those in the meeting to open their scriptures and read along. Perhaps it was as a result of someone being irritated by the noise of rustling scriptures. Perhaps it was someone with a hearing aid, whose aid frequency was tuned to pick up the rustling so well that it drowned out the rest of the speaker's voice. Perhaps it was because the meeting got delayed and disrupted by the folks struggling to find their scriptures, and open them up to the relevant page. I can't say for certain. But I did raise my eyebrows when the letter was read in advance to the High Council.

---

[314] Ephesians 4:14 "That we *henceforth* be no more children, tossed to and fro, and carried about with every wind of doctrine, by the sleight of men, *and* cunning craftiness, whereby they lie in wait to deceive;"

My candid reaction to that letter was that it diminished the office of those who signed the letter by the petty micro-managing of opening the scriptures during a sacrament gathering. I wondered in amazement that someone in the Church Office Building got the First Presidency to sign such a letter. I wondered at how, with all that threatens us today, opening scriptures in order to read along in sacrament meetings managed to become so important that the First Presidency would write and send a letter worldwide to be read in the stakes and wards. It was perplexity on stilts.

Beyond that my approach has been twofold: First, I have NEVER asked anyone to open their scriptures in a sacrament meeting since then. However, I have said in talks during sacrament that "I cannot ask you to open your scriptures and read along" in order to call attention to the policy. I have also said, when teaching outside of sacrament meetings, that I was free to ask them to read along in their scriptures "because we are not in a sacrament meeting." I do this to call attention to the policy. I think to call attention to it is to cause people to wonder at the pettiness and inconsequential nature of a letter from the First Presidency addressing the opening of scriptures in sacrament meeting.

These are just two examples. There are many. As I have said before, I pay very close attention to the church, what is said and done, and how relevant or irrelevant some position, letter, emphasis or program is in an absolute sense. I try to take it all in and reach my own conclusions. Looking at it all, I am quite concerned. Faithful, tithe paying and active, nevertheless quite concerned.

I believe if enough people were similarly concerned that eventually the "opinion polling" might obtain reasonable results. That is, the top would hear about reasonable concerns and learn of reasonable opinions, and then promulgate policies and send out statements accordingly. That, however, will require a great effort to call attention to the things that matter most, and clarity in pointing out the things that do not matter at all. We fret over trifles while things are burning down all around us. I wonder how long it will take for the polling to inform the Saints of the fire burning around them.

O That I Had Repented

National debt is nearly the entire annual gross domestic product.

The banking crisis in Europe is threatening to spread, and the US has committed billions to help prop up the imbalanced European socialist-democracies.

The money supply is shrinking at a rate comparable only to the years leading into the Great Depression.

I am reminded of the Nephites when they were denounced with these words:

> "O ye wicked and ye perverse generation; ye hardened and ye stiffnecked people, how long will ye suppose that the Lord will suffer you? Yea, how long will ye suffer yourselves to be led by foolish and blind guides? Yea, how long will ye choose darkness rather than light? Yea, behold, the anger of the Lord is already kindled against you; behold, he hath cursed the land because of your iniquity. And behold, the time cometh that he curseth your riches, that they become slippery, that ye cannot hold them; and in the days of your poverty ye cannot retain them." (Helaman 13:29–31)

As our own riches become "slippery" so that we cannot hold onto them, I think we get a taste of what the Nephites were allowed to experience because they could not distinguish between those who taught the truth and those who merely led them about while blind.

The prophecy continued with these additional words of wise, and still relevant counsel:

"And in the days of your poverty ye shall cry unto the Lord;
and in vain shall ye cry, for your desolation is already come
upon you, and your destruction is made sure; and then shall ye
weep and howl in that day, saith the Lord of Hosts. And then
shall ye lament, and say: O that I had repented, and had not
killed the prophets, and stoned them, and cast them out. Yea,
in that day ye shall say: O that we had remembered the Lord
our God in the day that he gave us our riches, and then they
would not have become slippery that we should lose them; for
behold, our riches are gone from us. Behold, we lay a tool
here and on the morrow it is gone; and behold, our swords
are taken from us in the day we have sought them for
battle. Yea, we have hid up our treasures and they have slipped
away from us, because of the curse of the land. O that we had
repented in the day that the word of the Lord came unto us;
for behold the land is cursed, and all things are become slippery, and we cannot hold them. Behold, we are surrounded by
demons, yea, we are encircled about by the angels of him who
hath sought to destroy our souls. Behold, our iniquities are
great. O Lord, canst thou not turn away thine anger from us?
And this shall be your language in those days. But behold,
your days of probation are past; ye have procrastinated the
day of your salvation until it is everlastingly too late, and your
destruction is made sure; yea, for ye have sought all the days
of your lives for that which ye could not obtain; and ye have
sought for happiness in doing iniquity, which thing is contrary
to the nature of that righteousness which is in our great and
Eternal Head. O ye people of the land, that ye would hear my
words!" (Helaman 13:32–39)

As always, the Book of Mormon remains the keystone of our
religion. A person can get closer to God by abiding its precepts than
through any other book.

I don't think Joseph Smith wrote it. I think he translated it. I
think it contains wisdom from an earlier, failed civilization that once
inhabited this land. I think their lessons should not be forgotten by

us. Because when we fail to learn them by precept, then we get to learn them by experience. And some of their experiences were quite difficult.

Catch Hold or Cling

There are two different words used by Nephi regarding contact with the "iron rod" or word of God. Joseph Smith translated the two words as "cling" or "clinging" for one, and "hold" or "holding" as the other.

The different word use raises the question of meaning. If they meant identical things, then the same word would have been translated. Therefore, there must be a reason for the different words.

Below are examples of the different words in the context of the record:

> And it came to pass that I beheld others pressing forward, and they came forth and caught *hold* of the end of the rod of iron; and they did press forward through the mist of darkness, *clinging* to the rod of iron, even until they did come forth and partake of the fruit of the tree. But, to be short in writing, behold, he saw other multitudes pressing forward; and they came and caught *hold* of the end of the rod of iron; and they did press their way forward, continually *holding* fast to the rod of iron, until they came forth and fell down and partook of the fruit of the tree. (1 Nephi 8:24, 30)

Some catch hold, then cling.

Some hold, then hold fast.

So the question becomes why the different description. Both of these different approaches result in the persons reaching the destination, then partaking of the fruit. But they are situated differently as they move along the process. Some are "clinging" and some are "holding" as they move toward their destination.

To "cling" implies something frantic, something charged with emotion, and something more desperate than to "hold." "Holding" seems calm, thoughtfully committed and more methodical than does "clinging." From this, I conclude that there are at least two kinds of people who will make their way to partake of the fruit of the tree of life in this world.

For one group, the process is unnerving, fearful, and emotionally wrenching. They cling on despite earth and hell. They fight to retain their grip, and they make heroic efforts in the opposition they face. They cling because they cannot relent, cannot relax, and know they face peril as they live their lives daily. For them their hopes are kept despite all their fears. They cling because they desire more than the opposition can deter them.

For another group, the process is less emotional, but nonetheless filled with determination. They are not as charged with fear, but face what comes to them calmly and with the assurance that the Lord's word is in their hands and will be a refuge that will bring them to eternal life.

I think there is another, more likely possibility, as well. There is not two groups, but only one. From time to time everyone faces moments of difficulty. The only way to stay with the rod is to cling. Then the seasons change, the storm relents, and calm returns. During those times when life improves, the person can continue to hold and move forward, but they have purchased the season of calm by the things they have endured in faith. Now they know it is only necessary to hold on, and all things will come to them.

I do not know of a life that gets lived without challenge, difficulty and seasons of despair. I believe all of us will at times be required to cling, and at others have the ability to hold the course. Whether it is the one season or the other, however, at the end of the journey you will lay hold on eternal life. Press on.

I Am the Lord That Smiteth

The people among whom Ezekiel lived were filled with sin; public and private. The prophet was inspired to deliver a serious warning to them inasmuch as they could not learn by being taught correct precepts, but only by harsh judgment. His warning included this statement:

> "The morning is come unto thee, O thou that dwellest in the land: the time is come, the day of trouble is near, and not the sounding again of the mountains. Now will I shortly pour out my fury upon thee, and accomplish mine anger upon thee: and I will judge thee according to thy ways, and will recompense thee for all thine abominations. And mine eye shall not spare, neither will I have pity: I will recompense thee according to thy ways and thine abominations that are in the midst of thee; and ye shall know that I am the Lord that smiteth." (Ezekiel 7:7–9)

I had a few thoughts about why and how such "judgments" could be easily be poured out upon us, as well.

From drug abuse to carnality, we are less civil and more dangerous as a population each year. If you would like to see the Lord "pour out [His] fury upon [us]" you only need to shut off the electrical power in Detroit or Los Angeles at night. We are filled with the savagery that will bring about our own punishment. When the electrical grid fails in larger metropolitan areas of the United States, it will be Americans killing Americans, without any need for an invasion by an enemy. God will not need to send a plague upon us. We become our own plague because of our wickedness.

In the aftermath of Hurricane Katrina, when the New Orleans Police Department was unable to keep order, and the National Guard had not arrived yet, there were days filled with violence, rape and murder. It did not take anything more than a brief lack of police

authority before the population was plagued with criminal misconduct, violence and killing.

What more fitting a way to "judge thee according to thy ways?"
What more apt a manner for "recompensing thee for all thine abominations?" It is our own choice to become our own undoing. Amazing, really.

Are our sins any less than that generation to whom Ezekiel spoke?
Americans have killed 40 million unborn (innocent) children. Hitler,
the great genocidal monster of the last century, only killed 6 million
in his perversity. We have selected the most innocent, and ended 40
million of their lives. As Christ put it: Truly we deserve a millstone
hung around our necks and to be drowned in the depth of the sea
for this wanton shedding of innocent blood.[315]

This great perversity is what we call a "right to choose," thereby
clothing an atrocity in the words of virtue. We call evil good and
good evil, and never take time to notice we fulfill prophecy as we do
so. (2 Nephi 15:20, using Isaiah 5:20 to describe us and our time. [316])
Freedom of choice, right to choose, tolerance, diversity, open and
free are all words implying virtue. They justify suppression of truth,
sexual misconduct, killing innocent unborn and curtailing freedom of
thought and expression. We are hardly able to recognize good from
evil, because everything destructive or debasing, advocated by those
addicted to a perversity, is called by them good. And any who oppose
these abuses are called evil, intolerant, oppressive, haters and ignorant.

It should not surprise any of us if the Lord should shortly pour
out His judgments upon us. All it would take is a prolonged failure of

---

[315] Matthew 18:6 "But whoso shall offend one of these little ones which believe in me,
it were better for him that a millstone were hanged about his neck, and *that* he were
drowned in the depth of the sea."

[316] 2 Nephi 15:20 "Wo unto them that call evil good, and good evil, that put darkness
for light, and light for darkness, that put bitter for sweet, and sweet for bitter!"

the power grid and we would unleash on ourselves our own direful judgments.

Personal Revelation

On the 13th of November, 1835, Joseph was instructing, and made the following comment (which has been often repeated):

> "[I]f God gives you a manifestation, keep it to yourselves." (*Joseph Smith Papers; Journals* 1:98)

This statement has been quoted as a basis to support the position that any person's revelation should NEVER be shared with another person; other than of course a revelation given to the church president. The statement needs to be understood, however, in light of later statements recorded by Joseph in the same volume of the *Joseph Smith Papers*.

On page 170 Joseph recorded that "angels ministered unto them, as well as myself." A little further down on the same page:

> "My scribe ...saw in a vision the armies of heaven protecting the Saints in their return to Zion." Still on the same page: "The vision of heaven was opened to these also, some of them saw the face of the Savior; and others were ministered unto by holy angels, and the spirit of prophesy and revelation was poured out in mighty power."

On page 171 Joseph recorded that those who were present "spent the time in rehearsing to each other the glorious scenes that transpired on the preceding evening, while attending to the ordinance of the holy anointing."

On page 174 Joseph recorded that his brother, William, "saw the heavens opened and the Lord's host protecting the Lord's anointed."

On page 182 Joseph recorded that Zebedee Coltrin "saw a vision of the Lord's House—and others were filled with the spirit and

spake in tongues and prophesied." Later on that same page, in footnote 361, this is included: "Oliver Cowdery also recorded that 'many
saw visions, many prophesied, and many spake in tongues.'" citing to
Oliver's Diary for 6 Feb. 1836.

It is apparent that Joseph's comment did not result in these early
Saints not speaking of the manifestations they received. Nor did Joseph exhibit any disapproval or concern about hearing of others
speaking of their spiritual manifestations. His comment, therefore,
needs to be understood in the context of the overall manner in which
spiritual experiences were experienced and shared among the early
church, even within a couple of months of the statement used to
justify criticism of any person saying anything about any manifestation they received.

Oddly, I do not think anyone should share anything with anyone
else unless the Lord, who gives manifestations, directs. When He
does, then I think objections are made at the peril of disrespecting
the Lord's command. (See e.g., Alma 8:25; 3 Nephi 23:9—where the
Lord required some of what Samuel had said to be added to their
scriptures which the Nephites had neglected to record.[317])

Answers to Prayers

I was asked why it seems there are seasons when a person can't
get an answer from God. Even when they have previously had wonderful contact, revelation, insights and blessings, there are times
when nothing is coming from God. It appears to be unrelated to

---

[317] Alma 8:25 "But behold, I have been commanded that I should turn again and
prophesy unto this people, yea, and to testify against them concerning their iniquities."
3 Nephi 23:9 "Verily I say unto you, I commanded my servant Samuel, the Lamanite,
that he should testify unto this people, that at the day that the Father should glorify his
name in me that there were many saints who should arise from the dead, and should
appear unto many, and should minister unto them. And he said unto them: Was it not
so?"

faithfulness or activity. Why, then, does God remain silent from time to time?

There are multiple reasons why this happens. It IS unrelated to God's love for the person.

The first and most common reason I have discovered is that you are already in possession of the answer. It was given to you by God and you have it, but you don't recognize it. It would be better to stop asking for an answer and instead ask to be able to see what you have already been given.

The second reason is that you need to struggle and make your own decision first, then to petition to know if the decision is right. It is not always appropriate to defer all decisions to the Lord. You must develop the capacity to make sound decisions on your own. The Lord will, of course, ratify the correct decision and warn you about the wrong one. But you need to develop the ability to decide first.[318]

Another reason, and perhaps the least common, is that the Lord knows that in your struggle you will eventually reach the correct decision. He must let you proceed on your own because the process of important. Even Abraham endured this process.[319] After he made the decision and traveled to the border, just prior to his entry into Egypt the Lord returned to him and prepared him for what he would encounter there.

There are also occasions wherein the Lord has determined to give you the answer, but you are not prepared for what is coming. There-

---

[318] D&C 9:7–9 "Behold, you have not understood; you have supposed that I would give it unto you, when you took no thought save it was to ask me. But, behold, I say unto you, that you must study it out in your mind; then you must ask me if it be right, and if it is right I will cause that your bosom shall burn within you; therefore, you shall feel that it is right. But if it be not right you shall have no such feelings, but you shall have a stupor of thought that shall cause you to forget the thing which is wrong; therefore, you cannot write that which is sacred save it be given you from me."

[319] Abraham 2:21 "And I, Abraham, journeyed, going on still towards the south; and there was a continuation of a famine in the land; and I, Abraham, concluded to go down into Egypt, to sojourn there, for the famine became very grievous."

fore, you are put through experience to develop. During this time, you are moving toward the answer that you are being prepared to receive. Once the preparation is over, the answer follows. It is possible that so much transpires between the request and the answer that you forget it was your petition to the Lord that set things in motion. Nevertheless the Lord was working to give you an answer all along.

There are occasions where the answer lies before you, and your path will intersect with the answer in the normal course. The apparent silence from the Lord is really the answer—Stay true and you will find it as you move along. These moments are what develop necessary patience. We are tempted to show ingratitude when these happen, thinking that it was our own ability which secured for us the answer, instead of the mercy of the Lord. That is a mistake.

The final reason is that you are mistaken about your worthiness or standing before God and you need to alter what you are doing. In this instance it is likely that you get an answer, but the answer is that you are in need of repentance or change. The change needs to precede an answer. Never ignore a warning that you are out of the way; it may be the kindest response of all. Get your life in order first, then the answer you seek will follow. Ingratitude to the Lord is often the first reason for needed repentance.

These are the reasons I have found for those seasons in which an answer is not forthcoming from the Lord.

Developing Your Faith

I've been thinking on the different kinds of questions I get, and what those questions reflect about the one asking. There are two conditions that cannot be overcome by me or any other person by answering your question. The first one is your insecurities. The other is your curiosity. Your insecurities about whatever is going on in your life will not go away because you received an answer to a question.

Your curiosity will not be satisfied by hearing a spiritual experience recounted by another person.

Insecurities are a result of a lack of faith. You deserve them. You have not acquired knowledge yet. You have them as a gift, as a warning that you have not yet received what you need. Nor have you developed faith yet. I've given you a post that repeats very important and true doctrine from the Lectures on Faith. It is a blueprint for how you develop faith. I cannot do it for you. Neither can Joseph or Jesus Christ. Faith comes from within you, developed by the same process through which every man who has ever had faith developed it. There are no shortcuts, no independent conferral by sprinkling something on you, and no method different than what has always been required. To the extent I am able to explain the process, I have done so in *The Second Comforter*. If you are still insecure, then you have not done what that book teaches you to do. Getting an answer from me, or from any other man, will not replace the hollow feeling inside you springing from the absence of saving faith.

The scriptures are filled with spiritual experiences and doctrine. Adding another account to those already there will not benefit you nor bring you closer to developing faith. It will not fill you. That is why my experiences have never been told. (Only in my testimony of the truthfulness of what I teach have I touched briefly upon my experiences.) The focus of all I have done is doctrine. Teaching correct principles will allow you to both govern and develop yourself.

Asking for details from my experiences will add absolutely nothing to you. Those experiences will only weaken you. It will also weaken me. It will make me seem more than I am. It will cause you to surrender to another the responsibility devolving upon yourself. You will only err in thinking that having another "spiritual story" to retell has made you closer to the Lord. It doesn't happen that way. Get your own spiritual experiences. Then, if you want more, keep them sacred. That is what I do. I teach principles. I do not reveal experiences.

I read many years ago about Abraham being the "friend of God." I read also in the D&C about the Lord calling some early Saints His "friends." As I reflected upon that word ("friend") I thought about what it meant ("friendship"). After pondering the word for many days, and observing the people around me, thinking about what I saw in society, and considered the sermons I heard in church, I reached the conclusion that there wasn't a "friend" of God upon the earth any longer.

As I considered the conclusion, I thought about it from God's perspective. What must it mean to a Heavenly Father who has no friend upon the earth. How must He sorrow over His children who have departed from friendship. The thought grew in me until I determined I would become the "friend" of God; not for my sake, nor for any benefit which may come to me because of it. I thought of it only as a way to honor Him; to show Him that despite earth and hell there would yet be another "friend" of His upon the earth.

I have remained true to that determination from that time till now. It defines the choices I have made, the opportunities I have forfeited, the places I have been, and the doors which have opened. I may not be much of anything in this world, but I do have a Friend whose love I value and whose companionship I cherish. If I were to tell you all the details of that it would do you no good and would betray trust.

Asking about it is the clearest indication that you have misunderstood both the process and what I am trying to do to help others.

Destroyer Rideth upon the Waters

A study by the Harvard Business School has concluded that government spending does not stimulate an economy. It stifles. You can read the study here.[320]

This was not the conclusion the study was expected to produce. It is not a welcomed study during a time when the whole commitment of the federal policy is predicated upon the opposite conclusion. Simply put, we're pursuing a course that won't/can't work.

It shows again, how foolish it is to trust in the opinions of men. I'm utterly convinced that opinions are misleading. I believe the scriptures counsel against using opinions as a basis for determining truth.

The Great Whore, which deceives the world, sits upon "many waters."[321] The definition of "waters" is given in verse 15.[322] These unstable waters are the "peoples, and multitudes, and nations." It is again a reminder of the original blessing given to Reuben, in which instability is compared to "water."[323] Great wars, overflowing armies and unstable political movements have all been compared to a flood of water.[324]

---

[320] http://www.people.hbs.edu/cmalloy/pdffiles/envaloy.pdf

[321] Revelation 17:1 "And there came one of the seven angels which had the seven vials, and talked with me, saying unto me, Come hither; I will shew unto thee the judgment of the great whore that sitteth upon many waters:"

[322] Revelation 17:15 "And he saith unto me, The waters which thou sawest, where the whore sitteth, are peoples, and multitudes, and nations, and tongues."

[323] Genesis 49:4 "Unstable as water, thou shalt not excel; because thou wentest up to thy father's bed; then defiledst thou *it:* he went up to my couch."

[324] Isaiah 28:2 "Behold, the Lord hath a mighty and strong one, *which* as a tempest of hail *and* a destroying storm, as a flood of mighty waters overflowing, shall cast down to the earth with the hand."
Jeremiah 46:8 "Egypt riseth up like a flood, and *his* waters are moved like the rivers; and he saith, I will go up, *and* will cover the earth; I will destroy the city and the inhabitants thereof."

Opinions of peoples, multitudes and nations are as "unstable as water." They flow, and ebb and move about in dangerous currents. Finding an opinion and adopting it as the basis for a church decision or policy is a study in learning which cannot bring you to the truth.[325]

Before this latest study, it was common wisdom that government spending was NEEDED in order to combat the recession. Now, it appears the solution will only mire the country in a more prolonged downward economic cycle. Opinions were gathered carefully before the commitment was made. Now, we have accepted only foolishness as our wisdom.

I have always thought the tools of industry have no place in a church which claims to be guided by inspiration. To the extent the church elects to employ opinion polling and focus group gathering to inform its decision, it will reach the wrong conclusions, make the wrong decisions, and go backward.

Inspiration does not lie within the opinions of the great and unstable waters. Indeed, the Destroyer rides upon the waters.[326]

Keys and Assignments

For the benefit of a worthy inquirer, who has the right to know:

Keys are related to assignments given. When the church gives someone an assignment, they receive the keys associated with performing the assignment. For example, when an Elder's Quorum President is called, he receives the keys to preside over the Quorum. With those keys the President has the large assignment (making the Quorum function) and is entitled to the smaller or more detailed assistance from the Lord to serve each quorum member's needs.

---

[325] 2 Timothy 3:7 "Ever learning, and never able to come to the knowledge of the truth."

[326] D&C 61:19 "I, the Lord, have decreed, and the destroyer rideth upon the face thereof, and I revoke not the decree."

If the President neglects his duties, despite the fact that the authority is conferred upon him, he lacks the power associated with the assignment. His keys become thereby wasted or lost.

Keys, however, are not limited to the church giving an assignment. When the Lord gives an assignment, commission or commandment to a person by His own voice, then the Lord similarly gives to the person the keys to accomplish the assignment, commission or commandment. By acting consistent with the duty devolving upon him, the man receives not only the larger assignment, but also the inspiration to accomplish the smaller or more detailed activities related to the assignment given to him.

An example from Nephi illustrates the point. Nephi was commanded to build a ship.[327] Nephi needed direction and instruction to accomplish the task given to him. Since he possessed the keys to accomplish the work, the direction was forthcoming from the Lord as it was needed and as Nephi inquired to obtain it.[328] In the process of asking and receiving direction as he fulfilled the assignment, Nephi learned other, greater things as well.[329]

Nephi saw in the assignment (keys) he had been given a direct relationship between fulfilling the assignment to build a ship and Moses' commission (keys) to deliver Israel from bondage. He used Moses as an example to his brothers to justify how the Lord could

---

[327] 1 Nephi 17:8 "And it came to pass that the Lord spake unto me, saying: Thou shalt construct a ship, after the manner which I shall show thee, that I may carry thy people across these waters."

[328] 1 Nephi 17:9–10 "And I said: Lord, whither shall I go that I may find ore to molten, that I may make tools to construct the ship after the manner which thou hast shown unto me? And it came to pass that the Lord told me whither I should go to find ore, that I might make tools."

[329] 1 Nephi 18:2–3 "Now I, Nephi, did not work the timbers after the manner which was learned by men, neither did I build the ship after the manner of men; but I did build it after the manner which the Lord had shown unto me; wherefore, it was not after the manner of men. And I, Nephi, did go into the mount oft, and I did pray oft unto the Lord; wherefore the Lord showed unto me great things."

assign someone as untrained as Nephi to build a ship.[330] It was an

---

[330] 1 Nephi 17:23–43 "And it came to pass that I, Nephi, spake unto them, saying: Do ye believe that our fathers, who were the children of Israel, would have been led away out of the hands of the Egyptians if they had not hearkened unto the words of the Lord? Yea, do ye suppose that they would have been led out of bondage, if the Lord had not commanded Moses that he should lead them out of bondage? Now ye know that the children of Israel were in bondage; and ye know that they were laden with tasks, which were grievous to be borne; wherefore, ye know that it must needs be a good thing for them, that they should be brought out of bondage. Now ye know that Moses was commanded of the Lord to do that great work; and ye know that by his word the waters of the Red Sea were divided hither and thither, and they passed through on dry ground. But ye know that the Egyptians were drowned in the Red Sea, who were the armies of Pharaoh. And ye also know that they were fed with manna in the wilderness. Yea, and ye also know that Moses, by his word according to the power of God which was in him, smote the rock, and there came forth water, that the children of Israel might quench their thirst. And notwithstanding they being led, the Lord their God, their Redeemer, going before them, leading them by day and giving light unto them by night, and doing all things for them which were expedient for man to receive, they hardened their hearts and blinded their minds, and reviled against Moses and against the true and living God. And it came to pass that according to his word he did destroy them; and according to his word he did lead them; and according to his word he did do all things for them; and there was not any thing done save it were by his word. And after they had crossed the river Jordan he did make them mighty unto the driving out of the children of the land, yea, unto the scattering them to destruction. And now, do ye suppose that the children of this land, who were in the land of promise, who were driven out by our fathers, do ye suppose that they were righteous? Behold, I say unto you, Nay. Do ye suppose that our fathers would have been more choice than they if they had been righteous? I say unto you, Nay. Behold, the Lord esteemeth all flesh in one; he that is righteous is favored of God. But behold, this people had rejected every word of God, and they were ripe in iniquity; and the fulness of the wrath of God was upon them; and the Lord did curse the land against them, and bless it unto our fathers; yea, he did curse it against them unto their destruction, and he did bless it unto our fathers unto their obtaining power over it. Behold, the Lord hath created the earth that it should be inhabited; and he hath created his children that they should possess it. And he raiseth up a righteous nation, and destroyeth the nations of the wicked. And he leadeth away the righteous into precious lands, and the wicked he destroyeth, and curseth the land unto them for their sakes. He ruleth high in the heavens, for it is his throne, and this earth is his footstool. And he loveth those who will have him to be their God. Behold, he loved our fathers, and he covenanted with them, yea, even Abraham, Isaac, and Jacob; and he remembered the covenants which he had made; wherefore, he did bring them out of the land of Egypt. And he did straiten them in the wilderness with his rod; for they hardened their hearts, even as ye have; and the Lord straitened them because of their iniquity. He sent fiery flying serpents among them; and after they were bitten he prepared a way that they might be healed; and the labor which they had to perform was to look; and because of the simpleness of the way, or the easiness of it, there were many who perished. And they did harden their hearts from time to time, and they did revile against Moses, and also against God; nevertheless, ye know that they were led forth by his matchless power

appropriate example. It illustrates how once the Lord gives an assignment to a man, the Lord entrusts the keys and provides the inspiration to accomplish the assignment.

Similarly, all the prophets who have been sent to warn Israel in any generation have been given the keys from God to accomplish their assignment. Even among people who no longer held such authority, the Lord would directly ordain those He commissioned during the Old Testament times (*TPJS*, 181).

When the church builds a temple and calls a temple president the one called to preside over the temple is the only one who can organize and run the temple. He has the keys and should be respected. Anyone who has an assignment or keys conferred upon them, by the church or by the Lord, has an assignment that should be respected.

Nephi's brothers and the royal court of King Noah all learned that it simply wasn't possible to terminate the mission of someone holding keys before they finished their assignment. (For Nephi, see 1

Nephi 17:48–55.[331] For Abinadi see Mosiah 13:2–5.[332]) Of course, once the assignment given the man has been completed, they are as

---

[331] 1 Nephi 17:48–55 "And now it came to pass that when I had spoken these words they were angry with me, and were desirous to throw me into the depths of the sea; and as they came forth to lay their hands upon me I spake unto them, saying: In the name of the Almighty God, I command you that ye touch me not, for I am filled with the power of God, even unto the consuming of my flesh; and whoso shall lay his hands upon me shall wither even as a dried reed; and he shall be as naught before the power of God, for God shall smite him. And it came to pass that I, Nephi, said unto them that they should murmur no more against their father; neither should they withhold their labor from me, for God had commanded me that I should build a ship. And I said unto them: If God had commanded me to do all things I could do them. If he should command me that I should say unto this water, be thou earth, it should be earth; and if I should say it, it would be done. And now, if the Lord has such great power, and has wrought so many miracles among the children of men, how is it that he cannot instruct me, that I should build a ship? And it came to pass that I, Nephi, said many things unto my brethren, insomuch that they were confounded and could not contend against me; neither durst they lay their hands upon me nor touch me with their fingers, even for the space of many days. Now they durst not do this lest they should wither before me, so powerful was the Spirit of God; and thus it had wrought upon them. And it came to pass that the Lord said unto me: Stretch forth thine hand again unto thy brethren, and they shall not wither before thee, but I will shock them, saith the Lord, and this will I do, that they may know that I am the Lord their God. And it came to pass that I stretched forth my hand unto my brethren, and they did not wither before me; but the Lord did shake them, even according to the word which he had spoken And now, they said: We know of a surety that the Lord is with thee, for we know that it is the power of the Lord that has shaken us. And they fell down before me, and were about to worship me, but I would not suffer them, saying: I am thy brother, yea, even thy younger brother; wherefore, worship the Lord thy God, and honor thy father and thy mother, that thy days may be long in the land which the Lord thy God shall give thee."

[332] Mosiah 13:2–5 "And they stood forth and attempted to lay their hands on him; but he withstood them, and said unto them: Touch me not, for God shall smite you if ye lay your hands upon me, for I have not delivered the message which the Lord sent me to deliver; neither have I told you that which ye requested that I should tell; therefore, God will not suffer that I shall be destroyed at this time. But I must fulfil the commandments wherewith God has commanded me; and because I have told you the truth ye are angry with me. And again, because I have spoken the word of God ye have judged me that I am mad. Now it came to pass after Abinadi had spoken these words that the people of king Noah durst not lay their hands on him, for the Spirit of the Lord was upon him; and his face shone with exceeding luster, even as Moses' did while in the mount of Sinai, while speaking with the Lord."

vulnerable to destruction at the hands of enemies as anyone else.[333]

When someone receives an assignment, and fulfills it with honor, they hold the keys of that assignment to all eternity.[334] They are expected to come to the great meeting when keys are returned to Adam and then, in turn, to Christ, preliminary to His return as the One whose right it is to preside over all things (*TPJS*, 157).

I suppose the best way to be invited to that meeting would be to obtain a key from the Lord, perform in strict conformity to the assignment He gives you, and become thereby entitled to return that key in the great assembly.

. . . For the rest, I'm not sure if this post will have any meaning.

Gifts Come from God

Question:

"In these days there are many holistic healing arts that area coming forward. EFT (tapping), angel therapy and readings, chakra work, Reiki, aura work, energy work, etc., etc. Are these gifts of the spirit? Are they gifts of the "right" spirit:)

---

[333] Mosiah 17:20 "And now, when Abinadi had said these words, he fell, having suffered death by fire; yea, having been put to death because he would not deny the commandments of God, having sealed the truth of his words by his death."
D&C 135:4 "When Joseph went to Carthage to deliver himself up to the pretended requirements of the law, two or three days previous to his assassination, he said: "I am going like a lamb to the slaughter; but I am calm as a summer's morning; I have a conscience void of offense towards God, and towards all men. I SHALL DIE INNOCENT, AND IT SHALL YET BE SAID OF ME—HE WAS MURDERED IN COLD BLOOD."—The same morning, after Hyrum had made ready to go—shall it be said to the slaughter? yes, for so it was—he read the following paragraph, near the close of the twelfth chapter of Ether, in the Book of Mormon, and turned down the leaf upon it:"

[334] D&C 128:21 "And again, the voice of God in the chamber of old Father Whitmer, in Fayette, Seneca county, and at sundry times, and in divers places through all the travels and tribulations of this Church of Jesus Christ of Latter-day Saints! And the voice of Michael, the archangel; the voice of Gabriel, and of Raphael, and of divers angels, from Michael or Adam down to the present time, all declaring their dispensation, their rights, their keys, their honors, their majesty and glory, and the power of their priesthood; giving line upon line, precept upon precept; here a little, and there a little; giving us consolation by holding forth that which is to come, confirming our hope!"

When someone is working with you on correcting old belief systems from childhood and they say they had a dream that might be relevant, should you trust that.? What do you feel about people who do angel readings? How can you discern so as not to be deceived or lead down an incorrect path. Many people who do this kind of work are not LDS...are they entitled to gifts of the spirit? Sometimes I have seen LDS people get involved with these modalities and leave the church or become inactive . . . others remain very faithful. I sometimes feel that people should be able to go to the source of all healing directly . . . Christ . . . and bypass these types of healings. But then again, sometimes I think perhaps people need these modalities to help remove blocks of low self-worth and self condemnation that block them from going directly to Christ for feelings of unworthiness and believing that Christ can heal them. I remember Jeffery Holland in a conference of the last couple of years say, "Christ can heal you and he can do it now!" (not his exact words). Anyway, I have wondered about this for a long long time. I hope you give me your opinion."

First, as to gifts:

I believe there are "gifts" given (or acquired) by people which are based on real sensitivities or talents. I believe they exist as part of the talents brought into this life. Some people have talent to sing, compose music, or create art. There are those who have developed spiritual gifts. There are many kinds of gifts, but they all come from God.[335]

Possession of a gift, however, does not mean a person will use that gift in conformity with God's will or plan. If a person does not seek to follow the Lord's will, they can be misled and use gifts for improper ends. People who fail to remain obedient, who begin to use

---

[335] Moroni 10:8 "And again, I exhort you, my brethren, that ye deny not the gifts of God, for they are many; and they come from the same God. And there are different ways that these gifts are administered; but it is the same God who worketh all in all; and they are given by the manifestations of the Spirit of God unto men, to profit them."

their gifts to gratify their pride or to achieve their ambitions can drift away from the light and take others with them. Just because a person possesses a gift does not mean they live their lives in conformity to truth. Nor does it mean they will not mislead you. Proper use of a gift should show gratitude to and promote faith in God.[336]

Second, as to modalities:

I do think that there are aids to faith that can help someone who is weak to still act in faith. Modalities that focus thought, bolster confidence and assist in believing the Lord can heal can aid in the process. In the end it is the authority of God and faith in Him that allows good things to follow. It comes from Him. If an act helps focus thought and confidence in Him, then the act is worthwhile.

The problems creep in when the modality is regarded as an independent authority apart from God. As soon as a person begins to view God as uninvolved, or that they can control the outcome independent of God's will, there is an opening for evil or deception. Gifts were not intended to produce a monetary profit and should not be practiced for money.[337]

Gifts belong to the body of believers and should be used to promote faith in God.[338]

---

[336] D&C 20:27 "As well as those who should come after, who should believe in the gifts and callings of God by the Holy Ghost, which beareth record of the Father and of the Son;"

[337] Acts 8:20 "But Peter said unto him, Thy money perish with thee, because thou hast thought that the gift of God may be purchased with money."

[338] D&C 46:10, 26 "And again, verily I say unto you, I would that ye should always remember, and always retain in your minds what those gifts are, that are given unto the church. And all these gifts come from God, for the benefit of the children of God."

Be Still and Know That I Am God

It is apparent from emails sent to the blog that some readers refuse to study carefully either the scriptures or what I have written. I will make yet another attempt to explain some important distinctions.

There is a difference between testifying that some principle is true and teaching others how to follow the principle, and discussing details of personal experiences which are not going to be meaningful and are not appropriate.

There are reasons why intimate details of temple ordinances are guarded by covenants they will not be revealed. It is true those covenants have been violated by many people. Some people have decided to reject what was offered, make themselves liars, and treat with contempt what should have been treated with care. All of that is between them and the Lord, with whom they made the covenant. Their violation of a trust does not detract one bit from the power of covenants kept by others.

We are not responsible for how others behave when they receive something that ought to be treated as sacred. We are all only accountable for how we individually treat such things.

It is appropriate for anyone to testify to the truth, that the Lord lives, and that He has and still does minister to men in the flesh. It is appropriate to explain that those blessings are predicated upon the same conditions for *any person* who will follow the law upon which such blessings are predicated. It is appropriate to explain what those conditions or laws are. It is appropriate to gather together in one continuous discussion the diverse elements scattered throughout the scriptures and put them into one convenient discussion of the whole. I have done that.

What is not important for anyone to know is the details of what goes on in a meeting between God and one with whom He deigns to appear. Joseph Smith for example remarked, concerning the First

Vision, "*many other things did he say unto me, which I cannot write at this time*" (JS–H 1:20).

Repeatedly the Book of Mormon draws a line and says that things were "*not lawful*" for man to write.[339] A person who does not understand the difference between the line that must be drawn and why it exists simply is not prepared to receive with gratitude what the Lord is offering.

The riches of eternity are offered by the Lord to you and each of you *directly*. It does not come from learning "secrets" from someone else. It comes by following the path. You do not need anything more than a description of the path. Follow it. Until you follow it, the heavens will remain shut against you. As soon as you follow it, you will have the results you would like to have.

Curiosity about sacred details that the scriptures repeatedly warn are not lawful to put into writing here in this fallen world, reveals an immaturity that should be overcome. If you want the details, learn them from the Lord. *Directly*. Without an intermediary. Teachers are commissioned by the Lord to reiterate the path by which they are to be obtained. He does not send someone to do the work for you. In-

---

[339] 1 Nephi 14:28 "And behold, I, Nephi, am forbidden that I should write the remainder of the things which I saw and heard; wherefore the things which I have written sufficeth me; and I have written but a small part of the things which I saw."

3 Nephi 26:16 "Behold, it came to pass on the morrow that the multitude gathered themselves together, and they both saw and heard these children; yea, even babes did open their mouths and utter marvelous things; and the things which they did utter were forbidden that there should not any man write them."

3 Nephi 27:23 "Write the things which ye have seen and heard, save it be those which are forbidden."

Ether 4:1 "And the Lord commanded the brother of Jared to go down out of the mount from the presence of the Lord, and write the things which he had seen; and they were forbidden to come unto the children of men until after that he should be lifted up upon the cross; and for this cause did king Mosiah keep them, that they should not come unto the world until after Christ should show himself unto his people."

Ether 13:13 "And I was about to write more, but I am forbidden; but great and marvelous were the prophecies of Ether; but they esteemed him as naught, and cast him out; and he hid himself in the cavity of a rock by day, and by night he went forth viewing the things which should come upon the people."

deed, you either do the work for yourself or it remains undone—
forever.

It is clear that some who want the most revealed to them are the
ones who have not yet read what I've written. You simply continue
to ask and ask again. *Study* what I've written *carefully* and *anyone* will
find it is all there. Several people have done so, and have received the
promised results. But they took care and devoted careful, solemn and
ponderous thought to the matters set out in what I have written.
That is what the writings were intended to produce, and why they
were commissioned to be written by the Lord. I know that the process is true, because I have lived it. I know that the descriptions provided in my writings are sufficient, because they have produced results akin to my own. You do not need more details from me. You
need to take seriously what I've already written. Actually, you don't
even need that. What I have written is taken from the scriptures,
primarily the Book of Mormon. If you understood the scriptures
you wouldn't even need what I've written. I have only been instructed
in how to bring the process together in a convenient single narrative,
building line upon line to a whole.

Careful, solemn and ponderous thought is what is needed. Not
frantic, exasperated and impatient demanding that someone tell you
something right now that will fix what is amiss in your life. Such
frantic conduct is likely to yield nothing.

I hope this aids in understanding what is appropriate and what is
over the line. If you want to know all the mysteries of God, He is
willing to reveal them. Not to the impatient, demanding and immature. But to those who develop a firm mind in every form of godli-

ness, including patience, persistence, faith, and sacrifice.[340] These things are not won cheaply. But they are won.

I think the words "be still and know that I am God" are more than just an admonition to 'shut-up.'[341] I think it is a formula. Let your anxieties pass over you. Leave them. Be calm. In the great calm of pondering over what He has given to you, you will "know" Him. Therefore, if you would like to know God, then ponder deeply and meditate on the things *He has already given to you*.[342] This is how Joseph Smith received the First Vision, Joseph F. Smith saw the Vision of the Redemption of the Dead, Nephi saw in vision the Lord, and Nephi son of Helaman would receive his calling and election. I can't give you a formula, I can't recite any additional vision and I can't tell

---

[340] Moroni 7:30 "For behold, they are subject unto him, to minister according to the word of his command, showing themselves unto them of strong faith and a firm mind in every form of godliness."

[341] D&C 101:16 "Therefore, let your hearts be comforted concerning Zion; for all flesh is in mine hands; be still and know that I am God."

[342] D&C 138:11 "As I pondered over these things which are written, the eyes of my understanding were opened, and the Spirit of the Lord rested upon me, and I saw the hosts of the dead, both small and great."
JS–H 1:12 "Never did any passage of scripture come with more power to the heart of man than this did at this time to mine. It seemed to enter with great force into every feeling of my heart. I reflected on it again and again, knowing that if any person needed wisdom from God, I did; for how to act I did not know, and unless I could get more wisdom than I then had, I would never know; for the teachers of religion of the different sects understood the same passages of scripture so differently as to destroy all confidence in settling the question by an appeal to the Bible."
1 Nephi 11:1 "For it came to pass after I had desired to know the things that my father had seen, and believing that the Lord was able to make them known unto me, as I sat pondering in mine heart I was caught away in the Spirit of the Lord, yea, into an exceedingly high mountain, which I never had before seen, and upon which I never had before set my foot."
Helaman 10:2–4 "And it came to pass that Nephi went his way towards his own house, pondering upon the things which the Lord had shown unto him. And it came to pass as he was thus pondering—being much cast down because of the wickedness of the people of the Nephites, their secret works of darkness, and their murderings, and their plunderings, and all manner of iniquities—and it came to pass as he was thus pondering in his heart, behold, a voice came unto him saying: Blessed art thou, Nephi, for those things which thou hast done; for I have beheld how thou hast with unwearyingness declared the word, which I have given unto thee, unto this people. And thou hast not feared them, and hast not sought thine own life, but hast sought my will, and to keep my commandments."

you about any visitation I have had that will absolve you of following the process by which God has become known to all those who have come to know Him since the time of Adam. All I can do is testify that the same path is open to *everyone*. But only on the same condition as it is available to all.

Christ's Ministry

We have an account of Christ's "ministry" to the Nephites beginning in chapter 11 of 3 Nephi and continuing through the 28th chapter. During the ministry Christ instructed, performed ordinances, (including the sacrament) blessed, healed, taught from scriptures, provided prophecy, and extended the promise of exaltation to many, including the Twelve He called. The full extent of what He did became so sacred that the account is interrupted and we are told that it was not lawful to put it into writing.[343]

Now, if you can take all that in, (and it is worth careful consideration to make sure you get the point) then you can begin to understand this statement recorded by Moroni about the visit between Christ and the Brother of Jared:

> "And now, as I, Moroni, said I could not make a full account of these things which are written, therefore it sufficeth me to say that Jesus showed himself unto this man in the spirit, even after the manner and in the likeness of the same body even as he showed himself unto the Nephites. And he ministered

---

[343] 3 Nephi 17:15–16 "And when he had said these words, he himself also knelt upon the earth; and behold he prayed unto the Father, and the things which he prayed cannot be written, and the multitude did bear record who heard him. And after this manner do they bear record: The eye hath never seen, neither hath the ear heard, before, so great and marvelous things as we saw and heard Jesus speak unto the Father;"
3 Nephi 26:16 "Behold, it came to pass on the morrow that the multitude gathered themselves together, and they both saw and heard these children; yea, even babes did open their mouths and utter marvelous things; and the things which they did utter were forbidden that there should not any man write them."
3 Nephi 27:23 "Write the things which ye have seen and heard, save it be those which are forbidden."

unto him even as he ministered unto the Nephites; and all
this, that this man might know that he was God, because of
the many great works which the Lord had showed unto him."
(Ether 3:17–18)

When Moroni wrote this it was nearly 400 years after Christ's
ministry to the Nephites. When he wrote this Moroni:

1. Had the records of Christ's ministry before him.

2. Had been personally visited by Christ.[344]

3. He also had personally been visited by the three Nephite disciples who were there when Christ appeared and called them as His
witnesses.[345]

4. Had the entire Jaredite record before him, including the portion that he would not translate due to its sacred character.[346]

When Moroni says that Christ "ministered" to the Brother of
Jared "as He ministered unto the Nephites" this is more than just an
appearance. It is more than just a conversation, with the Lord showing Himself to the man. It is more than merely giving the man an
understanding that He lives, that He is the Redeemer and Savior. It

---

[344] Ether 12:39 "And then shall ye know that I have seen Jesus, and that he hath talked
with me face to face, and that he told me in plain humility, even as a man telleth another in mine own language, concerning these things;"

[345] Mormon 8:10–11 "And there are none that do know the true God save it be the
disciples of Jesus, who did tarry in the land until the wickedness of the people was so
great that the Lord would not suffer them to remain with the people; and whether they
be upon the face of the land no man knoweth. But behold, my father and I have seen
them, and they have ministered unto us."

[346] Ether 4:5–7 "Wherefore the Lord hath commanded me to write them; and I have
written them. And he commanded me that I should seal them up; and he also hath
commanded that I should seal up the interpretation thereof; wherefore I have sealed up
the interpreters, according to the commandment of the Lord. For the Lord said unto
me: They shall not go forth unto the Gentiles until the day that they shall repent of
their iniquity, and become clean before the Lord. And in that day that they shall exercise faith in me, saith the Lord, even as the brother of Jared did, that they may become
sanctified in me, then will I manifest unto them the things which the brother of Jared
saw, even to the unfolding unto them all my revelations, saith Jesus Christ, the Son of
God, the Father of the heavens and of the earth, and all things that in them are."

would include the same kind of ministry as was had among the Nephites.

I believe the Lord's ministry in any age is the same. As the Redeemer, determined to bring to pass the immortality and eternal life of man,[347] it would only make sense that He would be determined to have those who receive Him be redeemed, promised eternal life, and instructed sufficiently to enter into their exaltation. This is why Christ says that He and the Father will "take up our abode with" such men.[348] That "abode" is the Father's House. More plainly, it is the Father's family. It is to become His son, begotten by the Father. Sonship requires initiation, and Christ's ministry would include all the required promises, rites and teachings to allow the person to lay claim upon eternal life.

"For these are they who are of Paul, and of Apollos, and of Cephas"

It has become very clear to me that there is an intangible and almost inexpressible difference between truth and error.

Satan quotes scripture to make a point in an argument with Christ, showing how he wants to justify his ends by resorting to scriptural/true principles.[349]

---

[347] Moses 1:39 "For behold, this is my work and my glory—to bring to pass the immortality and eternal life of man."

[348] John 14:23 "Jesus answered and said unto him, If a man love me, he will keep my words: and my Father will love him, and we will come unto him, and make our abode with him."

[349] Matthew 4:6 "And saith unto him, If thou be the Son of God, cast thyself down: for it is written, He shall give his angels charge concerning thee: and in *their* hands they shall bear thee up, lest at any time thou dash thy foot against a stone."

The accusations brought against Abinadi were scripture-based.[350] So were those brought against many others, including Christ. Indeed, the most frequent accusation against Christ related to the commandment to "keep the Sabbath day holy" and Him healing on the Sabbath.

I can see how people are almost completely taken in by the use of scriptural arguments or scriptural language, when they have never encountered the Holy Spirit, not received light and truth from God, and have not accepted guidance from a higher source.

Those who have light, and who use what light they have to accept more light, are going to find their way. Those who do not, and therefore, cannot have their path illuminated by a higher source, will be lost. They will be unable to distinguish between truth and error. Indeed, they will call good bad, and believe the truth to be a lie. It is inevitable.

This is why no man can be the guide for another. Everyone must stand on their own, acquire their own oil for their lamp, and stop leaning upon others to lead them.

I do not see that happening in any great numbers. Instead, I see fools loudly and stupidly proclaiming that it is always guaranteed safe to be led by men as long as you are careful about the men you follow.

No man will save you. *No not one.* You either follow them into the telestial kingdom in wherein you presently reside, or you figure out

---

[350] Mosiah 12:19–24 "And they began to question him, that they might cross him, that thereby they might have wherewith to accuse him; but he answered them boldly, and withstood all their questions, yea, to their astonishment; for he did withstand them in all their questions, and did confound them in all their words. And it came to pass that one of them said unto him: What meaneth the words which are written, and which have been taught by our fathers, saying: How beautiful upon the mountains are the feet of him that bringeth good tidings; that publisheth peace; that bringeth good tidings of good; that publisheth salvation; that saith unto Zion, Thy God reigneth; Thy watchmen shall lift up the voice; with the voice together shall they sing; for they shall see eye to eye when the Lord shall bring again Zion; Break forth into joy; sing together ye waste places of Jerusalem; for the Lord hath comforted his people, he hath redeemed Jerusalem; The Lord hath made bare his holy arm in the eyes of all the nations, and all the ends of the earth shall see the salvation of our God?"

how to get out of here.[351] Notice that these people followed TRUE or authentic messengers, yet they remain captured in a telestial existence for worlds without end.

They receive not the testimony of Jesus, which is the spirit of prophecy.[352]

I see benighted arguments couched in the language of scripture all the time. The clarity with which I can detect the errors made is not because I am smarter than other people. I am not. I can see clearly the difference between truth and error by the light given to me. I can't give that to you. Only you can acquire it. I can tell you how to acquire it. But in the end, you alone will either follow the pattern and obtain the results, or continue to live in the dark.

"And why stand we in jeopardy every hour?"

Every one of us needs to be challenged. None of us should be complacent about how we live, the words we speak or write, and the thoughts we entertain. If this blog does not stir you up and make you reconsider what you are doing and how you are living your life everyday, then it is a waste of time. If I am not personally challenging you, then I am not worth taking the time to read.

---

[351] D&C 76:98–101 "And the glory of the telestial is one, even as the glory of the stars is one; for as one star differs from another star in glory, even so differs one from another in glory in the telestial world; For these are they who are of Paul, and of Apollos, and of Cephas. These are they who say they are some of one and some of another—some of Christ and some of John, and some of Moses, and some of Elias, and some of Esaias, and some of Isaiah, and some of Enoch; But received not the gospel, neither the testimony of Jesus, neither the prophets, neither the everlasting covenant."

[352] Revelation 19:10 "And I fell at his feet to worship him. And he said unto me, See *thou do it* not: I am thy fellowservant, and of thy brethren that have the testimony of Jesus: worship God: for the testimony of Jesus is the spirit of prophecy."

It is a doctrine of the devil to tell you that "all is well."[353] The obligation of any true messenger is to continually cry repentance. Satan employs ministers to satisfy itching ears with a smooth message.[354] They lead people carefully down to hell. The Lord commissions His messengers to deliver the opposite message. If I am really engaged in working for Him, then the words should challenge, even offend you.

Only fools think there are institutional prerogatives that entitle people to God's favor. There is no magic ordinance. There is no certificate that can be issued to you or your group, by any person or institution, that entitles you to enter heaven. It does not exist. Those who believe there is some institutional voodoo that will guarantee you entrance into heaven are sadly mistaken.

Assume for a moment that you have indeed been given by the Father the promise of eternal life, what then? Are you entitled to rest while all around you the world is filled with unsaved souls?[355] Does such a promise remain yours if you do not labor all your remaining days to cry repentance and bring others to the tree of life so they may partake? Having entered into the Lord's "rest," does not the heir then owe it to everyone else they meet for the remainder of their lives to bring them with them?[356]

---

[353] 2 Nephi 28:20–21 "For behold, at that day shall he rage in the hearts of the children of men, and stir them up to anger against that which is good. And others will he pacify, and lull them away into carnal security, that they will say: All is well in Zion; yea, Zion prospereth, all is well—and thus the devil cheateth their souls, and leadeth them away carefully down to hell."

[354] 2 Timothy 4:3 "For the time will come when they will not endure sound doctrine; but after their own lusts shall they heap to themselves teachers, having itching ears;"

[355] Alma 13:12 "Now they, after being sanctified by the Holy Ghost, having their garments made white, being pure and spotless before God, could not look upon sin save it were with abhorrence; and there were many, exceedingly great many, who were made pure and entered into the rest of the Lord their God."

[356] D&C 18:15 "And if it so be that you should labor all your days in crying repentance unto this people, and bring, save it be one soul unto me, how great shall be your joy with him in the kingdom of my Father!"

There is no hour here when we are not in jeopardy.[357]

So when you read something on this blog or in a book I have written which challenges you, brings you up short, or makes you think that I may be speaking about you, then I have succeeded. On the other hand, if you believe you are justified by what you read here, then you miss entirely the obligation incumbent on both of us.

We all need to repent. If the Lord has extended to you the promise of eternal life, then you have moved to another plane of growth and challenge. That great promise opens the door for you to struggle and grow in your comprehension of what He has done. You still must learn how to exercise the new prerogatives given to you in the proper way. The challenges will not relent. We are designed for growth. It will not come to an end in this life. It is to prepare us for something far greater.[358] We must become as He is to be like Him.[359]

"Power" or "Authority"

In the church we have a regular system for ordination to give someone priesthood authority. It requires the candidate to be interviewed, found worthy, recommended by the presiding authorities (Bishop or Stake President) to a congregation who sustains the ordination before it is performed. The ordination takes place by the laying on of hands, is recorded, and a certificate is issued to the one ordained.

---

[357] 1 Corinthians 15:30 "And why stand we in jeopardy every hour?"

[358] D&C 132:20 "Then shall they be gods, because they have no end; therefore shall they be from everlasting to everlasting, because they continue; then shall they be above all, because all things are subject unto them. Then shall they be gods, because they have all power, and the angels are subject unto them."

[359] 1 John 3:1–3 "Behold, what manner of love the Father hath bestowed upon us, that we should be called the sons of God: therefore the world knoweth us not, because it knew him not. Beloved, now are we the sons of God, and it doth not yet appear what we shall be: but we know that, when he shall appear, we shall be like him; for we shall see him as he is. And every man that hath this hope in him purifieth himself, even as he is pure."

In contrast, the Lord's ordination among the Nephites required only His word to be spoken, and power was conferred:

> "And the Lord commanded him that he should arise. And he arose and stood before him. And the Lord said unto him: I give unto you power that ye shall baptize this people when I am again ascended into heaven. And again the Lord called others, and said unto them likewise; and he gave unto them power to baptize. And he said unto them: On this wise shall ye baptize; and there shall be no disputations among you." (3 Nephi 11:20–22)

It is interesting that the word used in His conferral of priestly right was "power" and not "authority." Consider the difference. Consider what it means for the Lord to speak unto a man and tell him that he has "power" from the Lord.

Is there a difference between having the "authority" to baptize, as we spread it about in the church today, and having the "power" to baptize as conferred by Christ? If there is, then what is that difference?

Good questions to ponder. Particularly as you consider President Packer's timely reminder of the general lack of power in the priesthood of today's church in his recent General Conference address, "The Power of the Priesthood."[360]

Have a Joyful Saturday

I have a dear friend whose daughter is getting married this month. I look forward to driving out to the wedding. We're planning to take my wife's Mini-Cooper and leave the top down. A day's worth of driving to and from the wedding is about as delightful a thing as I can imagine at the moment. I don't care if we're driving at night, the

---

[360] Packer, "The Power of the Priesthood", General Conference, April 2010.

seats have electric heaters and the stars overhead are as interesting as the daytime sky. More so in fact.

The greatest things we possess are our families and friends. They matter. They can endure to all eternity. Nothing will come with us from this fallen world other than the friends and family we acquire, the lessons we have learned, the covenants made with and ratified by the Lord, and the kind acts we have done. Everything else will dissolve back into the dust of this world.

Have a joyful Saturday. Do something kind for someone who dislikes you. Do something generous for someone who loves you. Go to bed tonight knowing that if this day were the one day chosen to judge your character that it is your best. Make the day holy by the way you live, the words you speak and the thoughts you entertain.

Heaven is stirred and Hell itself is shaken when even one soul lives such a day.

Spring

Spring is nearly gone (the solstice is coming soon) and we didn't get a garden planted until yesterday. We've had snow on our yard within the last three weeks. Late start.

The result of the abiding winter is nature has just begun to wake up. The evergreens are shooting out their new season's growth. I've been noticing again how even the most prickly evergreens, like the Colorado Blue Spruces, are so soft and fern-like in their new shoots. Pretty, and very soft and agreeable, in addition to being fragrant. We still get glimpses of Eden in the Spring, even in this fallen world.

Just before dark takes over the neighborhood each night the quail are hooting to get back together again. They get separated during their daily foraging and then want to regroup as a family before nighttime slumber. They will get in a tree or on a rooftop and begin to hoot. They make a funny little call. You can tell by the answer coming back which ones belong together. They hoot, get closer, re-call again, get closer, until finally they wind up together and quiet.

Deer have been wandering through the neighborhood all winter long. They seem to be clearing out now because the valley is getting warmer, and there's new growth on the foothills from the melting snow. The mountain tops are still under many feet of snow, so the deer won't really return to the high ground until another month or so.

There's an order to all this stuff. Wild and uncontrolled nature is organized, orderly, intelligent and the animal kingdom is divided into families. They feel joy at their companionship with one another as they fill the measure of their creation.

I am grateful each night, too, as my family gathers together to see each of us has made it through the day safely. There's a Divine hand that can be seen in family life. Even when there is difficulty and dis-appointment, the family is tied together by God and nature.

Preaching the Gospel to All Who Are Here

When I was over missionary work for my stake we would meet with the Mission President quarterly. The "Spanish Language Initia-tive" was where the primary missionary success was taking place in an area from Idaho to Wyoming and throughout Utah. The justifica-tion for the Spanish Language Initiative was rather an excuse. The stated reason was: "Can you imagine what will happen to the home base of the church with so many moving in if there isn't an effort made to convert them?"

Criticism has been leveled at the church for the eagerness with which the missionaries are being sent to teach illegal aliens. There are full time Spanish language missionaries being called to teach all over the United States. My wife has a friend living in Texas whose son was recently called to a Spanish language mission in Pocatello, Idaho.

Criticism has been based upon the Article of Faith which states we believe in "honoring, obeying and sustaining the law." The criticism is that there is some hypocrisy in seeking out and baptizing those who are illegal. The process seems to be lawless rather than sustaining the law.

At one point the church announced that law enforcement officers, judges and State prosecutors would no longer be called to be Bishops or Stake Presidents because it presented a conflict of interest for them to be a presiding church official over those who they were required to enforce the law. I do not know if that policy still exists, but it was the policy for some time while I was on the High Council.

I've thought the church's position was poorly articulated and deserving of criticism. The church ought to make a well-publicized statement justifying what is happening by adopting a straight-forward explanation that everyone can understand and agree is true. I wish they would announce the following, or something close to the following, as the their reason for the Spanish Language Initiative:

The Church of Jesus Christ of Latter-day Saints has an obligation to proclaim the Gospel. We believe in inviting all to come to the Gospel and be baptized. We would preach the Gospel to anyone, regardless of their race or nationality, wherever situated. Today there are millions of people welcomed into the United States by a national government that has refused to enforce any significant deterrent to cross-border crossing. Although such entry is nominally "illegal," even the current President of the United States, the country's chief law enforcement official, has proclaimed it is in the best tradition of the American people to welcome immigrants to the country. The Church of Jesus Christ of Latter-day Saints is not a law enforcement agency. It is powerless to make or enforce any immigration law or policy. If the national government does not prevent migration into the United States, we believe it is altogether appropriate to offer all who will receive the Gospel an opportunity to be taught and baptized here, just as we would do for the same people if they were located in another country.

This puts the responsibility upon the Federal government, where it belongs. It shows the church is powerless to affect the outcome of the migration. It also avoids the "can you imagine what it would be like if we didn't work to convert them" excuse, and puts it into a positive and reasonable light.

I do not think the church's actions deserve criticism. I do, however, think they ought to be more forthright about justifying and defending the effort to convert those whose presence here is nominally illegal. There's nothing wrong about preaching to such people.

D-Day

On this morning 66 years ago my father landed on Omaha Beach in the first wave of the invasion. He was a combat engineer, with the responsibility to blow up obstacles on the beach to let the tanks and equipment move about unimpeded. The battle, however, changed plans. He and everyone else there that morning needed to focus on the incoming fire and staying alive.

It didn't matter that the obstacles were left. No tanks arrived on Omaha Beach that day. The explosives were better used to clear away a path to the German emplacements on the top.

As my father was dying, nearly 50 years later, he wondered why his life was spared when so many of his friends died that day. A few years later when *Saving Private Ryan* was released it very much reminded me of my father.

I think of him every June 6th. It seems more clearly a day tied to him than either his birthday on February 20th or the day of his death November 20th. What a great man he was. Possessed with profound insight, tempered by the things he suffered, living in obscurity, quick to laugh, never angry and capable of giving wise advice. In all my life, I only saw him angry one time. But I think I heard him laugh every single day; oftentimes at himself.

If You Love Me, Receive Instruction from Me

John Hall and I were recently discussing the Gospel of John. He pointed out that Christ's words: "If you love me, keep my commandments" appear several times in the Gospel. He thought the words could be better translated to mean: "If you love me, act as a sentinel (or guard) ready to receive further instructions from me."

The current King James translation was based on the recognition that the cannon of scripture had closed and revelation had ended. Therefore they took those things into account as they rendered their translation.

For us, at least in theory, the cannon of scripture is not closed. Also, in theory, revelation is still possible.

There is an effort underway to redefine revelation and circumscribe its acceptable bounds. The coming view will be that revelation should only be expected which confirms that the church's authorities are speaking for God, and anything direct from God has ended. God has finished His work, and now given His authority to man.[361] If Nephi was a prophet (and he was) then that will become the church's position at some point.

It is our responsibility to receive revelation. It is also our responsibility to keep the narrowing boundaries as wide open as possible. Whatever the line is, you should live at that line to prevent it from drawing even tighter.

---

[361] 2 Nephi 28:5 "And they deny the power of God, the Holy One of Israel; and they say unto the people: Hearken unto us, and hear ye our precept; for behold there is no God today, for the Lord and the Redeemer hath done his work, and he hath given his power unto men;"

If you love Christ, stand as a sentinel ready to receive further instructions from Him.

Made in the USA
San Bernardino, CA
25 September 2015